BALL FOUR

The Final Pitch

Jim Bouton

**Original Ball Four
Edited by Leonard Shecter**

Bulldog Publishing
P.O. Box 188
North Egremont, MA. 01252
www.ballfour.com

Bulldog Publishing
P.O. Box 188
North Egremont, MA. 01252
www.ballfour.com

Library of Congress Cataloging-in-Publication Data
Bouton, Jim.
  Ball Four.
  Rev. ed. of: Ball four plus ball five, 1981
    1. Bouton, Jim.   2. Baseball players—United
States—Biography.   3. Baseball—United States.
  I. Shecter, Leonard.   II. Bouton, Jim. Ball four
  plus ball five.   III. Title.
  GV965.B69A3   1990   796.37'092 [B]   89-49151

ISBN 0-9709117-0-X

20   19   18   17   16   15   14

PRINTED IN THE UNITED STATES OF AMERICA.

For Laurie

CONTENTS

PREFACE

WRITTEN IN 1980; UPDATED IN 1990 AND 2000.

There was a time, not too long ago, when school kids read *Ball Four* at night under the covers with a flashlight because their parents wouldn't allow it in the house. It was not your typical sports book about the importance of clean living and inspired coaching. I was called a Judas and a Benedict Arnold for having written it. The book was attacked in the media because among other things, it "used four-letter words and destroyed heroes." It was even banned in a few libraries because it was said to be "bad for the youth of America."

The kids, however, saw it differently. I know because they tell me about it now whenever I lecture on college campuses. [These days I do motivational speaking to corporations and the "kids" are often gray or bald or paunchy.] They come up and say it was nice to learn that ballplayers were human beings, but what they got from the book was moral support for a point of view. They claim that *Ball Four* gave them strength to be the underdog and made them feel less lonely as an outsider in their own lives. Or it helped them to stand up for themselves and see life with a sense of humor. Then they invariably share a funny story about a coach, a teacher, or a boss who reminds them of someone in the book.

In some fraternities and dorms they play Ball Four Trivia, or Who Said That?, quoting characters from the book. And there is always someone who claims to hold the campus record for reading it 10, 12, or 14 times. Then they produce dog-eared copies for me to sign. I love it.

Sometimes when people compliment me about my book I wonder who they're talking about. A librarian compared *Ball Four* to the classic *The Catcher in the Rye* because she said I was an idealist like Holden Caulfield who, "viewed the world through jaundice colored glasses." Teachers have personally thanked me for writing the only book their nonreading students would read. And one mother said she wanted to build me a shrine for writing the only book her son ever finished.

The strangest part is that apparently there is something about the book which makes people feel I'm their friend. I'm always amazed when I walk through an airport, for example, and someone I've never met passes by and says simply, "Hey, *Ball Four.*" Or strangers will stop me on the street and ask how my kids are doing.

Maybe they identify with me because we share the same perspective. One of my roommates, Steve Hovley, said I was the first fan to make it to the major leagues. *Ball Four* has the kinds of stories an observant next door neighbor might come home and tell if he ever spent some time with a major league team. Whatever the reasons, it still overwhelms me to think that I wrote something which people remember.

I certainly didn't plan it this way. I don't believe I could have produced this response if I had set out to do it. In fact, twenty years ago when I submitted the final manuscript I was not optimistic. My editor, Lenny Shecter, and I had spent so many months rewriting and polishing that after awhile it all seemed like cardboard to us. What's more, the World Publishing Company wasn't too excited either. They doubted there was any market for a diary by a marginal relief pitcher on an expansion team called the Seattle Pilots.

With a first printing of only 5,000 copies I was certain that *Ball Four* was headed the way of all sports books. And then a funny thing happened. Some advance excerpts appeared in *Look* magazine and the baseball establishment went crazy. The team owners became furious and wanted to ban the book. The Commissioner, Bowie "Ayatollah" Kuhn, called me in for a reprimand and announced that I had done the game "a grave disservice." Sportswriters called me names like "traitor" and "turncoat." My favorite was "social leper." Dick Young of the *Daily News* thought that one up.

The ballplayers, most of whom hadn't read it, picked up the cue. The San Diego Padres burned the book and left the charred remains for me to find in the visitors clubhouse. While I was on the mound trying to pitch, players on the opposing teams hollered obscenities at me. I can still remember Pete Rose, on the top step of the dugout screaming, "Fuck you, Shakespeare."

All that hollering and screaming sure sold books. *Ball Four* went up to [500,000 in hardcover, 5 million in paperback], and got translated into Japanese. It's the largest selling sports book ever. I was so grateful I dedicated my second book, *I'm Glad You Didn't Take It Personally*, to my detractors. I don't think they appreciated the gesture.

One way I can tell is that I never get invited back to Old Timers' Days. Understand, *everybody* gets invited back for Old Timers' Day no matter what kind of rotten person he was when he was playing. Muggers, drug addicts, rapists, child molesters, all are forgiven for Old Timers' Day. Except a certain author.

The wildest thing is that they wouldn't forgive a cousin who made the mistake of being related to me. Jeff Bouton was a good college pitcher who dreamed of making the big leagues someday. But after *Ball Four* came out a Detroit Tiger scout told him he'd never make it in the pros unless he *changed his name!* Jeff refused, and a month after he signed he was released. For the rest of his life, he'll never know if it was his pitching or his name.

I believe the overreaction to *Ball Four* boiled down to this: People simply were not used to reading the truth about professional sports.

The owners, for their part, saw this as economically dangerous. What made them so angry about the book was not the locker room stories but the revelations about how difficult it was to make a living in baseball. The owners knew that public opinion was important in maintaining the controversial reserve clause which teams used to control players and hold down salaries. They lived in fear that this special exemption from the anti-trust laws, originally granted by Congress and reluctantly upheld in the courts, might someday be overturned.

To guard against this, the Commissioner and the owners (with help from sportswriters), had convinced the public, the Congress, and the courts—*and* many players!—that the reserve clause was crucial in order to "maintain competitive balance." (As if there was competitive balance when the Yankees were winning 29 pennants in 43 years.) The owners preached that the reserve clause was necessary to stay in business, and that ballplayers were well paid and fairly treated. (Mickey Mantle's $100,000 salary was always announced with great fanfare while all the $9,000 and $12,000 salaries were kept secret.) The owners had always insisted that dealings between players and teams be kept strictly confidential. They knew that if the public ever learned the truth, it would make it more difficult to defend the reserve clause against future challenges.

Which is why the owners hated *Ball Four*. Here was a book which revealed, in great detail, just how ballplayers' salaries were "negotiated" with general managers. It showed, for the first time, exactly how owners abused and manipulated players by taking advantage of their one way contract.

It turned out the owners had reason to be afraid. It may be no coincidence that after half a century of struggle the players won their free agency shortly after the publication of *Ball Four*. No one will know what part the book may have played in creating a favorable climate of opinion. I only know that when Marvin Miller asked me to testify in the Messersmith arbitration case which freed the players, I quoted passages from *Ball Four*.

The sportswriters, on the other hand, were upset at almost all the other things *Ball Four* revealed. Chief among these being that ballplayers will, on occasion, take pep pills, get drunk, stay out late, talk dirty, have groupies, and be rude to fans. The irony here, of course, is that if the *sportswriters* had been telling what went on in baseball there would have been no sensation around my book.

David Halberstam, who won a Pulitzer Prize for his reporting on Vietnam, wrote a piece in *Harper's* that was less a review of *Ball Four* than a commentary on the journalism of our times.

> He has written . . . a book deep in the American vein, so deep in fact that it is by no means a sports book . . . a comparable insider's book about, say, the Congress of the United States, the Ford Motor Company, or the Joint Chiefs of Staff would be equally welcome . . .

> As the book is deeply in the American vein, so is the reaction against it. The sportswriters are not judging the accuracy of the book, but Bouton's right to tell (that is, your right to read), which is, again, as American as apple pie or the White House press corps. A reporter covers an institution, becomes associated with it, protective of it, and, most important, the arbiter of what is right to tell. He knows what's good for you to hear, what should remain at the press-club bar. When someone goes beyond that, stakes out a new dimension of what is proper and significant, then it is the sportswriters and the Washington bureau chiefs who yell the loudest, because having played the game, having been tamed, when someone outflanks them, they must of necessity attack his intentions, his accuracy. Thus Bouton has become a social leper to many sportswriters and thus Sy Hersh, when he broke the My Lai story, became a 'peddler' to some of Washington's most famous journalists.

By establishing new boundaries, *Ball Four* changed sports reporting at least to the extent that, after the book, it was no longer possible to sell the milk and cookies image again. It was not my purpose to do this, but on reflection, it's probably not a bad idea. I think we are all better off looking across at someone, rather than up. Sheldon Kopp, the author and psychologist, wrote, "There are no great men. If you have a hero, look again: you have diminished yourself in some way." Besides, you can get sick on too much milk and cookies. And as far as damaging baseball goes, I haven't noticed any drop-off in attendance. The most obvious impact of *Ball Four* has been on sports *books,* although I'm not sure I want to claim credit for those results. Traditionally, sports books are written like this. Joe Shlabotnik has a good year (wins 20 games, bats .300, etc.). At the end of the season a sportswriter comes over to Joe's locker and says that money could be made from a book. The sportswriter says don't worry, he'll do the writing, all the player has to do is answer some questions into a tape recorder. The star's picture goes on the cover, the writer cranks it out in a month-and-a-half, and they split 50/50.

Publishers like sports books because, while they rarely make a lot of money, they never *lose* money. Quality is not important. Any book with a big-name player on the cover is guaranteed to sell 5,000 copies, enough to recoup the printing costs.

These books usually talk about how important it is to get a good night's sleep because the team sure needs to win that big game tomorrow. Since *Ball Four* things have changed. Now when an athlete and his ghost go in to pitch a book the publisher is likely to say, "How much are you willing to tell? If you're not going to open up, we're not interested."

Of course the player and the ghost promise to write things which have never been written before, with the result that each new book promises to go further than the last. There seems to be a contest to see which book can be the most shocking. I'm always startled to see these books advertised as, "More revealing than *Ball Four,*" or "More outrageous than *Ball Four.*"

What's interesting is that while the content of sports books has changed, *the process* for writing them remains the same. Where before a jock mouthed platitudes into a tape recorder for a few hours, now he tells raunchy stories into the recorder for a few hours. Sensationalism has become a substitute for banality. We've gone from assembly line gee-whiz books to assembly line exposes.

And people tell me I started it all. Sigh.

In spite of everything, I'm glad I wrote *Ball Four* and not because of the money or notoriety it has brought me. I'm glad I have it for myself. Here, presented forever in one place, are all those memories from a special time in my life. Sometimes, when I'm alone, I'll just open the book and read whatever is on that page. I almost always laugh out loud, not because I'm funny, but because the ballplayers are funny. People sometimes ask me if I made up all those stories and I tell them of course not. I can't write that well. I just quoted other people.

In 1969 I thought it would be a good idea to write a book and share the fun I'd had in baseball. The notion that it would someday change my life never occurred to me. Before I tell you about that in Ball Five and Ball Six and Ball Seven you should probably read *Ball Four*. It follows, along with the editor's foreword and the introduction, exactly as it was thirty years ago, unchanged except for typos and minor factual corrections.

In addition to Ball Seven, there is also a Rogues Gallery of 124 player photos, which I hesitated to add because I feared they might intrude on the reader's wish to imagine the players for themselves. This may be especially true for readers who have already read the book and have favorite images in mind.

But these concerns were far outweighed by my longing to immortalize this colorful cast of characters. Particularly the Seattle Pilots players who seem to have been sent to that expansion team for the express purpose of being in *Ball Four*. It's as if somebody had said, "This team's not going to win any games, but if someone writes a book it'll be a great ball club."

What is the attraction of the Seattle Pilots? I think the fact that they existed for only one year has made them special. Unclaimed by town or franchise, the Pilots are like the Flying Dutchmen, doomed to sail aimlessly without a harbor.

Or, as the decades pass, more like Brigadoon, the enchanted village that comes alive every hundred years. The Pilots played just one magic summer, then disappeared, existing now only in the pages of a book.

EDITOR'S FOREWORD

I can't even say this book was my idea. I'd known Jim Bouton since he first came up with the Yankees, was familiar with his iconoclastic views and his enthusiastic, imaginative way of expressing them, and it occurred to me that a diary of his season—even if he spent it with a minor-league team as he had the season before—might prove of great general interest. As usual, he was ahead of me. "Funny you should mention that," he said when I first brought it up. "I've been keeping notes."

Bouton talked into his tape recorder for more than seven months. Our typist, Miss Elisabeth Rehm of Jamaica, N.Y., did herculean work to keep up with the flood. There is nothing inarticulate about Jim Bouton. Before the season ended Miss Rehm had typed the equivalent of 1,500 pages (about 450,000 words) of double-spaced Bouton. From the beginning there was, fortunately, great rapport between us. I quickly found I did not need to spend a lot of time with Bouton pulling truth and anecdotes out of him. They were there, in abundance, starting with the very first tape from Arizona. We spent no more than five days together all season.

It may seem odd in an effort of this sort, but there were no disagreements between us. From the first we shared the opinion that the only purpose to adding to the huge volume of printed material that had been produced about baseball, was to illuminate the game as it had never been before. We resolved to reveal baseball as it is viewed by the men who play it, the frustrations and the meanness as well as the joy and the extraordinary fun. The difficulty is that to tell the truth is often, unfortunately, to offend. Bouton never flinched. It was not our purpose to offend, of course, but if in the process of telling the truth we did, so be it.

We had to make a decision, too, about the use of language. There is earthiness in baseball clubhouse language. To censor it, we felt, would be to put editorial omniscience between the reader and reality. Besides, we were not aiming this book at juveniles. Rate it X. The only thing we left out was repetitiveness.

The hardest part of editing Bouton's 1,500 pages was deciding what to leave out. There was so much that was so good, so incisive, so funny, that the choices were most difficult. In the end I managed to take it down to about 650 pages. The final cut, to about 520 manuscript pages, was made by both of us at the very last. We spent eighteen hours a day together for weeks, cutting, editing, correcting, polishing. There were arguments sometimes and frayed nerves, and we came to know each other in that special, complicated way that people who have worked very hard, very closely on a project they consider important come to know each other. I'm not sure how Bouton feels about it, but I believe I came away a better man.

LEONARD SHECTER
New York City, January 1970

INTRODUCTION

FALL 1968

I'm 30 years old and I have these dreams.

I dream my knuckleball is jumping around like a Ping-Pong ball in the wind and I pitch a two-hit shutout against my old team, the New York Yankees, single home the winning run in the ninth inning and, when the game is over, take a big bow on the mound in Yankee Stadium with 60,000 people cheering wildly. After the game reporters crowd around my locker asking me to explain exactly how I did it. I don't mind telling them.

I dream I have pitched four consecutive shutouts for the Seattle Pilots, and the Detroit Tigers decide to buy me in August for their stretch drive. It's a natural: the Tigers give away a couple of minor-league pheenoms, and the Pilots, looking to the future, discard an aging righthanded knuckleballer. I go over to Detroit and help them win the pennant with five saves and a couple of spot starts. I see myself in the back of a shiny new convertible riding down Woodward Avenue with ticker-tape and confetti covering me like snow. I see myself waving to the crowd and I can see the people waving back, smiling, shouting my name.

I dream my picture is on the cover of *Sports Illustrated* in October and they do a special "Comeback of the Year" feature on me, and all winter long I'm going to dinners and accepting trophies as the Comeback Player of the Year.

I dream all these things. I really do. So there's no use asking me why I'm here, why a reasonably intelligent thirty-year-old man who has lost his fastball is still struggling to play baseball, holding on—literally—with his fingertips. The dreams are the answer. They're why I wanted to be a big-league ballplayer and why I still want to get back on top again. I *enjoy* the fame of being a big-league ballplayer. I get a tremendous kick out of people wanting my autograph. In fact, I feel hurt if I go someplace where I think I should be recognized and no one asks me for it. I enjoy signing them and posing for pictures and answering reporters' questions and having people recognize me on the street. A lot of my friends are baseball fans, as well as my family and kids I went to school with, and I get a kick out of knowing that they're enjoying having a connection with a guy in the big leagues. Maybe I shouldn't, but I do.

Like someone once asked Al Ferrara of the Dodgers why *he* wanted to be a baseball player. He said because he always wanted to see his picture on a bubblegum card. Well, me too. It's an ego trip.

I've heard all the arguments against it. That there are better, more important things for a man to do than spend his time trying to throw a ball past other men who are trying to hit it with a stick. There are things like being a doctor or a teacher or working in the Peace Corps. More likely I should be devoting myself full-time to finding a way to end the war. I admit that sometimes I'm troubled by the way I make my living. I *would* like to change the world. I *would* like to have an influence on other people's lives. And the last time I was sent down to the minor leagues a man I consider my friend said, only half-kidding, I guess, "Why don't you quit and go out and earn a living like everybody else, ya bum ya?"

I was piqued for a moment. But then I thought, what the hell, there are a lot of professions that rank even with baseball, or a lot below, in terms of nobility. I don't think there's anything so great about selling real estate or life insurance or mutual funds, or a lot of other unimportant things that people do with their lives and never give it a thought. Okay, so I'll save the world when I get a little older. I believe a man is entitled to devote a certain number of years to plain enjoyment and driving for some sort of financial security.

You can always be a teacher or a social worker when you've reached thirty-five. That gives me five more years and I'm going to use them all. You can't always be a major-league baseball player. There are only a certain number of years—and I know how few they are—in which you can play baseball. And I think you can be a better teacher if you *have* played baseball, if only for the fact that the kids will listen to you more. I think I'll have more value at *anything* I do later on for having been a baseball player. I believe that, foolish as it is, Stan Musial has more influence with American kids than any geography teacher. Ted Williams is better known than any of our poets, Mickey Mantle more admired than our scientists. Perhaps I can put my own small fame to work later on.

Right now, the fact is that I love the game, love to play it, I mean. Actually, with the thousands of games I've seen, baseball bores me. I have no trouble falling asleep in the bullpen, and I don't think I'd ever pay my way into a ballpark to watch a game. But there's a lot to being *in* the game, a lot to having those dreams.

A lot of it is foolishness too, grown men being serious about a boy's game. There's pettiness in baseball, and meanness and stupidity beyond belief, and everything else bad that you'll find outside of baseball. I haven't enjoyed every single minute of it and when I've refused to conform to some of the more Neanderthal aspects of baseball thinking I've been an outcast. Yet there's been a tremendous lot of good in it for me and I wouldn't trade my years in it for anything I can think of. If you doubt me, take a look at my fingertips; I'm growing calluses on them.

So what follows, then, is not so much a book about Jim Bouton as it is about what I've seen and felt playing baseball, for a season, up and down with an expansion team, and for what has been for me so far, a lifetime.

Part 1 They Made Me What I Am Today

NOVEMBER

15

       I signed my contract today to play for the Seattle Pilots at a salary of $22,000 and it was a letdown because I didn't have to bargain. There was no struggle, none of the give and take that I look forward to every year. Most players don't like to haggle. They just want to get it over with. Not me. With me signing a contract has been a yearly adventure.

       The reason for no adventure this year is the way I pitched last year. It ranged from awful to terrible to pretty good. When it was terrible, and I had a record 0 and 7, or 2 and 7 maybe, I had to do some serious thinking about whether it was all over for me. I was pitching for the

Seattle Angels of the Pacific Coast League. The next year, 1969, Seattle would get the expansion Seattle Pilots of the American League. The New York Yankees had sold me to Seattle for $20,000 and were so eager to get rid of me they paid $8,000 of my $22,000 salary. This means I was actually sold for $12,000, less than half the waiver price. Makes a man think.

In the middle of August I went to see Marvin Milkes, the general manager of the Seattle Angels, and the future general manager of Pilots. I told him that I wanted some kind of guarantee from him about next year. There were some businesses with long-range potential I could go into over the winter and I would if I was certain I wasn't going to be playing baseball.

"What I would like," I told him, "is an understanding that no matter what kind of contract you give me, major league or minor league, that it will be for a certain minimum amount. Now, I realize you don't know how much value I will be for you since you haven't gone through the expansion draft and don't know the kind of players you'll have. So I'm not asking for a major-league contract, but just a certain minimum amount of money."

"How much money are you talking about?" Milkes said shrewdly.

"I talked it over with my wife and we arrived at a figure of $15,000 or $16,000. That's the minimum I could afford to play for, majors or minors. Otherwise I got to go to work."

To this Milkes said simply, "No."

I couldn't say I blamed him.

It was right about then, though, that the knuckleball I'd been experimenting with for a couple of months began to do things. I won two games in five days, going all the way, giving up only two or three hits. I was really doing a good job and everyone was kind of shocked. As the season drew to a close I did better and better. The last five days of the season I finished with a flurry, and my earned-run average throwing the knuckleball was 1.90, which is very good.

The last day of the season I was in the clubhouse and Milkes said he wanted to see me for a minute. I went up to his office and he said, "We're going to give you the same contract for next year. We'll guarantee you $22,000." This means if I didn't get released I'd be getting it even if I was sent down to the minors. I felt like kissing him on both cheeks. I also felt like I had a new lease on life. A knuckleball had to be pretty impressive to impress a general manager $7,000 worth. Don't ever think $7,000 isn't a lot of money in baseball. I've had huge arguments over a lot less.

When I started out in 1959 I was ready to love the baseball establishment. In fact I thought big business had all the answers to any question I could ask. As far as I was concerned clubowners were benevolent old men who wanted to hang around the locker room and were willing to pay a price for it, so there would never be any problem about getting paid decently. I suppose I got that way reading Arthur Daley in *The New York Times*. And reading about those big salaries. I read that Ted Williams was making $125,000 and figured that Billy Goodman made $60,000. That was, of course, a mistake.

I signed my first major-league contract at Yankee Stadium fifteen minutes before they played "The Star-Spangled Banner" on opening day, 1962. That's because my making the team was a surprise. But I'd had a hell of a spring. Just before the game was about to start Roy Hamey, the general manager, came into the clubhouse and shoved a contract under my nose. "Here's your contract," he said. "Sign it. Everybody gets $7,000 their first year."

Hamey had a voice like B.S. Pully's, only louder. I signed. It wasn't a bad contract. I'd gotten $3,000 for playing all summer in Amarillo, Texas, the year before.

I finished the season with a 7–7 record and we won the pennant and the World Series, so I collected another $10,000, which was nice. I pitched much better toward the end of the season than at the beginning. Like I was 4–7 early but then won three in a row, and Ralph Houk, the manager, listed me as one of his six pitchers for the stretch pennant race and the Series.

All winter I thought about what I should ask for and finally decided to demand $12,000 and settle for $11,000. This seemed to me an eminently reasonable figure. When I reported to spring training in Ft. Lauderdale—a bit late because I'd spent six months in the army—Dan Topping, Jr., son of the owner, and the guy who was supposed to sign all the lower-echelon players like me, handed me a contract and said, "Just sign here, on the bottom line."

I unfolded the contract and it was for $9,000—if I made the team. I'd get $7,000 if I didn't.

If I made the team?

"Don't forget you get a World Series share," Topping said. He had a boarding-school accent that always made me feel like my fly was open or something. "You can always count on that."

"Fine," I said. "I'll sign a contract that guarantees me $10,000 more at the end of the season if we don't win the pennant."

He was shocked. "Oh, we can't do that."

"Then what advantage is it to me to take less money?"

"That's what we're offering."

"I can't sign it."

"Then you'll have to go home."

"All right, I'll go home."

"Well, give me a call in the morning, before you leave."

I called him the next morning and he said to come over and see him. "I'll tell you what we're going to do," he said. "We don't usually do this, but we'll make a big concession. I talked with my dad, with Hamey, and we've decided to eliminate the contingency clause—you get $9,000 whether you make the club or not."

"Wow!" I said. Then I said no.

"That's our final offer, take it or leave it. You know, people don't usually do this. You're the first holdout we've had in I don't know how many years."

I said I was sorry. I hated to mess up Yankee tradition, but I wasn't going to sign for a $2,000 raise. And I got up to go.

"Before you go, let me call Hamey," Topping said. He told Hamey I was going home and Hamey said he wanted to talk to me. I held the phone four inches from my ear. If you were within a mile of him, Hamey really didn't need a telephone. "Lookit, son," he yelled. "You better sign that contract, that's all there's gonna be. That's it. You don't sign that contract you're making the biggest mistake of your life."

I was twenty-four years old. And scared. Also stubborn. I said I wouldn't sign and hung up.

"All right," Topping said, "how much do you want?"

"I was thinking about $12,000," I said, but not with much conviction.

5

"Out of the question," Topping said. "Tell you what. We'll give you $10,000."

My heart jumped. "Make it ten-five," I said.

"All right," he said. "Ten-five."

The bastards really fight you.

For my ten-five that year I won 21 games and lost only 7. I had a 2.53 earned-run average. I couldn't wait to see my next contract.

By contract time Yogi Berra was the manager and Houk had been promoted to general manager. I decided to let Houk off easy. I'd ask for $25,000 and settle for $20,000, and I'd be worth every nickel of it. Houk offered me $15,500. Houk can look as sincere as hell with those big blue eyes of his and when he calls you "podner" it's hard to argue with him. He said the reason he was willing to give me such a big raise right off was that he didn't want to haggle, he just wanted to give me a top salary, more than any second-year pitcher had ever made with the Yankees, and forget about it.

"How many guys have you had who won 21 games in their second year?" I asked him.

He said he didn't know. And, despite all the "podners," I didn't sign.

This was around January 15. I didn't hear from Houk again until two weeks before spring training, when he came up another thousand, to $16,500. This was definitely final. He'd talked to Topping, called him on his boat, ship to shore. Very definitely final.

I said it wasn't final for me, I wanted $20,000.

"Well, you can't make twenty," Houk said. "We never double contracts. It's a rule."

It's a rule he made up right there, I'd bet. And a silly one anyway, because it wouldn't mean anything to a guy making $40,000, only to somebody like me, who was making very little to start with.

The day before spring training began he went up another two thousand to $18,500. After all-night consultations with Topping, of course. "Ralph," I said, real friendly, "under ordinary circumstances I might have signed this contract. If you had come with it sooner, and if I hadn't had the problem I had last year trying to get $3,000 out of Dan Topping, Jr. But I can't, because it's become a matter of principle."

He has his rules, I have my principles.

Now I'm a holdout again. Two weeks into spring training and I was enjoying every minute of it. The phone never stopped ringing and I was having a good time. Of course, the Yankees weren't too happy. One reason is that they knew they were being unfair and they didn't want anybody to know it. But I was giving out straight figures, telling everybody exactly what I'd made and what they were offering and the trouble I'd had with Dan Topping, Jr.

One time Houk called and said, "Why are you telling everybody what you're making?"

"If I don't tell them, Ralph," I said, "maybe they'll think I'm asking for ridiculous figures. They might even think I asked for $15,000 last year and that I'm asking for thirty now. I just want them to know I'm being reasonable."

And Houk said something that sounded like: *"Rowrorrowrowrr."* You ever hear a lion grumble?

You know, players are always told that they're not to discuss salary with each other. They want to keep us dumb. Because if Joe Pepitone knows what Tom Tresh is making and Tresh knows what Phil Linz is making, then we can all bargain better, based on what we all know. If one of us makes a breakthrough, then we can all take advantage of it. But they want to keep us ignorant, and it works. Most ballplayers in the big leagues do not know what their teammates are making. And they think you're strange if you tell. (Tom Tresh, Joe Pepitone, Phil Linz and I agreed, as rookies, to always tell. After a while only Phil and I told.)

Anyway, on March 8, my birthday, Houk called me and said he was going to deduct $100 a day from his offer for every day I held out beyond March 10. It amounted to a fine for not signing, no matter what Houk said. What he said was, "Oh no, it's not a fine. I don't believe in fining people." And I'm sure it never occurred to him just how unfair a tactic this was. Baseball people are so used to having their own way and not getting any argument that they just don't think they *can* be unfair. When I called Joe Cronin, president of the league, to ask if Houk could, legally, fine me, he said, "Walk around the block, then go back in and talk some more."

After walking around the block and talking it over with my dad, I chickened out. Sorry about that. I called Houk and said, "Okay, you win. I'm on my way down." I salved my wounds with the thought that if I had any kind of a year this time I'd really sock it to him.

Still, if I knew then what I know now, I wouldn't have signed. I'd have called him back and said, "Okay, Ralph, I'm having a press conference of my own to announce that for every day you don't meet *my* demand of $25,000 it will cost *you* $500 a day. Think that one over."

Maybe I wouldn't have gotten $25,000, but I bet I would've gotten more than eighteen-five. I could tell from the negative reaction Ralph got in the press. And I got a lot of letters from distinguished citizens and season-ticket holders, all of them expressing outrage at Houk. That's when I realized I should have held out. It was also when Ralph Houk, I think, started to hate me.

The real kicker came the following year. I had won eighteen games and two in the World Series. Call from Houk:

"Well, what do you want?'"

"Ordinarily, I'd say winning eighteen and two in the Series would be worth about an $8,000 raise."

"Good, I'll send you a contract calling for twenty-six-five."

"But in view of what's happened, last year and the year before that, it will have to be more."

"How much more?"

"At least thirty."

"We couldn't do that. It's out of the question."

A couple of days later he called again. "Does $28,000 sound fair to you?"

"Yes it does, very fair. In fact there are a lot of fair figures. Twenty-eight, twenty-nine, thirty, thirty-two. I'd say thirty-three would be too high and twenty-seven on down would be unfair on your part."

"So you're prepared to sign now."

"Not yet. I haven't decided."

A week later he called again and said he'd sent me the contract I wanted—$28,000.

"Now, wait a minute. I didn't say I'd sign for that."

"But you said it was a fair figure."

"I said there were a lot of fair figures in there. I said thirty-two was fair too."

"Are you going back on your word? You trying to pull a fast one on me?"

"I'm not trying to pull anything on you. I just haven't decided what I'm going to sign for. I just know that twenty-eight isn't it."

By now he's shouting. "Goddammit, you're trying to renege on a deal."

So I shouted back. "Who the hell do you people think you are, trying to bully people around? You have a goddam one-way contract, and you won't let a guy negotiate. You bulldozed me into a contract my first year when I didn't know any better, you tried to fine me for not signing last year, and now you're trying to catch me in a lie. Why don't you just be decent about it? What's an extra thousand or two to the New York Yankees? You wonder why you get bad publicity. Well, here it is. As soon as the people find out the kind of numbers you're talking about they realize how mean and stupid you are."

"All right. Okay. Okay. No use getting all hot about it."

When the contract came it was like he said, $28,000. I called and told him I wouldn't sign it. I told him I wouldn't play unless I got thirty.

"No deal," he said, and hung up.

Moments later the phone rang. Houk: "Okay, you get your thirty. Under one condition. That you don't tell anybody you're getting it."

"Ralph, I can't do that. I've told everybody the numbers before. I can't stop now."

Softly. "Well, I wish you wouldn't."

Just as softly. "Well, maybe I won't."

When the newspaper guys got to me I felt like a jerk. I also felt I owed Ralph a little something. So when they said, "Did you get what you wanted?" I said, "Yeah." And when they said, "What did you want?" I said, "Thirty." But I said it very low.

Now, I think, Ralph really hated my guts. Not so much because I told about the thirty but because he thought I went back on my word.

Four years later Ralph Houk was still angry. By this time I had started up a little real-estate business in New Jersey. A few friends, relatives and I pooled our money, bought some older houses in good neighborhoods, fixed them up and rented them to executives who come to New York on temporary assignment. Houses like that are hard to find and Houk, who lives in Florida, needed one for the '69 season. After a

9

long search he found exactly what he wanted. Then he found out I owned it. He didn't take it. Too bad, it might have been kind of fun to be his landlord.

Of course, I may misunderstand the whole thing. It's easy to misunderstand things around a baseball club. Else how do you explain my friend Elston Howard? We both live in New Jersey and during my salary fights we'd work out a bit together. And he always told me, "Stick to your guns. Don't let them push you around." Then he'd go down to spring training and he'd say to the other guys, "That Bouton is really something. Who does he think he is holding out every year? How are we gonna win a pennant if the guys don't get in shape? He should be down here helping the club."

I didn't help the club much in 1965, which was the year the Yankees stopped winning pennants. I always had a big overhand motion and people said that it looked, on every pitch, as though my arm was going to fall off with my cap. I used to laugh, because I didn't know what they meant. In 1965 I figured it out. It was my first sore arm. It was my only sore arm. And it made me what I am today, an aging knuckleballer.

My record that year was 4–15, and we finished sixth. It wasn't all my fault. I needed lots of help and got it. Nevertheless my spirits were high waiting for my contract because of something Houk had said. He'd been painted into a corner with Roger Maris. There was a story around that after Maris hit the 61 home runs he got a five-year, no-cut contract. But he'd had a series of bad years and should have been cut. So to take himself off the hook with Maris, Houk said that anybody who had a poor year because of injuries would not be cut. Fabulous, man, I thought. That's me.

When I got my contract it called for $23,000, a $7,000 cut.

"But, Ralph, I was injured and you said . . ."

"You weren't injured."

"The hell I wasn't."

"Then how come you pitched 150 innings?"

"I was trying to do what I could, build my arm up, trying to help the team."

Somehow he remained unmoved. I guessed it was my turn to be humble. "Look, Ralph, I know that people think you lost the battle with me last year and I know some of the players are upset that I got $30,000.

10

So I know there are reasons you have to cut me. Tell you what. Even though I could stand firm on the injury thing if I wanted to, I'll make a deal with you. Cut me $3,000 and we can both be happy." He said okay.

After that, it was all downhill. Which is how come I was happy to be making $22,000 with the Seattle Pilots.

Part 2 "My Arm Isn't Sore, It's Just a Little Stiff"

FEBRUARY
26

Tempe

Reported to spring camp in Tempe, Arizona, today, six days late. I was on strike. I'm not sure anybody knew it, but I was.

I had signed my contract before I knew there was going to be a players' strike and I was obligated to report on time. I found that out at the big meeting the players had with Marvin Miller, the players' union leader, at the Biltmore in New York earlier this month. I'm much in sympathy with what Miller is doing and I think, given the circumstances, he won a great victory. I think the owners understand now that we're going to stick together—even the big stars, who don't have that much at stake. Still, I was going to live up to my contract and report on time. What made me change my mind was a phone call I made to Lou Piniella, a twenty-six-year-old rookie who'd been in the Baltimore and Cleveland organizations.

Since the Pilots were not a team yet we had no player representative, so the three or four Pilots at the meeting in the Biltmore were asked to call four or five teammates each to tell them what happened. I reached Lou in Florida and he said that his impulse was to report, that he was scared it would count against him if he didn't, that he was just a rookie looking to make the big leagues and didn't want anybody to get angry at him. But also that he'd thought it over carefully and decided he should support the other players and the strike. So he was not reporting.

That impressed the hell out of me. Here's a kid with a lot more at stake than I, a kid risking a once-in-a-lifetime shot. And suddenly I felt a moral obligation to the players. I decided not to go down.

The reason nobody knew I was on strike, though, was that I'd asked the Pilots to find a place for me and my family in Tempe. They couldn't. So I said that as long as there were no accommodations I couldn't report. I sort of took it both ways. You take your edges where you can. I learned that playing baseball.

As soon as I got to the park I went right over to Marvin Milkes' office and we shook hands and he asked me if I had a nice flight. He also said, "There's been a lot of things said about the strike and I know you've said some things about it, but we're going to forget all that and start fresh. We have a new team and everybody starts with a clean slate. I'm giving some people a new opportunity. I've got a man in the organization who is a former alcoholic. I've even got a moral degenerate that I know of. But as far as I'm concerned we're going to let bygones be bygones and whatever has been said in the past—and I know you've said a lot of things—we'll forget all about it and start fresh."

I said thanks. I also wondered where, on a scale of one to ten, a guy who talks too much falls between a former alcoholic and a moral degenerate.

I know a lot of guys on the club. Greg Goossen is one. He's a catcher, a New York Met castoff, and is up out of Triple-A. Two years ago I was playing against Goose in the International League. There was a bunt back toward the pitcher and Goose came running out from behind the plate yelling, "First base! First base!" at the top of his lungs. Everyone in the ballpark heard him. The pitcher picked up the ball and threw it to second. Everybody safe. And as Goose walked back behind the plate, looking disgusted, I shouted at him from the dugout, "Goose, he had to consider the source."

I guess I got to him, because the first time he saw me—two years later—he said, "Consider the source, huh?"

The only thing separating my locker from the boiler in the clubhouse is Roland Sheldon's. Rollie said it had only exploded once this spring, fortunately while the clubhouse was empty. Reminded me of my first Yankees spring training in St. Petersburg. I was just there for a look and shared a broom closet with Jim Pisoni, an outfielder. I think my number was 129 1/2. The higher the number, the worse chance they think you have of making the club.

The year I was given 56 was the year I made the club. Toward the end of spring training, Big Pete, the No. 1 Yankee clubhouse man, Pete Sheehy, said, "Listen, I got a better number for you. I can give you 27." I told him I'd keep 56 because I wanted it to remind me of how close I was to not making the club. I still wear 56. I'm still close to not making the club.

Sal Maglie is the pitching coach—Sal the Barber of the New York Giants, my boyhood hero. He still looks like he'd knock down his grandmother. He's got those big evil-looking black eyes. Looks something like Snoopy doing the vulture bit. He told me I'd be pitching five minutes of batting practice today and that I'd be the last pitcher.

That might mean something. It's one of the tiny things you look for all during spring training. You watch who you follow in batting practice, try to find out how many minutes you've pitched compared with other pitchers, decide whether you're with the good squad or the bad squad, whether the morning workout is more important than the afternoon workout. The Yankees would divide the squad into morning and afternoon groups and they'd always say it didn't mean a thing, just two groups for convenience. Except that the morning group always had

Mickey Mantle, Roger Maris, Elston Howard, Whitey Ford and guys like that. The afternoon group would have a bunch of guys named Dick Berardino. I never saw a guy hit or pitch himself off the afternoon list.

I'm not sure it's going to be that way here, though. They seem to have strung us all out pretty well. I can't really read anything into the way it's broken up. And that makes me nervous.

Before the first workout, Joe Schultz, the manager (he's out of the old school, I think, because he *looks* like he's out of the old school— short, portly, bald, ruddy-faced, twinkly-eyed), stopped by while I was having a catch. "How you feeling, Jim?" he asked. I wonder what he meant by that?

FEBRUARY
27

This is the first time I've trained in Arizona. I think I'm going to like it. The park is in a beautiful setting—the center of a desolate area, flat, empty, plowed fields in all directions. And then, suddenly, a tremendous rocky crag rises abruptly to look down over the park. At any moment you expect to see a row of Indians on horseback charging around the mountain and into the park shooting flaming arrows. I'd always heard you couldn't work up a sweat in Arizona. Not true. I ran fifteen or twenty windsprints and I can testify that anyone who can't sweat in Arizona hasn't tried.

The clubhouse here is kind of cramped and the Yankees would probably sneer at it, but there's a soda fountain—Coca-Cola, root beer, 7-Up, cold, on tap, freebie. If Pete Previte saw this he'd go crazy. Little Pete's the No. 2 Yankee clubhouse man and he had this mark-up sheet. Every time you took a soft drink you were supposed to make a mark next to your name so he'd know how much to charge you. He spent the whole day going around saying, "Hey, mark 'em up. Don't forget to mark 'em up. Hey, Bouton, you're not marking 'em up." And he'd never have enough orange juice, although that's what everybody wanted most. One time I asked him, "Pete, how come you're always out of orange juice?" And he said, "If I get it, you guys just drink it up."

We were running short sprints and I guess a couple of tongues were beginning to hang out because somebody yelled, "Marvin Miller, where are you now that we need you?"

But don't let baseball players kid you. All we did today was run about fifteen short sprints and Jim Ryun probably runs that much before he brushes his teeth in the morning. Baseball players are far from being the best-conditioned athletes in the world.

I think I detect a bit of Drill Instructor in Ron Plaza. He's the coach who gives us our daily calisthenics. He's got those California-tan good looks, All-American, and he says, "Gentlemen, today we're going to do some jumping-jacks." I don't mind the calisthenics, I think they're good for us. I just don't like the idea of Plaza looking as if he's enjoying himself. He reminds me of the DI I had who always called us "people." "All right, you people, today we are going to do fifty pushups, people." He looked like *he* was enjoying himself too.

And then there's always the coach who hollers, "Good day, good day to work." It could be raining a hurricane out there with mud up to your ass and some coach is sure to say, "Good day, good day to work."

Bob Lasko is in camp. I was glad to see him. He's a pitcher, righthanded, and we broke in together in the Rookie League in Kearny, Nebraska, in 1959. He's thirty years old, too, and he's never pitched a game in the major leagues. He's a real big guy and I remember he had a tremendous fastball and a great overhand curve. I used to try to model my motion after his. I always seemed to be better when he was around. We roomed together in Amarillo in 1961 and became close friends. His trouble was that the Yankees tried to hide him. He pitched in about thirty innings all season at Kearny. One time he got in a ballgame, struck out the side for three consecutive innings and they took him out of the game and put another pitcher in. The rule at the time was that if you didn't get drafted your first year the organization could keep you for three years without moving you up to a major-league roster. Since he pitched so few innings that summer, no one drafted him.

Bob told me today that he'd once complained about it. "I talked to one of the Yankee coaches," he said. "I told him I didn't think the Yankees had been fair to me and his neck started to get all red and he started to holler and damn, we almost had a fight, right there."

I asked him who the coach was.

"Ralph Houk," he said.

Still, some of it is probably Lasko's fault. He led a couple of leagues in earned-run average, but he seemed to have built up a sort of minor-league psychology. He was always an easy-going guy and as a result got pushed around. I know that in the big leagues, if you come to spring training real cocky it will antagonize a lot of the players but it will help your chances with management. They notice you and they say, "Look at that son of a bitch, boy he's really brazen. Let's stick him in there and see what he looks like." And a quiet guy like Lasko might never get a good look.

So why does he go on? For one thing, he's like me. He likes baseball. And there is still the hope that he can get just a few years in the big leagues. That would make getting a job in the future that much easier. Plus, it says here, you can't beat the hours.

FEBRUARY
28

Decided to get a haircut today. My hair was quite long and the sideburns were thick and heavy. I didn't want to have a longhair image, so I got a really short haircut and look like a stormtrooper. It's terrible, but it won't hurt me. You never can tell how spring training is going to go. I could be one of those borderline cases and the difference between making the team and not making it might be the length of my hair.

I wore a mustache all winter and thought I looked pretty good. Cut it off before I came down. Richie Allen can wear those porkchop

19

sideburns of his if he wants because he hits all those home runs. What's standing between me and *my* mustache is about twenty wins.

When I walked into the clubhouse with my new haircut, Sheldon said, "Now you look like the old Bulldog." Bulldog! That's what they called me when I was a big winner with the Yankees. Bulldog. *Gruff!* This is the impression I wanted to create all along. Maybe they'll think because my hair is short I got my fastball back. You got to use all your weapons.

One thing you *don't* do is what Steve Hovley did. He's an outfielder I played with in Seattle last year, twenty-four years old, intellectual type. He told Milkes that he wouldn't report until March 22 because he wanted to finish up some college classes. Milkes told him he'd never make the team if he waited that long and Steve said, well, he'd looked at the roster and didn't think he could make it anyway. Besides, he thought he could use another year or two in Triple-A.

That's a big mistake. No matter what the truth of it is, Milkes will now always think that Steve doesn't have enough desire to be a major leaguer. There are times you have to show hustle, even if it's false.

Lots of holler out there in the infield. "Fire it in there, Baby." "C'mon, Joey." "Chuck it in there." And the word for *that* friends, is false chatter. You don't hear it as much during the season because nobody's nervous and nobody has to impress a coach who thinks you're trying harder if you holler "Hey, whaddaya say?" You only hear it in spring training—and in high-school baseball. I remember when I was in high school, even if we lost the game, the coach would say, "I liked your chatter out there, a lot of holler. That's what I like to see." So if you couldn't hit, you hollered.

Another thing you need in spring training is a knack for looking busy. There really isn't much to do in spring training, and it's a lot like being in the army, where the sergeant will never say anything to you if you *look* like you're doing something. I mean just stopping to tie your shoelace, or walking along briskly as if you have someplace to go. That's what pepper games are, really: looking busy without actually doing anything.

Sheldon was talking about that today. He says what he does is walk around policing up the area and no one ever hollers at him for that. He also walks back and forth to the dugout as if he's on an important mission. "Do something," Shellie said. "Walk, bend, throw a ball into your glove, swing a bat, but don't be standing there with your legs crossed and your arms folded."

Also in camp is Steve Barber, pitcher, lefthanded, who was with the Yankees last year. Naturally we got to talking about Jim Turner, The Colonel, Southern Fried Chicken variety. Turner's the pitching coach over there and has been voted the champion frontrunner of the civilized world. In case you forgot, you could always tell how you were doing by the way The Colonel said good morning. If he said, "Well now, good morning, Jimsie boy," that meant you'd won your last two or three games and were in the starting rotation. If he nodded his head to you and said, "Jimbo, how you doin', how you doin'?" you were still in the starting rotation, but your record probably wasn't much over .500. If he just said, "Mornin'," that meant you were on the way down, that you'd probably lost four out of five and it was doubtful if you would be getting any more starts. If he simply looked at you and gave a solemn nod, that meant you might get some mop-up relief work, or you might not, but you definitely weren't starting anymore and would never get into a close game again. And if he looked past you, over your shoulder, as if you didn't exist, it was all over and you might as well pack your bag because you could be traded or sent down at any moment.

MARCH
1

Joe Schultz stopped by again to say a kind word. I noticed he was making it his business to say something each day to most of the guys. He may look like Nikita Khrushchev, but it means a lot anyway. I'm sure most of us here feel like leftovers and outcasts and marginal players and it doesn't hurt when the manager massages your ego a bit.

I was moved up from last to next-to-last, and then to second, for my five minutes of batting practice, and I've decided there's no significance to the position. My arm feels good; no pain, no problems. Every once in a while I let a fastball fly and it comes out of my hand real easy and seems like it took no effort. I can almost hear a voice in the back of my mind whispering, "You can go back to it, you can find it, you can find your old fastball and you'll be great again." Of course, I've heard that siren song in my head before and I've won a total of fourteen games in the last four years. So I'm going to stick with my knuckleball. I'll probably throw it 90 percent of the time, and if my other stuff comes around for me, I'll probably cut it down to about 40 or 50 percent. But I've got to remember that if it wasn't for my knuckleball I'd probably be back in New Jersey, raising chickens or something. Remember, stupid, remember!

One of the problems is that the hitters hate to hit against my knuckleball in batting practice. They don't like pitchers to work on anything out there. They want you to lay it in there and let them smash it over the fence. So I compromise. For each seven swings they get, I give them two or three knuckleballs.

Gerry McNertney (now there's one of the great names in baseball) was catching me today, and when I threw a knuckler that didn't do much I hollered in to him, "Is it better than Wilhelm's? Is it? Huh?"

Nert caught Hoyt Wilhelm when they were with the White Sox and he tried to be kind. He laughed and said, "Not bad, not bad." I asked Nert about Wilhelm's knuckleball and he said one of his problems was that he was throwing it about three-quarters because he didn't have the strength to come with it straight overhand anymore. He is, after all, at least forty-six by his own admission. Nert said it was only effective when he came straight over. "You seem to be throwing straight overhand all the time," he said, "and you should have success with it."

Things are looking up. Right now I'm thinking that I can do anything—start, relieve, be a long man or a short man. Or all of them together, every day, because the knuckleball doesn't take anything out of your arm. It's like having a catch with your sister. I'm starting to get that old fire in my stomach again.

There are some things I ought to explain about the knuckleball. I was about thirteen years old the first time I threw it. I was very little at the time, the littlest and skinniest kid in the neighborhood, but I could play ball. At least I could hit and run. Although I had a good arm, I couldn't throw very hard. So when I saw a picture on the back of a cereal package explaining how to throw the knuckleball, I thought I'd try it.

There was a picture of Dutch Leonard and a picture of how he held the ball, and about a paragraph explaining it. The knuckleball isn't thrown with the knuckles, of course. It's thrown with the fingertips, and the principle is to release the ball so that it leaves all the fingertips at the same time without any spin on the ball. The air currents and humidity take over and cause the ball to turn erratically and thus move erratically.

Wilhelm was doing pretty good with the Giants at the time, and that was another reason to try it—except that my hand was so small I couldn't hold the ball with three fingers like everybody else did. I had to hold it with all five. I still do. It's kind of freaky, I guess, but as a result I throw it harder than anybody else. Anyway, it took about a week before I could get it to knuckle at all. I remember once I threw one to my brother and hit him right in the knee. He was writhing on the ground moaning, "What a great pitch, what a great pitch." I spent the rest of the summer trying to maim my brother.

I used the knuckleball all the way through high school and college, about 50 percent of the time. I might have been the youngest junkball pitcher in America. After a couple of years in the minors, however, I started to get bigger and stronger and started to overpower people with my fastball. So I phased the knuckleball out.

I never really used it again until 1967. My arm was very sore and I was getting my head beat in. Houk put me into a game against Baltimore and I didn't have a thing, except pain. I got two out and then, with my arm hurting like hell, I threw four knuckleballs to Frank Robinson and struck him out. The next day I got sent to Syracuse. Even so, it wasn't until the last part of the next season that I began throwing it again. The idea that you've lost your regular stuff is very slow in coming.

Sal the Barber came over to me today and said, "You're looking smoother than I remember seeing you in the last few years. You're getting your body into it now. I remember thinking that you were using up your force before you even released the ball and looked as though you never released it the same way twice."

That made me feel pretty good. Then Bob Lemon, manager of the Pilots' Triple-A Vancouver club, came over and said, "Hello, Bill," and Mike Ferraro, an infielder, hollered while I was pitching, "Fire it in there Bob." Thanks a lot, Hank, thanks a lot, Sam.

MARCH
2

Tommy Harper, who's an infielder listed as an outfielder on the roster, reported today. He's certain to make this team, along with guys like Barber, McNertney, Gary Bell, Mike Hegan, Ray Oyler, Don Mincher, Rich Rollins and Tommy Davis. Harper just got out of the Air Force and they asked him if he wanted to re-up, as they call it. They told him he could come back for two years and they'd make him a staff sergeant. And he told them, "I wouldn't re-up for two years if you made me a general."

We had sliding and pick-off drills today and I noticed a lot of the guys having trouble. Lasko was standing next to me during one of them and said, "Hey, I thought this was a simple game."

It's tough in these drills to perform like you should perform because you're much better off in athletics if you do things instinctively. I suppose that's what they mean when they say baseball isn't a thinking man's game. If you have to think about it, you tend to do things mechanically rather than naturally.

I've always felt there were three kinds of athletes. First, there's the guy who does everything instinctively and does it right in the first place. I think Willie Mays is that kind of guy, and so was Mickey Mantle. I don't think these guys can articulate what they're doing, they just know what to do and they go out and do it. I put Yogi Berra in this category too. I remember Yogi standing around the batting cage trying to explain hitting to some of the guys and he started to talk about his hands and his legs and he couldn't make himself clear. Finally he said, "Ah, just watch me do it."

Second, there's the athlete who's educated. If they're pitchers they try to figure out the mechanics of rotation and the aerodynamics of the curve ball. If they're hitters they try to figure out force and velocity in relation to weight. Jay Hook comes to mind. He was a pitcher with an engineering degree from Northwestern University. He had all the tools: big, strong, good stuff. But he was always too involved with the mechanics of pitching. Ballplayers often say, "Quit thinking, you're hurting the club." I really believe you *can* think too much in this game, and Hook always did.

The third kind is the one who is intelligent enough to know that baseball is basically an instinctive game. I like to think that's me. So what *I* do kiddies, is work hard, stay in shape, practice—then, once I'm on the field I let my instincts take over. Also I don't smoke.

Euphoria: Bob Lemon called me by my right name.

Now a few hundred words about Frank Crosetti, coach. Cro, as we fondly call him, is fifty-eight years old, bald as an egg and, we all assume, rich as Croesus. We assume he's rich because he's always checking the stock tables and because between 1932, when he began to play for the Yankees, and 1968 when he left as a coach, he had pulled down some 23 World Series shares in addition to his considerable salary. And no one has noticed him spending very much of it. In addition, starting at age fifty, he elected—possibly through foolishness, more likely through greed—to collect his player pension. When the pension was raised by a considerable amount—only for those who had not yet started to draw on it—Cro sued to get the higher rate. He lost, but I haven't noticed any holes in his shoes.

I have to give him credit, though. He's out there every day, his beady little eyes shining, not an ounce of fat on him, taking calisthenics with all us kids and never missing a beat; jumping-jacks, pushups and everything. Another thing he does is get up every morning at 6:45 a.m. and take a long, pre-breakfast stroll. When he was with the Yankees, once in a while he'd run into some of us coming back from a night on the

25

town. We'd try to get by with a "Good morning, Cro, nice day." I doubt he was fooled. There was even some suspicion that Cro was turning in reports on the hours some players kept, although it has never been confirmed and must be considered a rumor.

Cro's a coach like every other coach, except his twin fortes are saving baseballs (he's a strong company man) to the point of jumping into the stands after them, and chasing photographers off the field. He's the self-appointed photographer-chaser of the Western world. If a photographer should just happen to step into fair territory during practice here's Cro, screaming from the other side of the field, "Hey, what're you doing? Get off the field!" He's got this high, squeaky voice, and when he was with the Yankees half the club was able to imitate it. So at night, when we'd be getting on a bus and you couldn't see individual players, Cro would get aboard and somebody would yell in his voice, "Hey, for crissakes, get the hell off the bus. What're you photographers doing on the bus?"

Don't get the idea that I consider Cro a lovable old man, butt of little jokes but a heart of gold. Like most coaches he's a bit of a washerwoman and sometimes a pain in the ass. I had an odd run-in with him when I was with the Yankees. The unwritten rule on the club was that if a pitcher was knocked out of a game early he could dress and watch it from the stands if he wished, just so long as he was back in the clubhouse after the game—in case the manager had a few nasty words to say to him. On this day we were playing a doubleheader and my wife, Bobbie, was up in the stands with the kids—I have three now, Michael, five, Kyong Jo, four, and Laurie three. I got knocked out early and decided to dress and watch the rest of the game in the stands with my family. After the game I'd get back into uniform for the second game.

Crosetti, who was coaching at third, spotted me in the stands and told The Colonel that I was in my streetclothes and looked like I was about to go home. So The Colonel, who loved to get this kind of information, told Big Pete to go up into the stands and get me. At first I thought Big Pete was kidding, but when I found out he wasn't I was burned up.

I got into my uniform and, when the game was over and Cro came into the clubhouse, I went over and told him to keep his big nose out of my business, that he was a goddam busybody and should have been watching the game instead of me. So he yelled back at me and I yelled back at him—bright, clever things that little boys yell at each other, and all of a sudden he jumped up and started punching me.

Now, *there's* a dilemma. I don't want to get hit, even by the skinny old Cro. At the same time I don't want to hit *Frank Crosetti,* for crissakes. So I sort of covered up and started backing off. Besides, I couldn't help it, I was laughing. At that point my friend Elston Howard, quickly sizing up the great dangers involved, came running over, threw a body block at me and knocked me down. I picked myself up, went over to my locker and sat down. I should have let it go at that. Instead I hollered over to Cro again to keep his nose out of my business and this was when Houk came over and said if I said one more word he'd knock me right off my goddam stool.

I didn't say another word. And that was the end of it, except you may be certain it was all recorded in my file, in red ink.

Hectic day for personal affairs. We moved out of the motel we'd been staying in where it cost us about $135 an hour and into a two-bedroom apartment. Nice place, heated swimming pool and all. Packing, loading, unloading, unpacking—the life of a ballplayer. It's one of the pains in the neck. On the other hand it's exciting, in a way, moving around, seeing new places.

The family loves it in Arizona. We've taken a few rides out into the desert and looked at the cactus and the beautiful rock formations, and the kids are excited about the weather getting warm enough so they can use the pool. Kyong Jo, the Korean boy we adopted, is doing great with his English. Every once in a while he'll burp and say, "Thank you." But he's getting the idea.

Got a big day tomorrow. Ten minutes of batting practice. I think I'll use the Johnny James (former Yankee pitcher) theory of batting practice. Under this theory you imagine you're in a game and you move your pitches around on the hitter, dust him off, throw sliders, the works. The hitters hate it. But it helped Johnny James make the team, at least for a while.

27

MARCH
3

When I was a kid I loved to go to Giant games in the Polo Grounds. And a little thing that happened there when I was about ten years old popped into my mind today. There was a ball hit into the stands and a whole bunch of kids ran after it. I spotted it first, under a seat, and grabbed for it. Just as I did, a Negro kid also snatched at it. My hand reached it a split second before his, though, and I got a pretty good grip on it. But he grabbed the ball real hard and pulled it right out of my hand. No complaint, he took it fair and square. I thought about it afterward, about what made him able to grab that ball out of my hand. I decided it had to do with the way we were brought up—me in a comfortable suburb, him probably in a ghetto. I decided that while I *wanted* the baseball, he *had to have it*.

Batting practice today. Arm felt fine after throwing, which is more than I can say for Steve Barber's. Two seconds after he threw he was in the trainer's room with an icepack on his elbow. And I haven't even had a twinge. It's kind of scary. Maybe I'm not throwing right.

Most pitchers are paranoid about their arms. You live in terror that you're going to wake up in the morning and not be able to pitch anymore. You wake up in the middle of the night and you make a throwing motion to see if it's going to hurt. In the morning the first thing you do is circle your arm just to see how it feels. In fact one of the reasons it takes injured arms so long to heal is that pitchers are constantly testing the aggravated part and making it worse. Trainers always tell you to give it a chance to get better, but what do trainers know about temptation? You got to *test*. I know sometimes I'll be out with my family, eating in a restaurant maybe, and all of a sudden I'll circle my arm over my head and I'm sure everybody thinks I'm calling the waiter or that I'm crazy. I'm just testing.

It's understandable. All a pitcher has is his arm. Pitching is a precise skill that requires a coordinated effort among many parts of the body.

One small hurt and it's all gone. Like a tiddly-winks champion with a hangnail.

The guy pitching batting practice before me, fellow by the name of Paul Click, who won't make the team, got hit with a line drive. Instead of ducking behind the screen in front of the mound he turned his back. I guess he thought that if he turned his back and closed his eyes the ball couldn't find him. He got it in the back of the head and it opened up a lot of skin. It reminded me of the time when I was pitching in Baltimore, six years ago. I threw a low outside fastball to Jackie Brandt. He held back on it and at the last instant reached out and hit a line drive right back at me. I never saw the damn thing. It smacked me on the jaw and opened me up for about twelve stitches. Those were the days when I gutsed it, so I jumped right up and said I wanted to pitch. "Ralph, I'm ready, I'm ready," I said. "I can pitch." Johnny Blanchard was the catcher. "Not with two mouths you ain't, Meat," he said.

They wanted to carry me off on a stretcher but I knew if my wife heard I was carried off the field she'd have a miscarriage. So I went off under my own power, bloody towel and all, and listened carefully for the ovation. I got it.

Ovations are nice and some guys sort of milk them. Like Joe Pepitone. If he had just the touch of an injury he'd squirm on the ground for a while and then stand up, gamely. And he'd get his ovation. After a while the fans got on to him, though, and he needed at least a broken leg to move them.

There was an intrasquad game today after the workout, and although I didn't have to stay to watch it I did. That's what you call showing desire. Jim O'Toole was pitching when I got there, and his curve wasn't sharp and he was walking a lot of guys. He's got about eight kids and spring training means more to him than a lot of other guys, but he was really laboring. I felt sort of sorry for him, but not very.

Let me explain. It was rather early to be playing an intrasquad game and I thought, "I hope nobody gets hurt." Then I had to amend that in my mind. I meant "I hope I don't get hurt." I've always wanted everyone to do well. If I'm not playing I root for my teammates. But I don't want them to do well at my expense. Even when I was in junior high school,

I'd sit there hollering encouragement and all the time I'd be saying, "Gee whiz, if he'd break his leg I could get in there and play." It's not exactly the perfect attitude, but it's the way I feel.

Last spring Fred Talbot said to me, "When I'm out there pitching, are you rooting for me, Bouton?"

"Yeah, Fred."

"Do you really hope I do well?"

"Yeah, Fred. But not at my expense."

What I should have said was, "Yeah, Fred, I hope you do well. I hope you have a helluva year down there in Triple-A." It ended up I landed in Triple-A and he stayed in the big leagues. When I was sent down we I had a record of 1–0. Talbot was 1–8. I still think about that.

The mindless grind of spring training produces, as you might guess, a sort of mindlessness. This morning Mike Hegan and I were partners in calisthenics and were locked in something that looked like the Twist. And I said to Mike, "Hey, this gives me an idea for a dance."

"Hey, that's right," he said. "We'll call it the Twist."

"Right, and we'll open a string of dance halls."

"Yeah, and we can call them the Peppermint Twist."

"Right."

"But we need a front man with a great name. How about Chubby?"

"Great. We'll call him Chubby Checker."

This conversation actually took place, Doctor.

Then some guy farted and everybody laughed, and about five minutes later, in a sudden burst of quiet, he farted again and somebody hollered, "Will somebody answer the phone! Some ass keeps calling."

Uniform-measuring day. This is always a waste. They measure everybody carefully and the uniforms arrive three sizes too big. Part of the reason is that everybody is wearing tight-fitting uniforms these days. Pepitone refuses to take the field if his uniform isn't skintight. Phil Linz used to say that he didn't know why, but he could run faster in tight pants. And I understand that Dick Stuart, old Dr. Strangeglove, would smooth his uniform carefully, adjust his cap, tighten his belt and say, "I add 20 points to my average if I know I look bitchin' out there."

Mike Marshall is a righthanded pitcher who was 15-9 in the Tiger organization last season. He's got a master's degree from Michigan State. He majored in phys. ed., with a minor in mathematics. He's a cocky kid with a subtle sense of humor. He's been telling everybody that the new lower mound, which was supposed to help the hitters, actually shortens the distance the pitcher has to throw the ball. It has to do with the hypotenuse of a right triangle decreasing as either side of the triangle decreases. Therefore, says Marshall, any psychological advantage the hitters gain if the pitcher doesn't stand tall out there will be offset by the pitchers knowing that they are now closer to the plate.

Clever fellow, Marshall. He has even perfected a pick-off motion to second base that's as deadly as it is difficult to execute. He says one reason it's effective is that he leans backward as he throws the ball. I asked why, and he said, "Newton's Third Law, of course." Of course. Except the last time I tried his pick-off motion I heard grinding noises in my shoulder.

Steve Hovley sidled over to me in the outfield today and whispered into my ear, "Billy Graham is a cracker."

Although I've enjoyed being in Arizona, there are things about training in Florida I'll miss. Every spring Phil Linz and I would have dinner at Las Novedades in Tampa and we'd order Cuban black-bean soup and *Pompano en papillot* and we'd have a bottle of wine and talk about our old days in the minor leagues (and the time Joe Pepitone stole an elevator). Even when Phil was with the Mets we'd make it a point to meet in Tampa and go to Las Novedades.

I had the same kind of relationship with Roger Repoz and Fritz Peterson, two others guys I roomed with on the Yankees. Roger and I had this one spot in Detroit, the Italian Gardens. We'd go there for linguine with white clam sauce and we'd have a bottle of wine, and then some more linguine and another bottle of wine, then maybe another bottle of wine, and we'd stagger back to our room. When Roger was sold we made a pact that any time we got to Detroit we'd go alone to the Italian Gardens and order linguine and drink wine and stagger back to the hotel in memory of the good times we'd had.

I know when I'm in Anaheim next I'll do what Fritz Peterson and I used to think was a lot of fun. We'd rent a little car and speed along the freeways playing Spanish music as loud as the radio would go and we'd go down to the beach or into the mountains. In San Francisco Fritz and I made an inspection trip to Haight-Ashbury where the hippies offered to turn us on with LSD. We were too chicken to try.

The first roommate I had in pro ball was a guy named Arturo Polanco and he couldn't speak a word of English. So he taught me Spanish and I taught him English. The first words he learned were "Son of a bleach." I think something was lost in translation.

MARCH
4

Mickey Mantle announced his retirement the other day and I got to thinking about the mixed feelings I've always had about him. On the one hand I really liked his sense of humor and his boyishness, the way he'd spend all that time in the clubhouse making up involved games of chance and the pools he got up on golf matches and the Derby and things like that.

I once invested a dollar when Mantle raffled off a ham. I won, only there was no ham. That was one of the hazards of entering a game of chance, Mickey explained.

I got back by entering a fishing tournament he organized and winning the weight division with a ten-pounder I'd purchased in a store the day before. Two years later Mantle was still wondering why I'd only caught that one big fish and why all the other fish that were caught were green and lively while mine was gray and just lay there, staring.

I also remember the time I won my first major-league game. It was a shutout against the Washington Senators in which I walked seven guys and gave up seven hits and had to pitch from a stretch position all game. They were hitting line drives all over the place and Hector "What a Pair of Hands" Lopez bailed me out with about four leaping catches in left field. When the game was over I walked back into the clubhouse and there was a path of white towels from the door to my locker, and all the guys were standing there, and just as I opened the door Mickey was putting the last towel down in place. I'll never forget him for that.

And I won't forget the time—1962, I guess it was—in Kansas City. I was sitting alone in a restaurant, eating, when Mickey and Whitey Ford came in and Mickey invited me to eat with them and picked up the tab and it made me feel good all over and like a big shot besides.

On the other hand there were all those times when he'd push little kids aside when they wanted his autograph, and the times when he was snotty to reporters, just about making them crawl and beg for a minute of his time. I've seen him close a bus window on kids trying to get his autograph. And I hated that *look* of his, when he'd get angry at somebody and cut him down with a glare. Bill Gilbert of *Sports Illustrated* once described that look as flickering across his face "like the nictitating membrane in the eye of a bird." And I don't like the Mantle who refused to sign baseballs in the clubhouse before the games. Everybody else had to sign, but Little Pete forged Mantle's signature. So there are thousands of baseballs around the country that have been signed not by Mickey Mantle, but by Pete Previte.

Like everybody else on the club I ached with Mantle when he had one of his numerous and extremely painful injuries. I often wondered, though, if he might have healed quicker if he'd been sleeping more and loosening up with the boys at the bar less. I guess we'll never know.

What we do know, though, is that the face he showed in the clubhouse, as opposed to the one he reserved for the outside world, was often one of great merriment.

I remember one time he'd been injured and didn't expect to play, and I guess he got himself smashed. The next day he looked hung over out of his mind and was sent up to pinch-hit. He could hardly see. So he staggered up to the plate and hit a tremendous drive to left field for a home run. When he came back into the dugout everybody shook his hand and leaped all over him, and all the time he was getting a standing ovation from the crowd. He squinted out at the stands and said, "Those people don't know how tough that really was."

Another thing about Mantle. He was a pretty good practical joker. One time he and Ford told Pepitone and Linz that they'd finally arrived, they were ready to go out with the big boys. Mantle told them to get dressed up, tie and all—this was in Detroit—and meet them in a place called The Flame. Mickey gave them the address and said to be sure to ask for Mickey Mantle's table.

Pepitone and Linz were like a couple of kids at Christmas. They couldn't stop talking about what a great time they were going to have with Mickey Mantle and Whitey Ford. They got all fancied up, hopped into a cab and told the driver to take them to The Flame. After about a half-hour the cab pulled up in front of a place that was in the heart of the slum section—a hole in the wall with a broken plate-glass window in front and a little broken-down sign over the door: The Flame. No Mantle. No Ford. No table.

Tommy Davis was in the training room having the ankle he broke in 1965 taped. I asked him if he thought it would ever be the same again and he said he doubted it, because it's supposed to take two years for a fracture and dislocation to heal and he was back playing after one. I'm sure that's true of a lot of injuries that athletes suffer. They come back too soon and the injury keeps recurring. Like I say, you can't beat the hours.

Freddie Velazquez was in the trainer's room too. He caught a foul ball on his big toe and it looked like a ripe tomato. The toenail was peeling off. He never made a sound while it was bandaged. Then he went out and played on it. Later Velazquez was talking Spanish to some of the other players and someone—I don't know who—yelled, "Talk English! You're in America now."

It was 55 degrees and blowing out there today, so I only watched a couple of innings of the intrasquad game. I was there long enough to see Marshall get hit pretty hard. Evidently the shorter hypotenuse didn't help him much. He just ran into Doubleday's First Law, which states that if you throw a fastball with insufficient speed, someone will smack it out of the park with a stick.

As penance for going home early I spent some time considering the possible fortunes of this ballclub. It's early, but it doesn't look bad at all. Except we're going to be hurting for starting pitchers. Gary Bell is probably the only legitimate starter we have. Which isn't bad for number 56.

In the back of my mind I see myself as a starter for this team. I think a knuckleball pitcher is better off starting. One reason is that there are usually men on base when a relief pitcher comes in. If his knuckleball is working well, you might get a passed ball and a run. If it's not working well—and often it's not—you get hit. With no one on base, though, this isn't too important. The argument is simple and crystal clear. If only somebody would listen.

I asked one of the sportswriters if Joe Schultz had said anything about the way I threw today and he said, "Yeah."

"Well, what?"

"He said, 'It's too early to tell.'"

My reporting late has made this the first spring I've ever been behind anybody getting into shape. Usually I'm ready to pitch in the early games, but it looks like I'm not going to be ready here. It's quite different from my last spring with the Yankees in 1967. I was really impressive, right from the beginning. I led the club in innings pitched with 30, and I gave up the fewest hits, fifteen, and no homers and only two or three extra-base hits. My ERA was .092, which means less than one run per game, and in one stretch I went nine innings without giving up a hit. At the end of spring training a newspaper guy said to Houk, "Wow, didn't Bouton have a great spring?" and Houk said, "You can't go by that too much. He always has a good spring." (The spring before I was 1-3 and had a 5.10 ERA.)

Another thing about that spring. This was after I'd pitched about 25 marvelous innings. Houk sat next to me in the dugout and told me, very confidentially, "You know, you're having a helluva spring, a better spring than Dooley Womack, and I think you're just the man we need in the bullpen."

What I wanted to say was: "I'm having a better spring than *who*? *Dooley Womack? The* Dooley Womack? I'm having a better spring than Mel Stottlemyre or Sam McDowell or Bob Gibson." That's what I *should* have said. Instead I just sat there shaking my head. He could've knocked me off my seat.

Instead he sold me to Seattle. Okay, so I had a lousy year there. That still doesn't mean Houk knew it all the time. You can make a lousy pitcher out of anybody by not pitching him. I'll always believe that's what Houk did to me. Besides, there's no way the Yankees can justify getting rid of a twenty-nine-year-old body for $12,000, and before the season is over I'm going to remind a lot of people that they did.

Steve Hovley and I had a discussion about Norman Vincent Peale's power of positive thinking. We agree it's a crock. Steve said it was like feeding false data into a computer. There comes a day when you realize you've been building a false sense of confidence and then it all breaks down and the dream is smashed.

I think that kind of thing happened with the Yankees. Houk used to tell us we were going to win the pennant, *we were going to win the pennant.* Then June rolled around and we knew we *couldn't* win the pennant, but instead of trying for second or third everybody threw in the towel and we finished ninth.

We might be building ourselves up to that kind of fall with this club. Everybody is saying we're going to be great. There's a difference between optimism and wishful thinking.

Not only did I have some tenderness in my elbow today but Sal told me I'll be pitching in the exhibition game Sunday. The tenderness will go away, but how am I going to pitch Sunday? I'm not ready. I haven't thrown to spots yet. I haven't thrown any curveballs at all. My fingers aren't strong enough to throw the knuckleball right. I've gone back to taking two baseballs and squeezing them in my hand to try to strengthen my fingers and increase the grip. I used to do that with the Yankees, and naturally it bugged The Colonel. The reason it bugged The Colonel is that he never saw anybody do it before. Besides, it wasn't his idea. "What are you doing?" The Colonel would sputter. "Put those baseballs back in the bag."

Immediately Fritz Peterson would pick up two baseballs and start doing the same thing. One day Fritz got Steve Hamilton and Joe Verbanic and about three or four other pitchers to carry two balls around with them wherever they went. It drove The Colonel out of his mind.

The following spring Fritz was removed as my roommate. The Colonel kept telling Fritz not to worry, that pretty soon he wouldn't have to room with "that Communist" anymore. And Fritz would say, "No, no, that's all right. I *want* to room with him. I *like* him. We get along great."

And The Colonel would say, "Fine, fine. We'll get it straightened out."

So one day Houk called me into his office and said, "Jim, we're switching around roommates this year. I think it will be good for everybody to have pitchers with pitchers, catchers with catchers."

"That's fine," I said. "I'm already rooming with a pitcher."

"Well, we want young pitchers to room with young pitchers, and since you've been with the club so long, we feel you deserve a single room. It's a status thing. Whitey and Mickey have single rooms, and we thought you should too."

I said that was fine with me and if he wanted Fritz to room with a young pitcher I'd take a single room.

Then Houk called Fritz in and said, "Bouton deserves a single room and you wouldn't want to stand in his way, would you?" Fritz said he wouldn't, so they put him in with Dooley Womack, young pitcher. He was three months younger than I.

The Yankees thought I was a bad influence on Fritz. They had some funny ideas about bad influence. What I did bad was talk to newspapermen and talk around the clubhouse about things that were on my mind, politics sometimes, and religion. That's breaking the rules. The word was around: don't talk to the newspapermen. Hell, baseball *needs* the newspapermen. So I broke a rule. But suppose you break the rules about staying up late and getting drunk. That's okay. It may hurt the team, but it's better than talking to newspapermen. You figure it.

As for teaching Peterson to do the wrong things, the only thing I ever taught him was how to throw that change-up he uses so effectively. And he still enjoys giving me the credit.

We were sitting around the clubhouse and I asked Sal the Barber about the days when he pitched for the Giants against the Dodgers. He said yeah, he'd never forget those days. "You know, it's a funny thing," he said. "When I pitched against the Dodgers I didn't care if it was the last game I ever pitched. I really hated that club. If I could've gotten that feeling everytime I pitched I'd have been a lot better pitcher."

I'll have that feeling at least a couple of times this year. When I pitch against the Yankees.

MARCH

6

Steve Hovley sidled over to me in the outfield and said, "To a pitcher a base hit is the perfect example of negative feedback."

Sal Maglie said he hadn't seen me working on my breaking ball, and he's right, because I haven't. So tomorrow I'll have to work on that too. Damn, I can't believe the games are starting so fast. Tomorrow's the first game and I don't even know who's pitching. Still, it will be kind of exciting to see how we do. I guess starting out with a new team is sort of like setting out to discover America. Sort of.

Gary Bell is nicknamed Ding Dong. Of course. What's interesting about it is that "Ding Dong" is what the guys holler when somebody gets hit in the cup. The cups are metal inserts that fit inside the jock strap, and when a baseball hits one it's called ringing the bell, which rhymes with hell, which is what it hurts like. It's funny, even if you're in the outfield, or in the dugout, no matter how far away, when a guy gets it in the cup you can hear it. Ding Dong.

At a pre-workout meeting Joe Schultz told us to learn the signs or it would cost us money. This is a lot different from Houk's theory. Houk's method was to be as nice to us as possible and if you missed a sign he would alibi for you. You could miss them all year and he would never get angry. I guess he figured that someday you'd come to like him enough to start paying attention to the signs. But the Yankees sure missed a lot of signs. Even when we were winning.

MARCH
7

Okay, boys and girls, tomorrow is my birthday and I'll be thirty years old. I don't feel like thirty. I look like I'm in my early twenties and I feel like I'm in my early twenties. My arm, however, is over a hundred years old.

Had our first spring-training game, the first real test for the shiny new Seattle Pilots. Today was the day. This was it. For keeps. The big one. Against Cleveland. Greg Goossen was the designated pinch-hitter under the experimental rule that allows one player to come to bat all during the game without playing in the field. "Are they trying to tell me something about my hands?" Goossen went around saying. "Are they trying to tell me something about my glove?" And after that he became the first Seattle Pilot to say, "Play me or trade me."

I was watching the game today for some signs of what kind of team we're going to have this year. There were lots of them, but I'm still not sure. Like we gave up two runs in the first inning on the first four pitches and I thought, "Oh, oh. Move over, Mets." But in our half of the first we scored five runs and we went on to get nineteen in the game. I couldn't believe it. I think the people in Seattle will now start believing we have a good team. And, my God, maybe we do. We scored all those runs without Tommy Davis, or Don Mincher or Rich Rollins. Or Jim Bouton, for that matter.

I've started slowly tossing the real big overhand curve ball that once made me famous. I also threw the knuckleball to Freddy Velazquez and was gratified when McNertney came over with the big knuckleball glove and asked Velazquez if he could catch me for a while. Still can't believe I'm pitching day after tomorrow, although mentally I've started getting ready—I mean I'm getting scared. I love to pitch when I'm scared. Of all the big games I've had to pitch in my life—and I'm including high-school games that were just as big to me as any major-league game—I always did my best work when I was scared stiff. In fact, if I'm not scared for a game I'll create some critical situations in my mind. Like, I'll pretend it's a World Series game and that it really counts big. I told Fritz Peterson about how I felt about being scared and one day before I was going to start a game he came over and whispered in my ear, "If you want to see your baby again, you'll win today."

After the game Bobbie and I were at a party with Gary Bell and his wife and Steve Barber and his. Gary's wife, Nan, said she'd been anxious to meet me since she'd read in the Pilot spring guidebook that some of my hobbies were water coloring, mimicry and jewelry-making. "Everyone else has hunting and fishing, so I figured you must be a real beauty. I mean, jewelry-making?" said Nan. "Make me some earrings, you sweet thing."

Then we got to talking about some of the crazy things ballplayers do. Nan told a story of the time she called Gary on the road to check on a flight she was supposed to catch. She called him at 4:30 A.M., his time, and his roommate, Woodie Held, answered the phone and said, without batting an eyelash, that Gary was out playing golf. And Nan shrugged and said, "Maybe he was."

My wife and I burst out laughing when Gary asked me if I'd ever been on the roof of the Shoreham Hotel in Washington. The Shoreham is the beaver-shooting capital of the world, and I once told Bobbie that you could win a pennant with the guys who've been on that roof. "Pennant, hell," Gary said. "You could stock a whole league."

I better explain about beaver-shooting. A beaver-shooter is, at bottom, a Peeping Tom. It can be anything from peering over the top of the dugout to look up dresses to hanging from the fire escape on the twentieth floor of some hotel to look into a window. I've seen guys chin themselves on transoms, drill holes in doors, even shove a mirror under a door.

One of the all-time legendary beaver-shooters was a pretty good little lefthanded pitcher who looked like a pretty good little bald-headed ribbon clerk. He used to carry a beaver-shooting kit with him on the road. In the kit there was a fine steel awl and several needle files. What he would do is drill little holes into connecting doors and see what was going on. Sometimes he was lucky enough to draw a young airline stewardess, or better yet, a young airline stewardess and friend.

One of his roommates, a straight-arrow type—Fellowship of Christian Athletes and all that—told this story: the pitcher drilled a hole through the connecting door and tried to get him to look through it. He wouldn't. It was against his religion or something. But the pitcher kept nagging him. "You've got to see this. *Boyohboyohboy!* Just take one quick look." Straight-arrow finally succumbed. He put his eye to the hole and was treated to the sight of a man sitting on the bed tying his shoelaces.

One of the great beaver-shooting places in the minor leagues was Tulsa, Oklahoma. While "The Star-Spangled Banner" was played you could run under the stands and look up at all kinds of beaver. And anytime anyone was getting a good shot, the word would go out "*Psst!* Section 27." So to the tune of "The Star-Spangled Banner" an entire baseball club of clean-cut American boys would be looking up the skirt of some female.

Beaver shooting can get fairly scientific. I was still in the minor leagues when we discovered that if you stuck a small hand mirror under a hotel room door—especially in the older hotels, where there were large spaces between the door and the floor—you could see the whole room just by looking at the mirror. This was a two-man operation: one guy on his hands and knees looking at the mirror, the other at the end of the hall laying chicky, as they say. We usually sprinkled some change around on the floor so you'd have a reason being down on it if anybody caught you.

Spot a good beaver and you could draw an instant crowd. One time in Ft. Lauderdale we spotted this babe getting out of her bathing suit. The louvered windows of her room weren't properly shut and we could see right into the room. Pretty soon there were twenty-five of us jostling for position.

Now, some people might look down on this sort of activity. But in baseball if you shoot a particularly good beaver you are a highly respected person, one might even say a folk hero of sorts. Indeed, if you are caught out late at night and tell the manager you've had a good run of beaver-shooting he'd probably let you off with a light fine.

The roof of the Shoreham is important beaver-shooting country because of the way the hotel is shaped—a series of L-shaped wings that make the windows particularly vulnerable from certain spots on the roof. The Yankees would go up there in squads of 15 or so, often led by Mickey Mantle himself. You needed a lot of guys to do the spotting. Then someone would whistle from two or three wings away, *"Psst!* Hey! Beaver shot. Section D. Five o'clock." And there'd be a mad scramble of guys climbing over skylights, tripping over each other and trying not to fall off the roof. One of the first big thrills I had with the Yankees was joining about half the club on the roof of the Shoreham at 2:30 in the morning. I remember saying to myself, "So this is the big leagues."

MARCH

8

Mesa

Today Joe Schultz said, "Men, you got to remember to touch all the bases." The occasion was a meeting after our glorious 19–4 victory in which one of the guys on the Cleveland club missed third base and was called out. So the lesson for today was "Touch those bases. Especially first."

A couple of things about spring training. Mike Ferraro, an infielder, was with the Yankees last spring. Bobby Cox got a big winter buildup and was supposed to have the third-base job there, but Ferraro had such a hot spring (sportswriters voted him the Yankees' outstanding rookie; he hit .351, Cox hit .186) they had to start the season with him at third. They let him play eleven games and when he didn't burn down any buildings they benched him and sent him to Syracuse. He feels that they never intended to use him at all but were embarrassed into it and were not unhappy when he didn't do well.

Then there was Duke Carmel. He was supposed to be the second coming of Joe DiMaggio, and they really gave him a good shot. But he didn't hit in Ft. Lauderdale, and I remember Whitey Ford saying to him, "Well, Duke, it looks like you just can't hit in southern Florida." We made a trip to Tampa and he didn't hit there either. "Well, Duke, it looks like you're just not a Florida hitter," Whitey Ford said. Then we played a few exhibition games in the South and Carmel didn't get a hit. "Well,

Duke," Ford said, "it looks like you just can't hit south of the Mason-Dixon line." When the season started it turned out Duke couldn't hit north of the Mason-Dixon line either, and finally he was sent down when he was about 0-for-57. If they hadn't wanted him to make it so bad they never would have held on to him that long. But they'd spent all winter building him up. And they'd built up Bobby Cox the same way. They wanted Cox to make it, not Ferraro.

The other thing is a story Johnny Sain once told me. Sain is not only the greatest pitching coach who ever lived, he's a man who tells the truth. And what he says, believe it or not, is that sportswriters actually play a part in deciding who's going to make the team. Sain said he sat in on many meetings where the performance of the individual player hadn't changed, but there had been two or three articles written about him and immediately the coaches and management tended to look at him in a new light. Sain says if there's not a lot of difference between players, the job will go to the guy who seems to be getting the most attention in the newspapers. Power of the press.

Tomorrow I'll be pitching three innings or less against Oakland, and I'm a little worried. My fastball isn't ready yet and my knuckleball is just marginal. Yet, as several people have pointed out to me, I need to accumulate some good statistics to throw at them when spring training is over. I can't say, well, I've been working on my knuckleball all spring and that's why I got clobbered.

My wife reminds me that I never got clobbered in Seattle when I was first working on my knuckleball and she suggests I go with it all the way. I give her opinion a lot of weight. We were both freshmen at Western Michigan when we met and all she would talk about was baseball. When I told her I was going out for the freshman team, she said, "You don't have to do that because of me."

I didn't tell her it wasn't because of her. And then, when she first saw me pitch she said, "That's a big-league pitcher if I ever saw one." So she's a hell of a scout. Knuckleballs. Hmm.

I've had some pretty good advice from my family. My dad especially. He helped pick the college I went to and got me into it. My services as a pitcher were not exactly in great demand. I pitched a no-hitter in my senior year in high school but I was only 5-10 and 150 pounds. My dad got a look at the Western Michigan campus, fell in love with the beauty of it, thought I'd love the baseball stadium and had me apply. I didn't hear anything for a long while, but my dad was real cool. He took a bunch of my clippings—all six of them—had copies made and sent them to the baseball coach there, Charley Maher. He wrote, "Here's a fellow that may help our Broncos in the future," and signed it "A Western Michigan baseball fan." A week later I was accepted.

It was my dad's cool that got me the bonus from the Yankees too. I'd been playing with an amateur team in Chicago in the summer of 1958 and nobody noticed me much until I pitched two good games in the tournament at the end of the season. I mean scouts would walk up to me and ask where they could find a player, but it was always somebody else. After those two games, though, the scouts were buzzing around me, wanting to take me to dinner, and there were a lot of rendezvous in cars and a lot of cloak-and-dagger stuff, and it was all a big thrill to me.

When I got home at about nine o'clock my mom and dad were playing bridge with some friends, and when I walked in the door I said, "Dad, you're not going to believe it, but I pitched the best game of the tournament and the scouts want to sign me. Dad, they're talking about real big money."

My dad looked at his cards. "Two no trump," he said.

He didn't really believe me. Then the phone rang and I said, "Dad, that's a scout on the phone, I know it is. What should I tell him?"

"Tell him $50,000," he said. "Three spades."

He still didn't believe me. I went over to the phone, and sure enough it was a scout from Philadelphia. "My dad says $50,000," I said. The scout said, "Fine. We want you to fly to Philadelphia and work out with the team."

That ended the card game.

I flew to Philadelphia, and it was great. I met Robin Roberts and Puddin' Head Jones and a lot of the other players. And they put me up at the Hotel Warwick, which had these leather-padded elevators that impressed me tremendously. I ordered a $10 meal, including three or four appetizers and a giant filet mignon. But I felt kind of guilty because all the time I was in Philadelphia it rained and I didn't get a chance to throw a single pitch. I went home and never heard from them again. For a long time I worried that it was because I spent so much on that meal.

I also went to Detroit, and I remember meeting Al Kaline and seeing Ted Williams smack five in a row into the upper deck in batting practice. I threw on the sidelines for the Tigers and all they would offer me was $10,000. I went home and talked it over with my dad and we decided the money the scouts had been talking was all a lot of baloney. Hardly any of the other clubs were interested anymore. I was discouraged, disappointed.

So my dad went to work on a form letter. "My son Jim is prepared to sign a major-league contract by Thanksgiving. If you are interested, please have your bid in by then." He sent the letter to about half the major-league clubs. The only club we fooled was the Yankees.

Jerry Coleman came out to talk to us, and my dad was careful to have baseball-team letterheads strewn around as if we were up to our ears in offers. Coleman authorized the local scout, Art Stewart, to go up to $30,000, and it was laid out this way: I'd get a $5,000 bonus, $5,000 a year in salary over the next three years, and I'd get the remaining $10,000 if I made it to the major leagues. It came to $10,000 a year—if I made it. A lot of bonuses weren't as big as they sounded.

But I was happy and my dad and I threw our arms around each other and congratulated each other on how smart we were to pull such a fast one on the New York Yankees. As it turned out I spent those three years in the minors and did make the Yankees, which means they made a pretty cheap investment. In recent years I've been kidding my dad about having sold me short in the first place and how a really astute father would have been able to get me at least $50,000 or $60,000.

MARCH
9

Tempe

Before the game today Rollie Sheldon was talking about old-timers. It's a funny thing, but athletes have improved tremendously through the years in every sport where performance can be objectively measured—track and field, swimming, etc. Yet in other sports, especially boxing and baseball, there are always people who say the old-timers were better—even unmatched. I don't believe that, and I was very interested when Sheldon pointed out some figures in the Hall of Fame book. Like, old "Hoss" Radbourne, who played before the turn of the century. He pitched the last 27 games of the season for his team and won 26 of them. Old Hoss was 5 feet 9 inches tall and weighed 168 pounds. Some hoss! Pony is more like it.

Some of the other heights and weights in the book were great. Wilbert Robinson was 5-9 and 215 pounds. Can you imagine what he looked like? Which reminds me of what Johnny Sain used to say on Old Timers' days: "There sure is a lot of bullshit going on in here today. The older they get the better they were when they were younger."

Pitched my three innings today and gave up two runs. I consider it a good outing, however. I struck out the first hitter I faced on four pitches, all knuckleballs. (Don't ask me who he was; hitters are just meat to me. When you throw a knuckleball you don't have to worry about strengths and weaknesses. I'm not sure they mean anything, anyway.) I noticed again that I throw a better knuckleball in a game than I do on the sidelines. Maybe because the juices start flowing.

I gave up only one hit, a line-drive single after I got behind on the count to Danny Cater—2 and 0 on knuckleballs. I had to come in with a fastball and he hit it pretty good. The only other well-hit ball was off a knuckler, but it was on the ground and went for an out.

In the three innings I walked two, committed an error (hit Bert Campaneris in the head trying to throw him out at first), was hurt by a passed ball (a real good knuckler that broke in on a righthanded hitter, went off McNertney's glove and back to the backstop) and a couple of sacrifice flies. Two unearned runs. So the old ERA starts off at zero.

In the shower room, Maglie told me he felt I needed my other pitches to set up my knuckleball. He also said he didn't want me to become strictly a knuckleball pitcher and that I should work on my curve, fastball and change-up. "Even if you don't throw it for a strike, just show it to them and let them know you have it," he said. I was glad to hear that from Sal. No matter what Bobbie says, I don't want to abandon myself completely to the knuckleball. I can still hear that lost chord.

MARCH
10

Mesa

Game called on account of rain. So we sat around the clubhouse and shot the shit. We're still in the process of feeling each other out. Because we're all sort of strangers there are no old, smoldering problems. Mostly we know each other only from playing against each other. Ray Oyler was saying that here Gary Bell is lockering next to him and for the last eight years Ray'd been screaming across the field at him, "Hey, sweetheart. Where's your purse, you big pussy?" Ray says it's all very strange.

The only guy here I ever hollered at was Jim Gosger. He was always just a marginal player with the Kansas City A's but he would hit me like he was Ted Williams. I used to scream at him, "What the hell are you doing hitting me? You're not good enough." And he'd say what hitters always say, even if you get them out. "Can't understand how you get anybody out with that shit you throw!"

There are days, I suppose, when we are both right.

Little Mike asked me today when I would be pitching for the Seattle Angels and I had to tell him it wouldn't be the Angels, it would be the Pilots. He got used to Angels last year when Seattle was a minor league affiliate of the California Angels. It's been rough on Mike. First it was the New York Yankees and then the Syracuse Chiefs, and just when he was getting used to Syracuse it was the Yankees again, and then the Seattle Angels, and now the Seattle Pilots. And let's hope it won't be the Vancouver Mounties. I've got to make this club and stay here all year if only so my son will know where his dad's working.

Saw a diagram of Sicks' Stadium (named after beer baron Emile Sicks) in Seattle today, and the power alleys—where the sluggers put away knuckleballs that don't knuckle—are 345 feet. Yankee Stadium is over 100 feet deeper in left-center and over 60 feet deeper in rightcenter. No doubt about it, I'm going to be a threat in old Sicks'.

MARCH
11

Tempe
Knuckleball to the rescue today. I pitched batting practice, and when I was warming up my elbow hurt on every pitch—except the knuckleball. It was impossible for me to get loose. So I gave each hitter three nothing fastballs and two knuckleballs, and the knucklers were really jumping. Afterward Sal came over and said, "It was really moving today." That's the first comment he's had on the knuckleball. Maybe I can make him a believer.

I guess it wasn't too good for my elbow, though. When I got through pitching it felt like somebody had set fire to it. I'll treat it with aspirin, a couple every four hours or so.

I've tried a lot of other things through the years—like butazolidin, which is what they give to horses. And D.M.S.O.—dimethyl sulfoxide. Whitey Ford used that for a while. You rub it on with a plastic glove and as soon as it gets on your arm you can taste it in your mouth. It's not available anymore, though. Word is it can blind you. I've also taken shots—novocain, cortisone and xylocaine. Baseball players will take anything. If you had a pill that would guarantee a pitcher 20 wins but might take five years off his life, he'd take it.

Reminds me of the dumb things I used to do when I was in high school. The idea in those days was that when your arm was overworked and inflamed you put heat on it. It is exactly the wrong thing to do. We did it anyway. First Atomic Balm, which is just about what you'd expect from the name. You wore that stuff in the shower and let the hot water run on it, as hot as you could stand it. Then there was this stuff called Heet! I'd paint that all over my arm and I'd lie on my bed in agony. Sometimes I actually burned off a layer of skin. Now *that's* dedication.

A couple of things about sore arms. When I was throwing the kind of fastball that made my hat fall off people would ask me, "Jesus, doesn't it hurt? It looks like your arm's going to come off." I thought it was a silly question because it felt just fine. But now when I try to throw that way it feels like all those people told me it should feel. It feels like my arm's going to come off at the shoulder.

The most painful thing about it is that you know you're damaging something. It's pain, but it's fear, too. Sometimes the pain is like you get when you bang your funnybone. It hurts like hell. Only when it's your funnybone you know it's a passing thing. When it's your shoulder you think you might be snapping a muscle or ligament and you'll never be able to throw again. Pain and fear are a tough combination.

I try to stay away from the club doctor. This is something I learned in my first season. I was at Auburn, N.Y., and I got hit with a line drive that broke the thumb on my pitching hand. The Yankees flew me to New York to see Dr. Sidney Gaynor. I walked into his office with my dad and he said, "Who are you?"

I told him my name and said the Yankees had told me to see him.

He pointed at my dad. "And who are you?"

"I'm Jim's dad."

"Anything wrong with you?"

"No."

"Then what are you doing here?"

"Well, I just came along with Jim."

"We don't need you. Stay out here."

He took me into another office, took the cast off my thumb and bent it every which way. Then he told me it was broken and that it should have a bandage instead of a cast and that I shouldn't bump it into anything.

My dad couldn't believe the way Dr. Gaynor had spoken to him and I said he must just have had a bad day. I was sure he wasn't that way all the time. But I found out later he *was* that way all the time.

When I had my arm trouble in 1965 I went to him and he put me through some stretching exercises and said, "You got a sore arm."

"Yeah, I know," I said. "It hurts when I throw."

He was offended. It was like I had told him he had gravy on his tie. "If it's sore, don't throw," he said.

"For how long? A day, a week?"

"I don't know," he said. He was growling by now. "When it starts feeling better then you can start throwing again." Real scientific.

I believe Dr. Gaynor was actually offended when you came to him with an injury. You were imposing on his time. I'm sure there were a lot of guys who chose not to go to him with injuries because they didn't want to take his guff. I know I did. Mickey Mantle and Whitey Ford would go to other doctors sometimes and once Mantle got a vitamin shot from a quack who used an unsterile needle, and almost missed a World Series with a bleeding abscess on his hip.

MARCH
12

I overheard Lou Piniella having a heated discussion with Joe Schultz and, nosy as I am, I asked him what it was about. Piniella said that a couple of players had heard Joe tell a sportswriter yesterday that if Piniella couldn't throw any better than he was throwing he wouldn't make the club. Lou said his arm had bothered him last year and he just wanted to nurse it this spring. I can understand why he was upset. He's only been here two weeks and that's not enough time to get your arm ready or for them to decide that someone could make the club or not make it. It's ridiculous, particularly since Lou hit .300 last year with a Triple-A club and he was one of their $175,000 draftees. Sounds like somebody up there wants to unload Lou Piniella.

Either that, or Joe Schultz is pushing the panic button. It's a managerial disease Johnny Keane fell victim to when he managed the Yankees. John was a good, decent man, and no doubt there was lot of pressure on him. He seemed to feel that each day was the most important day of the season and it started right with the opening game of spring training. John always seemed willing to sacrifice a season to win a game. And this caused a lot of long-range problems. Guys played when they were hurt and then were out longer than they would have been if they hadn't been pushed back too soon. Mantle used to love to tell about his conversations with Keane. He said they'd go like this:

"How do your legs feel today, Mick?"

"Not too good."

"Yes, but how do they feel?"

"It hurts when I run, the right one especially. I can't stride on it or anything."

"Well, do you think you can play?"

"I don't know. I *guess* I can play. Yeah, hell, what the hell. Sure, I can play."

"Good. Great. We need you out there. Unless you're hurt— unless it really hurts you. I don't want you to play if you're hurt."

"No, it's okay. I hurt, but it's okay. I'll watch it."

"Good, good. We sure need you."

After a while we used to joke in the outfield. I'd go over to Mick and say, "Mick, how does your leg feel?"

"Well, it's severed at the knee."

"Yes, but does it hurt?"

"No, I scotch-taped it back into place."

"And how's your back?"

"My back is broken in seven places."

"Can you swing the bat?"

"Yeah, I can swing. If I can find some more Scotch tape."

"Great. Well, get in there then. We need you."

Poor Steve Barber was in the training room today getting some diathermy on his shoulder. He says his arm doesn't hurt. Ballplayers learn after a while that you don't tell anybody you have an injury if you can possibly avoid it, even a teammate. It might get back to the coaches, get spread around and be blown up out of all proportion. More important, it's because you don't want to admit it to yourself.

MARCH
13

Pitched three innings, gave up five hits, one of them a tremendous home run over the left-field fence by a guy who caught me in Seattle last year, Tom Egan. Tommy Davis said he could follow the flight of the ball pretty good, until he lost it in a cloud. A very bad day for the knuckleball. It just didn't knuckle. The overhand curve was working pretty good and some of the fastballs hopped pretty good. Who knows, maybe my old motion is coming back. The sirens are still singing.

Steve Barber went three innings and pitched pretty well. Maybe his arm doesn't hurt him after all—except that he was in the diathermy machine again this morning. Steve reminds me of a guy who was with the Yankees for a while, Billy Short. He was a little lefthander with a face on him like a kewpie doll. He was constantly getting diathermy and ultrasound on his arm. He even wanted to use a machine between innings, and once he asked the trainer if he could bring the ultrasound out to the bullpen so he could get it on his arm during the game in case he had to warm up.

I know exactly how he felt. I've wanted ultrasound on my arm between pitches sometimes. Or novocain.

I was judge in an age contest today. Bill Stafford, Ray Oyler, Don Mincher and Tommy Davis. I said Oyler looked oldest. They laughed, because that made Oyler a four-time winner. In the book, Tommy is twenty-nine, the rest thirty, Oyler included, which made me glance into the mirror myself. I still look to be in my mid-twenties. I'm glad the mirror doesn't reflect what's in my arm.

Mike Marshall was in the Tiger organization for a while and he says that, like the Yankees, they frown on players telling reporters the truth. A reporter asked Mike what he was being paid and he said he didn't feel he could say, but it was less than the minimum. The reporter printed it and asked how the hell the Tigers could be paying their No. 1 reliever less than the minimum. So Mike got called in by Jim Campbell, the general manager. Campbell wasn't angry that Mike was making less than the minimum, but that he told.

I asked Mike if he'd ever talked to Johnny Sain about contracts and he said he hadn't. Sain gives you good advice on how to get money out of a ballclub. John's a quiet guy and follows most of the baseball rules about keeping your mouth shut, but he's not afraid to ask for money if he thinks he deserves it. He was with the Boston Braves in 1948, the year they won the pennant. It was Spahn and Sain and then, dear Lord, two days of rain. Warren Spahn and Sain were the staff and Sain really put it to John Quinn, who was the general manager. Sain had had a big argument in the spring about his contract and signed for less than he wanted. Now the team was just home from a western trip and fighting for the pennant and Sain went to Quinn and said, "I'd like to talk about my contract."

"We'll talk about your contract next winter, when it comes up," Quinn said.

"No, I'd like to talk about it now," John said.

"What the hell," Quinn said. "You signed a contract and we're going to stick by it. We can't renegotiate a contract during the season."

"Well, you're going to renegotiate this one," John said.

"What the hell do you mean by *that*?" Quinn said.

"I'm supposed to pitch Thursday," Sain said. "But unless you pay me what I wanted in the beginning I'm not pitching."

That meant it would be Spahn and rain and pray for a hurricane, and then maybe a flood. So Quinn tore up his contract and gave him a new one, and John won 24 games. He used to say to me, "Now, don't be afraid to climb those golden stairs. Go in there and get what you're worth."

Those golden stairs.

Ruben Amaro is here with the Angels and I was happy to see him. We were good friends in New York. He's the kind of guy, well, there's a dignity to him and everybody likes and respects him. He's outspoken and has very strong opinions but he never antagonizes people with his positions the way I sometimes do. I wish I could be more like him.

Roger Repoz is with the Angels too, and I asked him if he had linguine last year in our restaurant in Detroit. He said he was keeping the faith.

More conversation about positive thinking today. When I pitched in the World Series in '63 and '64, I won two out of three games and the only thought that went through my mind before and during the game was, "Please don't let me embarrass myself out there." No thought of winning or losing. If you told me beforehand that I would lose the game but it would be close and I wouldn't be embarrassed, I might well have settled for that. I was terrified of being humiliated on national television and in front of all my friends. Now, that's certainly not positive thinking, and yet I was able to win ballgames. Maybe there is a power to negative thinking.

MARCH
14

Arm felt pretty good today after pitching yesterday and I don't know whether to attribute it to the aspirin or the bottle of beaujolais I polished off at dinner. Or maybe it was the ice I put on my elbow.

Marty Pattin pitched today and looked good. He reminded me of when I was a young phenom. Straight overhand pitcher, good rising fastball, hard overhand curve. He's a little guy but cocky, with lots of guts. When I saw him throwing free and easy like that it really made me want to find my old stuff.

I looked over Maglie's record today and noticed that he had his best years after coming back from the Mexican League and was thirty-three years old. So I'm wondering if I'm not going to end up being a fastball, curveball pitcher again this year. But then I remember what it was like last year; how frustrating it was to find my motion and get my rhythm, and how I'd get hit and then not get any regular work. All of which tells me I better stick to the knuckleball.

I guess you could say I'm torn.

Ding Dong Bell gets his first start against Arizona State U. tomorrow and he says he's not ready. I told him it's no sweat because if anybody makes this team it's going to be old Ding Dong, no matter what happens this spring. He said he realized that, and he's going to go out there and just keep from getting hurt.

Pitching against a college team, you can't look good no matter what. If you do well, they're just college kids. If you don't, you're a bum. Yet the kids are in better shape than we are and can be a pain in the ass.

Batting practice is the time to stand around in the outfield and tell each other stories. At first we all sort of kept our distance, standing fifteen feet apart and doing the job the way it's supposed to be done. By now, though, we're standing in clumps of five or ten and take turns catching whatever fly balls happen to come our way.

It was Dick-Stuart-story-day today, and this one was about the time Johnny Pesky was managing the Red Sox and Stuart was playing for him and showing up late for a lot of things. For some reason this upset Pesky, so he called a meeting to talk about MORALE. Stuart was late for it. In fact he didn't show up until about half an hour before the game (three is considered about right) and he walked right into the middle of the meeting. All eyes were on him as he opened the door to the clubhouse and, without missing a beat, opened his doublebreasted jacket, paraded to the center of the room with his hips swinging, did a pirouette and said, "And here he, is nattily attired in a black suede jacket by Stanley Blacker, with blue velvetine pants and shoes by Florsheim. The handkerchief is by Christian Dior." Everybody went nuts. Even Pesky had to laugh.

Stuart's a beauty. I remember a game we played against him in Boston with Earl Wilson pitching. On the first pitch of the game somebody hit a foul pop fly between the catcher and first base and Earl ran over to call who was supposed to catch the ball, and he made a tragic mistake. He called Stuart. The ball dropped to the ground in front of him with a sickening thud.

Earl picked up the ball and stormed back to the mound. The next pitch was another pop fly, this one in fair territory. Earl ran over screaming at the top of his lungs, "I got it! I got it!" He wasn't taking any chances. At the last second, guess who ran into him and spiked him? Dick Stuart. The ball went flying and the runner got two bases.

Now Wilson's got a spiked left foot and a man on second and he's steaming mad. The next pitch is a ground ball on the first-base line and Earl runs over, picks it up, whirls to throw to first and Stuart isn't on the bag. First and third.

Wilson slammed his glove down and walked toward the dugout like he was quitting right there, but he thought better of it and came back to the game. And Stuart? Stuart was his usual jovial self. He knew he had bad hands and there was nothing he could do about it.

Curt Blefary is another guy with classically bad hands. When he was with Baltimore, Frank Robinson nicknamed him "Clank," after the robot. Once the team bus was riding by a junkyard and Robinson yelled for the driver to stop so Blefary could pick out a new glove. (If you're going to shake hands with a guy who has bad hands you are supposed to say, "Give me some steel, Baby.")

Speaking of hands, there's the story of the player who was sound asleep on an airplane when suddenly it ran into some turbulence. He woke up and promptly threw up. But just before he messed all over himself he managed to reach up and catch most of it in his hands. The guy sitting next to him, with perfect aplomb, turned to him and said, "Good hands."

15

I'm not sure I'm going to like Don Mincher. I keep hearing that big southern accent of his. It's prejudice, I know, but everytime I hear a southern accent I think: stupid. A picture of George Wallace pops into my mind. It's like Lenny Bruce saying he could never associate a nuclear scientist with a southern accent. I suppose there are people in baseball who are as turned off by my northern accent, and I've often thought that the best way to get through professional baseball is never to let on you have an education.

Well, Mincher was talking about going to see a Johnny Cash show, and I imagine when he talks about Johnny Cash it's like the Negro players talking about James Brown. Lots of times in the clubhouse you'll have a radio on and every once in a while it gets switched back and forth between a soul-music station and a country-western station. If you're going good you get to hear your kind of music. In the Yankee clubhouse, western music dominated. In the Horace Clark Memorial Lounge you heard the music from the Virgin Islands and soul music. In the trainer's room, where Mickey Mantle was king, you'd hear the Buck Owenses and Conway Twittys.

Went to the rodeo with the family, and when they played "The Star-Spangled Banner" Mike said, as he does every time he hears it, "Dad, they're playing the baseball song again."

We were toasting marshmallows in the backyard and I was sharpening a stick to put through the marshmallows when I sliced off most of the tip of my left thumb. I went to the clubhouse to have it repaired. Someone saw the ugly slice and immediately a crowd formed, as it always does when something gory is on exhibit. We like to say about ourselves—we baseball players—that we're ghouls. I remember one time it was standing room only in Ft. Lauderdale when Jake Gibbs got hit on the thumb and they had to drill a hole through his nail to relieve the pressure. I had a front-row seat myself. The drill boring through the nail started to smoke and when it hit paydirt Jake jerked his hand and the drill was ripped out of the trainer's hand and here's Jake's hand waving in the air with the drill still hanging from the hole in his nail. One of the great thrills of the spring.

Looking at Steve Barber doing his jumping-jacks during calisthenics I realized that his pitching arm is all bent and much shorter than his right arm. That's from throwing curveballs. It's almost as deformed as Bud Daley's arm. Bud, who had polio as a boy, pitched for the Yankees for a while. The polio left him with a crook in his right arm. It didn't bother him, even when the players would make fun of it. Sometimes there would be twenty-five guys in front of the dugout, all of them catching the ball with a crooked arm.

When I told Barber he looked like Bud Daley, he laughed and said, "Yes, but Daley didn't have to pitch with that arm, only catch."

Barber was in the diathermy machine again today and then looked pretty good in batting practice. I've been taking aspirin. My arm hurts and I didn't do as well pitching BP as Barber. Maybe there's something to that diathermy machine.

The only thing I think of these days when I go out to pitch is how my arm feels. My concern used to be about how my curveball was breaking and whether I could get the fastball over. Now I think about my arm. Hell, once the hitter gets up there I can always make adjustments and find something to throw him. But if your arm hurts, that's it.

I've had a lot of conversations with my arm. I ask what the hell I ever did to it. I ask why won't it do for me what it used to do in the old days. I whisper lovingly to it. Remember '64? Remember '63? Wasn't it fun? Things could be like that again. Just one more time, one more season. It never listens.

When I was shaving today, a rookie beside me reminded me of how old I am for this game. His name is Dick Baney; he's a young kid and has a great fastball. I hate him. "Hey, I wrote you a fan letter that you never answered," he said.

I thought, hell, he's so young, it might be true. "When did you write it?" I asked.

"When I was about six," he said.

If there's one thing I hate it's a smart-ass rookie. I know a lot about smart-ass rookies. I was one myself. The guy I got on when I came to the Yankees was Jim Coates. Actually he got on me first. He'd say, "Get a few years in the big leagues before you pop off." Or he'd get on me about my number being too high. And I'd get on him about being so skinny. One time in the trainer's room, I asked him if those were really his ribs or was he wearing a herringbone suit. That one drove him up the wall.

He'd lisp at me when I was going in to pitch. "Is she going out and try it again today? Is she really going to try today?"

And I'd say, "Yeah, Coates, I'm going out there and hammer another nail into your coffin."

Another time I said, "Hey, Coates, you endorsing iodine?"

And he said, cautiously, "Why?"

"Because I saw your picture on the bottle."

MARCH
16

We had a visit from Commissioner Bowie Kuhn today. The visit was preceded by the usual announcement from the manager: "All right, let's get this thing over with as quickly as we can." What it really means is: "Okay you guys, you can listen. But don't ask any questions."

The commissioner said that baseball is a tremendous, stupendous game and that it didn't need any drastic changes, that we simply needed to improve our methods of promotion. One of the things that none of us should do, he said, is knock the game. He said if we were selling Pontiacs we wouldn't go around saying what a bad transmission it has. In other words, don't say anything bad about baseball.

He said he was pleased with the settlement that had been made with the players but he felt there was too much bitterness in the dispute. I felt there was an unspoken warning there to be careful of things we said that could be interpreted as bitterness toward the owners. Imagine being bitter toward the owner of a baseball club.

Kuhn also talked about the integrity of the game and how he felt it's one of the only sports that the average fan knows in his heart is completely honest. (I wonder what the football, basketball and hockey people would say to *that*.) I'm not sure all fans feel that way, but I really don't think there is any gambling at all inside baseball. I may be naive, but I don't think there's any gambling, or any intentional passing along of information.

Kuhn got a nice round of applause and nobody asked any questions. Then he left with Joe Reichler, the Commissioner's personal caddy. Commissioners come and go, but Joe will always be with us. Some guys were made to be permanent caddies.

All of which for some reason reminds me of one of our bullpen occupations: choosing an All-Ugly Nine. Baseball players are, of course, very gentle people. If we happen to see some fellow who is blessed with a bad complexion we immediately call him something nice, like "pizza face." Or other sweet little things like:

"His face looks like a bag of melted caramels."

"He looks like he lost an acid fight."

"He looks like his face caught on fire and somebody put it out with a track shoe."

Some famous all-uglies are Danny Napoleon ("He'd be ugly even if he was white," Curt Flood once said of him); Don Mossi, the big-eared relief ace on the all-ugly nine (he looked like a cab going down the street with its doors open); and Andy Etchebarren, who took over as catcher from Yogi Berra when the famed Yankee receiver was retired to the All-Ugly Hall of Fame.

Lost to Arizona State 5–4 yesterday, and would you believe that Joe Schultz and Marvin Milkes are steaming? In fact one of the pitchers who was taken out of the game got cut today—Bill Edgerton. He figured to get cut because he was one of the five or six guys who were asked to move their lockers to the visiting-team locker room. Of course, they were told it had nothing to do with their ability or status, just that some guys had to move. By coincidence, most of them were cut today. The only one I was really interested in was Greg Goossen, whom I'd come to like, mainly because he had the ability to laugh at himself.

That's what Milkes and Schultz should have done about losing to Arizona State—laugh. Or at least not take it so damn seriously. Except they probably think that the fans and writers are going to draw a lot of conclusions about a game like this and, alas, they're probably right. You can't educate everybody about baseball in two weeks.

Lou Piniella has the red ass. He doesn't think he's been playing enough. He's a good-looking ballplayer, 6–2, handsome, speaks fluent Spanish and unaccented English. He's from Tampa. He says he knows they don't want him and that he's going to quit baseball rather than go back to Triple-A. He says that once you get labeled Triple-A, that's it. I suggested to him that this wasn't the year to quit because the Seattle people were bound to make mistakes in their early decisions and I thought there would be a shuttle system between Vancouver and Seattle and that guys who didn't stay with the club the first month might be called up real quick. But he said he was going to quit anyway and force them to do something. And since he cost $175,000 in the expansion draft he figures they'd rather make a deal for him than lose him altogether. He's probably right. A lot of decisions in baseball are based upon cost rather than ability. Cost is easier to judge.

Now that the cut-down season is here we'll soon be talking of deaths in the family. At least that's what we did with the Yankees. When a guy got cut we'd say he died. Fritz Peterson would come over to me and say, "Guess who died today." And he'd look very downcast and in the tones of an undertaker read the roll of the dead.

A player who wasn't going well was said to be sick, very sick, in a coma or on his deathbed, depending on how bad he was going. Last year when I was sent to Seattle, Fritz asked me what happened and I said I died.

"You can't die," Fritz said. "You're too good to die."

Like Mae West once said, goodness has nothing to do with it.

On the Yankees the Grim Reaper was Big Pete. Once he whispered in your ear that the manager wanted to see you, you were clinically dead.

I remember toward the end of one spring training, Don Lock, an out-fielder with a pretty good sense of humor (he needed it, having spent a lot of years in the Yankee chain trying to break into an outfield of Tom Tresh, Mantle and Maris), barricaded his locker. He hung sweatshirts across the top, crossed out his name, piled up his gloves and shoes in front to form a barrier, then snuggled inside the locker holding a bat like it was a rifle, and fired it at anybody who came near. It was good for a few laughs, but in the end the Grim Reaper got him anyway.

Another way Big Pete would let you know you had died was by not packing your equipment bag for a road trip. There would be a packed bag in front of every locker except yours. Rest in peace. It's kind of like, "All those who are going to New York City, please step forward. Not so fast, Johnson."

When I warm up tomorrow I'll be trying to recreate in my mind an abstract feeling I get when I'm throwing well. It can't be explained. It's a *feeling,* the feeling you get when you're doing something right, a sort of muscular memory. I find the best way to arrive at this feeling is to eliminate all other thoughts and let my mind go blank. Sometimes, when you can't find this feeling while you're warming up, panic sets in. It's one of the reasons I like to use a double warm-up. The interval between the two warm-ups gives me a chance to think about what I did and to see if I can't make some corrections.

If this sounds insane, it may be.

MARCH
17

Scottsdale

Had a long chat with Steve Hovley in the outfield. He's being called "Tennis Ball Head" because of his haircut, but his real nickname is Orbit, or Orbie, because he's supposed to be way out.

Hovley is anti-war and I asked him if he ever does any out-and-out protesting in the trenches. He said only in little things. For instance, when he takes his hat off for the anthem he doesn't hold it over his heart. I feel rather the same way. The whole anthem-flag ritual makes me uncomfortable, and when I was a starting pitcher I'd usually be in the dugout toweling sweat off during the playing of the anthem.

We agreed we're both troubled by the stiff-minded emphasis on the flag that grips much of the country these days. A flag, after all, is still only a cloth symbol. You don't show patriotism by showing blank-eyed love for a bit of cloth. And you can be deeply patriotic without covering your car with flag decals.

Hovley said he didn't mind being called Orbit. "In fact I get reinforcement from it," he said. "It reminds me that I'm different from them and I'm gratified."

What's different about Hovley is that he'll sit around reading Nietzsche in the clubhouse and sometimes he'll wonder why a guy behaves a certain way. In baseball, that's a revolutionary.

I must say, though, that things are changing. When I first came up with the Yankees, there was intolerance of anybody who didn't conform right down the line—including haircut and cut of suit. But as the old-timers disappear, there seems to be more freedom, more tolerance.

Hovley and I got to talking about the strange relationship between baseball managers and players, and the fact that players seldom talk to managers about anything. "I ran into Joe Schultz in the shower the other day," Hovley said, "and suddenly we were all alone. I really didn't know what to say to him. The only thing I could think to say was, 'Who's going to play third this year?' or 'How many pitchers are you going to take north?' So when he said, 'Hi, Steve, how are you?' I said, 'Fine,' and immediately started lathering up my face so I wouldn't have to talk to him anymore."

I was shocked when I got to the ballpark today—figuring I was going to be the starting pitcher and go five innings or so—to be told by Sal that I was the third pitcher and that I'd only go one or two innings. Immediately my mind started churning. Does this mean I'm being put on the shelf? I've heard that last-two-innings talk before in my career and it always means, "See you later."

But it was needless worry. Dick Baney, who started and was told to go as far as he could, got nailed early. Four runs in four innings. Stafford came in for two innings and looked terrible. So I was in there in the seventh.

I started off great. I gave the first guy all knuckleballs and got him on a grounder. To the next guy I threw five beautiful knuckleballs. He missed the first two for strikes. Then he fouled three of them off and I figured now I've got him. He must be expecting another knuckleball, because every knuckler I threw him was knuckling better than the one before. Surely he isn't looking for a fastball.

I looked in for the sign and the catcher was thinking the same thing. So I cranked up and gave him a fastball, hoping to sneak it by him, and he snuck it over the left-field fence. Tommy Davis, my friend, once again lost sight of the ball when it went behind a cloud. I hate to think how far he might have hit it had we not fooled him so badly.

After the game Sal said I'll probably pitch again tomorrow, which means they now must be thinking of me as a short-relief man. I'd like to pitch an inning or so the day after tomorrow because that's when we play the Giants. I was always a Giant fan when I was a kid and I'd like to pitch against Willie Mays so I can tell my brother what it feels like. Whenever we played stickball as kids we'd take turns being the Giants and Dodgers. I pitched to Willie Mays hundreds of times, only it was my brother, batting righthanded even though he was lefthanded so he'd look as much like Willie as possible. Now I'd like a shot at the real thing, with a baseball instead of a rubber ball. I think it will be a fair match. Both of us are near the end of our careers. He's had a few more lucky years than I have, but we're both over thirty and that's a great equalizer.

Whitey Ford always said that the way to make coaches think you're in shape in the spring is to get a tan. It makes you look healthier and at least five pounds lighter. Following Ford's postulate I was sitting on the bench in the sun while Baney was pitching. This gave me an opportunity to listen in on the pearls of Sal Maglie and Joe Schultz, who were also getting some sun. These pearls are of a special kind, absolutely valueless at best, annoying enough to upset your concentration at worst. For instance, a big hitter was up with two men on base and as Baney looked in for the sign, Joe Schultz hollered, "Now get ahead of this guy." And Sal hollered, "Get something on this pitch. He's a first-ball hitter."

And just as he cranked up to throw, somebody (I couldn't tell who) yelled, "High-ball hitter. Keep the ball down."

If he takes all this advice Baney has to throw a strike at the knees with Chinese mustard on it. What the hell, if you could throw that kind of pitch every time you wanted to you wouldn't need any coaching. Christ, you'd have it made.

But Baney isn't Superman. He got behind. Ball one, low in the dirt.

The next piece of advice was, "Got to get ahead now. Nothing too good."

"Nothing too good" means don't throw it down the middle and "got to get ahead" means don't throw him a ball. In other words, hit a corner.

Of course, he still has the other advice ringing in his ears. So now he's supposed to hit a corner, low on the knees, with a hard fastball. This is wonderful advice. Ball two. Ball three.

"Got to come in there now, but not too good."

That's really beautiful advice. Especially with a good hitter up there who may well be swinging at 3 and 0. Sure enough, Baney threw a good fastball—belt high. It got hit into center for a double and two runs. And as the ball went out there Sal shook his head and said, sadly, "Too high, too high."

How many inches are there between the belt and the knee? How many pitches can you control to that tolerance? How many pitching coaches are second-guessers? Answers: Eighteen inches. Very few. Most.

And this kind of bullshit goes on during most ballgames. The same things are said over and over in the same situations. They all come to the same thing. They're asking you to obey good pitching principles; keep the ball down (most hitters are high-ball hitters), don't make the pitch too good (don't pitch it over the heart of the plate), move the ball around inside the strike zone and change speeds (keep the hitter off balance), and get ahead of the hitter (when you have two strikes on a hitter and two balls or fewer, you may then throw your best pitch as a borderline strike and the hitter will have to swing to protect himself).

This is the essence of the battle between the pitcher and the hitter, and it doesn't do any good to yell this kind of advice to a pitcher in a crisis situation. He knows it as well as he knows his name. But pitching coaches use shouted advice as protection. If they shout enough advice they can't be wrong.

Old Chicken Colonel Turner was a master at this. He'd sit in the dugout and shout to Stan Bahnsen, "Now, keep the ball down, Bahnsen," and Stan would throw a letter-high fastball that would get popped up into the infield and The Colonel would look down the bench and say, "The boy's fastball is moving. The boy's fastball is rising." Two innings later, same situation, the very same pitch, home run into the left-field seats. The Colonel looks up and down the bench and says very wisely, "Got the ball up. You see what happens when you get the ball up?"

Then you'd get a weak lefthanded hitter up in Yankee Stadium and somebody would throw him a change-up and he'd hit it for a home run into the short porch and The Colonel would say, "You can't throw a change-up to a lefthanded hitter, boys. Not in this ballpark." A week later a guy would throw the same pitch to the same kind of hitter and the guy would be way out in front and The Colonel would say, "Change-up. One of the best pitches in baseball. You can really fool the hitter with it."

Whatever the result, The Colonel always knew the cause. And in the little world of baseball, he is not alone.

Merritt Ranew hit a pinch-hit home run that tied the game up in the ninth inning. He got a very cold reception in the dugout. The reason is that nobody wants to play extra innings in a spring game. It happened that we scored two more runs in the inning and won it, but it was a narrow escape and nobody was very happy with Ranew. By coincidence I have a soft spot in my heart for extra-inning games in the spring and believe that every player—at least every player who doesn't have the team made—should feel this way. I made the Yankee ballclub in an extra-inning spring game.

This was in 1962, and I wasn't even on the roster. They asked me to pitch the ninth inning of a game against St. Louis when we were behind by a run. We tied it up in the bottom of the ninth, so I wound up pitching five scoreless innings and lost it on an unearned run. But four days later I got to pitch in another game, and then two more, and I made the club. If I'd pitched only one inning in that first game they might never have taken another look. In fact, all the scrubeenies pray for extra innings in the spring. Or at least they should.

MARCH
18

Tempe

We lost an 8–5 ballgame today and I did my part, giving up two runs in a single inning. There was a triple on an ankle-high knuckleball (I hate triples off ankle-high knuckleballs), and then Tommy Davis lost a fly ball in the sun and it fell for a double.

When I was a kid I might have run out there and kicked him in the shin. I actually used to do that. I would stop the game and scream at a kid if he made an error, and everybody hated me for it. In recent years, though, I've turned full circle. I may say to myself, "Ah, Tommy, you should have had that," but I go out of my way to show absolutely no reaction. I don't pick up the resin bag and slam it down, and I don't kick dirt, and I don't stare out at the player.

The reasons are selfish. First of all, people think terrible thoughts about you when you do that kind of thing, and I don't like people to think terrible thoughts about me. Secondly, you get on a player that way and he may miss the next play too. So I say nothing.

While warming up to come into the game I was wondering if my wife was in the park. I enjoy playing baseball better when I know there are friends or family watching. It's a bit of hot dog in me. I got a special kick when my parents and my brothers used to come to a ballgame because it seemed like I was putting on a special performance just for them. I've pitched some of my best games when I knew I had left a lot of tickets for my countless admirers. The longest game in the American League was played in Detroit a few years ago. I pitched the last seven innings for the Yankees in a 22-inning game and there were fifteen Bouton passes sitting up there behind the dugout, all relatives of my wife. I really think I did better because I knew they were there. Sometimes, when I know there are no friends or family present, I pretend they're home watching on television, thousands of them. You take your ego trips, I take mine.

Lost the game today, so we had a chance to prove we could be more silent than thou. After a loss the clubhouse has to be completely quiet, as though losing strikes a baseball player dumb. The radio was blaring when we came into the clubhouse and Joe Schultz strode the length of the room, switched it off and went back to his office. After that you could cut the silence with a bologna sandwich. The rule is that you're not supposed to say anything even if it's a meaningless spring-training loss. Feeling remorse has nothing to do with it. Those who did poorly in the game and those who did well, even those who didn't play, all are supposed to behave as if at a funeral.

The important thing is to let the manager and coaches know you feel bad about losing. I'm sure they believe that if you look like you feel bad about losing then you're the type who wants to win. So you go along with the little game. And they played this game real hard with the Yankees when I got there, but every once in a while Phil Linz, Joe Pepitone and I would giggle about something after a losing game and we got some pretty nasty stares from the old guard.

This was what was behind the famous Phil Linz harmonica incident. It was in 1964, when Yogi Berra was manager, on a bus ride from Comiskey Park to O'Hare airport in Chicago. It was hot, we were tied up in Sunday traffic, we'd blown a doubleheader, we'd lost four or five in a row, we were struggling for a pennant and tempers were short. Linz was sitting beside me, stewing because he hadn't played, and all of a sudden he whipped out a harmonica he'd bought that morning and started playing "Mary Had a Little Lamb." The reason he played "Mary Had a Little Lamb" was that it was the only song he knew how to play. He really played very respectfully and quietly, and if "Mary Had a Little Lamb" can sound like a dirge, it did.

Yogi, who was sitting in the front of the bus, stood up and said, "Knock it off."

Legend has it that Linz wasn't sure what Berra said, so he turned to Mickey Mantle and asked, "What'd he say?"

"He said play it louder," Mantle explained.

Linz didn't believe that. On the other hand he didn't stop. In a minute Yogi was in the back of the bus, breathing heavily and demanding that Linz shove that thing up his ass.

"You do it," Linz said, flipping the harmonica at him. Yogi swatted at it with his hand and it hit Pepitone in the knee. Immediately he was up doing his act called, *"Oooooh,* you hurt my little knee." Pretty soon everybody was laughing, even if you're not supposed to laugh after losing, especially a doubleheader.

And that was really all of it, except that I should point out that in the middle of it all Crosetti stood up and in his squeaky voice screamed that this was the worst thing he'd ever seen in his entire career with the Yankees.

Ray Oyler was racked up at second base by Glenn Beckert of the Cubs, and when he came back to earth he was heard to call Beckert a son of a bitch. This is not on the same order as motherfucker, but he didn't have a lot of time to think.

It has become the custom in baseball to slide into second base with a courteous how do you do, so when somebody does slide in hard everybody gets outraged and vows vengeance. A few years ago Frank Robinson slid into Bobby Richardson with murderous aplomb and the Yankees were visibly shocked. *How could he do that to our Bobby? We'll get him for that.* Actually this was a National League play and the Yankees simply weren't used to it.

Before the game, Joe Schultz asked me how the old knuckleball was coming along and I said fine. I was ready to pitch. Indeed, I added, it was my opinion that if a knuckleball pitcher got himself into proper shape he could probably pitch every day because the knuckleball takes almost nothing out of your arm. I was about halfway through this little speech when I noticed that Schultz was staring over my shoulder into the blue, blue sky. If I had said I just cut my grandmother's throat from ear to ear, he would no doubt have said, "Fine, fine."

Managers don't like to be told who should play and who shouldn't, and who should be a starting pitcher and who shouldn't, and when Joe started feeling I was telling him I should be a starter he turned me off. I shouldn't have said anything. I should have just lathered my face.

MARCH
19

Phoenix

Two talks today from my main men, Schultz and Maglie;
one okay, the other terrible.

Schultz said we weren't in shape and that we were making physical
mistakes that we wouldn't if we were—in shape, I mean. (I'm not sure I
understood that.) But then he obviously felt he'd hurt our feelings and
tried to take it all back. "Shitfuck," he said, using one of his favorite
words ("fuckshit" is the other). "Shitfuck. We've got a damned good
ballclub here. We're going to win some games."

I agree. I don't see how we can avoid it.

What Schultz is afraid of, I guess, is that we might get down on
ourselves and then, well, the losing might never stop. Baseball players are
a special breed for getting down on themselves. When they do, it's look
out below.

The meeting with Maglie was disappointing, largely, I guess, because he was my hero when I was a kid and I expected a lot out of him.
Also because he didn't get along with Dick Williams, the Boston Red
Sox manager. I count that as a good sign because managers, being what
they are, often don't get along with coaches who have something on the
ball. I thought Sal Maglie might turn out to be another Johnny Sain.
Afraid not.

Maglie started out saying, "Look, you guys got to concentrate out
there. You're not concentrating."

Now what the hell does that mean? There are about thirty pitchers
here, young and old, and not one of them isn't concentrating when he's
pitching. I mean I *know* nobody is out there thinking about going out
to play golf or about how the beer is going to taste after the game. If
anything, most of us are concentrating too much, getting too tense, trying to do too much. Johnny Sain always told guys who had control problems that they were trying too hard to throw the ball to a specific spot,
not that they weren't concentrating. Sain would compare pitching to a
golfer chipping to a green and say that if you tried for the cup you might

miss the green. The thing to do was just hit the green, pitch to a general area.

Control was our big problem, Sal said. We've walked eighty and struck out only forty and the ratio should be the other way around. He's absolutely right. But he's got the wrong reason.

Then he surprised me by mentioning my name. "Some of you guys think you can get by on only one pitch," he said. "You can't do it. Nobody is a one-pitch pitcher." He added: "Bouton, they're just waiting for your knuckleball. You got to throw something else."

In the immortal words of Casey Stengel, "Now, wait a minute." Are we trying to win ballgames down here or are we trying to get ready for the season? What I have to learn is control of the knuckleball. And I'm not going to learn it by throwing fastballs. I tried to explain that to Sal after the meeting and he said, well, yes, but I should have some other pitches to set up the knuckleball.

I said I agreed with him 100 percent. I said it because I'm in a shaky position here and the first thing you got to do is make the ballclub, and you don't make ballclubs arguing with pitching coaches.

Afterward in the outfield we talked about one-pitch pitchers. Ryne Duren was a one-pitch pitcher. His one pitch was a wild warm-up. Ryne wore glasses that looked like the bottoms of Coke bottles, and he'd be sort of steered out to the mound and he'd peer in at the catcher and let fly his first warm-up pitch over the screen and the intimidation was complete. All he needed was his fastball and hitters ducking away.

And just for the hell of it I got into a conversation with Maglie about when he was a great pitcher, and I asked him what he used to get the Dodgers out with in his glory days with the Giants. "Ninety-seven snappers," Sal Maglie said.

So much for one-pitch pitchers.

Anyway, Gary Bell said not to worry about Maglie. "Last year in Boston he told one of the newspaper guys I'd never last throwing across my body," Gary said. "Chrissakes, I've been here fourteen years. You think he meant I'd never last past fifty?"

71

MARCH
20

Tempe

Day off, so I'll take the opportunity to discuss the beanball. Everybody asks.

When I used to throw very hard I was always concerned that I would let a fastball go and hit somebody in the head. Occasionally I would dump somebody by accident and I'd run right up to the plate to see if he was all right. I fractured Wayne Causey's arm with a fastball and I felt terrible about it for days.

The beanball (it's sometimes called "chin music") is a weapon. Hitters don't like pitchers throwing at them, and there are guys in the league who have a reputation for not hitting as well after they've been thrown at a few times. Nor do I look down on pitchers who use it as a weapon. They're probably shrewder than I am. I'm just not a crafty person, I guess, especially when it comes to pitching. I probably should have cheated more. I should have thrown a spitter. I should have used a mudball. I didn't, and I'm not sure why, except that when I was successful throwing real hard, I didn't need to. And when I was going bad, I was so bad nothing would help.

Only once in the years I've been pitching has anybody ever ordered me to throw a duster. It was last year at Seattle and Joe Adcock, a man I like, was the manager. I came into a game in relief and John Olerud, the catcher, came out and said, "Joe wants you to knock this guy on his ass."

I couldn't believe it. So I said something clever. "What?"

"Joe wants you to knock this guy on his ass."

"I just got in the game. I got nothing against this guy."

"Well, he says to knock him on his ass."

"Bullshit," I said. "I haven't thrown that much. I'm not sharp enough to know where the hell I'm throwing the ball. I'm not going to do it. You go back there and tell him that you told me to knock him down and that I refused and if he wants to say something afterward let him say it to me."

Adcock never said a word.

I mean, what if I screw up a man's career? I'm going to have that on my conscience for . . . well, for weeks maybe.

The fact is, though, that I once did throw at a guy. I mean to maim him. His name was Fred Loesekam. He was in the White Sox organization and he was a bad guy. He liked to slide into guys spikes high and draw blood. During warm-ups he liked to scale baseballs into the dugout to see if he could catch somebody in the back of the head. He even used our manager for target practice. So I took my shots at him. We all did. Once I threw a ball at him so hard behind his head that he didn't even move. The ball hit his bat and rolled out to me, and I threw him out before he got the bat off his shoulder.

When you throw a ball behind a hitter's head you're being serious. His impulse is to duck backwards, into the ball. If you're not so serious and all you want to do is put a guy out for a piece of the season, you aim for the knee. An umpire will give you two or three shots at a guy's knee before he warns you. Mostly, though, I hardly ever brush anybody back on purpose. And if I throw a knuckleball high inside, the hitter might decide to just take it on the chin and trot down to first base.

And don't believe it when you hear that a pitcher can throw the ball to a two-inch slot. A foot and a half is more like it, I mean with any consistency. When I first came up I thought major-league pitchers had pinpoint control, and I was worried that the best I could do was hit an area about a foot square. Then I found out that's what everybody meant by pinpoint control, and that I had it.

Of course, hitters hear things from the bench: "Stick it in his ear!" That's almost as good as throwing at a hitter because now he thinks you're going to, and that's half the battle. I know not what course others may take, but for me, my most precious possession is the three balls I'm allowed to throw before I walk somebody. If I give up one of them merely to frighten the hitter, I'm giving up half my attack. I decided long ago I couldn't afford that.

MARCH
21

Death came calling today. Joe Schultz gathered a bunch of guys in his office and told them that because of space requirements they'd have to work out on our other field with the Vancouver squad. "You're not cut," Joe said. "Your stuff is still in your locker and you're still on the team. Don't draw any conclusions from this."

It wasn't really death. It was just the priest coming to your bedside to say a few choice Latin words. Among the casualties were Steve Hovley, Rollie Sheldon, Skip Lockwood and Jim O'Toole. One of the guys who got the call, Lou Piniella, didn't go into Joe's office, but sort of sulked outside. "Come on in, Lou," Joe said. "It's not going to be anything bad." Lou knew better.

Piniella is a case. He hits the hell out of the ball. He hit a three-run homer today and he's got a .400 average, but they're easing him out. He complains a lot about the coaches and ignores them when he feels like it, and to top it off he's sensitive as hell to things like Joe Schultz not saying good morning to him. None of this is supposed to count when you judge a ballplayer's talents. But it does.

Besides, Schultz has his problems. They're named Tommy Davis, Wayne Comer, Jose Vidal and Jim Gosger, and somebody has to go. I'm sure that whoever is sent down will be the best of them.

The fellow I feel rather sorry for is Rollie Sheldon. His record is about the same as mine, except he's got fewer walks, and I'll wager he's wondering why I'm still here and he's getting the message. All I can think is that my knuckleball made me a better bet, a stickout among the mediocrities. Of course, a couple of poor performances by me and Joe Schultz will be telling me I don't have to worry either.

I was also rather sad about Claude "Skip" Lockwood. Hate to lose a funny man. The other day we were talking about pitching grips in the outfield (it was the day after I'd been mildly racked up by a couple of doubles) and Lockwood asked me, "Say Jim, how do you hold your doubles?"

About a week ago Lockwood said, "Hey, the coaches are calling me Fred. You think it means anything?"

"Don't worry about it, Charley," I told him.

And today he came over and said he was a little confused, that he didn't know which field he was supposed to be working on. He said he guessed things were getting better for him. "Last week I didn't know who I was. Now all I don't know is where."

I should point out that the Lockwood case is a perfect example of what happens to a guy who reports an injury. He was scheduled to pitch in one of the first two exhibitions but came up with a sore arm. Four days later he went to Sal and said he felt fine. This was almost two weeks ago. He still hasn't pitched. When he asked Schultz about it the dandy manager said, "I didn't want to take a chance with your arm."

That's a crock of crap. What it amounts to is having a reason to cut a young guy. If you can cut him for some reason other than his pitching it's just that much easier on your psyche. Decisions, decisions.

It's also why, when you ask Steve Barber, while he's sitting in the diathermy machine, if he's having trouble with his arm, he says, "No, no. I'm just taking this as a precautionary measure."

Sure enough, after the two workouts today on the two fields, the Grim Reaper struck. Five or six of the guys who were told not to worry this morning were cut this afternoon. Sheldon, Goossen, Lockwood, Bill Stafford and a couple of guys I don't know.

As I drove home after the game I passed the Vancouver practice field and saw Goossen working out at first base. He's hard to miss, with his blocky build and blond, curly hair, working without a hat. I was already missing him and the nutty things he does and I thought here's a field that's only about fifty yards away and yet it's really hundreds of miles away, the distance between the big leagues and Vancouver. Those guys all work out at different times, change in different locker rooms, listen to different coaches. They moved into a different world when they got cut from the big club. There were no tears, no sympathy, no farewells and no handshakes. And no one goes down to that field to tell Goose to hang in there. One day he's here and the next he's gone. It happens every day and it's a reality to all of us, yet I can't help thinking how strange it is. There should be more fanfare when a guy leaves, more goodbyes, more hang-in-theres. And once in a while maybe we should stop when we drive by the practice field and give Goose a wave and let him know we still like him and that he's still alive.

MARCH
22

There was a notice on the bulletin board asking guys to sign up to have their cars driven to Seattle. Price $150. The drivers are college kids. I think I'd prefer Bonnie and Clyde. I say this because I remember college and how I drove an automobile in those days and I would not have hired me to drive my car. Still, a lot of guys put their names on the list—very tentatively.

Baseball players' words to a beautifully tender song (Actually Overheard in the Clubhouse Division): "Summertiiiime, and your mother is easy."

Steve Hovley was dancing to a tune on the radio and somebody yelled, "Hove, dancing is just not your thing."

"Do you mind if I decide what my thing is?" Hovley said.

So I asked him what his thing was. "I like sensual things," he said. "Eating, sleeping. I like showers and I like flowers and I like riding my bike."

"You have a bike with you?"

"Certainly. I rent one. And I ride past a field of sheep on the way to the park every day and a field of alfalfa, and sometimes I get off my bike and lie down in it. A field of alfalfa is a great place to lie down and look up at the sky."

I sure wish Hovley would make the team.

When I got to the ballpark this morning I ran into Frank Kimball, one of the young catchers. He was standing under the eaves in order to keep out of the pelting rain, his soggy equipment bag beside him. I knew, but I asked anyway. "What's up?"

"I just got sent down."

"Too bad. When did you find out?"

"They did it chickenshit. They told me in the office when I went to get my paycheck."

"You mean Joe didn't tell you?"

"No. And when I went back to him to ask him what the story was he said he was sorry, he forgot to tell me."

Eccch.

I haven't been pitching very well and I think that as a result my sideburns are getting shorter. Also, instead of calling Joe Schultz Joe I'm calling him Skip, which is what I called Ralph Houk when I first came up. Managers like to be called Skip.

I'm scheduled to pitch in the doubleheader they have scheduled tomorrow. I'll be at Scottsdale to pitch against the Cubs and a good outing by me could clinch a spot on the staff—maybe. What I've got to concentrate on this time is control and throwing other pitches besides the knuckleball. Whatever Sal Maglie says, Jim Bouton does. I'll impress the hell out of him with my curve and fastball and I'll just use the knuckler to get them out.

MARCH
23

Scottsdale

We lost a heartbreaker in the tenth, 7–6, but my heart wasn't broken. Indeed, I counted it as a pretty good day. Sorry about that, folks. I pitched three innings, gave up two hits and no runs and was ahead of most of the hitters. I used a good mixture of fastballs, overhand curves, change-ups and knuckleballs. Take that, Sal Maglie.

Going in to pitch those three innings I told myself that it was life or death, that everything depended on the way I pitched, that my dad was extremely interested in how I did and I would be calling him after the game. It was a good psyche job. Not only did I give up no runs, I popped up Ernie Banks and I popped up Ron Santo, both on knuckleballs. After each inning I looked up at my wife in the stands and we exchanged smiles, and in the last inning I pounded my hand into my glove in triumph and when I looked up at her she was as happy as, in the immortal words of Harry Golden, a mouse in a cookie jar.

My wife actually believes that it's possible, through concentration, to transfer strength from one person to another. She believes that during the game she transferred her strength to me and I pitched well. She is, of course, a nut.

A revelation about Joe Schultz. Mike Hegan has been hitting the hell out of the ball and at this point is to the Seattle Pilots what Mickey Mantle was to the Yankees. Today he was hit on the arm by a fastball, and when Joe got to him and said, "Where'd you get it, on the elbow?" Hegan said, "No. On the meat of the arm, the biceps."

"Oh shit, you'll be okay," Joe said. "Just spit on it and rub some dirt on it."

Hegan couldn't move three of his fingers for an hour. But it didn't hurt Joe at all.

Riding beck to Tempe I had a beautifully serene feeling about the whole day, which shows how you go up and down an emotional escalator in this business. It was my first really serene day of the spring and I felt, well, I didn't care where the bus was going or if it ever got there, and I was content to watch the countryside roll by. It was desert, of course, with cactus and odd rock formations that threw back the flames of the setting sun. The sun was a golden globe, half-hidden, and as we drove along it appeared to be some giant golden elephant running along the horizon and I felt so good I remembered something Johnny Sain used to talk about.

He used to say a pitcher had a kind of special feeling after he did really well in a ballgame. John called it the "cool of the evening", when you could sit and relax and not worry about being in there for three or four more days; the job done, a good job, and now it was up to somebody else to go out there the next day and do the slogging. The cool of the evening.

Of course, there's the converse. If a pitcher doesn't do well, he has three or four days to contemplate his sins. A hitter is back in there the next day, grinding his teeth and his bat. Still, I was feeling so good that I began to think about pitching against the Yankees, and what it would be like going back to Yankee Stadium and facing them. I had all four of my pitches working today, and I had good control, and I thought how much fun it's going to be to get back to the Stadium and toy, really *toy* with them. They haven't even seen my knuckleball. It could really be a picnic.

I think coach Eddie O'Brien is going to prove a gold-plated pain in the ass. He must think he's Frank Crosetti or something, because when I reached into his ballbag he said, "What are you going to do with it?"

"I'm going to count the laces," I told him. "And then I'm going to juggle it."

Later on O'Brien noticed some of the guys were eating sunflower seeds in the bullpen. "Hey, none of that," he said. "No eating in the bullpen."

"Not even sunflower seeds, Eddie?"

"Nothing. Not even sunflower seeds."

Eddie O'Brien will have to be clued in on what happens in the bullpen. Maybe the way to cure him is to make him head of the refreshment committee.

Ran my long foul-line-to-foul-line sprints in the outfield and kept myself going by imagining I was Jim Ryun running in the Olympics: I'm in the last fifty yards and I'm going into my finishing kick and thousands cheer. If I'm just Jim Bouton running long laps very little happens. Let's see. Here's the World War I flying ace . . .

Bill Stafford and Jimmy O'Toole got their releases today. Stafford hopes to hook on with the Giants (I don't see how) and O'Toole is shopping around. I've had some big discussions with O'Toole. His father is a cop in Chicago and was in on the Democratic Convention troubles. I'd been popping off, as usual, about what a dum-dum Mayor Daley was and O'Toole said hell, none of those kids take baths and they threw bags of shit at the cops, and that's how I found out his father was a cop. Even so, I feel sort of sorry for him because he's got about eleven kids (I should feel more sorry for his wife) and he seemed a forlorn figure as he packed his stuff. I told him good luck but somehow I didn't get to shake his hand, and I feel bad about that.

It's funny what happens to a guy when he's released. As soon as he gets it he's a different person, not a part of the team anymore. Not even a person. He almost ceases to exist.

It's difficult to form close relationships in baseball. Players are friendly during the season and they pal around together on the road. But they're not really friends. Part of the reason is that there's little point in forming a close relationship. Next week one of you could be gone. Hell, both of you could be gone. So no matter how you try, you find yourself holding back a little, keeping people at arm's length. It must be like that in war too.

MARCH
24

Tucson

On my way to the park today I passed the Vancouver practice field and spotted Sheldon over there playing pepper. It gave me a sinking feeling. There but for the grace of the knuckleball go I. Not that it still can't happen. I still may not fit in with Schultz's plans. What we need is a lefthanded pitcher, starter or reliever, and I can see a trade for one. But where does an aging righthanded knuckleballer fit in? Vancouver?

I know I felt differently after those good three innings yesterday, but I'm already tossing around in my mind how I'll react if I'm sent down. I'll take it calmly, see, and say to Joe, "Skip, I know you've got a lot of things on your mind and you didn't really have the chance to give everybody the amount of work that would have helped them the most.

But I don't want to be a problem. I'll go to Vancouver and do a good job there and expect to be called up after a month of the season goes by."

On the other hand, would that be the best approach? Maybe I could talk him out of it. Maybe I could get a couple of more chances to pitch and then he'd wind up cutting somebody else.

There's a third possibility. Maybe right now, at this very moment, I've got the team cinched. Dream city.

Jake Gibbs of the Yankees once ordered pie a la mode in a restaurant and then asked the waitress to put a little ice cream on it.

A sportswriter came up to Darrell Brandon today and asked him where he thought the club would finish. "Where did Joe Schultz say?" Brandon asked.

"Third," the reporter said.

"Put me down for third too," Brandon said.

Obviously I'm not the only worried guy in this camp.

We had dinner with Gary and Nan Bell and he said that if he could pick a place to play it would be Boston. He said he didn't like Cleveland because Gabe Paul would interfere in his personal life. (Nobody interferes in Gary Bell's personal life, not even his wife.) But Boston was money paradise. He said guys with 12-12 seasons there would automatically get a $5,000 raise.

I'd heard that about Boston. The year Dick Radatz had his big year was the year I won 21. We both had two years in the big leagues and we were both young phenoms. While I was trying to get $20,000, a $9,000 raise, Radatz was going to $41,000. Radatz told me that at a banquet and said that if he'd really battled them he could have gotten $45,000 or $50,000. I absolutely refused to believe him. But Bell said it was true. Good grief, $41,000! The bastards were *stealing* my money.

25

Marvin Miller is coming around tomorrow to hand out some checks for promotions the Players' Association was paid for. So everybody was busy reminding everybody else not to tell the wives. We get little checks for a lot of things, like signing baseballs, which are then sold. In our peak years with the Yankees we were getting around $150 for signing baseballs. It's all pocketed as walking-around money. The wives don't know about it. Hell, there are baseball wives who don't know about the money we get for being in spring training, or that we get paid every two weeks during the season. John Kennedy, infielder, says that when his wife found out about the spring money she said, "Gee whiz, all that money you guys get each week. How come you've never been able to save anything?" And John said, "We just started getting it, dear. It's a brand-new thing."

Joe Schultz asked Wayne Comer, outfielder, how his arm felt. Comer said he wasn't sure, but that every time he looked up there were buzzards circling it.

Tommy Davis has been having trouble with his arm too, which was why he was playing first base when I came into the game against the Indians with runners on first and third and one out. Second and third, really, since before I drew a breath the guy stole second. Rich Sheinblum, outfielder, rookie, was up and I threw two curve balls to him for a 1-and-1 count. He missed a knuckleball and then hit a one-hopper hard and deep to first. I covered and got Sheinblum, and when the guy tried to score from third I nailed him with a strike to home plate. Two thirds of an inning. Another perfect Bouton day.

One of the dumb things I do sometimes is form judgments about people I don't really know. Case history: Jack Hamilton, pitcher, Cleveland Indians. He was with the Angel organization last year and played with me in Seattle, which is where I got to know him. Before that I

MARCH
26

Tempe

Six cuts today. You walk into the clubhouse and you see a guy packing his bag and you both try not to look at each other. Most guys won't pack until they know everybody is busy on the field, but sometimes you surprise somebody in there and it's always awkward.

Steve Hovley was one of the six. He was able to smile and say it came as no surprise to him and that Vancouver is a very nice town.

I was surprised to see Merritt Ranew get cut. He's been hitting well and we're short of lefthanded hitters. Very strange.

Got another flash from Eddie O'Brien today. I had a minor eye infection and was wearing dark glasses in the bullpen and O'Brien said, "What's with the shades?"

"I'm having trouble with my eyes."

"Well, I don't think you should be wearing shades down here."

"But, Eddie baby, the doctor says I have to. Do you want I should get a note from him?"

"Well, if the doctor says so . . ."

MARCH
27

Yuma

Our first big road trip today to Yuma, Arizona, and we did what ballplayers do at the start of every trip—stand around the airport, inspect the threads and make funny comments: like, if a guy is wearing a turtleneck that's too big for him, "Who gave you that turtleneck, Bronco Nagurski?"

You can start fights if you get on a guy about something meaningful, like race or religion. But you can kid a guy about his clothes, or about the way he looks. We couldn't decide, for example, whether Sal Maglie looked more like an Indian chief or Mafia enforcer. But we didn't tell him.

Me: "If you're a customs official would you check Maglie's bag?"

Bell: "I'd strip him to his shorts."

Then there was Gabe Paul, Jr.'s, haircut. Worst haircut I ever saw. It was military all around, except on top, where it was kind of new left. Ugh. Ray Oyler's comment was, "Hey, Gabe, where'd you get that nice razor cut?"

Today Joe Schultz said, "Many are called, few are chosen." He said it out of the clear blue, several times, once to Lou Piniella. Said Lou: "Is that a bad sign?" I said I didn't know. But I did. And it was.

Would you believe that we were playing a ballgame in Yuma, the winter home, as they say, of the San Diego Padres, which is a place you pass through on the way to someplace else, a place that doesn't even have a visiting clubhouse, so that we had to dress on the back of an equipment truck, and in the middle of a game before about twelve people, one of them yelled at us, "Ya bums, ya!" I mean, would you believe it?

Although we won the game Joe Schultz wasn't impressed. There were a couple of minor dumb plays, so Joe had a meeting on the bus. One of the things he was upset about was that one of the guys asked, "Who do we play tomorrow?"

Said Joe: "Boys, if you don't know who you're going to play you don't have your head in the game."

The guy who asked the question was Lou Piniella, and now he knows what Joe meant by "Many are called, few are chosen." Goodbye Lou.

Still, at the end of the meeting I wanted very much to say, "By the way Joe, who *do* we play tomorrow?" But I'm not pitching all *that* well.

Today Joe Schultz also said, "Put your hat on."

He said it to me.

Five minutes later Eddie O'Brien came over and said, "See, what'd I tell you? Put your hat on."

You would think that managers have too much on their minds to notice things like that. But they don't. I know, for one example, that Al Lopez hated Bob Shaw because he was blond and handsome and used to keep his hat off as much as possible so the girls in the stands could get a good look. And one day Lopez called out of the dugout to him, "Shaw, I see you with a different broad every night. You must be a lousy lay."

We were doing windsprints and Gary Bell was having a terrible time because of certain local poisonous fluids he'd encountered the night before. We decided that Eddie O'Brien would let him off if he got a note from his bartender.

Bell is a funny man and, along with Tommy Davis, is emerging as one of the leaders of the club. He's got an odd way of talking. Instead of saying, "Boy, that's funny," he'll wrinkle up his face and say, "How funny is that?"

Or he'll say, "How fabulous are greenies?" (The answer is very. Greenies are pep pills—dextroamphetamine sulfate—and a lot of baseball players couldn't function without them.)

There is an odd sort of sexual liberation among baseball players— a verbal one. It's considered perfectly all right to make sexual remarks about your wife and other players' wives. It's a nothing-sacred game, and Bell is one of the leading practitioners. "When I get home I'm going to knock my old lady's eyebrows off," he'll say. Or he'll go up to Ray Oyler and say, "Ray, when you come to the ballpark tomorrow will you bring my socks? I left them under your bed."

Sometimes you'll get this kind of conversation:

"Gee, your wife was great last night."

"Oh, she wasn't all that great."

"You should have been there earlier. She was terrific."

After the game today many of us repaired to the local pub and spent the fading hours of the afternoon drinking beer. Johnny Podres, the old Dodger who seems to be making it with the San Diego Padres (that's sort of nice, Podres of the Padres), was there, feeling little pain, and took it upon himself to straighten me out as a pitcher. "Listen, Jim, let me show you what you used to do and what you're doing now."

Pretty soon there was a beer glass where my right leg was supposed to be, an ash tray for my left foot and martini glasses for the length of my stride, and he was going through all my motions, two ways. Of course, I had to do it too, and after a while we drew a pretty good crowd. What he was saying was that I had to get my body into the ball and that I should hold my weight back and let it go all at once. It was sound advice and it embarrassed the hell out of me.

Still, it was a good afternoon. I was pleased that Podres should care and that he remembered my old motion and there was that little stirring in my belly that maybe he was right, maybe I could still find the old magic. But then I remembered baseballs disappearing into clouds and I smiled and tried to sit down. "One more time," Podres said. And all the guys said, "Yeah, one more time, Bouton, and this time get it right." So I did it one more time, wishing I could drink beer faster and get drunker.

On the airplane, Darrell Brandon, sitting next to me, said, "You like to read a lot, don't you?"

"Yeah," I said cleverly.

"Does it make you smart?"

He wasn't being sarcastic. I think he really wanted to know. "Not really," I said. "But it makes people think I am."

Actually I was somewhat embarrassed by the question. In fact I *do* like to read on airplanes, but when I do I'm not in on the kidding and the small talk, so as a result I'm an outsider. I've resolved not to be an outsider this year. I'm not reading so much and no one can accuse me of playing the intellectual. And here I get caught up in a magazine article and Darrell Brandon is asking if reading makes you smart.

A little more about the new Bouton image. If the guys go out to a bar after a game for a few drinks, I'm going too. I'm going to get into card games on airplanes. I don't like bars much, and card games bore me, but I'm going to do it. If you want to be one of the gang, that's one way to do it.

It's odd, but you can be seven kinds of idiot and as long as you hang around with the boys you're accepted as an ace. Johnny Blanchard of the Yankees was an ace. He was just another jocko, but he was an ace because he was always out with Mickey Mantle and the boys, drinking, partying, playing cards. Every once in a while, just to enhance his image, he'd smack some poor guy off a bar stool and that was great. Johnny Blanchard was one of the boys.

Why should I be one of the boys? Why should I yield to the jockos? Oh, I'm not going to hold back if something comes up I feel strongly about, but I'm going to soft-pedal it a bit, at least at the beginning, until I'm sure I can make this club. I really believe that if you're a marginal player and the manager thinks you're not getting along with the guys it can make the difference.

I'm positive that the one reason Houk got rid of me was that I'd made a lot of enemies on the club (including Houk, I guess) simply because I refused to go along with the rules they set up.

Here's an example. I always felt that players should cooperate with the press, and when the Yankees got angry at me for talking too much to reporters I was quoted as saying, "Well, I don't get angry at them for *not* talking to reporters, why should they get angry at me because I do?" And that made it even worse.

Or they'd make a rule, because of some story or other, that nobody should talk with this or that reporter. So when he came into the clubhouse I'd give him a big smile and talk with him and be seen having lunch with him, just to let them know I wasn't going to buy that nonsense.

In September 1966 when the Yankees were in ninth place, 26 1/2 games out of first place, Murray Olderman of Newspaper Enterprises Association, asked me what I thought was wrong with the Yankees. After carefully examining our statistics and lofty place in the standings I said, "I guess we just stink." The headline in the papers the next day said "Bouton: Yankees Stink." The distortion was only minute.

Houk called me into his office. "Olderman made you look bad," he said. "The players are all upset. I'm sure he misquoted you. You've got to be careful when you talk to these guys."

"Well, he didn't really misquote me," I said.

Houk didn't think that was enough. He thought I should say more. I asked him like what. And he said I should apologize to the players. I said I would. And I did. I'm not sure what for, though. I mean, boy, did we stink.

Then there was the matter of talking too much, not to reporters, to the guys. You see, you *could* talk about the war in Vietnam, only you had to say, "Look at those crazy kids marching in the street. Why don't they take a bath?" Or you could say, "What right does Rev. Groppi have to go out in the streets like that? He should be in the pulpit where he belongs." If you said these things, no one would accuse you of talking politics, because you were *right*.

On the other hand, if you said things like, "We've got no right to be in Vietnam," or that, "Rev. Groppi is certainly making his religion relevant up there in Milwaukee," then you shouldn't be talking about things like that, because you were *wrong*.

And it could cost you too. When Joe Garagiola was running "The Match Game" on television, a lot of the Yankees, almost all of them, were getting on the show. I mean even Steve Whitaker. And me, the articulate Jim Bouton, spontaneously witty, always at ease in front of the camera, never got a call.

This year, though, it's a new Bouton. At least until I win some ballgames.

MARCH
28

Holtville

Mike Hegan has been hitting like fury. He does that from time to time. His history is streaks. He's either hitting .450 or .150.

I wondered if he ever got any help from his father, who has been in baseball twenty years and is now a Yankee coach. Mike said he never did. In fact, when he was growing up he hardly saw his father at all, and to this day they seldom talk about baseball.

The help he gets is from his mother. He said that he believed it was she who put him into his current hot streak. She knows a lot about hitting and she sends him little reminders all the time of what to do and think about while he's hitting. She's a big reader of golf manuals and applies them to baseball, sending him helpful hints for the duffer that actually help.

We don't have a hitting instructor here. So I've been thinking that maybe Mike Hegan's mom, since she has such a good record . . . ah, I don't think Eddie O'Brien would go for it.

When Lou Piniella said he'd been to a palm reader the other day the guys wanted to know what she'd told him.

"She told me I was hitting in bad luck," Piniella said.

Today, while we were sitting in the bullpen, Eddie O'Brien, the All-American coach, said, just after one of our pitchers walked somebody in the ballgame: "The secret to pitching, boys, is throwing strikes."

Gee, Eddie! Thanks.

I came in to relieve in the ninth and got the last out. After the game, Joe Schultz had the whole team run around the bases and then said, "Okay, everybody in—except Bouton and Baney. I want to see you two."

Baney got this horrified look on his face and said, "Oh, my God!"

I couldn't resist, so giving him my sincere look, I said, "This is it."

He turned pale and moped over to Joe, slowly, as if attached to a large rubber band. But all Joe wanted was to tell us that we had to run some extra laps since we were in the bullpen and weren't able to run when everybody else did.

I never saw anybody run laps looking so happy as Dick Baney. Unless it was Jim Bouton.

Wayne Comer got into an argument with an umpire, and they were jawing back and forth. The last thing said was, "All right, Comer. You'll be sorry you said that."

And he probably will. Umpires do get even with people, even good umpires. I remember when George Scott first came up to Boston. He must have irritated Ed Runge somehow because the word came out from Elston Howard that when Runge was behind the plate and Scott was hitting, the strikes wouldn't have to be too good.

The first pitch I threw to Scott was about six inches off the plate. Strike one. The second pitch was eight inches outside. Strike two. The third pitch was a curve in the dirt. Scott swung and missed. He never had a chance.

Runge is one of the more powerful umpires in the league, mostly, I suppose, because he's a real good one. He's been wearing these long, gray sideburns that look just great against his tan. He is a striking figure out there. I asked him if he thought he could get by wearing the burns during the season and he said he didn't know, that Joe Cronin, the league president, hadn't seen them yet. But I'm betting on Runge. He's got power.

There was the time, for example, when Steve Whitaker was with the Yankees and bitched to him on a couple of calls and Runge told Mickey Mantle, "You better straighten that boy out."

That night Mantle and Whitaker ran into Runge at a restaurant and Mantle told Whitaker he'd better go over and apologize. Whitaker said the hell he would. But after Mantle explained to him what it might mean to his batting average he succumbed. Just call him *Mr.* Runge.

One would have thought Comer was through arguing with umpires, but I guess he's a slow learner. The other day he got himself in trouble with another umpire by getting on his son, who is trying to be an umpire. The son told the father and the father told Tommy Davis that Comer better come up swinging. He meant he wasn't likely to get any balls called.

Sure enough the first pitch to Comer was a high curve and he called it strike one. Comer didn't even look back. He swung at the next pitch and hit a line drive off the fence for a triple. The ump looked over to our bench and said, "See, it makes him a better hitter."

Rich Rollins has a good story he tells in the same vein. It goes back to when we were playing against each other in the Class-B Carolina League. Rich had hit two home runs in the first game of a doubleheader and the club had some deal that anybody who hit three home runs in one day would get $300. So the other players on Rollins' team told him to go to our catcher, Norm Kampshor, and get him to tell him what was coming by offering him half the money.

Rollins: "I didn't want to do it at first. I said I didn't think it was right, but they said hell, it was common practice, and there I was just out of school and didn't know a damn thing. So I told Kampy I needed another home run and that he'd get $150 if he told me what was coming. He didn't even hesitate. Just said sure.

"And not only did he tell me what was coming, but after a while he started asking me what I'd like to have thrown. And I'd say fastball, or change, and I'd get it."

The big joke, of course, was that I was the pitcher at the time.

"You know, I really felt sorry for you," Rollins said. "There you were sweating your guts out trying to make the big leagues and not only did I know what was coming, but I was calling your game for you."

In the end, though, the joke was on Rollins. Calling my game for *me,* he managed only one double in four times at bat. And if he had come to me, I probably would have grooved one for him. Not for money, just for the hell of it.

Sorry kids, things like that happen. Phil Linz was batting .299 going into the last game of the season at Modesto and asked the other catcher to help him get to .300. "When you come up I'll have the third baseman play real deep," the catcher said. "All you have to do is lay down a bunt and beat it out."

That's exactly what happened. Phil got the hit for his .300 average and got the manager to take him out of the game. Now it's in the record books forever that Phil Linz hit .300.

The same thing happened with Tommy Davis. He was hitting .299 for the Mets and playing against his old teammates, the Dodgers. Johnny Roseboro was catching. "Hey, Baby, you're my main man," Davis said. "How about a little help?" Roseboro said sure and told him what was coming. Davis got his hit and had his .300 batting average.

MARCH
29

Palm Springs

Tommy Davis is loose and funny and a lot of guys look to him, not only Negroes. Everybody sort of gravitates toward him and his tape machine, and he's asked his opinion about things. Like, "Hey Tommy, what kind of town is Palm Springs?"

So far I haven't heard any of the white guys say, "Tommy, what are you doing for dinner tonight?" Maybe it will come. Maybe.

At least Tommy is no Elston Howard. The best way I can explain Howard is to recall the day Jimmy Cannon, the elderly columnist, Howard, his wife Arlene and I got involved in an argument about civil rights; Arlene and I on one side, Cannon and Howard on the other. Arlene and I were the militants.

The guys are grumbling about Joe Schultz. I'm not sure if it's serious or just the normal baseball grumbling. Joe has been insisting that the guys do more running and more pick-ups, and nobody likes that, so they're sniggering behind his back and calling him things like "Step-and-a-Half" because he walks with a slight limp.

I hope it doesn't get to be the kind of thing the Yankees had with Johnny Keane. None of the guys were happy when Houk moved up to general manager in 1964, and they didn't like Yogi Berra as a manager, and they hated Keane. They constantly grumbled about Keane, and when he'd, say, flash the bunt sign, they'd say to themselves, "What the hell does Keane know about our style?" They never respected anything he did. So they'd make a half-hearted attempt to bunt and pop it up or hit into a double play. Then the newspaper guys would ask them what was the matter and they'd say they didn't know, they were trying just as hard as they always did. The hell they were.

I mean if Houk flashed the bunt sign they'd think, "Oh boy, what a genius." And they'd lay down the bunt. It's a mental thing. If you're going to give physically 100 percent you have to be giving mentally 100 percent. Except how can you give 100 percent for a guy you call Squeaky or Midget or other rotten things?

MARCH
30

Holtville

Now about Roger Maris. Roger fought a lot with the people in the stands, especially in Detroit, where he used to give them the finger. He and the fans would get to calling each other names and then Maris would roll out his heavy artillery.

"Yeah? How much money are *you* making?"

Roger was making $70,000 a year.

After a while every time Maris got into an argument the guys in the dugout would say, "C'mon Rodg, hit him with your wallet."

Thinking about the great Rodg reminded me of a brief encounter. One day there appeared a clipping on the bulletin board in the Yankee clubhouse. It was a quote from me after Mel Stottlemyre had hit an inside-the-park home run, which is very hard for a pitcher to do. One of the writers came to me after it and said, "What were you thinking when Stottlemyre was going around the bases?" It was a nice, silly question, so I gave him a nice, silly answer. I said I was hoping that Stottlemyre would fall down because if he hit an inside-the-park home run it would put pressure on all us other pitchers to hit inside-the-park home runs, and who needed that? And now it's on the bulletin board like I was serious.

I asked around to find out who put it up, but I couldn't, although I eventually decided it must have been either Clete Boyer, another one of my boosters, or Maris. So one day when they were standing together in the outfield I went over and said, "I wish you guys would tell me who put that clipping up on the board, because I'd like to get my hands on the gutless son of a bitch who did it."

And although Maris had already denied to me that he put up the clipping, he said, "Don't call me gutless."

Somehow I managed not to get into a fight with him. But I felt I'd won the battle of wits. Which is probably why he didn't own up to posting it the first time I asked him. He didn't want to contend with my rapier-like mind.

Maris' friend Clete Boyer was the kind of guy who would always tell me to be careful who I brought into the clubhouse. Yet he led the league in hosting the offspring of clothing manufacturers. The way it worked, he'd get free sweaters and in return he'd have to bring the sons of the manufacturers into the clubhouse where they could run around, ask for autographs and make pests of themselves. He and Maris got the sweaters, and we got the kids.

And a final word about my favorite baseball writer, Jim Ogle, of the Newhouse papers. Ogle was a Yankee fan and he reacted to players purely on how much they were helping the Yankees to win. Charm, personality, intelligence—nothing counted. Only winning. Ogle didn't have even the pretense of objectivity. He was the only writer in the pressbox who would take the seventh-inning stretch in the Yankee half.

Once at a winter press conference, when the Yankees were announcing the signing of three or four guys, Stan Isaacs, who writes a really good column for *Newsday,* on Long Island, passed a note to Houk. It said: "Has Ogle signed his contract yet?"

Isaacs may not have known how ironic he was being. In fact Ogle's ambition was always to work for the Yankees. But they would never give him a job.

Not that this prevented him from doing little jobs for them. Like when I was sent down he was on television with Yankee broadcasters and said that it wasn't so much that I was pitching poorly, but because of the kind of person I was. He said that none of the players liked me and there were some terrible things about me he couldn't even talk about. This left it up to the public imagination. What was I? Rapist, murderer, dope peddler? Jim Ogle wouldn't say.

MARCH
31

Tempe

It's getting to be, as the boys say, nut-cutting time. And it was not good news to hear that we're going to start the season with only nine pitchers. Besides that, we traded Chico Salmon to Baltimore for Gene Brabender, "a hard-throwing righthanded country boy," said Steve Barber. I look at the pitching staff and I see six guys who have it made: Diego Segui, Marty Pattin, Jack Aker, Gary Bell, Steve Barber (including sore arm) and, because he had such a good year in Triple-A, Mike Marshall. Add Brabender and we have seven. So all spring there have been maybe thirty pitchers fighting for two spots on the staff.

I like to think I'm in pretty good shape. I haven't been scored on my last three or four times out and I've looked pretty good. But if they decide to keep, say, two lefthanders, where am I? Or suppose I get bombed tomorrow? Now I know what life on a tenterhook is like.

I thought the Salmon trade was pretty good for us because we didn't really have a spot for him. But he was very disappointed. He slammed the door when he left Joe's office. I know he counted on going to Seattle. He spent the winter up there and went to a lot of promotional dinners and leased an apartment and rented furniture, the works. Now it's Baltimore instead. Life in the big leagues.

Jack Aker, who's been our acting player representative, called a meeting today to elect a permanent player rep and alternate. Aker has quite a bit of experience in that area. He was the player rep in Kansas City when the players had all that trouble with Charley Finley and he's the most qualified guy on the team. He was elected with no opposition.

Tommy Davis nominated me for alternate, which both surprised and pleased me. Don Mincher seconded. Then someone nominated Gary Bell and the two of us left the room. Gary won it by one vote, and Tommy Davis kidded that Mincher had switched and voted for Bell.

Don was embarrassed, but I don't blame him. He doesn't know me that well and Gary's been around a lot longer.

Actually it felt rather good to lose by only one vote. When I was with the Yankees I once campaigned for player rep and didn't come that close.

Understand that *nobody* campaigns for player rep. Mostly you get the job the way Aker did. "All right, who wants to be player rep? Aker? Okay, Aker, you're the player rep."

But I campaigned with the Yankees because I wanted to dump Clete Boyer, and I guess that worked because when we had nominations he stood up and said, "I want to quit this fucking job." Also I actually thought I had a chance of winning and that I was probably the best man for the job.

So I mimeographed a two-page statement on why I felt I would be a good player rep and what qualities I thought we should look for and why I felt I met those requirements. I added some silly things in order to keep it all rather light, like I wanted to be a player rep so I could get to ride in a big airplane and write player rep on my jockstrap.

I got three votes. One of them was on an absentee ballot by Fritz Peterson. He had to leave, but left it for me in case I needed it. I never embarrassed Fritz by casting it. So everyone thinks I got only two votes. Let history record it was three.

APRIL

1

Four pitchers were cut before the game—Dick Baney, Dick Bates, Buzz Stephen and Bob Lasko. I walked in on Lasko in the clubhouse and he was sipping coffee and had a smile on his face.

"What are you so happy about?" I said.

"The pressure is off," he said. "The pressure is off and I'm going to Vancouver, which means I'll be with my family."

I don't think I'd have taken it quite that well.

I got into the game, pitched two innings and looked good. I gave up a run, unearned. The catcher dropped a foul pop and then the hitter walked. He scored on a double, which was the only well-hit ball off me. I had a good assortment of stuff and was able to throw fewer knuckleballs, which must have pleased Sal Maglie.

After the game John Morris and Darrell Brandon got it. So one lefthander, Bill Henry, and I had made it. It's a good feeling, but if I had known all along what the odds were I'd have been less optimistic and more nervous.

Brandon has taken being sent down pretty hard, although he did have a poor spring. He took a long time packing his bag and after we were through with our workout he was still in the clubhouse, just sitting there in front of his locker, looking as though he hoped Schultz might change his mind and tell him it was all a mistake. No one went over to talk to him. It was sad and strange.

When I came to the park and saw Baney, Bates and Stephens packing, I started to smile. I was so relieved it wasn't me. And knowing that with them gone it would be that much easier for me, I felt this silly grin pop out on my face, so I bit my lip to get it off and turned into my locker. I didn't want anybody to see me smiling. I didn't want to *be* smiling. But I was, I was.

Anyway, we're down to twenty-five players now with a nine-man pitching staff, which means if we do anything, we'll add a pitcher, so I feel fat, safe and secure. Also I know that if I don't make it, or if I don't get to pitch, it'll be because I wasn't good enough. It won't be on my mind that someone is trying to sabotage me the way I felt when I was with the Yankees. Even if it isn't true, even if Houk wasn't out to get me, even if all the times I had to go into ballgames without having enough time to warm up properly, and if all the times I would go ten days without so much as throwing a ball in batting practice, were all accidental, it seemed to me I was being set up to be canned.

Like we all knew Piniella would be canned and it happened today. He was traded to Kansas City for Steve Whitaker and John Gelnar, a played against him in the minors and considered him stupid, a hard-throwing guy who didn't care whether or not he hit the batter. In the majors I figured him for a troublemaker because he used to get into fights with Phil Linz. Nobody fights with Phil Linz.

Then, when Hamilton hit Tony Conigliaro in the eye a couple of years ago and put him out for the season, I thought, boy, this guy is some kind of super rat. But when I played with him in Seattle I found he was just a guy like everybody else, honestly sorry he'd hit Conigliaro, a good team player, a friendly fellow who liked to come out early to the park and pitch batting practice to his kids. All of which made me feel like an ass.

The Unsinkable Molly Brown almost was sunk tonight. Unsinkable is what we call Laurie, our youngest. She's only three, but a tough little broad. This spring alone, for example, she's been bitten by a dog, hit in the head by a flying can of peas and had nine stitches sewed into her pretty little head. Nothing puts her down. Tonight, though, the kids were playing in the bedroom and suddenly we heard shattering glass followed by Laurie crying. Seems her head had made contact with a jalousie, resulting in broken glass and a bit of blood. The reason she had made such violent contact is that Kyong Jo had pushed her, and the reason he had pushed her is that I had told him to. I told him to push her because little girls are very often pests to little boys and the best way to get rid of little girl pests is to give them a gentle push. Only it's not supposed to result in blood, and poor Kyong Jo was severely chastened. He had this look of terrible shame on his face. Fortunately little Laurie wasn't hurt much. No stitches were required and we were able to reassure both her and Kyong Jo. After all, she *is* the Unsinkable Molly Brown.

pitcher. It was a giveaway. Bound to happen, though. Lou just wasn't their style.

We were talking about what we ought to call Brabender when he gets here. He looks rather like Lurch of the "Addams Family," so we thought we might call him that, or Monster, or Animal, which is what they called him in Baltimore last year. Then Larry Haney told us how Brabender used to take those thick metal spikes that are used to hold the bases down and bend them in his bare hands. "In that case," said Gary Bell, "we better call him Sir."

Hey, funny thing. This isn't a real bad ballclub. It hits like hell. We have six guys hitting over .300 and Hegan is hitting over .400. We're scoring a lot of runs. We've won five in a row this spring and we're nearly back to .500. And the Angels have yet to beat us. Maybe we really *can* finish third.

APRIL

2

John Kennedy says he knows the reason he's been hitting so poorly this spring. The low mound has screwed up his swing.

We had a meeting on catchers' signs today and I was glad that it was decided to use the pump system rather than the finger system. I have trouble with the finger system because I can't see the fingers. But the pump system is fine. It's not how many fingers are involved, but how many times they are flashed.

You use the pump with an indicator, which can be changed if you're worried about somebody reading you. Let's say you number your pitches this way: 1-curveball, 2-fastball, 3-change, 4-knuckleball or slider or screwball or whatever odd pitch you happen to have. The fifth pump starts the cycle again. Now, say the indicator, which can be changed from inning to inning, is three. That means the first pump is for the change, second pump the knuckleball, third back to number one, the curve. And so forth.

It's simple, and I wish I'd worked something like that out with the Yankees. I used to make Jake Gibbs wear white adhesive tape on his fingers so I could count them.

The other signs will work on a similar principle. Some sample signs: touching the left side of the chest is the take, right side of the chest is the bunt, touching the left leg is the steal and right hand to the right leg is hit-and-run. The principle here is that hitting signs are above the belt and running signs are below. The takeoff is wiping the hand across the letters and the indicator will be touching the right arm. That is, no sign is valid until after the right arm is touched. As a variation you can make the sign the second one after the indicator is flashed. Or the third. That way even if somebody knows all your signs he can't tell what you're putting on.

Speaking of signs, I'm reminded that when I came to the Yankees and Yogi Berra was catching, if there was a man on first he'd call nothing but fastballs. That was so he would have a better chance if the guy was trying to steal. In fact Yogi liked to call mostly fastballs because they're the easiest to catch. I understand that part of the difficulty between Berra and Sain goes back to the days when Sain pitched to him and he couldn't get him to call anything but fastballs.

I am, of course, an optimist. Each year I'm certain I'm going to be great again. Every winter I get a questionnaire from *Sport* magazine on picking the pennant races and I always pick myself as Comeback of the Year. Each year I believe it. Each winter I pay a college kid $5 three nights a week to catch me in a gym. Each year I'm certain.

And here I go again. I'm more positive than ever. My arm feels great. I've made the ballclub. I'm starting to throw like I used to throw, and I'm thinking I'll be a reliever for a while and then I'll do well in long relief and get a spot start now and then. Then I'll complete a ballgame and along around June they're going to stick me into the rotation and I'm going to wind up winning a flock of games, just like I did when I first came up to the Yankees. I see the team doing real well and I see me as one of the keys to our success. I see myself as one of the reasons we might finish third or fourth, I see myself as a goddam hero. That's what an optimist is, isn't it? A goddam hero.

The bench was treated to a lovely Sal Maglie second-guess today. Steve Barber was pitching and he had men on second and third with Jim Fregosi up. On 3 and 2 Barber threw a change and Fregosi lunged, hit it to left and knocked in both runs. As soon as the ball was hit, Maglie, who was standing next to Schultz, snapped his fingers and said, "Son of a bitch—3-and-2 change. That goddam 3-and-2 change."

Whenever something goes wrong, Maglie is quick to show disgust, especially if Schultz is around. I guess he wants the manager to know he's in the ballgame and that he doesn't take adversity calmly. But I was surprised about him fussing over a 3-and-2 change, because I think it's a helleva pitch. In a spot like that the hitter is looking for something the pitcher throws often, like the fastball, or if he's got good control of his curve he might throw that. So the off-speed pitch in that situation really throws the hitter off.

Later on I asked Sal about it. "Sal," I said sweetly, "I saw you get mad at the change-up Steve threw Fregosi. What's your feeling about the change on 3-and-2?"

"It depends on the situation," says Sal.

"I've had pretty good success with the 3-and-2 change."

"Well I did too," says Sal. "I remember once I threw one to Stan Musial with the bases loaded and he was so surprised he just stood there with the bat on his shoulder. Strike three."

We kicked that around for a while and Sal wound up saying that the 3-and-2 change was a helluva pitch, if you threw it to the right guy.

But not to Jim Fregosi. By Barber. Today.

APRIL
3

Bill Henry retired today, just like that. First he makes the team, then he walks in on Joe Schultz and announces his retirement. Joe told us about it and said that he admired the man, that he had a lot of guts to walk out.

John Morris, who was brought up from the Vancouver squad to replace Henry, was pretty frisky, like he'd just gotten a reprieve from the Governor. He said he had some long talks with Henry—which is something, because when you say hello to Henry he is stuck for an answer—and thinks he quit because he was holding back a young player. "What am I doing keeping younger guys from a chance to earn a living?" he said to Morris. "I'm forty-two years old. I've had thirteen years in the big leagues. I don't really belong here."

During the meeting Joe Schultz said, "It takes a lot of courage for a guy to quit when he thinks he can't do the job anymore."

So I opened my big yap and said, "If that's the case a lot of us ought to quit."

Which gave Sal Maglie the chance to say, very coolly, "Well, use your own judgment on that."

I'm not sure Sal likes me.

Today Joe Schultz said, "Well, boys, it's a round ball and a round bat and you got to hit it square."

APRIL
4

Packing day. Baseball players and their wives are very good packers. I can pack for a two-week trip in less than an hour and my wife has moving the whole family down to a science. I'm sure this will prove very valuable to us later in life. Especially if I become a big-game hunter. Or an astronaut. Of course it helped that Mike Marshall arranged, on a split-second timetable, to have our cars shipped to Seattle by rail. Maybe *he* should be running the Long Island Rail Road.

APRIL
5

San Diego

Gary Bell is my roommate. Good roommate. Good beaver-shooter. He tells a story about a guy who climbed a palm tree to shoot some beaver and got stranded when the tide came in. I wonder where the hell that palm tree was.

I think it should be known that when Whitey Ford was pitching for the Yankees he set up a table with a checkered tablecloth in the bullpen. On the table there was an empty wine bottle with a candle in it. Also hero sandwiches. Whitey Ford had style.

Bruce Henry, the Yankee road secretary, is one of my main men. He hated to buy bats for me. He always claimed I didn't need them. When he finally did, he had them inscribed not with my name, but my batting average—.092. And once when I complained that the people I'd given passes to were upset about getting poor seats, he said, "How'd they like the price?"

Wayne Comer says that Mayo Smith, the Tiger manager, once said to him, "Wayne, I think you're going to hit .290 this year—but you're going to be doing it in Montgomery, Alabama."

I am reminded that not long ago I ran into Bob Smith of the old "Howdy Doody" show at a Rexall in Ft. Lauderdale, and was able to sing to him the Howdy Doody theme song at the toothpaste counter:

It's Howdy Doody time,
It's Howdy Doody time,
Bob Smith and Howdy too,
Say Howdy do to you.

Let's give a rousing cheer,
Cause Howdy Doody's here.
It's time to start the show,
So kids, let's go!

Bob Smith went out of his gourd.

I also count myself as having a rather large store of answers to trivia questions.

Q. Who was the dog and who was the villain in Rootie Kazootie?
A. Galapoochie Pup and Poison Sumac.
The end of spring training always brings out the best in me.

APRIL
6

We played Vancouver before coming here to play San Diego a doubleheader for our last two exhibition games. I pitched two innings in the first game and gave up two runs. My arm felt good but I had poor control of my knuckleball. I asked Maglie if there was a chance I could get some more work in the second game. He said no. His reason was that they still had a couple of minor-league pitchers to look at. I said hell, I thought the team was set, and why didn't he ask Joe if he could squeeze me in. But he wouldn't. So I went to Joe. At the precise moment I started to explain why I thought I needed more work, Joe Schultz took a huge bite out of the liverwurst sandwich he was eating, got up off his stool, went to the Coke machine and mumbled something to me through his full mouth and over his shoulder. I didn't pitch. That's how I know what he said.

Part **3** And Then I Died

APRIL
7

Seattle

Today, the day before opening day, Joe Schultz said, "Well, it's back to the old salt mine, boys."

Later he encountered Tommy Davis and asked if that was "an old Budweiser" he was pouring down. "No, a Coke," Davis said.

And Joe Schultz said, "That's not too good for the old sto*macho.*"

Joe Schultz calls Jose Vidal "Chico," which is Spanish for "boy."

APRIL
8

Anaheim

Opening day—or Opening Day. Depending on how you feel about it.

I got a wire from Toots Shor in Anaheim before the game. It said, "Good luck, Jim. I hope you pitch often and win many games." Who says Toots never talks to has-beens?

Actually I don't know Toots that well. I've been in his place a few times and once when I was going bad he told me my whole problem was that I was striding three inches too far and if I just shortened up on the stride by those three inches everything would be fine. I was so desperate I actually tried it. It didn't help.

Everyone works out pregame nervousness in his own way. Tommy Davis was standing in the middle of the clubhouse taking a hitting stance with no bat in his hands, anticipating the pitch, striding into it, checking his swing and then going back and doing it all over again. It reminded me of a guy going over his notes just before a final exam, knowing all the time it wasn't going to do any good. If you don't have it by now, Tom, you're not going to.

There was a lot of grousing about the uniforms. It isn't only that they don't fit (no baseball uniforms fit, possibly because you are carefully measured for them). It's that they're so gaudy. I guess because we're the Pilots we have to have captain's uniforms. They have stripes on the sleeves, scrambled eggs on the peak of the cap and blue socks with yellow stripes. Also there are blue and yellow stripes down the sides of the pants. We look like goddam clowns. The only worse-looking uniforms are the ones they wear in Vancouver.

Naturally we won the first game. Beat the Angels 4–3. Mike Hegan hit the first home run for the Pilots and Joe Schultz, jumping up and down in the dugout, clapped his hands and actually yelled, "Hurray for our team."

When we came into the clubhouse, all of us yelling and screaming like a bunch of high-school kids, Joe Schultz said, "Stomp on 'em. Thataway to stomp on 'em. Kick 'em when they're down. Shitfuck. Stomp them. Stomp them good."

Already we're better than the Mets.

APRIL
9

Made my pitching debut today. Threw two fastballs to Hoyt Wilhelm, the elderly knuckleball pitcher who may one day be my idol. Got him out.

It took about a day into the season for us to be like every other ballclub, not just an expansion team full of strangers. I'm going out after the ballgame and have a few beers with the guys, maybe six or seven, which makes me blind. There is unquestionably a close feeling among the guys who go out and drink because they hash over the ballgame and it gives us all a feeling of common purpose. Slogan: The team that drinks together stays together.

Other things that draw a team together:

You're riding down the street in the team bus and you see a guy walking along with a big beer belly and his pants hanging below it and you say, "Mincher in ten years."

Or a guy is hanging on to a lamppost, a wino in a drunken stupor, severely defeated by life. "That's what happens when you can't hit the curve ball."

Marty Pattin does a pretty good Donald Duck. Before he pitched the opener he was going around the clubhouse saying in Donald Duck that you got to be loose, *quack*, you got to be loose. He was whistling in the dark. Later I found out he'd gone to bed at seven the night before and stayed in bed until noon. That's seventeen hours. I wonder if he got any sleep.

Today Joe Schultz said to the clean-shaven Rocky Bridges, Los Angeles coach, "Hey Rocky, how's your old mustache?"

Joe Schultz also said to Lou Johnson of the Angels, a man whom disaster has robbed of a piece of his left ear, "Hey, what's new, Half-Ear?"

Add to the saga of Mike Marshall: The other day he had a blister on his hand and the trainer told him the best way to help it was to keep it soaked in a cup of strong tea. A lot of guys would have told the trainer to shove the tea up his bippy, but Mike took the advice. Now he was walking around with his hand in a cup of tea—on the bus, in the clubhouse, sitting on the bench during the game and in his hotel room. So his roommate, John Kennedy, told everybody he had a nut for a roommate. Tea all over the goddam room. Even in his bed.

That's the way you become a nut. You have guts enough to walk around all day with your hand in a cup of tea.

APRIL
10

A few more words about Eddie O'Brien and Ron Plaza. O'Brien is one of the fairly famous basketball O'Brien twins who played with Seattle from '49 to '53. Actually his job is athletic director at Seattle University, but he had four years in the big leagues with the Pirates—as infielder and pitcher—and now he's here as a friend of management (or because his brother is in city government) to get his fifth year in on the pension plan. You only need four now, but Eddie's after five and no one's going to stop him.

Plaza was a coach under Schultz in Atlanta when it was still a minor-league city, and that's one of the ways you get to be a coach in the big leagues.

Coaches have little real responsibility, so it seems to me they should, at the very least, try to help club morale—cheer guys onward and upward, make jokes and smooth out little problems before they become big ones.

O'Brien and Plaza are officious types, though, and cause more trouble than they smooth over. And because they try to find things to do they become nothing but annoyances. Like O'Brien will say to Jack Aker, "Jack, you're in the bullpen tonight." Jack has been in the bullpen for eight years.

Another example: It is customary for players to pair off and throw easily on the sidelines before a workout or a game. So as I reached into the ballbag to grab some baseballs for the guys, Plaza said, "What are you going to do with those baseballs, Bouton?"

"I'm just going to take three or four out to the field because a few guys asked me to."

"Just take one."

"Yes, sir."

Steve Barber was in the diathermy machine again, all day, and I asked him again how it felt. "Better," he said, "fine, great. It just bothers me a little until I get loose and then there's no sweat." It's killing him. He hasn't been able to pick up a baseball and he was supposed to start today and didn't.

Standing around the outfield the conversation turned to religion. Don Mincher said he came from a very religious home and used to go to church every Sunday where people did things like roll in the aisles. He said there was a big circle of numbers on the church wall and when your number came up with somebody else's number you had to visit them and have a prayer meeting. As he got older Minch would say, "Well, let's have a few beers first." They didn't think that was very religious of him.

This afternoon Gary Bell and I went to Pershing Square (in Los Angeles) to listen to some of the old ladies in sneakers tell us to be prepared to meet our maker. I confess I enjoy rapping with them and usually wind up assured that eternal salvation is beyond my reach.

Later on we came across a group that was into the Indian thing and they were chanting *Hari Krishna Rama Rama,* etc., and I got to talking to one of them, who said that their religion simply was to reaffirm love of God regardless of the particular religion, and I thought that was fair enough and we hung around enjoying the chanting and sitar music.

Then a priest, probably about fifty-five years old, happened by and got into conversation with one of the group. When he left I asked what it was about. "He said this was a religion that didn't belong in this country," the young man said. "He said we already had enough religions in this country and that we should go back to India or wherever it was we came from."

Going over the hitters is something you do before each series, and before we went against the mighty Angels, Sal Maglie had a great hint for one of their weaker hitters, Vic Davalillo. "Knock him down, then put the next three pitches knee-high on the outside corner, boom, boom, boom, and you've got him."

Everybody laughed. If you could throw three pitches, boom, boom, boom, knee-high on the outside corner, you wouldn't have to knock anybody down. It's rather like telling somebody if he'd just slam home those ninety-foot putts he'd win the tournament easily.

APRIL
11

Seattle

Home again at Sicks' Stadium, graveyard for pitchers, home-run heaven, the major leagues. The clubhouse is small and crowded and there's no rug, just rubber runners on the cement floor and the lockers are small and close together, and there was a lot of grousing about it, and Joe Schultz said, "It's just like the old winter league. You've got to follow the crowd."

Gary Bell pitched and beat the White Sox, 7–0. Mincher hit two home runs. Tomorrow the world.

APRIL
12

Before today's game Joe Schultz said, "Okay men, up and at 'em. Get that old Budweiser."

APRIL
13

Pitched against the Chicago White Sox today and got bombed. Three runs in an inning-and-a-third. My knuckleball just doesn't seem to be ready yet. I can't get it over the plate consistently, and when I get behind I have to come in with my fastball, which somehow isn't too fast. So I got ripped for long hits, including one Don Pavletich hit over the left-field wall.

There were other problems. Pete Ward's a lefthanded hitter and I threw him a knuckler that was about a foot off the ground, outside. This is the kind of pitch he should have missed by a foot if he swung but he followed it all the way and belted it deep to center. It was caught against the wall, but it scored a run from third and I was damn relieved it didn't go out. That he was able to hit it at all is an indication that I wasn't throwing the knuckleball hard enough, probably because I was so worried about getting it over.

Pavletich hit a fastball, the first pitch I threw, and I thought, "Jesus, I didn't even get a chance to throw him a knuckler." It was supposed to set him up. So much for setting people up with my fastball, Sal Maglie, you fink. As soon as he hit it I said to myself, "Oh Christ, what a way to start. It's going to be a long time before I'm in there again." And I wondered how many innings I'd have to pitch in order to redeem myself and whether I'd be coming to bat in the next inning (sure enough) and subject to being pulled for a pinch-hitter (and I was).

We were behind like 4–0 when I came in and 7–0 when I left, and I have to admit I didn't cry when the other guys got clobbered too. You stand out less in a crowd.

After five games, our record is 3 wins and 2 losses. And we've scored a lot of runs. The team looks good. Tommy Harper is doing a helluva job at second base and I thought he'd be one of our weak spots. Ray Oyler's been fine at short and we've had some outstanding catches in the outfield. Third place doesn't look impossible. And if you don't count me, our pitching looks pretty good. Except for Steve Barber. Joe Schultz is upset with Barber because he has a sore arm. It's not as unusual as it sounds. Managers get angry at injuries. An injury is beyond a manager's control and he doesn't like anything he can't control. So if you're out too long with an injury he gets angry at you. The logic is almost perfect.

Johnny Keane was particularly prone to this kind of thinking. I remember going to Joe Soares, the Yankee trainer, and telling him my arm was bothering me and that I probably shouldn't throw and suggesting that he tell Keane.

"*You* tell him," Joe said. "The last time I told him anything he chewed my head off."

A kid named Tom Berg, who belongs to the Seattle organization and goes to school here, came over to work out with the club. And before the workout he was in the clubhouse shaving off his nice long sideburns. He got the word that Dewey Soriano, who is the president of the club, thought he would look better with shorter sideburns. Well, I think Dewey Soriano would look better if he lost weight.

I'm not getting enough pitching in, even as a short man, which is what I guess they've decided I am (although why they would want to bring in a knuckleballer with men on base, I can't understand). I need lots of work on my knuckleball and I'm not getting it. My other pitches aren't that bad, except they don't get anybody out, so I'm going to concentrate on the knuckleball. Last summer I threw to a catcher for about fifteen minutes every day, just knuckleballs, and if I was needed that night, I could still pitch. But Sal is not very enthusiastic. A couple of times I've asked him if I could warm up and he said, "You've been throwing the whole damn day." He was referring to the fact that I had played catch in the outfield before the game. The man's got big eyes.

The trouble is that coaches and managers have a thing about being strong for the ballgame. They don't realize that sometimes you can be too strong—sacrifice sharpness for strength. With a knuckleball, this can be particularly costly. I've tried to talk to Sal about this. I say, "Sal, I'd like to talk about my knuckleball."

And he snaps, "What?" and he's already looking at something over my shoulder. My impulse is to say that my Aunt Frances has a great knuckleball and would he like to give her a look. But when Sal snaps, "What?" he gives you the impression he doesn't want such a long answer.

If he had a liverwurst sandwich I'd expect him to take a big bite.

With Hovley gone, Mike Marshall is probably the most articulate guy on the club, so I asked him if he had as much trouble communicating as I've had and he said, "Of course. The minute I approach a coach or a manager I can see the terror in his eyes. Lights go on, bells start clanging. What's it going to be? What's this guy want from me? Why can't he be like everybody else and not bother me? It's almost impossible to carry on a conversation or get a direct answer to a direct question."

In baseball they say, "He's a great guy. Never says a word."

Like a lot of players, Jack Aker chews tobacco. But he's only been at it for two years and doesn't do it well. Hasn't learned to spit properly. As a result his uniform is always covered with brown spots.

All people who chew tobacco should have happen to them what happened to Steve Hamilton of the Yankees. Steve is an ace with chewing tobacco. Most players chew only on the field, Hamilton even chews at home and has a spittoon in the middle of his living-room floor. He says he also has a wife, which I don't altogether believe. Anyway he got careless once while pitching in Kansas City. He swallowed his chaw. So he turned around and gave it up, along with his cookies, on the back of the mound. In front of all those people.

I've felt like that on the mound too, and I don't even chew tobacco.

APRIL
14

I died tonight.

I got sent to Vancouver.

My first reaction: Outrage.

Second reaction: Omigod! How am I going to tell Bobbie? The *problems*. Where to live? How to get rid of the place we'd already signed a lease on in Seattle? What would happen to the $650 deposit? Moving again. *Again*. And we just got here.

But mostly outrage.

We'd lost a 2–1 game to Kansas City when Sal came over and said, "Joe wants to see you in his office."

My heart started racing. I mean Joe never wants to see me anywhere. So I knew. At the same time I thought, "Nah. It's too early. I've really only pitched the once. How can they tell anything from that? Maybe it's a trade? Or maybe he's just sore at something I've done. Let's see, what have I done lately?"

It takes a lot longer to tell it than to think it. As soon as I got into his office Joe Schultz said, "I hate to tell you a thing like this after such a close loss."

I almost laughed in his face. As though I'd be so broken-hearted over losing a lousy ballgame that I couldn't bear anything more, even a small thing like being sent to the minors.

Then Joe said he had to send me to Vancouver, and I thought, "What the hell, I'll go out with some class." I told him I would have done anything to help the club and that I really felt bad about having to leave it.

"I know," Joe Schultz said. "You work hard and you do all your running and you did everything we asked of you. We just didn't think your knuckleball did that much in Arizona and we wanted to see what it looked like when it got out of the light air, and it didn't look like it was coming around like we thought it should. We need pitching bad."

So I said, "Well, if I do real good down there, I'd like to come back."

I expected him to say, "Of course. You do good down there and we'll yank you right back here, stick you in and you'll win the goddam pennant for us." Or something reassuring like that. Instead Joe Schultz said, "Well, if you do good down there, there's a lot of teams that need pitchers."

Good grief. If I ever heard a see you later, that was it.

So I said thanks a lot and left.

I went back to my locker and there was a Coke sitting there that I'd opened. I gave it to Mike Marshall and opened a beer. This was not a night for Cokes. I threw my half-eaten corned-beef sandwich in the wastebasket and went over and told Gary Bell what had happened. He was kind of shocked, but as I started throwing stuff into my bag I could feel a wall, invisible but real, forming around me. I was suddenly an outsider, a different person, someone to be shunned, a leper.

Jose Vidal was the first guy to come over and say he was sorry to see me go. Velazquez was the second. And at that point I really felt close to them. Don Mincher came over and told me to hang in there—and, you know, I really was wrong about him. He's a good fellow.

I stopped by to shake hands with Gene Brabender and Tommy Davis, but I missed Tommy Harper and Jack Aker and some of the other guys. I realized I didn't have any money with me to pay the clubhouse men, so I told them I'd send a check. Then I picked up my bag and walked out. It felt lousy.

I suppose the man I'm most outraged at is Sal Maglie. The Screaming Skull, as he is being called (because he looks like a character in a movie of the same name), said the second really lucid thing to me that he has all spring. The first was, "Don't talk to the fans." And the second, "Joe wants to see you in his office."

116

That was all. No goodbye, no suggestions about what I should work on, or what I needed to improve, or what I had done wrong this spring, or what pitch I should work on. Not even a hang in there. Silence. I can't believe this is Sal the Barber, my idol.

I stopped by to see Marvin Milkes, and he wasn't any help either. I told him I was running into some big and sudden expenses and could he do anything about it, and he said—and this was beautiful—"Well, you didn't show us much all spring" (10 games, 19 innings, 16 hits, 11 walks, 5 strikeouts, 3.25 ERA). If I *had* shown much more I wouldn't be getting sent down. I felt like kicking him in the shins, but I said, "Hell, I had a better spring than four or five guys. In fact, I'm healthy, which is more than you can say for at least two of the guys." What I didn't say, but what I thought, was: "What about Steve Barber? He hasn't been able to pick up a baseball. He had a brutal spring. What's this love affair with Barber? Why can't he go on the disabled list?" Ah, the hell with it.

One of the worst things about getting sent down is the feeling you get that you've broken faith with so many people. I know my mother and father were rooting real hard for me, and all my friends back home, and they'll all feel bad—not for themselves, but for me.

Quitting altogether crosses my mind. But I won't. I *can't*. I'm convinced I can still get out big-league hitters with my knuckleball. I *know* I can. I know this is crazy, but I can see the end of the season and I've just won a pennant for some team, just won the final game, and everybody is clamoring around and I tell them, "Everybody have a seat. It's a long story."

I could be kidding myself. Maybe I'm so close to the situation that I can't make an objective judgment of whatever ability I have left. Maybe I just *think* I can do it. Maybe everybody who doesn't make it and who gets shunted to the minors feels exactly the way I do. Maybe too, the great cross of man is to repeat the mistakes of all men.

Part **4** I Always Wanted to See Hawaii

APRIL
16

Yesterday Bobbie and I drove up to Vancouver with the kids to look for a place to live. We found a nice home about twenty minutes from the ballpark, near the beach. We had to put down $480, which represented the first and last month's rent, May and August, and we had to give postdated checks for June and July. The owner is concerned that there might be another shift. He's not taking any chances.

In the meantime I still have that $650 deposit in Seattle and don't know if I'll be able to get that back. And we haven't received the $100 deposit we left in Arizona. That's $1,230. I lead the league in deposits. Fortunately there's a baseball rule that says when a player is transferred he's not responsible for the remainder of his rent, so we won't be liable for any more money, but we might not be able to get the $650 back if we can't rent to somebody else.

A lot of players don't have the problems we do because they leave their families at home and live in hotels. That's for one of two reasons. They're just starting out and don't make enough money. Or their kids are old enough to be in school and they don't want to take them out. These guys have their families with them only two months of the season. I don't know if I'll last long enough to have to make that kind of decision.

The Vancouver Mounties (little Mike is going to have a terrible time with that one) are still in Phoenix and I won't join them until they come home. They play in Tulsa first, so I called Bob Lemon, who's the manager, and asked if he intended to use me as a starter right away and he said no, he planned to use me in relief and that I might as well wait for them to get home.

So I got permission to work out with the Pilots. I felt terribly awkward in the clubhouse and I saw that the guys also felt funny about me being there. They had these strange looks on their faces, and I felt I had a rare and communicable disease.

Driving over to the park I thought about what I would say to them. "They made a mistake, realized it and asked me to come back." But nobody would believe that. Or if I was going to pitch batting practice, I could have told them that Sal and Joe decided that I hadn't been mean enough and I was going to show them how many guys I could knock down. But it was raining and there was no batting practice. So I ran in the outfield and threw to McNertney for about twenty minutes and to Larry Haney for fifteen. I threw strictly knuckleballs, which is what I'm going to be now, a knuckleball pitcher and nothing else. My wife was right. No more kidding myself, no more trying to bring along four or five mediocre pitches. I'm all through listening to managers and coaches about how much or how little I should be throwing. *I'm in business for myself.* As long as there's going to be no special protection for me, I've got to make all my own decisions. Sal always wanted me rested in case I had to pitch eight innings of relief, which I never did. So now I'm going to throw as much as I think I have to.

There was a meeting before the game with Minnesota, which I did not, of course, attend. Gary Bell filled me in. They were going over the Twins' lineup—it's a tough one—and the conversation went about like this:

"Pitch him high and tight."

"Hell, he'll hit that one over the left-field wall. You got to pitch him low and away."

"Pitch him away and he'll go to right field on you."

"I don't know about all of that. I do know you got to curve him."

"Oh no, he's a hell of a breaking-ball hitter."

Finally, Sal Maglie: "Well, pitch around him."

When the meeting was over, Gary added up the pitch-around-hims and there were five, right in the beginning of the batting order. So according to Sal Maglie, you start off with two runs in and the bases loaded.

It's like the scouting reports we used to get on the Yankees about National League teams. We'd get the word that this guy couldn't hit the good overhand curve. Well, *nobody* hits the good overhand curve. In fact, hardly anybody throws the good overhand curve. It's a hard pitch to control and it takes too much out of your arm.

And the word on Tim McCarver of the Cards was that Sandy Koufax struck him out on letter-high fastballs. Which is great advice if you can throw letter-high fastballs like Koufax could.

Anyway, I guess Gary didn't pitch around enough of the Minnesota hitters because they bombed him out in the first inning with three runs. We lost it, 6–4—I mean *they* lost it. There were several relief pitchers in the game and I could have sworn I saw Joe Schultz waving for his knuckleballer, but he was already gone to Vancouver.

One of the reasons I'll probably be playing baseball for the next few years is that I really don't have a career waiting for me outside. I'd find it hard to work for some big company. I'm not a nine-to-five type. I have a vague hope I might be able to work into television or politics somehow, and my friend Jim Jacobs and I have talked about making films. Jim, who once was the world's greatest handball player, has done great things with old fight films and we've talked about working up a baseball film and possibly films on other sports. But I'm not ready for that yet.

The only thing I'm involved in now is that real-estate venture. My brother Pete handles the business during the season, but there's really not much more than bookkeeping to it, since we do all the buying and selling when I'm home. Even so, it doesn't seem to be the kind of thing that would ever keep me occupied full time. So I'm a baseball player. A Seattle Pilot—pardon, a Vancouver Mountie. A Vancouver goddam Mountie.

I listened to the Pilots game over the radio and wouldn't you know it, I found myself rooting for them. When the Yankees sent me down all I wanted was for them to get mashed. Even now I hope they finish lower in their division than the Pilots do in theirs. I can't explain it, but that's what I feel. The only bad thing I wish for the Pilots is that they get into a lot of high-scoring games; win them, but need pitching help.

APRIL
17

Got a letter today from two girls who were members of my fan club. They'd read the article in *Signature* about us adopting Kyong Jo and wanted to congratulate us and wish me luck with my new team. I really liked that fan club. I enjoyed being a big league player and having people recognize me and having little kids get a charge out of meeting me. I remember what it was like when I was a kid and what a thrill I got just watching Willie Mays climb out of a taxicab. So the fact that I had my own personal fan club (would you believe an annual dinner and a newspaper called *All About Bouton?*) always pleased me. Of course I realized how old I'm getting and how quickly time passes when I heard that one of the fan-club members was in Vietnam. It just doesn't seem right that a member of my fan club should be fighting in Vietnam. Or that anybody should be.

The fan club started in 1962 when these two kids—George Saviano and Al Gornie—came to me and asked if they could start one. I told them to cool it until I did something. I didn't want them to waste a lot of time and energy on someone who might not be around too long. Of course I talked to them. I figure that's part of the game. Besides, I enjoyed it.

Not everybody agrees. I was a big New York Giant fan when I lived in New Jersey as a kid and then we moved to Chicago. I used to go to all the Cub–Giant games out there. And I remember once leaning over the dugout trying to tell Al Dark how great he was and how much I was for him and, well, maybe get his autograph too, when he looked over at me and said, "Take a hike, son. Take a hike."

Take a hike, son. Has a ring to it, doesn't it? Anyway, it's become a deflating putdown line around the Bouton family. Take a hike, son.

Having made the move to Syracuse a couple of times and then to Seattle and now to Vancouver makes me a member of a not-very-exclusive club. Us battered bastards of baseball are the biggest customers of the U.S. Post Office, forwarding-address department. I've seen letters chasing guys for months, years even. Sometimes you walk into a clubhouse and there's a letter on the table for a guy who was released two years ago. A guy like Rollie Sheldon still has mail coming to him in Yankee Stadium, and once they start forwarding, it can be a year before it catches up.

One of Gary Bell's parting lines about me was, "Here comes the guy who opened and closed a checking account in three days." True. We have taken the money out of our Seattle account and will deposit it in Vancouver. But we're optimistic. We're leaving a few dollars in the Seattle account in case I get called up later this summer. I should say *when* I get called up.

APRIL
18

Tacoma

There's nothing like walking into a minor-league clubhouse to remind you what the minors are like. You have a tendency to block it. It was cold and rainy in Tacoma when I went there to meet the Vancouver club and the locker room was shudderingly damp, small and smelly. There's no tarpaulin on the field, so everything is wet and muddy and the dirt crunches underfoot on the cement. The locker stalls are made of chicken wire and you hang your stuff on rusty nails. There's no rubbing table in the tiny trainer's room, just a wooden bench, and there are no magazines to read and no carpet on the floor and no boxes of candy bars. The head is filthy and the toilet paper is institutional-thin. There's no batrack, so the bats, symbolically enough, are stored in a garbage can. There's no air-conditioning and no heat, and the paint on the walls is peeling off in flaky chunks and you look at all of that and you realize that the biggest jump in baseball is between the majors and Triple-A. The minor leagues are all very minor.

There's no end to the humiliation. The kid in the clubhouse asked me what position I played.

The Vancouver team never got to the clubhouse because the game was called off before they left the hotel. So the uniforms never got there and I sat around in my underwear feeling sorry for myself. Whitey Lockman, the Tacoma manager, passed through and I told him I had just seen his most famous double, the one he hit before Bobby Thomson's home run in 1951, on television again. He enjoyed being reminded.

I went out to work in my long underwear with a warm-up jacket over the top and I thought to myself, "Damn, I wish somebody could see me out here being this conscientious—Whitey Lockman maybe, or a scout." If they only knew how hard I was willing to work and how much I was willing to sacrifice they'd know I'll make it back and that they ought to buy my contract now, at a bargain price. If I have a good year

I'm not going to forgive these other ballclubs who passed me up. Even the Mets had a shot. They didn't even nibble.

APRIL

19

Tonight I told Bob Lemon that I'd made a tactical mistake this spring in trying to do too much and that what I wanted to do from now on is what I did at the end of last summer—throw knuckleballs. I told him I also wanted to work out a program of throwing on the sidelines before the game for about ten minutes even if I'd be pitching a lot in the games. The idea is to maintain the feeling you need to throw the knuckleball and at the same time prevent the arm from getting too strong. If it's strong you have a tendency to bring it through too fast and you impart spin to the ball.

And Lemon said, "You throw any pitch you want and you throw it as often as you want and set up any working program you want. It's all up to you."

Gee, how am I going to handle all that responsibility?

For me, one of the savers of being in the minors is that it makes me an underdog. I like to be an underdog. I've always been the guy who never was the big phenom but that came out on top unexpectedly. When I was a kid—my brother and I and a couple of other kids—used to challenge eight guys to basketball games, two against one. Often we'd win and the other guys just couldn't believe that four could beat eight. The answer is that the underdog role is fun to play, and easy, because there's no pressure. You've got nothing to lose.

I enjoy the fact that my high school (Bloom Township HS, Chicago Heights) has decided to award a trophy that is given every year not to the guy who is the best, but to the one who shows the most desire and works the hardest. The trophy is called the "Jim Bouton 110 Percent Award."

Not that you can't carry that sort of thing too far. In 1959, I guess it was, I weighed 150 pounds and decided I should put on a lot of weight in order to throw a better fastball. So I ate. I ate a lot. I ate five meals a day, all very rich. In six weeks I put on 30 pounds and wrecked my stomach permanently. I don't have an ulcer, but there's an inflammation that won't quiet down, and I have to take Maalox every day. The fastball went, the stomach stayed.

How much running should a pitcher do? The idea, of course, is to be in good physical shape. However, it's quite possible to be both out of shape and a good pitcher. As Johnny Sain says, "You don't run the damn ball across the plate. If running did it, they'd look for pitchers on track teams." It's one of the reasons he's such a popular pitching coach.

There are pitchers who tell you that they've played for men who made them run miles a day and some who made them run hardly at all and that it never made any difference in their pitching. Personally, I've never been out of shape, so I wouldn't know.

The problem for a long-relief man is that he doesn't want to tire himself out before a game in which he may pitch eight innings. But if he doesn't run and then he doesn't pitch, he very quickly is out of shape. A short man can stay in shape just pitching. And then there's Mickey Lolich, who doesn't look like he's in shape to do anything but pitch. One of the nice things about baseball is that there are no rules you can't break.

Had a talk with Bob Tiefenauer about his knuckleball and he said he'd recently gotten a good tip from Ed Fisher. He says that when you're pitching with the wind at your back (which is very bad for the knuckler) you throw the ball harder. This seems to keep it out ahead of the wind and it knuckles pretty good. Tief says it sounds crazy, but there's logic to it and it seems to work. I'll have to remember that.

I've been thinking about my options in life these days. There aren't many. If I do poorly here I could easily be dropped. I don't think they want to pay $22,000 to some guy to pitch Triple-A. On the other hand I could be sold or traded, or brought back to Seattle. I don't think they want me back there, though, or Schultz wouldn't have said that about a lot of clubs needing pitchers. I see by the boxscores that a lot of pitching staffs are getting bombed. It's a lot different than last year.

Washington lost 6–0, and I wonder if they can use some pitching help. I sure would like to be with a club in the East, because if there's anything I want to do before I'm through it's win a few games in Yankee Stadium, and being with Washington would give me some extra shots at them. If this sounds like a grudge, it's only because it is.

Got my first inning of pitching in for the Vancouver Mounties and I was only super. We were leading 15–3 when Bob Lemon asked me if I wanted to pitch an inning. I said sure and went in to pitch the ninth. I struck out the first hitter on four knuckleballs. I struck out the second hitter on five knuckleballs. And I really wanted to strike out that third guy because striking out the side is the kind of thing that gets back to the big club. But the third hitter grounded out on a 1-and-2 knuckler. Still, it was almost too easy.

Corky Evans was the catcher. He's a good, enthusiastic kid. He caught me in the bullpen when I warmed up and he'll be catching me on the sidelines before the games. He's so enthusiastic he actually jumps around and says happy things when one of our guys gets a hit. In fact the first time he jumped up and started cheering I looked around to find out what had happened. All that happened was we got another one of about twenty hits. So at least he won't be grumbling about having to catch my knuckler.

Meal money in Triple-A is $7.50 a day. In the big leagues it's $15. I don't know if they mean to have you eat half as much or half as well.

Most baseball people have two ages, real and baseball. The older they get, the greater the discrepancy between their numbers. Some of the players were clever enough to cheat by two or three years as soon as they signed and thus were more valuable throughout their careers. I made the mistake of telling my real age right along and now it's too late to start lying. All this explains why Bill Monbouquette was able to say a couple of years ago that he was thirty-one. I was twenty-nine at the time, and I remember him pitching for the Red Sox while I was still in school.

The greatest all-time age put-on was engineered by Rollie Sheldon. When he signed he told scouts that he was nineteen. The Yankees brought him into spring training as a twenty-year-old phenom, and he won the James P. Dawson award as outstanding rookie of the spring, and just before the team went north it was discovered that he'd spent three years in the Air Force and three years in college and that he was actually twenty-six. By now, though, there was nothing anybody could do. And if he'd told them his real age he never would have had a chance.

I've also been reflecting on Joe Schultz. I'm afraid I'm giving the impression I don't like him or that he's bad for the ballclub. Neither is true. I think Joe Schultz knows the guys get a kick out of the funny and nonsensical things he says, so he says them deliberately. If there's a threat to harmony on the club I think it comes from the coaching staff.

On the other hand, it has been said that harmony is shit. The only thing that counts is winning.

Dick Baney is a fashion plate—I mean in a baseball uniform. There is a right way to wear a baseball uniform and a wrong way, and in order to do it right you have to break some rules. Like you're not allowed to cut your baseball socks. But if you don't cut your socks you're nothing.

I'm referring to the outside socks, the colored ones. Underneath you wear long white socks that are called sanitaries. Over those go the colored socks with the stirrups under the feet. This leaves narrow halfmoons of white showing. It has become the fashion—I don't know how it started, possibly with Frank Robinson—to have long, *long* stirrups with a lot of white showing. The higher your stirrups the cooler you are. Your legs look long and cool instead of dumpy and hot.

The way to make stirrups longest, or what are called high-cuts, is to slice the stirrup and sew in some extra material. It's against the rules, but Baney ignored them. Not only that, he took his uniform to a tailor and had it made so form-fitting the whole thing looks like it was painted on. He says this is important and the reason he did poorly his first time out was that: "I looked down at myself and I looked like a clown. I figured if I look like a clown I must be pitching like a clown, and so I did."

Do you know that ethyl chloride can be fun? This is a freezing agent kept around to cut the pain of cuts, bruises, sprains and broken bones. It comes in a spray can and it literally freezes anything it touches; hair, skin, blood. Also ants, spiders and other animals.

The way you have fun with ethyl chloride is spray it on a guy who isn't looking. First thing he knows there's a frozen spot on his leg and the hair is so solid it can be broken off.

Or you spray it on crawling creatures. They're frozen, they thaw and they resume their appointed rounds. Once we froze and thawed one bug thirty times just to see if it could be done. It can.

Hot-feet, or hot-foots, depending on your attitude toward the language, can also be fun if your life is drab and empty and puerile and full of Phil Rizzuto. I once gave Phil my famous atomic bomb hot-foot, which consists of four match heads stuck inside another match. It was such a lovely hot-foot his shoelaces caught fire and the flames were licking at his pants cuff.

One of the great hot-foots (hot-feets?) of all time was administered to Joe Pepitone by Phil Linz. The beauty part was that Pepitone was giving a hot-foot to somebody else at the time and just as he started to turn around and grin at the havoc he had wrought, a look of horror crossed his face and he began to do an Indian dance. The hot-footer had been hot-footed (feeted?) himself. Joe Pepitone is a gas.

APRIL
20

Vancouver

Today I got hung with a loss I didn't deserve, but possibly merited. It happened because a perfectly lovely knuckler got by the catcher. In the ensuing confusion, during which I personally covered home plate on a close play, the run scored amidst great argument. The man was out, but the umpire disagreed.

Merritt Ranew was the catcher, and although he's a fine fellow he had a lot of trouble with the knuckleball. Lemon suggested I stop off at the ballpark in Seattle on my way home (we haven't moved yet) and pick up McNertney's big glove. When I got to the stadium I spent a half-hour wandering around yelling to get somebody's attention. I couldn't, so I finally climbed over the fence in left field and went all the way to second base and screamed at the top of my lungs, "Is there anybody here?" No answer. "Christ," I thought, "anybody who wants to could come into this place, dismantle it and take it away by morning. I found the glove in the clubhouse and after I climbed back over the fence I noticed a sign that said: WARNING, GUARD DOG PATROLLING AREA. I could just see the papers the next morning: "Former Seattle Player Ripped to Shreds at Second Base."

APRIL
21

Honolulu
There are compensations to being in the minors. Like Hawaii. Arrived here today and it's beautiful. On the airplane, if you're Leo Marentette you play gin rummy. Leo used to be in the Tiger organization and the first thing he asked me was "How's Moon Man?" which is what the Tigers called Mike Marshall, the way the Pilots called Steve Hovley "Orbit." Leo took $70 meal money from Darrell Brandon and the word is that he bought rights to Jerry Stephenson, a gin-rummy mark, for the five-hour plane ride.

On the plane I discovered that Greg Goossen is afraid to fly. On the takeoff he wrapped himself around his seatbelt in the fetal position, his hands over his eyes. Then, as we were landing, he went into frenzied activity, switching the overhead light on and off, turning the air blower on and off, right and left, opening and closing his ashtray and giving instructions into a paper cup: "A little more flap, give me some more stick, all right, just a little bit, okay now, level out."

I asked him, "What's the routine?"

"I always feel better when I land them myself," Goose explained.

Hawaii is not exactly like the rest of the minors. The first thing they did at the ballpark was line us up on the foul line, where two Hawaiian girls presented each of us with a lei and a kiss on the cheek. When the girl got to me I bent her back over my knee and kissed her like they do in the movies. Nailed her a hell of a kiss, if I say so myself. For another there's a topless nightclub in the Polynesian Hotel, where we're staying, and the girls who work there live in the hotel. There's nothing minor league about that at all, at all. I mean, Kearney, Nebraska, was never like this.

Having been sent to the minors for at least parts of the last three seasons now, I've become somewhat defensive about it. It's disturbing to be considered a failure, to have a stigma attached to you just because you're sent down.

For the fact is, that by any sane comparative standard, I'm much better at my job, even in Triple-A, than most successful professional people are in theirs.

As a Triple-A player I'm one of the top thousand baseball players in the country, and when it's considered how few actually make it out of the hundreds of thousands who try, it's really a fantastic accomplishment. So I don't feel like a failure, and anybody who is guilty of thinking I am will be sentenced to a long conversation with Joe Schultz's liverwurst sandwich.

Not that there aren't little annoyances to being in the minors. Players have to do things that coaches do for them in the big leagues—like shag balls. Baseballs are thrown in from the outfield during batting practice and someone has to gather them up and give them to the batting-practice pitcher. In the minors the job is done by the pitcher who pitched the night before. I had forgotten this little duty when I was sold to the Seattle Angels, and when I was reminded I said—facetiously, of course—"But I'm a name player." And I had another nickname: Name Player.

Name Player got off the bus today and went off to inspect the Honolulu playing field where some of the Angel players I had played with last year were working out. I could see the surprised looks on their faces when they saw me. Jimmy Reese, the coach, hollered over at me, "Hey, Bouton, what are you doing down here?"

"That's what happens when you have a bad inning," I said.

Pitched again today and did not have another bad inning. It was my third appearance in three days, and the dear knuckler has been jumping. One pop-up, one groundout, one strikeout. I know this is the kind of work I need, but I'm wondering why they're pitching me so often. They have fourteen pitchers on the staff. Could it be that somebody in Seattle thinks I need the work? Or maybe they want a last look before they release me? *Release me?* Good grief.

Things are going so well I'm thinking of how much the family will enjoy Vancouver. It's a beautiful town, with the mountains coming right down to the edge of it. We've taken a place near the beach and it should be lovely indeed.

I'm really riding that emotional rollercoaster these days. In spring training I was going good and getting to pitch a lot. I led the club in appearances and I was excited about making the team. And then I didn't. All of a sudden I'm at a new low, like some crazy Dow Jones chart, and I have to start all over. Now I've pitched well in four games and I feel like the rollercoaster is on the way up, and that if I have three or four more good appearances I might even get called back to Seattle. In baseball you're only as good and as happy as your last appearance.

I read in the paper that Hoyt Wilhelm says there are only four guys throwing the knuckleball consistently in the major leagues—Wilbur Wood, Eddie Fisher, Phil Niekro and himself—and the reason is that you don't learn to throw the knuckleball, you have to be born with it. I wonder if I was born to throw the knuckleball and have been wasting myself all these years.

Jim Coates pitched against us tonight and beat us 4–1. Coates, as has been noted, could pose as the illustration for an undertaker's sign. He has a personality to match. He was the kind of guy who used to get on Jimmy Piersall by calling him "Crazy." Like, "Hey, Crazy, they coming after you with a net today?"

Piersall used to get mad as hell and call Coates a lot of names, the most gentle of which was thermometer, but it didn't seem to hurt the way he played. I remember a game in Washington. Piersall was playing center field and Coates was giving him hell from the Yankee bullpen. Piersall was turning away from the game to give it back when somebody hit a long fly ball to left-center and Piersall had to tear after it. All the time he was running he was screaming at Coates, and when he got up to the fence he climbed halfway up it, caught the ball, robbing somebody of a home run, and threw it in. But not for a second did he stop yelling at Coates.

Coates was famous for throwing at people and then not getting into the fights that resulted. There'd be a big pile of guys fighting about a Coates duster and you'd see him crawling out of the pile and making for the nearest exit. So we decided that if there was a fight while Coates was pitching, instead of heading for the mound, where he was not likely to be, we'd block the exits.

There was, of course, no fight. We'd all rather talk than fight.

APRIL
22

My great roomie, Bob Lasko, has led me down the trail of sin and perdition and gotten me smashed on *mai tais* (pronounced "my ties"). This is a Hawaiian drink brewed by the evil gods of the volcanoes and no fit potion for a clean-cut American boy like me. I could barely make it back to my room and turn on the tape recorder. (Can you sing a book?)

I almost can't believe it, but I was in another ballgame tonight. Pitched two-and-a-third innings, gave up one hit, a double by Bob Rodgers, one walk and no runs. I'm throwing the knuckleball for strikes. I'm almost feeling sorry for the hitters. And I *am* feeling guilty about the amount of work I'm getting when a guy like Lasko is getting almost none. But not very.

One of the natural beauties of Hawaii is the bullpen refreshment. There is a terrific soup sold in the ballpark called *siamin* (pronounced "sigh-a-min"), which contains native goodies, noodles, pork and herbs. Beats Cracker Jacks every time.

APRIL
24

I've been poisoned by *mai tais* twice more and sunburned once in the past two days. I also pitched in two more games, coming in both times in the ninth inning with a one-run lead and giving up no hits and no sweat. After the game tonight I walked by Jimmy Reese and he said, "What are you doing in this league?"—which made me feel very nice indeed. Could all this be due to the sun and the *mai tais?* Is it all just an illusion?

I've pitched six days in a row and everybody thinks I'll soon be called up. Hey, up there, you listening?

I called my wife during the seventh inning tonight because I didn't think I'd be used again, and just as the operator was asking her if she'd take a collect call, Sheldon came back to tell me there was a call for me to warm up. In fact, when Lemon gave the signal, the guys in the bullpen pretended they didn't understand in order to give Sheldon time to come get me. I thought he was kidding until I saw the terrorized look on his face. So I hung up, went in and saved another. Another day, another save.

APRIL
25

It's great to be young and in Hawaii. Not only did I pitch in my seventh straight game and get my third save, but I had a smashing bowl of siamin, corn on the cob and teriyaki out in the bullpen. Major league bullpen.

We get up around ten in the morning, put on our bathing suits, go down to the beach for three or four hours, come back to have a nice homecooked meal (we all have kitchenettes and share the cooking), do some shopping and get out to the ballpark at around five. Sheldon brings a radio down to the bullpen and always asks if we want to listen to a ballgame or music. Sheldon, you must be kidding.

Talk in the bullpen turned to Joe Schultz, and I recounted what he'd told me when he sent me down. Everybody was surprised that I didn't get the recording: "This is a recording. Pitch two or three good games and you'll be right back up here again. This is a recording."

Sheldon recalled the moment the Grim Reaper cut him down. He was in the outfield shagging and Sal Maglie stood at third base and hollered at the top of his voice, "Hey, Sheldon, Joe wants to see you in his office." Everybody in the outfield heard.

"I was so embarrassed, I turned red," Sheldon said. "I had the impulse to holler, 'Find out what he wants.' I'm still sorry I didn't."

Also a beaver-shooting story was told. It seems that the Detroit bullpen carried a pair of binoculars and a telescope. The binoculars were used to spot an interesting beaver in the stands and then the telescope was used to zero in. So when the guy using the binoculars spotted a likely subject he'd say, "Scope me."

Strange bullpen incident tonight. Some dum-dum fan came by with his girl, who was wearing tight slacks, bare midriff and revealing top. Naturally we all looked pretty hard. "What the hell you guys looking at?" he said. Since we figured he could guess, we didn't say. So he started yelling and giving us the finger and like that until somebody said, "You don't like it, big boy, come on over and we'll talk about it." (It's not unusual for players to get into shouting matches with fans and yell things like "Go check your wife, there's a ballplayer missing.")

The girl pulled him away, but he must have complained to a cop or somebody, because pretty soon it got back to Lemon that there had been an incident in the bullpen. Between innings he ran out and chewed us all out, not for getting into a fight with a fan just for not paying attention to the game. "You guys are having enough trouble getting anybody out," he said. He really knows how to hurt a guy.

When he left there was much consternation over him talking like that to our man Bill Ferrell, who happens to be nineteen years old and has a perfect pitching record, and in his only time at bat he got a base hit. We call him "1 and 0" and "A Thousand," and what he should have told Lemon is that *he's* not having any trouble getting anybody out.

The reason I suffer from *mai tai* poisoning so often is that the other guys can drink them with no effect at all while I get drunk. They insist I come along so that they can, as they say, put the hurt on my body. Then in the morning they invite me for breakfast so they can observe the havoc they have wrought. While they gorge themselves on the veranda, I bathe my eyes with Murine.

All of which decided us on two things about playing baseball in Hawaii: that in addition to the $7.50 meal money, there ought to be a beverage allowance; and that if a guy's home team was Hawaii and he was called up to the big leagues he might decide he didn't want to go.

APRIL
26

After seven straight appearances I didn't get into the game tonight. We lost 5–1, and after the game Lemon called me into his office and said, "You mad at me?"

"No, why?" I said.

"Because I wasn't able to get you into the game tonight."

We laughed. A winner's laugh.

Dick Bates got called up today. Not me, not Darrell Brandon. Dick Bates. We were sitting around the hotel pool when Sheldon arrived and asked us if we'd heard about Bates. We said no. When he told us, at first I thought he was kidding. Then I got pissed off. I was sure I'd be next. You just can't tell what goes through their minds up there, though. Like Lemon was telling me that after last night's game he was talking to Milkes on the phone, giving him the statistics of the ballgame, and when he got to where I came into the game he said, "And guess who relieved?" And Milkes said, "Him again?"

"Yep," Lemon said, "and he got a save. And do you know he's thrown 80 strikes and 47 balls so far?" (This is good even if you're *not* throwing the knuckleball.) Milkes was impressed. The point I started to make is that Milkes told Lemon that Edgerton had looked pretty good but that "they're beginning to get to him." When Lemon asked how many games Edgerton had pitched in, Milkes said two. *Beginning to get to him!* For crying out loud.

At the end of our talk I was going to ask Lemon about the possibility of getting a start or two while I was down here. Just then Bob Lasko came along and asked when he was going to pitch next and I didn't have the heart to say anything. I was afraid Lemon would give me a start and cut into Lasko's time. Really.

A note here about motivation. Marv Stachle has been talking about quitting after this season. He's been bouncing up and down between Triple-A and the majors for nine years now without getting close to his four years in. Now he says he just wants to have a good year, not because he expects to go anywhere, but for pride.

My own reaction is that pride counts.

When I called my wife after my third save, there was a gathering of Vancouver Mounties outside the phone booth. So on the bus today I was asked if I always call home after a save or a win and I said yes, I did. And Greg Goossen said, "Big deal. It means about three phone calls a year."

Corky Evans, my catcher, doesn't drink, smoke or swear. He spends his spare time reading *Field and Stream* and writing three letters to his girl every day and reading the three letters he gets from her in return. Corky doesn't even go out for a milkshake. So tonight Bob Lemon said to him, "Hey, Corky, if you go out looking for broads tonight, make sure you take that big glove."

I was glad to hear the score of the Seattle game tonight—sort of glad. They lost 14–2. I would rather they won 15–14.

APRIL
27

I was on a radio show after the ballgame last night and today the guys were kidding me about the gift. In the majors it's usually something worth $25 or $50, but in the minors it's a choice: you can have a "best wishes for the rest of the year" or an "everybody's rooting for your comeback."

Although I gave up my first earned run tonight, I got my fourth save. Right after the game we catch a midnight flight back to the mainland. I feel like a conquering hero returning.

APRIL
28

Seattle

I bummed a ride to Vancouver with Lemon rather than fly up with the team so I could have an afternoon at home. Lemon had to stop off for a conference with Milkes and Schultz. At three in the afternoon he called me. "You don't have to come back with me," he said. "Enjoy the day with your family and call Milkes tomorrow."

"What does that mean, Bob?"

"I don't know, Meat. Just call Marvin tomorrow."

My wife and I spent the rest of the day trying to figure the percentages. First, of course, it could mean I was being called up by the Pilots, and since they're home, I could join them tomorrow. It could also be that the Pilots are trying to make a trade and if it goes through there'll be an opening on the staff. If the trade doesn't go through, I'll be heading back to Vancouver. On the other hand, they may be trying to get a pitcher in a trade and if they do, it's also back to Vancouver for me. But if they *don't* get the pitcher, then I'll be called up. Finally, it could be that I may be involved in a trade.

We're covered for houses here and in Vancouver. But suppose I'm traded. I don't think I can afford any more deposits. And another thing. My wife just got through buying a bunch of beach toys for the kids. And this afternoon, before the phone call from Lemon, the kids ran around the neighborhood saying goodbye to their friends of two weeks. Tomorrow morning they may be saying hello again.

Part **5** The Yanks Are Coming,
The Yanks Are Coming

APRIL
29

Hello again.

The news came this morning. "Hrrrmph," Marvin Milkes said, or words to that effect. I was back with the Seattle Pilots. Not only that, but I had an hour-and-a-half to get my ass to the clubhouse and into uniform. Not only that, right after the game we're going on a road trip, first stop Minneapolis. Not only that, my suitcase has gone on ahead to Vancouver. Not only that, my hang-up suit bag is up there too and doesn't even have my name on it. Not only that, I'm inordinately happy.

I'm so happy I wasn't able to sleep last night, just thinking about being happy. So I got out of bed at four in the morning and spent two hours writing notes for a speech I'd like to deliver to Sal Maglie and/or Joe Schultz.

This is what I decided to say:

"I've given a lot of thought to this. In fact it's all I've thought about for weeks. Number one, the knuckleball. I'd like you to understand it takes a feel to throw it, not strength. So I think I have to throw fifteen minutes on the sidelines to a catcher every single day, no matter how many days in a row I've pitched, or how many innings I might be expected to go that night.

"Number two, we have to adjust our thinking on walks. Walks are inevitable with a pitch that jumps around so much. What's more important, when you're a knuckleball pitcher, is the total number of walks and hits. For instance, for Vancouver I pitched eleven innings and gave up four hits and seven walks, a total of eleven baserunners. If this were three walks and eight hits it wouldn't be as good because runners move faster and farther on base hits than they do on walks. Also I think it's wrong to throw a fastball to a good hitter with a 3-and-2 count unless I've got a big lead, and I think it's wrong to throw a fastball 3 and 1 in a close game, and it's wrong to throw a fastball 3 and 0 when a home run or hit would beat me. In every case I'd rather walk the guy with my best pitch than let him beat me with one swing at my worst.

"I'd also like to say that I don't mind talking about the mistakes I've made in certain situations. Some people call it second-guessing, but I don't. It's good to go over mistakes—after the game. What I want to eliminate is too many hollered instructions during the game. For example, if somebody hollers out to me, "Make him hit the ball," I think he means I should throw a fastball or slider, since I'm always trying to throw every knuckleball right down the middle anyway. I have to choose my own pitch, and chances are it's the knuckleball.

"Now, about that start. I think it's possible that someday I could pitch every three days with only two days of rest, or every four days, and relieve in between. I know I did it last year and Marvin Milkes can be a witness to that. The only other knuckleballer who is as young and strong as I am is Niekro, and he's starting every four days now. It's taken the Braves a long time to come around to the idea that a knuckleball pitcher can be a starter, but they have and the results are great. I'm so convinced this could be done that I'd be willing to go to the minors and prove it. In fact, the very nature of the pitch is such that it's more adaptable to starting than relieving. A starting pitcher doesn't have to worry about coming in with men on base.

"Finally, I don't think it's fair to compare me right away with guys like Niekro, Wood, Fisher and Wilhelm. They're top pitchers and I think I should be allowed to be only fair or even mediocre for a while—say, a month or six weeks. After all, the other guys have had years."

That's my speech. Now I wonder if I can pry anybody away from his liverwurst sandwich long enough to hear it.

When I got to the clubhouse today it was as though I'd never left. It was fun being back with all the guys again, and I really laid my week in Hawaii on them.

Sal and I had our big conversation.
Sal: "Hi, what time'd you get in?"
Me: "Eight yesterday morning. From Hawaii."
Sal: "Humglmpf."
That was it.

Marty Pattin won the game for us tonight with a two-hitter. He had a no-hitter going into the eighth and I thought, how could anybody not know he's pitching a no-hitter. The fans were cheering while Pattin was picking up the resin bag. We won 2–0, and I walked into the clubhouse feeling happy with myself for having given the ballclub such a tremendous lift that Pattin went out and pitched a two-hitter.

I was also gratified that Joe Schultz had me warming up, along with Jack Aker, in the ninth. This was a close game and he had me warming up. L'il old me.

MAY
1

Minneapolis

I started warming up before the game today in Minnesota and it was so damn cold—and the American League ball is definitely bigger than the Pacific Coast League ball—that I couldn't get the damn thing to break at all. Every single knuckleball I threw was rolling over, or spinning sideways, and I started to panic. I could feel the sweat break out on me, and I was cold and sweaty at the same time. Here was Lemon sending in good reports on me, I thought, and here I was letting him down. Not only that. When they get a look at this junk they're going to think all I have is a minor-league knuckleball. Baseball people think like that. And I thought if I didn't have a good knuckleball *right now* they'd send me down again and I'd *never* come back up.

Of course, when I got in the game my knuckleball was great. I came in with the bases loaded and promptly went to 3 and 1 on the hitter. What do I do now? Fastball or knuckleball? Before I was sent down it probably would have been the fastball. I threw the knuckleball and got a grounder to first base for the out at the plate. Then I struck out the next hitter to end the inning. I saved all three runs from being charged to my roomie.

I pitched two more innings, throwing only one fastball. Not a ball was hit out of the infield. We lost, 4–1.

Dick Bates was sent back down to make room for Darrell Brandon. I'm not sure what they think they're doing, but at a guess front offices are more interested in players who are far than those who are near. They were more interested in Bates than Brandon and Bouton, but only until they saw Bates up close.

We also just bought John O'Donoghue and when Gary Bell and I walked into the coffee shop this morning he was sitting there. Gary said that when ballplayers get up in the morning and go into the coffee shop and see a player from a different organization sitting there, "Everybody starts stepping lightly."

Gary has come up with a good nickname for Freddy Velazquez. Freddy just sits there in the bullpen, warming up pitchers, and he never gets into a game and just looks sad. So Gary calls him Poor Devil.

Last night Gary and I stayed up late talking about real estate and what future there might be in it for him as investor or salesman or broker and I suggested he might get involved by reading some real estate books. Gary is a typical ballplayer in some ways in that he doesn't seem to have any plan for himself, nothing to fall back on. The day he's out of baseball is the day he'll start thinking about earning a living. And then it could be too late.

We stayed up so late talking that I needed a nap in the bullpen. Fortunately the Minnesota bullpen is out of sight. So I slept four solid innings before going into the game. There may be better ways to earn a living, but I can't think of one.

Gary wasn't very happy, of course, after being knocked out in the fifth. He had a couple of beers and said, "Maybe we ought to break out those real estate books pretty soon." Then he had a better idea. He suggested that tonight the two of us go out and see what we could do about restructuring parts of San Francisco (we were to leave for Oakland after the game).

"San Francisco," Gary said, "is absolutely going to catch hell."

I was sitting in front of my locker this afternoon and suddenly someone walked over to me and there was a shadow on the newspaper I was reading. My heart started thumping. I could almost hear Sal Maglie say, "Joe wants to see you in his office." That's what insecurity is.

Today Joe Schultz said, "Hey, I want to see some el strikos thrown around here."

I'm always fascinated by what people say during infield practice. It's a true nonlanguage, specifically created not to say anything. This one today from Frank Crosetti as he hit grounders: "Hey, the old shillelagh!"

Had a big talk with Sal Maglie today. Not *the* big talk, with note cards and all that, which I carry around waiting for the right, quintessentially right, moment. It went about like this.

Me: "Sal, I've made some decisions about my knuckleball and I'd like to talk them over with you."

Sal: *"Mblvckd?"*

Me: "Yes. Well, I think I've got to throw the knuckleball all the time and forget about my other pitches."

Sal: "Of course. Christ, if you don't do that you won't get anybody out. That's your bread and butter."

Me: "Another thing. I've got to throw the ball for about fifteen minutes before the game to get the feel of it. I don't worry about tiring my arm. Strength means nothing to me."

Sal: "Certainly. Absolutely. Otherwise you can't stay sharp with it."

So I went back to my locker and tore up my index cards. Well, the truth of it is I tried to talk to Joe Schultz on the airplane, but every time I checked he was asleep. When he was awake, I had some second thoughts. Translation: I didn't have the nerve. I decided he would take it as me, Jim Bouton, trying to give orders to him, Joe Schultz. So I, Jim Bouton, said "Aw, the hell with it."

Now I've got permission to do it my way anyway. Sal Maglie. Love that man.

The man I love had quite an adventure tonight. Darrell Brandon pitching, and with Rod Carew on third base he's using a full wind-up. At the last moment he decides to take a look over at Carew, who's taking a pretty good lead. So he backs off the rubber and Sal yells at him, "For crissakes, get the hitter. The runner isn't going anyplace."

So Darrell winds up and lets fly. *And Carew steals home.*

When Darrell comes into the dugout at the end of the inning, Maglie lets him have it. "Dammit," he says. "You *know* you've got to pitch from the stretch in that situation."

Eddie O'Brien has finally been nicknamed. "Mr. Small Stuff." It's because of his attention to detail. Says Mr. Small Stuff, "Put your hat on." He said that to me today. Also to Mike Hegan. We were both running laps at the time.

Another thing Eddie O'Brien does is stand next to you when you're warming up. I think he does it so he can be near the phone when it rings. He has to answer it. One of these days I'll beat him to it and when Schultz asks for O'Brien I'll say, "He ain't here," and hang up. Add dreams of glory.

Oh yes. As I went out to pitch he said, "Throw strikes."

I don't think Eddie O'Brien understands this game.

Maybe nobody does. Like when I went out to do some throwing on the sidelines before the game Sal Maglie said, "Do your running before you throw."

"Gee, Sal," I said agreeably, "I don't like to throw when I'm plumb tuckered out from running. I'd rather throw first, then run."

So Sal said, triumphantly, "What if it rains?"

"If it rains, then I'd rather have had my throwing in than my running."

At which point Ron Plaza said, to no one in particular, "Aw, c'mon, let's go."

I went. But first I did my throwing. And it didn't rain.

MAY
2

Oakland

Talked to my wife and she said there were some interesting things in the Seattle paper about my knuckleball. The quotes from Joe and Sal were that, well, it was better than it was before. Then there was a quote from Billy Martin, the bold and brash (as they say) manager of the Twins, which said it was a "helluva" knuckleball. The thought naturally occurred that Sal and Joe are not yet willing to make that kind of commitment to my knuckleball.

The knuckleball was fine tonight against Oakland—when it knuckled. When it didn't, it got hit for two home runs. That was in the first of three innings I pitched. One ball was completely still. It must have looked like a watermelon floating up there. Float like a watermelon, fly like a rocket. The other rolled a bit and was hit just as hard. On the other hand, I threw only four pitches in the whole three innings that didn't do what they were supposed to do. It's aggravating, of course, that two of them were hit out of the park, but the others jumped so much that I struck out Reggie Jackson and Rick Monday, and the rest were tapped for pop flies and grounders.

After the game, McNertney told me that Sal Bando thought it was a better knuckler than Wilhelm's because it breaks more sharply and it's thrown harder. I'm not sure how to take that, since it was Bando who hit one of the homers off me.

Meanwhile, in the dugout, I found out from Darrell Brandon that Sal had thrown a fit when the home run was hit. He had a toothpick in his mouth at the time and he threw it hard on the ground (so hard a tree may yet grow on the spot) and said, "Jesus, he's got to start throwing something else. They're just waiting on that knuckleball."

I think McNertney understands the situation better. "Keep throwing it," he said. "It's getting better. Had a real good one tonight that was really jumping down. So a couple of them spun and they hit them out. But you got to go with it. Even 3 and 0."

It was a weird game. We were behind 4–0 and 6–1 and tied it at 6–6. They went ahead 8–6, and we damn near came back again but lost it 8–7. Now we're six games under .500 and in last place, and something is going to happen around here. Marvin Milkes is not a guy who will sit around in a situation that calls for panic.

This afternoon Gary Bell and I hired a car and drove up to the Berkeley campus and walked around and listened to speeches—Arab kids arguing about the Arab-Israeli war, Black Panthers talking about Huey Newton and the usual little old ladies in tennis shoes talking about God. Compared with the way everybody was dressed Gary and I must have looked like a couple of narcs.

So some of these people look odd, but you have to think that anybody who goes through life thinking only of himself with the kinds of things that are going on in this country and Vietnam, well, he's the odd one. Gary and I are really the crazy ones. I mean, we're concerned about getting the Oakland Athletics out. We're concerned about making money in real estate, and about ourselves and our families. These kids, though, are genuinely concerned about what's going on around them. They're concerned about Vietnam, poor people, black people. They're concerned about the way things are and they're trying to change them. What are Gary and I doing besides watching?

So they wear long hair and sandals and have dirty feet. I can understand why. It's a badge, a sign they are different from people who don't care.

So I wanted to tell everybody, "Look, I'm with you, baby. I understand. Underneath my haircut I really understand that you're doing the right thing."

Emmett Ashford was behind the plate tonight and did an especially good job calling the knuckleball. A couple of times I threw it knee-high and the ball seemed to drop into the dirt. But it was only after it had crossed the plate, so he called both of them strikes. Some umpires call the pitch where the catcher catches it, not where it crosses the plate. If he catches it as a ball, it's a ball. But Ashford was great.

He missed one pitch. It was when a guy was stealing second and McNertney came out of his crouch to get the ball. This blocked Ashford's view and he called it a ball. I yelled at him. "But Emmett, it was a perfect strike." That's all I said, and it was true, but I felt guilty about having said anything at all. I try to be especially nice to Ashford because everybody else harasses the hell out of him. He's not exactly the best umpire, but he is far from being terrible. He doesn't miss that many calls, and when he does, he misses them on both sides, like any good umpire. But other umpires talk behind his back. Sometimes they'll let him run out on the field himself and the other three who are holding back in the dugout will snigger. I hate that kind of stuff. I mean, I don't mind it when it's pulled on a ballplayer. But Ashford, for goodness sakes.

And, of course, the players pick it right up. As soon as he makes a bad call they start yelling, "Oh, that hot dog son of a bitch." Sure he's a flashy umpire and sure he does a lot of showboating. That's what got him into the big leagues in the first place. It's his bread and butter. Instead of bitching the players ought to give him credit for hustling. He hustles every minute he's out there, which is more than you can say for some umpires.

It's not hard to understand why he's resented, though. They feel he doesn't belong in the big leagues with his way of umpiring. Besides, he's a Negro, and they believe he's here just *because* of that.

It must be terrible for Ashford. When you're an umpire and travel around the big leagues in a group of four and three of them are white and the kind of guys who let you run on the field by yourself—well, it can make for a very lonely summer.

I know about lonely summers. In my last years with the Yankees I had a few of them. You stand in a hotel lobby talking with guys at dinnertime and they drift away, and some other guys come along and pretty soon they're gone and you're all alone and no one has asked you what you're doing about dinner. So you eat alone. It must happen to Ashford a lot. And it's one of the reasons I can't bring myself to argue with him.

Encountered Marvin Milkes sitting in the lobby tonight, and whether he knows it or not that's fairly nerve-racking. Anytime a general manager is on the road with his club there's a feeling that a trade is in the works. From the way things are going here, I get the feeling that the front office watches the game, and when you throw a strike you're immediately in their plans for the near future, and when you throw a ball you're on the trading block. The players go up and down like some crazy yo-yo, and what that looks like most is a panic operation.

Brought a copy of the *Berkeley Barb* back to the clubhouse and several of the guys were crowding around to read it when John Kennedy said, "Bouton, I bet you bought that paper." I told him I had. "Now, how did I know it was you bought that paper?" he said. Dunno, John. Extrasensory perception?

MAY

3

Steve Barber pitched a pretty good game while I was down on the farm, but he was in trouble again yesterday, loading up the bases with none out in the first. He said he couldn't get loose on the sidelines, and the only time his arm bothers him is when he's loosening up. He says once he gets into the game he's fine.

Oh.

Another thing Sal Maglie looks like is the friendly neighborhood undertaker. You can just see him standing in the mortuary doorway saying, "Oh yes, we have something very nice for you in mahogany." And Gary Bell recalled the old Digger O'Dell line, "Well, I'll be shoveling off now."

The friendly undertaker really put it to Marshall the other day. He told him that if he didn't use better judgment on the selection of his pitches, they'd be called from the bench by S. Maglie, pitching coach. Mike was furious. Any pitcher would be. As Johnny Sain has pointed out, a pitcher will in the course of his career throw to thirty or forty catchers, work for ten or fifteen managers and pitching coaches. If he let all those people tell him what to throw he'd never amount to anything but a confused pitcher.

Anyway, the discussion with Sal seemed to do something for Marshall because he went out today and pitched a fine game. He lost 3–2, but in his heart a pitcher counts that as a victory, just as the hitter counts as a hit the sharp line drive that somebody makes a leaping catch on. Marshall went all the way and gave up only four singles, probably the only four mistakes he made in the game. Well, five. The other one was not getting enough runs.

I was warming up late in the game in case Marshall's sturdy arm should falter, which, considering the closeness of the game, was rather encouraging. After I gave up those two home runs I naturally went to the bottom of the pile. But I think two good innings after that redeemed me.

The other man warming up was John O'Donoghue. He's pitched one scoreless inning for the club so far and that puts him right on top. Indeed, the way things are, any new man is No. 1 until he gets hit, which is soon enough.

Today's Marvin Milkes' stories concern Gene Brabender and Merritt Ranew. The Bender's been having a tough time—thirteen runs in seven innings, or terrible enough to receive serious notice. So Milkes told him he has three more starts to straighten out, and if he doesn't do well in them he could just mosey down the road.

Ranew was called up to fill in for Larry Haney, who had to put in some service time. Ranew had been hitting like .400 at Vancouver and in his first game here he got two hits. Today he got another and he's hitting the ball good every time up. So Marvin Milkes told him, "You keep hitting the ball like that and you'll be back up here again sometime."

And never is heard a discouraging word.

MAY
4

Darrell Brandon wanted a start and got it, just by asking for it. He also got shelled, lasting an inning and a third. He thinks he knows what happened. "I was good last night," he said. "I stayed in my room. Called my wife. Drank nothing stronger than orange juice. Then I read from the Gideon Bible and went to sleep. Then I last an inning and a third and I got two greenies in me I got to work out in San Francisco. Never again."

As for me, I was only as good as I had to be last night and I also lasted an inning-and-a-third and three earned runs. That puts me on the bottom of the heap again and depresses the hell out of me. I figure two like that and my ass is back in Vancouver.

We were playing trivia on the back of the bus the other day, and among the questions were:

What was the name of Roy Rogers' dog?

What was the name of the cat in the Buster Brown Show?

What three pitchers were sent down to the minor leagues with less than five innings of work among them?

The answers are Bullet, Midnight, Dick Bates, Bill Edgerton and Jim Bouton.

Brandon and I felt so badly about the whole thing we dragged Gary Bell off to a Chinese restaurant and I ate bird's nest soup, which disgusted them both.

Gary Bell and I have become the Falstaffs of the back of the bus. Gary entertains with quotes, anecdotes and insults, and when he goes back to his real-estate book I do my routines. In a trivia game recently I asked who the moderator of "You Asked For It" was. The answer was Art Baker, which led me into my "You Asked For It" routine. "We have a letter from a listener, Mrs. Sadie Thompson of Jablib, Wisconsin.

"Mrs. Thompson writes: 'Dear Art, I've always wanted to see a cobra strike an eighty-year-old lady. I wonder if you can arrange this on your show.'

"Yes, Sadie Thompson out there in Jablib, we went all the way to India for you and not only did we get a cobra, we got a bushmaster, the most deadly snake in the world. And right before your eyes the snake will be placed into a glass cage with sweet little white-haired Mrs. Irma Smedley. Here comes the snake into the cage, and just look at that sweet little old lady tremble. The snake strikes and that's it, ladies and gentlemen, the end of Mrs. Irma Smedley. Remember now, it's all because *you asked for it.*"

The boys ate it up. Sick humor is very big in the back of baseball buses and "You Asked For It" is almost as good as "Obituaries You Would Like To Read." Tune in next week, folks.

Some of the mores and manners of the back of the bus crew. Others who usually sit in the back are Oyler, Mincher, Kennedy, Hegan, Rich Rollins (The Listener), Gene Brabender (Lurch), Pattin (who does the Donald Duck) and Gosger (who does a splendid Porky Pig). The middle of the bus is dominated by Tommy Davis and his groovy tape machine, and the quiet guys sit in front, guys like Gus Gil and Freddy (Poor Devil) Velazquez. Mike Marshall also sits in front looking for somebody to play chess with him. I've played with him a few times and he'll thump me pretty bad. But then when he sees me start to lose interest he'll let me come close to beating him. That turns me on again for a while. He makes me feel like the donkey chasing the carrot on a stick.

One of the favorite back-of-the-bus games is insulting each other's wives, sisters, mothers and girlfriends. Some of the guys, among them Brabender and Marshall, refuse to participate in this game, but sometimes they're in it anyway. That's because any man who laughs when another man's wife or mother is insulted is automatically chosen as the next victim. Back-of-the-bus is a very rough business.

MAY
6

Seattle

The worst part of playing baseball is that you become a part-time father. I feel as though I've been on the road for a month—first with the Pilots, then with Vancouver, now back with the Pilots again. It's not terribly tough on a man and his wife, in fact absence often makes them appreciate each other more. But it's unsettling to the kids. They don't have a man around, and then when they do, well, you don't feel like disciplining them. You just want to enjoy them.

Before the game with the Red Sox tonight, we terrified pitchers huddled together and whispered about the power that club has. We decided that if Fenway Park in Boston is called "friendly," then the stadium here would have to be considered downright chummy. After the pitchers took batting practice, we were wondering if we should stay in the dugout and watch the Red Sox hit. We decided it would not be a good thing for us to see.

We saw enough in the game. They beat us 12–2. Brabender started and went four innings, having thrown nearly 100 pitches. It was not all his fault. There were about four errors behind him and we wound up emptying the bullpen. I came in with two runners on and stranded them and had a perfect inning-and-a-third. Then Brandon, Aker and Segui were stomped. So I should be back on the top of the heap again. Baseball isn't such a funny game.

I was asked if I'd go to a women's club dinner and say a few thousand well-chosen words and I said sure. I sort of like that kind of thing. Besides, it shouldn't hurt my standing with the front office, knowing I'm a guy who does that well. My only condition was that I be allowed to bring my family along. I'm away enough without leaving them to make a speech.

MAY
7

I caught Joe Schultz without a liverwurst sandwich today, backed him into a corner and asked him, gently, about my chances of starting a game. I talked fast. I told him that I felt strong enough to go nine innings with the knuckleball and that I could relieve besides if he needed me.

So Joe said, "We got four starters now."

I told him I knew that and that I didn't want to bump anybody. I just wanted him to keep in mind that I was available and could step in at any time. I pointed out that a knuckleball pitcher *should* be a starter, like Niekro in Atlanta.

So Joe said, "He doesn't throw all knuckleballs."

I told him he throws 90 percent knuckleballs, sometimes more.

So Joe said, "He throws only about 80 percent knucklers. The rest of the time he throws curveballs and fastballs and change-ups."

I wanted to tell him, well, maybe, but if I were a starter I'd have time to warm up properly and work in all those other pitches. I decided to let it ride. Because even if I do get a start I'm going to throw 95 percent knucklers. I've been through that war. So I said, "I think I can do the job. Give it some consideration."

He said he would, which is better than nothing. Somewhat.

Warming up in the bullpen tonight I got back the good knuckler, the one I had last year. They moved like a bee after honey, and I was throwing them real hard. Haney was catching and he said, rubbing a knee, that he'd never seen anything like it. "If you can just get someone to catch you," Haney said, "you'll be all right."

MAY
8

Another day off. Took the family on a ferry ride to the Olympic Peninsula. Stayed at a cabin on a lake and hired a little motorboat, and I don't know who had more fun, me or the kids. Pitching seemed very far away.

MAY
9

Mike Marshall pitched a helluva game tonight, shutting out Washington 2–0. A two-hitter, one of them by Frank Howard, called Capital Punishment. McNertney and I had a talk about the game when it was over. He said Mike called about 30 percent of his pitches, less than the usual 50 or so. Mike has some interesting ideas on what kinds of pitches should be thrown. He thinks a completely random pattern is best, that the hitter should never have an inkling of what's coming next. As a result, if a guy gets a hit off a curve ball he may get a curve the very next time up. On the other hand, McNertney believes that if you get a guy out on fastballs, you keep throwing him fastballs until he proves to you he can hit them. As for me, I throw the knuckleball.

Incidentally, the pitching staff was happy to learn tonight that Marvin Milkes had stationed a man outside the ballpark to measure the home runs that the Senators hit out of sight. Instead Marshall threw his two-hitter. Take that, Marvin Milkes.

The meeting before the game was marvelous. When we went over the hitters, Gary Bell had the same comment on each one: "Smoke him inside" (fastball inside). Frank Howard, McMullen, Brinkman, Epstein—every hitter. "Smoke him inside," said Gary Bell.

It got to be funny as hell after a while, because not only did he get no opposition, but he was taken seriously. According to the gospel of Gary Bell you pitch to the entire Washington team by smoking them inside.

I guess Marshall smoked them on the inside.

Chatted with Brant Alyea, the outfielder, about what was happening with the Washington club. He said Ted Williams was doing a fantastic job. "I'm just beginning to realize that baseball is at least 65 percent psychological," he said. "Williams has these guys so psyched they actually think they're great ballplayers. Brinkman's starting to think he's a hitter for crissakes and he's hit .200 all his life. Now he's up to .280. The team is up, the guys are emotionally high and Williams actually has them believing they're winners."

I wonder how he is with the pitchers.

The big confrontation is coming closer. The Yankees will be in town in a couple of days and I've been invited to appear at the sportswriters and sportscasters dinner on Monday afternoon. The idea is us against them. Mel Stottlemyre for the Yankees, me for the Pilots. I hope I can pitch against the Senators before the Yankees get here so I can show Joe Schultz how ready I am. I'm scared stiff the Yankees will get away without me pitching against them. At the same time I'd hate to get into one of those lost-cause games against them. I want them when they can feel the game in their guts.

MAY
10

Big meeting today. The way it happened, Marvin Milkes has been reading in the papers that some of the players aren't happy. So he suggested to Jack Aker that a meeting be called so the players could air their gripes. At the meeting, which lasted about twenty minutes, there were complaints about the beds in some of the hotels, the lack of a roof over the bench in the bullpen, the bare cement floor in the clubhouse and the absence of a watercooler in the clubhouse. Imagine having to take our greenies with beer. Big things like that.

It was also pointed out that when an exhibition game is scheduled for a Monday at the end of a road trip (as several are), the players should be permitted to go home Sunday night for at least a half-day at home. (This led to a certain amount of hilarity. The suggestions were that a half-day at home is just enough, or too much, and that a better place to spend the half-day was Las Vegas.) My gripe was that I thought that any ball hit into the yellow seats in left field should be a ground-rule double instead of a home run.

My own belief about the whole thing is that the players have only one serious gripe—the behavior of the coaches. But since they were all sitting right there no one complained.

When the meeting was over Aker asked Gary Bell what he thought about it all and he said, "Smoke him inside." Gary Bell is a beautiful man.

The sad truth about baseball, I'm afraid, is that there is not enough in it to occupy a man's mind. In desperation they turn to insignificant things and blow them up. Example: It was cold in the bullpen tonight, so I ran into the clubhouse and picked up three parkas. While I was at it I asked Curt Rayer, the trainer, if he could get some handwarmers going for us. Later, Larry Haney came out of the clubhouse and gave me a hot-water bottle he'd hidden under his jacket.

"Thanks," I said. "How come you had to smuggle it?"

"Curt didn't want any of the coaches seeing a hot-water bottle come out here," Haney said.

After the game Curt said I had bugged out at least half the coaching staff. Ron Plaza had overheard me asking for handwarmers and he told Curt it wasn't cold enough for them, and then somebody, maybe Joe Schultz, had said, "The hell with it, no handwarmers." Curt said everybody was very upset that I should ask for them, so he'd sent out a quiet hot-water bottle. It had been a warm day, so I guess the idea of handwarmers in May boggled the little minds.

This reminded me of something that happened the other day. Joe Schultz called me over and I thought he wanted to talk about my knuckleball, or pitching in general, or perhaps the state of the nation. Instead, with a straight face, he asked me whether I had any lightcolored sweatshirts or did I have only the dark kind I was wearing. I told him I had about fifteen dark sweatshirts since the other clubs I had been with all had dark blue sweatshirts. I said I used the dark ones in practice before the game, then changed to the Pilots' light blue for the game.

He considered that for a while, then finally nodded and said, "I guess that's okay."

Joe Schultz has yet to say a word to me about my knuckleball. Not even, "I guess that's okay."

I don't suppose I should care about any of this, except it *is* important to me to have a warm hand when I throw the knuckler. But even if I didn't need it, why should anybody care that I wanted it? And I would like to think that Joe Schultz has more important things to think about than the color of my sweatshirt.

At the meeting before the ballgame Sal Maglie said, "Okay, let's get some runs." He was kidding. We've been scoring a fantastic number of runs, which is either a tribute to our hitters or the size of this ballpark. Tonight, for example, we were losing to the Senators 11–3 in the sixth inning. First we came back to tie it, then we won 16–13. We ran through the whole pitching staff and only Gary Bell and I came out with any glory. I had a wicked knuckleball.

At one point, with a man on first, as I was about to release the ball, Ron Plaza yelled, "Throw it to first!" It disconcerted me enough so that the pitch was way off the plate. My impulse was to warn Plaza not to yell at me once I had released the resin bag and to shove those handwarmers up his bippy. But I managed to contain it.

Bell pitched the ninth inning and got them out. It was a minor miracle because he's supposed to pitch tomorrow and ran fifteen windsprints before the game and ate three sandwiches in the fourth inning. When he came into the clubhouse in the seventh to put on his supporter he asked no one in particular if it was too late to take a greenie.

How fabulous are greenies? Some of the guys have to take one just to get their hearts to start beating. I've taken greenies but I think Darrell Brandon is right when he says that the trouble with them is that they make you feel so great that you think you're really smoking the ball even when you're not. They give you a false sense of security. The result is that you get gay, throw it down the middle and get clobbered.

During the game the public-address announcer explained where to pick up the ballots to vote for "your favorite Pilot." I thought it necessary to remind the people sitting near the bullpen that your favorite Pilot did not necessarily have to be good.

The Yankees have lost thirteen out of fourteen now and I feel so bad about it I walk around laughing. Actually I just say that. In fact I'm beginning to feel sorry for some of the guys. The guy I care most about is Fritz Peterson, and he's doing well. He won the only game they won in the last ten days.

I'm still not sure about the Pilots. Sometimes I think the pitching staff can develop enough to help. Other times it looks like a bad staff. I sometimes think that a Marty Pattin should be able to win twenty and then I realize he's going to have all the ups and downs new pitchers in the big league are prone to. The same with Mike Marshall. He pitches a good game and they expect a lot of him. But what the hell, if he wins ten games he'll be doing great.

The other starters don't look so good. Gary is not really ready yet, and neither is Brabender. Barber has been taking cortisone shots in that elbow that hasn't bothered him all spring and he can't lift a baseball, much less comb his hair. Maybe Joe Schultz will consider *me* as a starter. If he started me in two or three games I might surprise him. But I think Sal has drummed it into his head that I can't be any good throwing the knuckleball all the time. My only chance is if they get desperate.

More baseball-player paranoia. First guy up in the bullpen today was Jack Aker. Second guy to go in was O'Donoghue. Then me. When O'Donoghue was called in, Darrell Brandon said, "That does it. I'll never go into that trainer's room again."

"Why not?" I asked.

"Because I was getting diathermy on this stiff neck I got and Joe Schultz spotted me and asked if I was all right. I said yeah, I was okay, but he probably thinks there's something seriously wrong with me. That's what I get for going into that goddam room."

MAY
11

With the Yankees coming in I'm beginning to feel like it's World Series time, my own personal World Series. I started out thinking that I was going to come in in the ninth inning and strike out the side, or start a game and pitch nine, but right now I don't care about winning or losing. I just don't want to embarrass myself.

Frank Howard drove in five runs with two home runs and a single against us and we beat the Senators anyway, 6–5. It was three straight over them, but all I got out of the evening was a marvelous nickname given to Frank Bertaina, a pitcher, by Moe Drabowsky, also a pitcher, when they were with Baltimore. Bertaina, Drabowsky decided, was not too smart, and was flaky besides. So Drabowsky called him "Toys in the Attic."

This is the kind of nickname that could be turned around into an offensive weapon. There may be no bigger flake in organized baseball than Drabowsky. Once, out in the bullpen in Anaheim, he picked up the phone, called a number in Hong Kong and ordered a Chinese dinner. To go.

Brabender was the pitcher tonight and he looked pretty good giving up two runs before tiring in the fifth. He was throwing the ball good and I think he's coming around. On the other hand, there's the continuing sad saga of Steve Barber. The only thing he's done lately is pull a hamstring while running in the outfield. So now, as he gets diathermy on his shoulder, he gets icepacks on his leg. He says he feels fine, except for a little tightness in his shoulder.

The story on him, I understand through the grapevine, is that he was asked to go to the minors until he's ready to pitch. As an eight-year man, however, he had the right to refuse, and did. He can be sold or traded to another major league team or given his release. That's all. And since they paid $175,000 for him in the expansion draft Barber will no doubt be around until he's able to pitch enough batting practice to get his arm in shape enough to pitch. I'm not sure I'd do the same in Barber's place. On the other hand, I'm not sure I wouldn't.

My taste in clothing is, I'm afraid, conservative. Tonight, though, I did show up in a rather mod outfit and John Kennedy said, "Hey, look at Bouton. He's getting there."

Maybe so. But I told him it's taking me so long to get there that by the time I do, everybody will be someplace else.

The first thing I felt when the Yankees showed up at the park today was embarrassment. That's because our uniforms look so silly with that technicolor gingerbread all over them. The Yankee uniforms, even their gray traveling uniforms, are beautiful in their simplicity. John O'Donoghue said that when Johnny Blanchard was traded to Kansas City he refused to come out of the dugout wearing that green and gold uniform. I would guess it's the only feeling I've ever had in common with Blanchard. At any rate, Blanchard never came out except to play the game, but I steeled myself and ran over to chat with the guys. There were a lot of visitors—Crosetti, Hegan, Kennedy, me. There was a lot of kidding and a lot of laughing, and this was one time Crosetti didn't feel it necessary to enforce the rule against fraternization.

Then the game. It was fantastic, unbelievable and altogether splendid. We scored seven runs in the first inning and made them look like a high-school team. They threw to the wrong bases. Their uniforms looked great; they looked terrible.

It reached the point where we were going nuts in the bullpen, jumping up and down and screaming and hollering. And suddenly I wasn't embarrassed by my uniform, I was embarrassed for the Yankees. They looked so terrible. Cheez, I wanted to beat them bad, but this was ridiculous. Seven runs. I wound up telling the guys to sit down and cool it.

It was not a cool night, though. A big fight, two benches and two bullpens empty and fifty guys milling around on the field. What a lovely war. It started when Marty Pattin threw one over Murcer's head. In his previous at-bat Murcer had hit a home run, and that sort of thing will sometimes result. So Murcer got on base and then came in high on Oyler, head first and fists flying.

The rule is that you're not allowed to just sit there when your teammates are in a fight, so everybody came off the bench and out of the bullpen and the only guy who sat there was Crosetti. I guess he was paralyzed by the choices involved. Too bad. I was hoping he might mix it with The Chicken Colonel and maybe they'd both get spiked or something.

I was very careful to keep a big smile on my face when I reached the scene of action. I didn't want anybody to think I was angry or serious. By and large nobody is serious about these baseball fights, except the two guys who start them. Everyone else tries to pull them apart and before long you've got twenty or thirty guys mostly just pulling and shoving each other. The two guys who started it have so many guys piled on top of them they couldn't reach for a subway token, much less fight.

At the bottom of the pile Murcer and Oyler found themselves pinned motionless, nose to nose. "Ray, I'm sorry," Murcer said. "I lost my head."

"That's okay," Oyler said. "Now how about getting off me, you're crushin' my leg."

"I would," Murcer said, "but I can't move."

There are a few guys on the Yankees I knew would love to have a shot at me, especially Fred Talbot, who I don't think would know the meaning of the word quit if he ever got into a fight with me. So I kept one eye out for Fred and the other for my friend Fritz Peterson.

I sort of circled the perimeter of action with both arms out to fend off any blind-siders and here came Fritz running toward me. He was laughing his head off and we grabbed each other and started waltzing like a couple of bears. He tried to throw me off balance and I tried to wrestle him down and all the time we were kidding each other.

"How's your wife?" I said. "Give me a fake punch to the ribs."

"She's fine," he said. "You can punch me in the stomach. Not too hard."

Finally he got me down and we started rolling around. Two umpires came running over and told us to break it up. "But we're only kidding," I said, protesting. "We're old roommates."

"Break it up anyway," the umpire said. Which made me think that here are two of four umpires breaking up a playful little wrestling match while there's a war going on nearby with 40 guys piled on each other. I guess they both recognized that they were in a very safe place.

After the game Fritz and I went out to dinner and I asked him what he would have done if Talbot or somebody else from the Yankees came over to help him out.

"I'd have had to tackle the guy," Peterson said.

The most interesting thing about the fight was Houk's reaction to the police, who came on the field to break it up. When he saw them he went out of his skull. "What the hell are cops doing on the field?" he shouted. "I've never seen cops on the field before. They ought to be at the university where they belong."

What he didn't understand, of course, is that the very thing that made *him* angry at the sight of cops is the same thing that puts kids uptight seeing them on campus.

It's not altogether surprising that the Yankees got into a fight. When I was with the club and we lost a few games Houk would have a meeting and he'd say something like, "Now, don't anyone be afraid to start something. If you get into a fight we'll all be with you."

Houk believed that fights woke teams up and made them play better. He also used the clubhouse meeting for effect. Like before the game with us he asked Len Boehmer, the catcher, how to throw to Hegan. "When Hegan was in our organization," Boehmer said, "they used to get him out with fast balls down the middle."

"Good," Houk said. "Meeting's over."

I think somewhere about the middle of the first inning they wished they'd had one.

One of my favorite Houk meetings took place before a game with the Red Sox during a losing streak in 1963.

"I just got to looking at these two lineups," he said, "and I thought I ought to compare them for you. Take the leadoff man. They got Mike Andrews. We got Bobby Richardson. Any comparison there? No. Number two we got Tom Tresh and they got Rico Petrocelli. (This was when Petrocelli was just coming up and Tresh was just off rookie of the year.) Could you imagine trading Tresh for Petrocelli? Third is Carl Yastrzemski and Roger Maris. Well, Yastrzemski is not a bad player, so maybe there's a standoff there. But look who's batting fourth! Jim Pagliaroni and Mickey Mantle. Now who the hell is Pagliaroni?" It broke up the whole clubhouse and really made his point.

The Yankees know I've been throwing the knuckleball and they all asked me how it was coming. I told them great. I think Chicken Colonel Turner is worried about it, concerned that I might have come up with a good one. This wouldn't show him in a very good light since he never even talked to me at the end, much less encouraged me to experiment. But get this. While I was warming up in our bullpen he told a couple of Yankee players, "You know, when we sent Bouton to Syracuse, the year before last, I told him to start throwing that knuckleball, but he wouldn't listen to me."

MAY
13

I think I should have a chance to pitch against the Yankees tonight. It's Stottlemyre against Gary Bell, and my roomie has been giving up runs. Against Stottlemyre we could easily be down a couple of runs by the fourth or fifth inning and then pinch-hit for Bell. At least I'm hoping I'll be first up. It hasn't been happening that way. I've been pitching better than Aker, and although Segui has won our last two games, he's been hit both times. Last night Schultz had O'Donoghue and Aker warming up and then O'Donoghue and Segui in a short situation. So why do I think it will be me tonight? Because I'm an optimist, that's why.

If I do get in, and if I should win, I'll send for Jim Ogle and insist he interview me. I wonder if he talks to rapists.

Hot flash! Whitey Ford's Italian restaurant in the bullpen has a real rival in the Baltimore bullpen: wienie roasts.

The pitchers' game is in full operation, and it's been costing me a few bob. The reason is that a system of bets and fines has been set up, and one of the fines is for fraternizing with the opposition. With the Yankees in town this has already cost me $2. On the other hand, I have had some satisfactions. One of the games is splitting the pitching staff into two teams during batting practice, with the losing team having to drop 50¢ into the kitty. I'm a terrible hitter in batting practice, possibly because I'm a terrible hitter in games. I'm so bad they call me Cancer

Bat, and when they made up the teams I was, naturally, thrown in at the end. When one of the guys on the other team complained that Bell's team had all the good hitters, he said, "Whaddayamean? We got Bouton." That seemed to mollify the opposition. So the first night of competition I got four line-drive singles and led my team to victory. That'll teach them to fool around with the Bulldog.

Another fund-raiser is electing the leading "fly" at the end of each road trip, the guy who had the worst trip for bugging people, being a pest, just flying them. The man elected is charged a dollar. Also, if you get caught eating at the table after a game with Charley uncovered, that costs a dollar. (On the Yankees this would have kept both Elston Howard and Yogi Berra broke. They were famous for dragging Charley over the coldcuts.)

The money goes into a kitty and at the end of the season it will be spent on a lavish party, for pitchers only. Gene Brabender is commissioner of the kitty and sergeant-at-arms because he's so big, and I'm secretary-treasurer, I'm not sure why. Perhaps because I look so honest.

An outfield game is making up singer-and-actor baseball teams purely on the sound of their names. Example—Panamanian. Good speed, great arm, temperamental: shortstop Jose Greco. Or big hardhitting first baseman; strong, silent type: Vaughn Monroe. And centerfielder, showboat, spends all his money on cars, big ladies man, flashy dresser, drives in 75 runs a year, none of them in the clutch: Duke Ellington. Finally— great pitcher, 20-game winner five years in a row, class guy, friendly with writers and fans alike. Stuff is good, not overpowering, but he's smart, has great control and curve ball, moves the ball around: Nat King Cole.

If you think this is a silly game, you haven't stood around in the outfield much.

Another one about passing time. Larry Haney says that in the Baltimore bullpen Dave Leonhard, who went through Johns Hopkins with a 3.9 average (that's out of a possible 4.0, kids) prepares quizzes on various subjects for the fellows: history, current events, literature, personal idiosyncrasies of players on the club. Sounds almost as good as singer-and-actor baseball teams.

And then we played a game of baseball. We knocked Stottlemyre out and won 5–3. I warmed up in the bullpen, not to pitch but just to keep my knuckleball sharp. It's been four days since I've been in a game. And I don't see much chance of getting in tomorrow either. Mike Marshall is pitching and he's been throwing real good. Bill Burbach is pitching for them and we should rack him up. He's a high-ball pitcher, and this is the wrong park to pitch high in. And I haven't been getting into games we win at all.

MAY
14

Shows what I know. We lost. We should have won. We were losing 3–2 going into the eighth and they brought Aker in. Jack's been getting bombed while I've had two good appearances in a row, and I thought I was ahead of him. But that's not what Joe Schultz thought. So he brought Aker in and he got ripped for a triple and a homer and now it's 5–2 and the game is about gone. So guess who got called in? Jim Bouton, or Lost Cause, as they say around the French Foreign Legion. I had a good inning. Call it pretty good. Roy White got to a mediocre knuckleball for a double down the first-base line. Then Pepitone connected solidly for a weak little roller down the firstbase line and I personally tagged him out. They got zero runs.

In the bottom of the ninth, though, Gus Gil hit a double with two on and suddenly it's 5–4 and I wonder if Joe Schultz is sorry he brought in Aker instead of me. Better relief and we'd have won the game. Even so, it's one run and a man on second with none out and inside I'm jumping up and down because if we win it's seven straight losses for them and a victory for me, my first win of the season and against the New York Yankees. Just like in my dreams. Except that we don't score and lose.

I wonder if their general manager, Lee MacPhail, noticed my knuckleball.

MAY
15

Boston

Off day for travel to Boston. As dusk fell Gary Bell and I went out to celebrate the fact that we've won five of our last six. We chose Sonny's as the ideal place, and it was, because when we returned to our hotel it was three-thirty in the morning and we were still able to have a long discussion about the world, the ghettos and civil rights (all of which we disagree about). We also decided that it would be a good idea, at each baseball game, to allow a fan to suit up and play in the game. Just announce on the public address that if there are any fans in the stands who think they could do a good job at any position, to come down and draw lots for the privilege. We could designate him as our wild-card fan.

And so to bed, after deciding that we are both promotional geniuses.

MAY
16

I knew I was going to enjoy this day. I just didn't know how much. It was going to be a good day because my brother Bob was coming up from Fairfield, Connecticut, to see the game and also Bill Morehead III of Harvard and Pittsburgh would be there. Morehead once sent me a long involved questionnaire about the knuckleball. He said he wanted to be a pitcher for Harvard and since he had hurt his arm he thought his only chance was to learn to throw the knuckleball. I called him on the phone and told him that answering the questionnaire would take too long and wouldn't teach him that much anyway and suggested he come down to Connecticut when I worked out there in a gym with my brother. He came down twice and I think now he understands the principle of it. It's just a matter now of him working on it. In any case, I was looking forward to seeing him.

So with friends in the stands I had my greatest night of the season. I pitched three innings against the Red Sox—the eighth, ninth and tenth—and shut them out with no hits. In the eleventh we scored six runs, and although the Red Sox came back with five in their half, while I paced up and down in the clubhouse cursing the other relief pitchers, we won 10–9 and I ended up with my first big W, as we baseball players call it. It was my first major league win earned with the knuckleball. I don't think I threw more than a couple of fastballs during the three innings. The knuckleball was just great. So was the company after the game.

MAY
17

I thought it would be a good time to talk to Maglie. He was shagging balls thrown in to second base from the outfield, and I got him between shags. I told him about my conversation with Schultz and his thought that I couldn't be a starter because I had only one pitch. I told him that Niekro said after his last game that he'd thrown 95 knucklers out of 104 pitches.

"Well, you can do that if it's breaking," Sal said.

"Fine," I said. "Then I can throw it all the time."

"But they start looking for the damn thing," Sal said. "And if it doesn't break you got nothing else."

"What about Wilhelm?" I said. "They wait for *his* knuckleball."

"He throws that slider of his once in a while."

"Sure, but they don't look for his slider. They look for his knuckleball. And what about when you threw the curve ball?"

"When I was pitching they always looked for the curve," he said, not without a certain pride.

"But you threw other pitches, didn't you?"

"Oh yeah."

"But they always looked for your curve, right?"

"Yeah, but they just couldn't hit it. They tried, but they couldn't."

Even after all that he wouldn't admit that it didn't matter if the hitter was looking for it as long as the pitch was good enough.

What I think is going on here is something in Sal Maglie's head. He said in spring training, in front of everybody, that you can't get by with one pitch. Now he doesn't want to admit he might have been wrong.

Then we played the game and it was lousy. Gary got beat real bad. It was especially tough because he wanted so much to do well in his old ballpark and when they announced his name before the game he got a standing O, which is an ovation. There were 30,000 people in the park and it was exactly the kind of day in which you want to look good against your old club, and in honor of the occasion Gary put down at least three greenies. They didn't do a bit of good.

I sat down next to him in the clubhouse afterward and said, "Hang in there, Rooms. Tonight we'll go out and celebrate until we forget what happened. Besides, you got nothing to worry about. We've both done our jobs and we both have some good years behind us and a game like this doesn't really matter."

"Yeah, you're right, Rooms," he said. "But when we're all through celebrating my loss tonight and when we get back to our room, we're going to start working on that knuckleball."

MAY
18

Today I've been thinking about God and baseball, or is it baseball and God? In any case, this rumination was caused by the sight of Lindy McDaniel of the Yankees. Although I've never met him, I feel I know him pretty well because of this newsletter he sends out from Baytown, Texas, called "Pitching for the Master." One of the first I got from him—and all the players receive them—was a complete four-page explanation of why the Church of Christ was the only true church. The dogmatism of this leads to the kind of thinking you find in the Fellow-ship of Christian Athletes and in *Guideposts* and *The Reader's Digest*. The philosophy here is that religion is the reason an athlete is good at what he does. "My faith in God is what made me come back." Or "I knew Jesus was in my corner." Since no one ever has an article saying, "God didn't help me" or "It's my muscles, not Jesus," kids pretty soon get the idea that Jesus helps all athletes and the ones who don't speak up are just shy or embarrassed.

So I've been tempted sometimes to say into a microphone that I feel I won tonight because I don't believe in God. I mean, just for the sake of balance, to let the kids know that belief in a deity or "Pitching for the Master" is not one of the criteria for major-league success. But I guess I never will.

Tonight I was making some notes in the bullpen and Eddie O'Brien was slowly going out of his mind with curiosity. Finally he sneaked over and snatched the paper out of my hand. I snatched it right back. That's all Mr. Small has to find out—that I'm writing a book. It'll be all over for the kid.

MAY
19

Front running is not limited to coaches. Here's what I mean. I've had about three appearances lately in which I haven't given up any runs. But no one bothered to talk to me. As soon as I win my first game, though, I'm on an interview show back to Seattle and they want to know the whole Jim Bouton story. "Give it to us from the beginning, Jim. Tell us all about it."

Hell, I could write a book.

It's like what happened to Diego Segui. About a week ago, Segui won two games. He pitched about two innings and gave up two runs and then about four innings and gave up two more runs. He was pitching lousy, but he was in there when our team was scoring runs, so he got credit for two wins. And so the reporters started coming around. "Gee, Diego, you're starting to win ballgames. Tell us what you're doing different."

He wasn't doing anything different, except maybe pitching worse. All they care about is results. "The world doesn't want to hear about labor pains," Johnny Sain used to say. "It only wants to see the baby."

MAY
20

Washington

It's been four days since I had my great night in Boston and I still haven't appeared in a ballgame. It's goddam depressing. I haven't even been the first or second man warming up. Hell, I'm going backward. One more good outing, I guess, and they'll ship me out.

Two trades today. We sent outfielder Jose Vidal to the Yankees for outfielder Dick Simpson. We also traded Aker for my old friend Fred Talbot. This is a little disturbing because Talbot and I didn't care too much for each other over there in New York. We're exact opposites. He's country and I'm city, and I always felt uncomfortable around him.

It's interesting, though, to see the Yankees trade Talbot, the guy they decided to keep instead of me two years ago. And they traded him for a guy who is, or at least should be, below me on the pitching totem pole over here. I believe Seattle would have wanted more than Talbot for me in a trade.

Marty Pattin, Donald Duck (his great routine is where he has Donald reaching orgasm), pitched a strong game tonight. In the eighth he gave up a home run to Mike Epstein after walking Frank Howard and we lost 6–5. Marty did not do Donald Duck tonight.

I mistakenly thought there would be a meeting tonight to elect a new player rep. I was sure Gary Bell, who was assistant rep, would get it.

I also thought I'd like to be Gary's assistant, so I asked Larry Haney, who was sitting next to me, if he would nominate me, and the minute I asked him I realized I'd made a mistake. Larry got a big grin on his face and immediately got up to tell the guys that I'd asked to be nominated. On the spot it was decided to add this to the list of fines our pitchers pay into the party kitty for various infractions, so I was assessed an *ex post facto* dollar fine for campaigning.

MAY
21

Today Mr. Small came out to the outfield where the pitchers were running and said, "Gentlemen, from now on we can all run with our hats off. It's really silly for us to run with our hats on, because the band gets all sweaty and ruins the hat."

"How come you weren't able to think of that a few weeks ago?" I asked him.

"Well, it wasn't as warm then and we weren't sweating at the same rate we are now."

Oh.

We've been running short of greenies. We don't get them from the trainer, because greenies are against club policy. So we get them from players on other teams who have friends who are doctors, or friends who know where to get greenies. One of our lads is going to have a bunch of greenies mailed to him by some of the guys on the Red Sox. And to think you can spend five years in jail for giving your friend a marijuana cigarette.

There's a zany quality to Joe Schultz that we all enjoy and that contributes, I believe, to keeping the club loose. Last night he got thrown out of a ballgame for the first time after disputing a home run that everybody knew was foul except the umpires. But that's not what he got thrown out for. He got thumbed out for offering the plate umpire his glasses, a very obvious gesture, which I enjoyed all the way out in the bullpen.

On the bench he's always saying all kinds of silly things. Like the other night when we scored six runs in the eleventh and the Red Sox scored five in the bottom half, he said, "Had them all the way." He gives a countdown on the outs when we're ahead. "Only eight outs to go—oops, only seven." And he's running up and down the dugout and jumping around like a little kid. At the same time he's letting Harper run on his own and letting the guys hit and run, and he doesn't get angry when they get thrown out stealing. It makes for a comfortable ballclub.

The knuckleball is groovy and still I can't get into a game. Tonight they could have put me in early with a 4–0 lead and Brabender pitching in a lot of trouble. They warmed me up, which means they're now thinking of me as a long man, which isn't a very good sign because there aren't many chances for a long man to get into a game when it matters. When they need short relief, both Segui and O'Donoghue get into the game.

Intellectually, I can understand Schultz's thinking. He has a lot of confidence in Segui, who was a top reliever last year, and O'Donoghue is his lefthanded relief man and does pretty well against lefthanders. Still, it gets me angry when the phone rings and it's not for me. After a while I cool off and think how I would have felt about the position I'm in now while I was with Vancouver, or in spring training, when I wasn't sure I was going to make the team. Also, the team is managing very well without me. We're playing heads-up ball. The guys on the bench are alive, and when the other team makes a mental error we take advantage of it right away. We're hitting the hell out of the ball, and we're even getting the breaks, which is part of it too. Besides, California is losing a lot of games, and what I see again in the crystal ball is third place.

What I also see in my crystal ball is that I'm the only guy in the big leagues who may finish behind his team. I was so embarrassed tonight I wanted to go off and join a monastery. We had the voting for player rep. Bell handled the meeting so well that it was impossible not to vote for him. Good for him. He'll enjoy driving the free car this summer, at least until he's traded.

176

The team doesn't take voting for player rep seriously. If it did Mike Marshall would have been elected. He's the most qualified guy on the club; bright, well read, knows a lot about the pension plan and is just the man for persistence and the paperwork. (Like he handled the shipping of our cars without a hitch and no fuss.) Except that he wasn't even nominated, because the vote for player rep is more of a popularity contest.

Which doesn't say much for me. Don Mincher, Tommy Harper and I were nominated for assistant. Tommy got six votes, Mincher got seventeen. I got one. I couldn't even break my Yankee record. I shudder to think what would happen if I wasn't trying to be one of the boys. I seem to be bearing up well under all of this. Inside, though, I'm a mess.

MAY
22

On the way to the ballpark tonight Ray Oyler, sitting in the back of the bus during a bumpy ride, discovered an erection. He promptly offered to buy the bus from the driver.

My pal Sal told me tonight that I was throwing too damn many pitches in the bullpen. He clocked me last night, he said, and I threw 180, which is like a game-and-a-half, and I never even got into the game.

When I tried to explain again that the knuckleball is not like other pitches he looked over my shoulder into the setting sun and said, "Yeah, no more throwing in the bullpen unless I tell you to warm up."

"Look, Sal, can't we talk this over?"

"No," he said striding off. "If you want to talk it over, talk to Joe." Fuck you, Sal Maglie.

I walked directly into Joe's office and told him I needed to throw a lot in the bullpen and that if he needed me for five or six innings early in the game that was fine, because I wasn't throwing until late in the game.

So Joe said, "All right."

"All right, I can throw on my own out there?"

"All right, I'll talk to Sal about it."

I saw Sal and Joe talking on the field a few minutes later, then Sal came over to me in the outfield and said, "It's exactly what I said to you before. You just got to cut down on your throwing in the bullpen."

I could feel my neck getting red. "When I talked to Joe he seemed to think I could throw on my own whenever I felt I needed it."

"Oh yeah, you can throw on your own," Sal said. "But just watch it and make sure you're ready to pitch if we need you."

Here's how Mike Marshall got into his most recent trouble. He was taken out of the ballgame in Boston the other night after giving up a grand-slam home run to Carl Yastrzemski. He told the writers that he should have finished the game. What he meant, of course, was that he should have been good enough not to give up the home run and good enough to hang in there. His remarks were interpreted as criticism of Joe Schultz for taking him out of the game. So pretty soon it got around the clubhouse that Mike was on the manager for something that was his own goddam fault and I ended up explaining that Mike had been misinterpreted. But the players were not anxious to give Mike the benefit of the doubt. Now Mike's in trouble with the newspapermen, the guys and probably Joe Schultz. Can't anybody around here understand English?

In the bullpen Talbot revealed an awful truth about Joe Pepitone. He has two different hairpieces. He's got a massive piece, which he wears when he's going out, and a smaller one to wear under his baseball cap. He calls it his game piece. On opening day he was wearing his game piece and hadn't put it on very well. So when he was forced to take his cap off, there it was, sitting on his head all askew. He was so embarrassed he tried to hide his head in the shoulder of the guy standing next to him. Kiss me, Joe baby.

Pepitone took to wearing the hairpieces when his hair started to get thin on top. And the hair he still has is all curly and frizzy when he lets it grow long. So he carries around all kinds of equipment in a little blue Pan Am bag. Things like a hot comb, various greases and salves, glue for the hairpiece, hair-straightener—and even a hair-dryer. He carries it wherever he goes, on the buses to the park, on airplanes. You never see him without that little blue bag. At any rate, one day Fritz Peterson and

I, a bit bored during a game we were winning about 6–2, went into the clubhouse and filled his hair-dryer with talcum powder. Then we cleaned it up, left it where he had and went back to watch the game. By this time it was 6–3, and then they tied it up and we lost it, 7–6, in extra innings. And one of the reasons we lost is that Pepitone struck out in a clutch situation.

So everyone was tired and angry and upset and you could hear a pin drop in the clubhouse, because after a loss that's the way it's supposed to be. After a while Pepitone came out of the shower and turned his hair dryer on. *Whoooosh!* Instant white. He looked like an Italian George Washington wearing a powdered wig. There was talcum powder over everything, his hair, his eyebrows, his nose, the hair on his chest. Of course, everybody went crazy. Loss or no, they all laughed like hell. To this moment, Pepitone never knew who turned on the powder. He always thought it was Big Pete Sheehy. Wrong again.

Gary Bell was hit again tonight, four runs in less than five innings. I relieved him with two on and two out and got Paul Casanova to pop up. They pinch-hit for me in the next inning, so I had a total outing of one-third of an inning.

In the clubhouse Gary was sitting in front of his locker sucking up a beer and I told him to hang in there.

"Rooms, my career is over," he said. "The Big C has got my arm."

"Besides that, how're you feeling?" I said.

"I feel fine," he said. "This is my fifth beer."

Ranew tells me that Vancouver sent Bob Lasko to Toledo, which is another Triple-A team in the International League. It burned me up because here's Lasko, a guy with ten or eleven years in professional baseball, most of it in Triple-A, bouncing around all over the country, playing for three, four, five different organizations in thirty or forty different towns, all without his family, and now, in the twilight of his career he gets a chance to play in his own home town and he gets sent to Toledo.

There's no justification for this. No one can tell me there wasn't another pitcher they could have sent to Toledo instead. I bet no one even realized Vancouver is home to Lasko. So one day, if Lasko ever makes it in the big leagues and has a good year, the owner will scream bloody murder if he tries to get an extra thousand in salary.

Don Mincher goes up to people and asks for a cigarette. When they give him one he pulls out a pack, puts the cigarette into it and puts it back into his pocket. Then he walks off.

There is often homosexual kidding among the players. Tonight Ray Oyler combed his hair forward and started mincing around the clubhouse, lisping, "Hello, sweetheart," or "C'mere, you sweet bitch." Then Gary Bell said, "Ray, you convinced me. You really are queer." And Ray said, "Well, it doesn't make me a bad person."

MAY
23

Cleveland
Flying in to Cleveland last night I thought about life in this great American city and decided that if you were going to crash on a Cleveland flight it would be better if it was an inbound flight.

Jose Cardenal was in center field fixing the legs of his tight pants and Talbot recalled the time in winter ball when Cardenal refused to play for three days because his uniform wasn't tight enough.

Joe Schultz had a short meeting before the game and said that we have enough ability to win a lot of games if we just used our common sense out there, just used our heads. So I went out and played like I had left my head back in the hotel room. You wouldn't think it was possible for me to play dumb baseball, considering my charm, intelligence and good looks. But I played dumb baseball.
The first inning was fine. I came in with the bases loaded and one out and got Cardenal to hit a one-hopper right back to me for the DP,

pitcher to catcher to first base. That's good. What I did in the next inning was bad.

With one out (Alvis struck out on a knuckleball), Hawk Harrelson doubled down the left-field line. No complaint, he hit a pretty good knuckleball. Then there was a little bouncer in front of the plate. Instead of settling for an out at first, I tried to get Harrelson going into third. I didn't have much chance of getting him and made a bad throw besides. So instead of two out and a man on third, I've got runners on first and third, one out. Larry Brown then hit one into right for a single, Harrelson scoring. The other runner was headed for third and the throw from right field was wild, over third and into the dugout. It shouldn't have mattered, because I should have been over there backing up the play. Instead I stood on the mound watching, like it was a John Wayne movie, while the second run scored and Brown went all the way to third.

I got the next two hitters and was unscathed in the following inning. I rate the performance fair because I got away with no runs in a bases-loaded situation. But there is no excuse for playing such dumb baseball.

MAY
24

Fred Talbot invited me out to dinner with his roommate, Merritt Ranew, after the game. It's a sign that we're living through a reincarnation with the Seattle Pilots. I found myself enjoying their company. Could I have been wrong about Talbot? Me, Jim Bouton, wrong?

I had planned to ask Joe—or my pal Sal—if I could start the exhibition game Monday against Spokane, but today I noticed that Gary Timberlake is around. He said he'd been called up to pitch the exhibition game. He was with our double-A team. He's going to fly from Cleveland to Seattle, pitch against Spokane and then go back to the minors. I guess they want to look at him. I mean they *know* what I can do. Or do they?

Steve Barber started the game tonight and pitched four innings, giving up two runs. He was taken out when his arm stiffened up. The situation was discussed in the bullpen.

Bell: "His next start will probably come next July."

O'Donoghue: "Or later."

Me: "Depending on how his arm feels."

MAY

25

At the pregame meeting the discussion was about how to pitch to Alvis. Ron Plaza pointed out to Mike Marshall that the way we play him will depend on how he's pitched. And Marshall said he didn't know yet. "I have to wait until I get out there," he said.

If no one else understood what he meant, I did. The way he pitches to any given hitter depends on how he feels at the moment, what his instincts tell him.

This was just one more reason to count him as a weirdo. And yet there's nothing weird about it at all.

Take something that happened in the 1964 World Series (when young fireballer Jim Bouton won two games). Bill White, lefthanded hitter, good power, is the subject. I usually throw lefthanders a lot of change-ups, but his first three times up I threw him none. I don't know why, I just didn't. Fourth time up I struck him out—on a change. The next day the quote from White in the papers was: "I waited all day for that change-up and he never threw it. Then I gave up looking for the damn thing and started looking for the fastball and here it came."

If I'd been required to come up with a pregame plan on how to pitch White, I'd have committed myself to throwing him the change and I would have thrown one early in the game and he'd have clobbered it. But nobody was asking me to stick to a plan and, I think instinctively, I did the right thing.

It may have been the last time.

MAY
26

I'm trying so hard to be one of the boys I'm even listening to country music. And enjoying it. The back of the bus is the country-music enclave, and most of the players are part of it. So far, though, we've not been able to swing over city boys like Tommy Davis, Tommy Harper and John Kennedy. I think we'll get them in the end, though. Maybe with a bull fiddle.

Back at the hotel, Gary and I talked about the relationship between country and city guys on a ballclub, which is intertwined with the relationship between whites and blacks. There are lots of walls built up between people, and I pointed out that if I'd never roomed with Gary I would still think, "Oh, he's just a dumb Southerner." So probably the solution is to have people live together. I mean we still disagree about a lot of things—religion, politics, how children should be raised—but because we've been able to talk about these differences, spend so many hours together, we've been able to at least understand them. How's that for a solution? Put people together in a hotel room in Cleveland.

Getting on the airplane in Cleveland we ran into the Kansas City Royals. There was a lot of conversation because we're both expansion teams and a lot of us have been rescued from the same junkpile. The funniest line was about Moe Drabowsky. They said he was sick on the bus the other night and puked up a panty girdle.

MAY
27

Seattle
It's been a great trip for the Seattle Pilots. We took two out of three in Boston, Washington and Cleveland, and since we won

three straight before we left home we're now only two games under .500 and I'm beginning to think we might have a shot at the divisional title. Of course, we'd need a little help. Maybe a small air crash involving the Minnesota and Oakland clubs. Nothing serious. Just a few broken arms and legs.

We'll know better after this next series. The Baltimore Orioles are in town. Which reminds me of a cartoon I once saw. It showed a little boy forlornly carrying a glove and a bat over his shoulder. "How'd you do, son?" his father asks. "I had a no-hitter going until the big kids got out of school," the kid says.

Another round of musical lockers today. John Gelnar was called up from Vancouver and Darrell Brandon was outrighted to Tucson. Brandon didn't take it very well. I was sitting next to him when Eddie O'Brien said, "Joe wants to see you."

"Oh, oh," Brandon said.

"Can't be that, Bucky," I said. "It's the wrong time."

When he came out of Joe's office he said, "Tucson. They outrighted me to Tucson. Boy, this just kills me. What am I going to tell Liz? She just got up here and we just got settled in and now we've got to move again."

At that moment I happened to look across the room—and there was Steve Barber getting his road uniform refitted. I guess he wants to look good while sitting in the diathermy machine. "You son of a bitch," I said to myself. "You're the guy who won't go down in order to help the club. Instead you hang around here, can't pitch and now other guys are sent down because of you." I got tremendously pissed off just thinking about it.

Talbot and I got to talking about Houk in the bullpen and we agreed that sometimes the man is 99 percent pure bullshit. "I was 0 and 8 last year," Talbot said, "and he came around to tell me he was taking me out of the rotation, not because I was pitching bad but because he thought the club was pressing too much behind me." That's called having smoke blown up your ass.

I tried to let Joe know that I haven't been pitching much lately. "I sure could use a workout," I said.

And Joe Schultz said, "If you need a workout go down to a whore-house."

Second best suggestion of the day. Going over the hitters it was decided that we should pitch Frank Robinson underground.

Ray Oyler (dubbed Oil Can Harry because he always looks as though he had just changed a set of rings) hit a home run into the left-field corner that must have traveled all of 305 1/4 feet. "As soon as I hit it, I knew it was out," he said. They have named the spot after Greenberg Gardens. They're calling it Oil Can's Corner.

Sitting in the bullpen it suddenly occurred to me that no one had said anything about Brandon being sent down. Not a word. It didn't seem right to me. A guy shouldn't be forgotten that quickly. At the very least we should have burned a candle.

MAY
28

Bobbie and I were talking about our plans for this fall and discussed the possibility of buying a trailer and taking a slow trip cross-country. On the other hand, we might ship the car, fly home and spend some time up at Cape Cod. Or we might wait until December and go sit on a warm island someplace. And why shouldn't we go to Europe?

What it all boils down to is money. If I get a raise next season we could afford to do any of these things. But if I have a bad season and they don't like this book, I may not even get a contract. So we decided that what I probably should do is get them to give me a contract at the end of this season, before they know about the book. Of course, the kind of contract I get will depend on what kind of season I have, and so all of it—plans, trips, contract—boils down to my knuckleball.

I had another Crosetti pulled on me tonight. When I was with Vancouver, the baseball coach at the University of Oregon called me and asked if I would talk to one of his kids about the knuckleball. I said sure and arranged to see the kid in Tacoma. As it happened I got called back by the Pilots and he had to come down to Seattle. Now this is a rainy night, the tarpaulin is on the field, there's nobody in the stands and it's an hour-and-a-half before game time. I've got this kid standing behind me while I'm throwing on the sidelines and here comes an usher to tell me I can't have an unauthorized person on the field. I explained what I was doing, but the usher said that Mr. Crosetti had sent him out and that the kid would have to leave. I gritted my teeth and told him that the kid was staying and if Cro didn't like it he could come over and tell me himself. He never did.

Jim Pagliaroni joined the club tonight and is going to be a welcome addition. He was describing a girl that one of the ballplayers had been out with and said, "It's hard to say exactly what she looked like. She was kind of a Joe Torre with tits." This joke can only be explained with a picture of Joe Torre. But I'm not sure any exist. He dissolves camera lenses.

Joe Schultz was put away by Earl Weaver of the Orioles tonight. We had a two-run rally going when Weaver came out of the dugout and pointed out that we were hitting out of order. Seems that Joe had made out two lineup cards and given the umpires the wrong one. Weaver, who spotted it right away, let us hit until we got something going and then we had to call it all back. Since we lost the game 9–5, and since there was no telling how many runs we might have scored that inning, Joe's face was very red indeed. I don't think he'll be telling us to keep our heads in the game again very soon.

Pitched one inning tonight and the greatest hitters in the American League were at my mercy. I struck Frank Robinson out on four absolutely hellacious knuckleballs; Boog Powell swung at two and missed for another strikeout, and Brooks Robinson popped up. The way that ball was moving, it's almost impossible for anyone to hit it solidly. They're at my mercy, I tell you.

Of course, since we were behind I was taken out for a pinch-hitter after my inning. Which means I'm still just a mop-up man. Maybe when the doubleheaders start piling up they'll give me a start. I can't wait.

MAY
30

I almost missed a ballgame today. It was Friday and I assumed we were playing our usual night game. I planned to spend the afternoon with the family at an art museum and I was lying around in my pajamas reading stories to the kids at one-thirty when the phone rang. It was Gary Bell.

"Where the hell are you?" he said.

"Where the hell are *you?*" I countered cleverly.

He told me. I flew in eight different directions, and the kids were scurrying around looking for my shoes and socks, and my wife was running after a shirt, and I felt like Dagwood Bumstead going to the office in the morning. I arrived at the ballpark at one-forty-five, fifteen minutes before game time, only two hours and forty-five minutes late, having missed running, batting practice and infield practice.

Almost to a man the guys were nice about it. I had a big grin on my face when I walked into the clubhouse and got a round of applause, and a lot of the guys told me they were glad I could make it today. Except Fred Talbot, who waved a little Yankee at me. "Jesus Christ, eleven years in baseball and you don't know whether it's a day game or night game."

I was absolutely not prepared to say I gave the umpire the wrong schedule card if Joe Schultz said anything to me, but he never said a word. Nobody was mad, including Maglie, who said it was a good thing I'd run the day before in my backyard. He was kidding about the fact that it rained yesterday and I called and asked whether I should come in or whether I could just run in my backyard. All the whole thing cost me was $10 to the pitcher's kitty for being late and $1 for missing infield.

I once came late to a game when I was with the Yankees—a World Series game. I wasn't pitching or anything, and it had rained all morning and I assumed, correctly, that there would be no batting practice, so I came in time for infield. But they'd called a pregame meetng and I missed it, so when I walked into that clubhouse there wasn't a single smile. Everyone was highly offended that I should take the Yankees and baseball and the World Series so lightly as to show up forty-five minutes before game time. I could have stayed out all night and come to the game with a hangover and I would have been forgiven. But I couldn't come late.

We split two games with the Orioles and lost our first today to the Tigers. So we've lost two out of three to the big kids and who knows where it will all end.

Fred Talbot had a marvelous story about Mel McGaha, who had a short run as manager of the Kansas City A's. McGaha called a meeting during spring training for eight o'clock on a Friday night, an unforgiveable sin. Guys had to leave their families and dinner parties and come in from all over the place. When they got there, McGaha said, "Boys, I'm glad you all got here tonight. We're not really having a meeting. I just wanted to see how quick we could all group up if we had to."

With the Tigers in town I've tried to call Johnny Sain and talk with him about my knuckleball and tell him how well I've been doing since I came back from Vancouver. I've missed him at the hotel a couple of times, but I'll keep trying.

I know Detroit needs relief help and they could get me cheap. If he looks in the newspaper he'll see a 4.2 ERA, although since I've returned from the minors it's only a bit over 3.0. In my last ten appearances I've given up one earned run, walked three and struck out eight. I've given up only five hits in eight innings. Of course, my own club doesn't seem very impressed, but that's another story.

I get the feeling that Sal and Joe just don't trust me. I think they're convinced that I need more than just the knuckleball to get by for more than an inning or two. One of these days they're going to need me for five or six innings and I'll show them. I'll show them. I'll show them. I think I'll show them.

Now they're talking about using Talbot as a starter, and this reduces *my* chances, except that the seer my wife went to this winter told her that our fortunes wouldn't rise until June. So I guess I won't get a start until then.

Do I really believe all of that? No, I don't.

Before we left the park today we were told that tomorrow's game would start at twelve-fifteen because of national television and that we'd have to take batting practice at ten-thirty. "Ten-thirty?" said Pagliaroni. "I'm not even done throwing up at that hour."

MAY
31

Tony Kubek and Mickey Mantle were here to do the TV broadcast and before the game Mickey was down in the clubhouse. With me standing right there, Joe Schultz says, "Mickey, what do you think of a guy who comes to the ballpark fifteen minutes before the game starts?"

Mickey shook his head sadly. "I know he's got some strange ideas," he said.

Don Mincher was worried about appearing on national television. "My mother's going to watch this ballgame in Alabama," he said, "and she's going to notice first thing that I'm not using the batting helmet with the earflap on it. And tonight she's going to be on the telephone, guaranteed, asking me why I'm not wearing my earflap."

Between innings of the game I got up in the bullpen and worked with the iron ball Mike Marshall keeps out there. Talbot was certain I was only doing it so I would get on television, and maybe I was, partly. After the third time up Talbot said, "Jesus Christ, Bouton, why don't you just run across the field and slide into second base and get it over with?"

The people who watched this game on television saw some of the dumbest baseball ever played this side of a sandlot. I hope Kubek and Mantle pointed it out to all the Little League, high-school and college players who were watching, but somehow I doubt it. So I'll do it here. It started in the first inning when Joe Sparma walked Tommy Harper, leading off, on four-straight pitches. Hegan was the next batter. Ball one. On ball two, way over Hegan's head, Harper tries to steal second and is thrown out. Sparma *still* hasn't thrown a strike. Two more balls and Hegan's on first base. Sparma has thrown eight balls in a row and he's got one out.

Tommy Davis up. First pitch, ball one. Second pitch is shoulder high, a ball, but he swings at it and tops it down the third-base line. He had no business swinging, of course. By now he should have been wondering if Sparma would *ever* throw a strike. Instead of wondering, he's thrown out at first. In the meantime, with two out and second base all his very own, Hegan decides to try for third. It's very important that he go to third base because he can score from there on a base hit. He can also score from second on a base hit. So he needs to go to third base like Frank Howard needs more muscles. Of course, he's out from here to there, and Sparma is out of an inning in which all he threw was ten pitches—all balls.

A couple of innings later Al Kaline, of all people, steals third with two out. Can't imagine what he was thinking of.

To cap it all off, we lost the game 3–2, and I didn't get into it. Diego Segui did. Since my win in Boston two weeks ago I've made just four appearances and pitched a total of four-and-a-third innings. We got starters around here who get knocked out in the second and third inning and this relief ace can't get any pitching in. I'm getting psycho about it, starting to feel the way I did in New York: that there's some kind of conspiracy to keep me out of ballgames just when I'm starting to throw good. I even have this morbid fear that someone in the front office has discovered I'm writing a book and is trying to work me out of the system. Then there's this weird one. It occurs to me that the Yankees may have prevailed upon Milkes, or the Pilot organization, to soft-pedal me so that I won't embarrass them. These two clubs have made quite a few trades and I know it embarrasses the Yankees to have Hegan doing so well here. So maybe they said, "Do us a favor, don't let Bouton look good." My wife says that soon the voices will be after me.

Maybe my problem is that I'm not merchandising my product properly. Knuckleball. It's got no pizzazz. How about Super Knuck? Or maybe I can borrow one of Satchel Paige's names for a pitch: Bat Dodger. Why not Super-Knuckling Bat Dodger? Or High-Velocity Super-Knuckling Bat Dodger? Nah. It's got to be short and snappy. Maybe tomorrow I'll ask Sal to think of a name for my pitch. He'll probably say how about working on that pitch they call The Curve?

Got a letter congratulating me on my great victory in Boston from Fritz Peterson today. It's an indication of how far down I've fallen when one miserable win calls for congratulations. Fritz said a lot of guys on the Yankees agreed that I had a real good knuckleball. Then he wrote: "It's a good thing Jim Turner taught you that pitch before you left New York."

There was also something about Fred Talbot. Fritz said that Talbot seemed to have changed a lot in the last year and that I'd probably like him now. I showed Talbot the letter and he said, "That son of a bitch. I thought he always liked me." I guess Fred *is* changing. The other day, after he won in Cleveland, I reminded him that he'd already matched last year's output of wins (one). A couple of years ago he'd have gotten angry. Now he just laughed.

Of course, he was damn lucky to get that win. We had an 8–2 lead in the fifth, and when he went in to pitch I told him all he had to do to get the win was to keep from getting a heart attack. I admit he pitched well. He gave up only three hits in five innings. But I couldn't help a feeling of jealousy stealing over me like green slime. Here I'd been scraping and scuffling, pitchin' in mop-up situations all year long, and I end up scratching together just one win, against Boston no less, in extra innings, and here comes Fred, he's with the club just ten days, and he absolutely waltzes to a win. Oh well, it'll make my comeback speech at the Americana Hotel that much more interesting.

The latest adventure of Mike Marshall has him feuding with Sal Maglie about his screwball. A screwball is a curve ball that breaks in the opposite direction of a curve ball: when thrown by a righthanded pitcher it breaks in on a righthanded hitter. Mike wants to throw screwballs and Sal wants him to throw curve balls, so they're at each other all the time.

"Why don't you just throw screwballs and tell Sal they were curve balls?" I suggested.

"I would," Marshall said. "But then the catchers tell Sal what I'm throwing."

See, the catchers are angry at him for trying to call his own game. So they go back to the bench and commiserate with Sal when he complains about the way Marshall is pitching. Mike won fifteen games last year and until recently he's been our most effective pitcher. They haven't disproved any of his theories. Why can't they just leave him alone?

I'm afraid Mike's problem is that he's too intelligent and has had too much education. It's like in the army. When a sergeant found out that a private had been to college he immediately assumed he couldn't be a good soldier. Right away it was "There's your college boy for you," and "I wonder what our genius has to say about that?" This is the same kind of remark Sal and Joe make about Marshall.

I think Sal and Joe put me right up there with Marshall in the weirdo department. They don't believe that my kind of guy can do the job, so when I *am* successful they're surprised. When Fred Talbot does the job, well, he's from the old school, blood and guts, spit a little tobacco juice on it.

Another thing. When I was winning a lot of ball games my double warm-up was a great idea, an innovation, maybe even a breakthrough. After I hurt my arm, the double warm-up became a terrible idea. It was sapping my strength. In fact it was downright weird.

JUNE

1

We came from behind three times tonight to beat the Tigers 8–7. I pitched a third of an inning, coming in with a man on second. I got Tom Matchick on a ground ball back to me on a 3-and-2 count. After the game I told Joe Schultz that the reason I went to 3-

and-2 was that I needed the work. "I figured you were doing *something* out there," Joe Schultz said.

In the clubhouse Joe delivered his usual speech: "Attaway to stomp 'em. Stomp the piss out of 'em. Stomp 'em when they're down. Kick 'em and stomp 'em." And: "Attaway to go boys. Pound that ol' Budweiser into you and go get them tomorrow."

This stuff really lays us in the aisles.

Jerry Neudecker was the umpire at third base. His position is just a few steps away from our bullpen and he stopped by, as umpires will, to pass the time between innings.

"Why is it that they boo me when I call a foul ball correctly and they applaud the starting pitcher when he gets taken out of the ballgame?" says Neudecker.

Says I: "Because, Jerry, the fans recognize the pitcher as being a basically good person."

He laughed.

Actually I think umpires can be too sensitive. They have this thing about a word. You'd think it was sticks and stones. The word is motherfucker and it's called the Magic Word. Say it and you're out of the game. I have only one question. Why? Now think about that.

One of the things baseball players take pride in is their crudity. The day Brandon was sent down, for example, Gary Bell, who is his friend, asked if he would mind leaving his tapes so the guys could continue to listen to his good music while he was gone. Which is like the guy in spring training who went up to a rookie and said, "Hey, if you get re-leased, can I have your sweatshirts?" The crudity takes other forms. Like the fellow who rooms with the great chick hustler. The hustler will spend all of his time pounding the streets, spending money in bars, working like hell at running down girls. His roommate just lounges around the room, watching television, taking it easy. And he does great just taking his roommate's leavings.

Then there's the tale Jim Gosger told about hiding in a closet to shoot a little beaver while his roommate made out on the bed with some local talent. Nothing sneaky about it, the roommate even provided the towel for Gosger to bite on in case he was moved to laughter. At the

193

height of the activity on the bed, local talent, moaning, says, "Oh darling, I've never done it *that* way before." Whereupon Gosger sticks his head out, drawls "Yeah, surrre," and retreats into the closet.

After he told us the story, "Yeah surrre," became a watchword around the club.

"I only had three beers last night."

"Yeah, surrre."

And I've known ballplayers who thought it was great fun to turn on a tape recorder under the bed while they were making it with their latest broad and play it back on the bus to the ballpark the next day.

Johnny Sain returned my call this morning and we had a long talk. I told him how my knuckleball was going and he asked me what pitch I was using for my off-pitch to go with it when I needed a strike. I said fastball. He suggested I use a slider instead. His reason is that when a hitter is looking for a knuckleball and gets something else, he thinks, "Fastball!" He may have time to adjust. But if the ball does something, has a little movement to it, he'll be fooled.

I said I'd try it, sort of cut my fastball a little and see if it would move. I asked him if he could use an elderly righthanded knuckleball pitcher in Detroit and he said, "No chance. We've got four pitchers now who've all pitched less than ten innings this year. That Mayo Smith (the manager) is not a very good man to pitch for. The last guy to pitch a good game is his man, and he overuses him and neglects everybody else. There are three or four pitchers on the club he doesn't even talk to."

He told about what had happened with a guy named Mike Kilkenny. He's a lefthanded pitcher and Sain had been teaching him to get lefthanders out by coming sidearm on them. It can be a really effective pitch. But Kilkenny pitched in an exhibition game recently and, with the bases loaded, he came sidearm on a lefthanded hitter and plunked him in the ribs. Said Smith: "When I saw you come sidearm I liked to die. You take that goddam sidearm pitch and shove it up your ass."

So here's another case where the manager is trying to make rules for his pitchers that go right over the head of the pitching coach.

Not long ago John went home for a day and Smith took the pitchers to the outfield and ran them hard, foul line to foul line. Sain was angry when he found out. So he went into Mayo's office and said, "Is this the pitching staff that led all baseball in complete games last year?"

"Yes, it is," Mayo said.

"Well, are we going to follow a formula that I used last year or one that hasn't been successful here for twenty-five years?"

"I guess we'll stick with what's been successful," Mayo said.

But he didn't like it. I'd bet right now the Tigers don't win the pennant again.

I told John about the trouble I'd been having getting enough work and how they always want to save me for the seven innings I never pitch. John laughed and said that he personally was a believer in throwing before a game, and that what he does is take a guy out of sight into the bullpen and let him work. He said if a pitcher is just throwing on the sidelines his arm can bounce back in 20 minutes. He's been able to sell pitchers on that, but it's hell selling managers.

JUNE
2

Big meeting before the game about personal appearances and autograph signing. It was proposed that we charge no less than $100 for any personal appearance and no less than $100 an hour for autograph-signing sessions. I said I didn't think it was a very good idea because it would work a hardship on the lesser-known player who could not command such a large fee. A player like Harper or Mincher or Davis might get that kind of money but a Gus Gil or a John Gelnar, guys who might be offered $25 or $50 for an appearance, might never get any shots at all. I suggested that it be left up to the individual what he wants to take for an appearance.

So Steve Barber said, "This is a big-league town and these people are going to have to learn to go big league."

And Don Mincher said: "If we go for $25 and $50 we'll never get it up there where it belongs."

And Brabender said, "If you want to dance, you've got to pay the fiddler." (This got a big laugh because it's what we say to a guy who's been out drinking the night before and has to do a lot of running with a bad body to get the alcohol out of his system.)

And O'Donoghue said: "We made that mistake in Kansas City, where the guys went for $25 or $50 and that's all we could ever get."

So I said: "Well, if a guy doesn't want to go for $50 he doesn't have to. He can pass it on to one of the lesser players. Besides, suppose it's a friend, or a good cause or something."

Then Joe Schultz said: "Well, whatever you do, I think you should all get together on it and everyone do the same thing. Hell, you guys are big-league ballplayers. Just make it a club rule and everybody will stick to it."

So much for my doctrine of laissez faire. The tyranny of the majority over the minority will always be with us. The vote was unanimous, except for my abstention. If someone offers me $25 or $50 and can't afford more, I'll take it.

The next thing we talked about was signing autographs for kids before the ballgame. Apparently there is a league rule that supposedly prohibits players from signing autographs when they're in uniform on the field. The rule is ignored. Some players were upset by this. Said Brabender: "If you don't feel like signing and you say you're not allowed to and some other guy comes up behind you and starts signing, you look like an ass."

So Joe Schultz said: "Make it my rule—no autographs once the gates open. No autographs at all."

Great. If a kid comes to the ballpark and wants an autograph, when the hell is he going to get it if not before the game starts? Of course, he can stand around outside in the dark for an hour or so after the game and hope he can stop us when we're rushing to get home. Who wants an autograph that bad? Especially from a Seattle Pilot.

At the end of the meeting Gary Bell brought up the fact that when we're in Baltimore next time we've been asked to go to Washington to attend a clinic Ted Kennedy is running for underprivileged children. Did anyone want to sign up? Mike Marshall signed, and Marty Pattin signed, and I signed. But before I did I stood up and said, "Now, wait a minute. We've got a free clinic here, right? For underprivileged kids? Well, isn't there some way we can get these kids to kick in their lunch money or something to us?"

Almost everybody laughed.

Ah, the ballgame. Steve Barber started. The last time he got a big lead but had to leave in the fifth. That's how Talbot got his quick win. The rule is that the starter can't get credit for the win unless he pitches five full innings.

Sure enough we score three in the first, two in the second and another in the third. We've got a 6–0 lead and it looks like Barber is having trouble out there. He's twitching his arm and cranking it around and doing a lot of fussing. So Talbot goes down and tells Maglie, as a joke, that he's absolutely ready, that his arm never felt better, just in case they should need him. Now every time Barber throws a ball Talbot holds up his hands in the sign of a T—for Talbot.

In the fifth, when Barber walks a couple, the call comes—for me. With two out I'm all set to go in and collect my Big W when Barber, the rat, goes ahead and gets the third out on a pop-up. Says Talbot: "Ah, sit down. No chance now. All you can get is a save or your ass kicked in." And he went down and told Sal his arm felt terrible.

I pitched the sixth, seventh, eighth and ninth, gave up three hits, one home run—Ken Harrelson took me over the left-field wall on a high knuckleball. And all I wound up with was a save.

I had a great knuckleball when I went in, but I lost it in the eighth. I got by on fastballs. In the bottom half we took an awful long time hitting so I asked Sal if I could try throwing a little to get the feel of the knuckleball back. "Nah," he said. "You're doing all right. Besides, it would look horseshit."

I was rooting for Steve Barber to look horseshit tonight and get his ass shipped out. Instead he had good stuff out there, good enough for them to keep him another month even if he can't pitch. I suppose down deep I'd like him to do well enough to make a contribution to this club. I think we have a chance to move now. We're in third place, only four out of first. And we're scoring all kinds of runs—six, seven a game. And we haven't been shut out. Not once. If we get some decent pitching, why, for goodness sakes, maybe we can win the pennant.

Talbot is in rare form these days. Like he was telling us how it used to be in the sheet-metal shop of the industrial school he went to. When they were taught how to weld, the first thing they did was weld the door shut when the teacher left the room. The next thing they did was weld every tool in the place onto a metal tractor, which was kept in the center of the room. And for kicks, they'd heat a steel bar until it was red hot, let the color cool out of it and then ask the new boy to bring over the metal bar. All it would cost was the skin off his hand.

JUNE
5

Baltimore

Arrived in Baltimore today, which is always depressing. The town puts you down, and the hotel is dingy, and they don't have bedboards, which means my back will ache tomorrow, and my roomie is supposed to pitch tomorrow and he's got a worse back than I have. It's dreary. Besides, I'm still suffering from having given up two earned runs in an inning-and-a-third the other night and losing the ballgame besides.

Even the newspaper depressed me tonight. I read where they're discussing the possibility of an integrated Davis Cup team in South Africa and a fellow named Alf Chambers, president of the South African Lawn Tennis Association said that the discussions had nothing to do with protests of other countries. And the increase in the number of swimming pools in Harlem has nothing to do with the riots and the troop withdrawals having nothing to do with the protest movement and the baseball owners broadened our pension coverage not because of any strike but out of an innate sense of fair play. Yeah, surrre.

And why is it, I ask myself, that baseball players are allowed to smoke during a game and that it's all right to sneak a smoke in the runway or even to go back into the clubhouse for a goddam cigarette, but if you take a candy bar out to the bullpen you get all kinds of static.

The bed in this hotel in Baltimore makes me think these bad thoughts. I think I'll go wash out my brain with soap.

JUNE
6

D.C. Stadium is being renamed Robert F. Kennedy Stadium and there are dedication ceremonies and those clinics that Marshall, Pattin and I signed up for. The Baseball Commissioner's office called Bell to ask if he could get guys like Sal Maglie, Joe Schultz, Tommy Davis, Tommy Harper and Don Mincher to attend. Sal said he had plans for tomorrow. Harper said he didn't want to go. Mincher said he would go, and Schultz sort of agreed. Tommy Davis said he would make the clinic if he could.

In the bullpen during the game the conversation turned to many things (Fred Talbot on the American destroyer that was cut in half by the Australian aircraft carrier: "The bastards must have been playing chicken out there"). But especially the talk was about the strike in the spring and the players who signed their contracts despite it—like Pete Richert of Baltimore. He said he had to sign his contract because he was just buying a house and the story was that he'd borrowed the money from the club and if he'd borrowed it from the bank he'd have had to pay a high interest rate. O'Donoghue thought this was justification enough. I said I didn't think so. I said that *everybody* could use the money, and that those who didn't sign were risking the owner's getting angry at them besides. And what about the marginal players? And the rookies? A lot more was at stake for them than some high interest rate on a loan.

There *was* agreement about the large number of Atlanta Braves who had signed. And we agreed *that* was all Paul Richards' fault. He put a tremendous amount of pressure on his players and I guess I blame them a helluva lot less than I do Richert.

And then Carl Yastrzemski's name came up because he'd just ignored the strike and Gary Bell said, "Didn't surprise me. Carl Yastrzemski is for himself first and second and the hell with everybody else."

Gee, Gary, Carl Yastrzemski?

Yes. Besides, during the strike Yastrzemski called several superstars in an attempt to form a separate committee and settle things without the Players' Association. Fortunately they told him to take a hike, son.

I don't think the only bad guys in this thing were the few players who caved in. Richards was particularly beautiful, calling Marvin Miller "a mustachioed four flusher." And many others were willing to take a strike and use Triple-A players and flush the game right down the drain if necessary. These are the same guys who want us to think they're sportsmen who run the game out of civic pride. They're not in this thing for money. They're not. We know because that's what they tell us. And we believe. Like Clete Boyer once told me that Dan Topping, former Yankee owner, was all for the players and a wonderful man. I asked him how he knew. And he said, "Ralph Houk told me."

Mike Marshall was sitting against the fence in the bullpen watching the ballgame. In order to get close to the fence he turned his cap around backward and used the leather band to protect his head from the cold steel. Without saying a word, Eddie O'Brien lifted the hat off his head and put it on him peak-front. "I don't want Joe getting on me because you guys are wearing your hats backward," he said.

With that, Marshall took his hat off, slammed it on the ground and said, "How's that? I don't have it on wrong now, do I?"

All the Orioles are wearing their socks with high cuts, like Frank Robinson, and no one seems to object. I watched very closely and saw no lack of spirit on the club as a result of these high cuts. Of course, the club is winning, but I don't know whether they're winning because of their socks or because a lot of them aren't wearing hats during batting practice.

If you ever see a baseball player stick his tongue out at someone in the stands it's not because he's mad at anybody. It happens to be a form of beaver shooting. The player scouts the stands for good-looking girls, and if he catches a doll's eye he sticks out his tongue. If she looks away, it means she's not interested. If she smiles, something might come of it. It's called shooting stingers.

Roomie got shelled out of the game in four innings. The Orioles are so hot right now it could happen to anybody. But poor Gary took it pretty hard. After I pitched my third of an inning I went into the club-house. "Rooms, I'm diving off the hotel tonight," he said. "Something's happening to my body. I'm going to be dead in six months."

Jim Gosger came over to cheer him up. "Hey, Gary, who's going to drive to Vancouver, you or I?"

Just then Marty Pattin walked by. "Hey, Pattin," Gary said. "Your shoes are terrible. Try and get some new shoes before I'm traded, will you?"

"You better get them before tomorrow morning," I said, trying to be helpful.

I felt bad for Gary. I also felt hungry. "Tell you what," I said. "Let's go out and get something to eat. Then we'll go out and tie one on."

"Rooms, I'm not hungry," Gary said. "Just thirsty."

"You're on an empty stomach," I said. "Let's go somewhere nice. We'll have cocktails and wine with dinner, then we'll do the town up right. But you got to get something to eat."

"Don't worry about me, Rooms," he said. "You're a great roomie and I love you. You've been teaching me new things. You've told me about the stars and the planets and I don't believe in Noah's Ark any-more, and you're making a non-believer out of me. I appreciate that, Rooms, but I got to go drinking tonight."

So Gary Bell went drinking, without his roommate. I didn't hear him come in.

There was another somewhat revolting development tonight. Ac-tually it's a continually revolting development that I haven't wanted to admit is happening. The catchers are getting tired of catching me—and scared because the little darling dances so much it not only can strike out a batter but break the catcher's finger. So they've been beefing. The other day Haney went to Sal Maglie and said he believed I was throwing too much. He said he thought it was bad for my arm.

I don't blame Haney. Or Pagliaroni, who doesn't want to catch me either. And I've told them that. I'm liable to take their living away from them. It's like Ranew told me once. "What if I've got to go up there and hit and I've got a bone bruise from your goddam knuckleball? Like you hit me on the knee tonight. It could have been my hand. Then I can't do my job."

I agreed with him, so I went over to Eddie O'Brien and said, "Eddie, old pal, how about you putting on a mask and catching me?"

"It's not my job to warm up pitchers," Eddie said.

"Why not? The bullpen coaches on the other teams warm up the pitchers."

"What if I get hurt?"

"That's a tough thing, Eddie," I said. "If you get hurt it's not as bad as if some other guy gets hurt and can't play when he's needed."

"Oh hell, there's not that much chance of getting hurt," he said. "I've seen guys get hurt on sliders. But if you think I ought to be catching your knuckleball, take it to the manager."

"I don't want to bother him with something so unimportant. It's so small I think it's a decision *you* can make."

"It's not my job."

And that's the way it went.

"As soon as the game is over I'll tell Joe our exact discussion," he said finally.

"Not after a loss," I said.

"If the point has to be brought up, it has to be brought up."

As it happened, I pitched to one hitter, Frank Robinson. He belted a line drive to the centerfielder. So I got out of that.

Then they pinch-hit for me and I felt empty, like a hungry man cut off after his shrimp cocktail. I told Sal I needed a pitching fix and that I was going out to the bullpen to throw. "That's your whole trouble," Sal said. "You're throwing too damn much."

Some trouble, I thought. I've only had one bad outing since I came back from Vancouver. What the hell was he talking about? Except that I knew. I was asking to do something unorthodox, and unorthodoxy does in baseball what heresy does in the priesthood.

I set my bulldog jaw. "I need to throw," I said. "And I'm goin' to throw."

"Oh, crissakes. If you have to throw, go ahead."

But by this time he'd made his point to everybody in the dugout. I was being a weirdo again.

Later on Mike Marshall said that while I was throwing in the bullpen Joe Schultz kept walking down to the end of the dugout to look out at me. He'd come back each time shaking his head. And in the shower after the game Sal was telling the catchers that I was throwing too much. Know something? The catchers agreed.

JUNE
7

This was the big day for the underprivileged kids of Washington, D.C. It was a pretty big day in the life of the Seattle Pilots too.

Breakfast with Mincher, Pattin and Marshall, and of all things, we got to talking about old Guess Who? Not vindictively, you understand, rather the way you talk about something funny that happened last night. Mincher said we were missing something by being out in the bullpen, that Maglie was great in the dugout—especially when Marshall was pitching. "If a guy hits a fastball when Marshall is out there," Minch said, "Sal says, 'Son of a bitch, he's throwing that fastball too much.' In the very next inning a guy will get a hit on a curve ball and Sal says, 'Son of a bitch, why doesn't he go to his fastball more?'"

"I try to sit next to him whenever I can," Mincher said.

At ten o'clock, five of us boarded the bus for Washington: Joe Schultz, Don Mincher, Mike Marshall, Marty Pattin and I. On the bus were six Orioles: the bullpen catcher Charley Lau, outfielders Dave May, Paul Blair and Don Buford, coach Billy Hunter and Jim Hardin, the pitcher.

During the one-hour ride, Joe Schultz was asking around about what kind of deal we were getting into and he found out that we were going to the Sheraton-Park Hotel, where we'd be assigned a playground in which to conduct a clinic. After that we were all going to the stadium for the dedication. "Oh shitfuck," Joe Schultz said. "I didn't think it was going to be like that. Oh fuckshit." He seemed agitated.

At the hotel things seemed pretty well organized. Everybody's name was on a list and they gave out tags and the addresses of the playgrounds and assigned drivers to take us out. Naturally this all took a while and we were standing out in the corridor waiting when Joe Schultz said to Mincher, "Shitfuck, Minch, what do you say? Let's get the hell out of here."

Mincher hesitated for a moment and it was all over. Schultz had his man. "Hell, I'm getting out of here and grabbing a cab," Joe Schultz said.

"Crissakes, don't leave me behind," Mincher said. "I'm going with you."

And the two of them left the hotel and took a cab back to Baltimore.

Ah, shitfuck.

At the end of the day, after the clinics and the elimination races for the kids at the playgrounds and the meet at the Stadium, and after guys like Sam Jones and Red Auerbach and Jim Beatty and a lot of Olympic swimmers and pro-football players had made their little talks and done what they could—little as it was—for the black kids of Washington, D.C., we took the bus back to Baltimore and Mike Marshall said he thought he understood what had happened with Joe Schultz and Don Mincher.

"I could see it coming," Marshall said. "Joe couldn't cope with the situation. He wasn't in charge. He was forced to follow along. It was frustrating to him not to know what the plan was and he's neither intelligent nor competent enough to be at ease with the unknown. That's why he surrounds himself with other people, coaches, who are as narrow as he is. He wants to rule out anyone who might bring up new things to cope with. He wants to lay down some simple rules—keep your hat on straight, pull your socks up, make sure everybody has the same color sweatshirt—and live by them."

And it was obviously true. Like on the bus going to Washington, Joe Schultz and I were sitting across the aisle from each other. I handed him the sports section of the paper and when he was through with it I asked him if he wanted to read the rest of the paper. "Nah," he said. "I don't read that."

There's no comfort for Schultz in the front of a newspaper. When he wants comfort he can get it from somebody like Mincher. I don't think Joe would have gone back to Baltimore alone, and I don't think Mincher would have either. But they gave each other just enough support to do it together. They were less afraid, both of them, of running out than they were of facing this great unknown that involved so many people.

Talking about Joe Schultz reminded Marshall of something that happened the other night. Although we had just blown a game to the Orioles, when Schultz came back into the clubhouse he was smiling. Mike thought that was kind of strange until he heard Schultz say, to nobody in particular, "Lou Brock stole his 25th base tonight. That's 25 out of 25."

And Mike Marshall thought, "My God. The man's living in a dream world. He still thinks he's with the Cardinals."

I had a long talk with Marty Pattin on the bus. He's had a tough, interesting life. He's from Charleston, Illinois, and his mother and father were separated when he was a baby and he was shipped off to live with his mother's folks. He was still a junior in high school when his grandfather died, so he moved into a rooming house and tried to work his way through the rest of high school. It was then he met a man named Walt Warmouth who helped him get through school—not only high school but college. Warmouth owned a restaurant, and Marty worked there and got his meals there, and every once in a while he'd get a call from the clothing store in town and be told he could pick out a suit and a bunch of other stuff and it was all paid for. They never would tell him who had paid, but Marty knew anyway. "The guy was like a father to me," Marty said. "And not only to me. He must have sent dozens of kids through school just the way he did me." Marty has a masters degree in industrial arts, and when he can he likes to help kids. That's why he signed up for the clinic.

What a terribly lonely life Marty must have had. Hell, it was a traumatic experience for me just going away to college and living in a dorm with a bunch of other kids. And here's Marty, still in high school, living in a rooming house. Not only that, but he goes on to become an All-American boy, complete with all the good conventional values. Like he was telling the kids at the clinic that sure it was difficult to throw a ball well or be a good basketball player. It was difficult to do a lot of things, but that they were all capable of doing a lot of difflcult things if they were willing to work hard and practice. I guess he ought to know.

I also thought that what these kids need is not a half-hour of conversation with some big-name guy who's just passing through. What they need is day-to-day attention from people like Marty's grandparents and Walt Warmouth and full-time workers in the ghettoes. And once again I wished I had the guts to chuck baseball and go out and do something for somebody besides myself. And getting mad at myself for *not* being able to do it, I look around for somebody else to blame and I decide, what the hell, one less goddam bomb and we could have somebody working full time in every one of those sixteen playgrounds in Washington they sent us famous athletes to.

It wasn't a half-hour after I got back from Washington that the phone rang in our room. It was Gabe Paul telling Gary Bell that Marvin Milkes wanted to see him.

"Rooms, what do you think it's going to be?" Gary said as he got dressed.

I told him it must be something about the Players' Association. I told him it might be that they found out I was writing a book and they wanted to check with him on how it was coming along. I told him that maybe Milkes was lonely and just wanted somebody to talk to. But we both knew.

Gary was gone only fifteen minutes. When he opened the door he said one word. "Chicago."

To the White Sox, for Bob Locker.

He sat on the edge of the bed and I could see the thoughts racing through his mind. How do I move? What do I do with my car? Who's on that club? Any friends? It's like, I suppose, when you're wounded. You don't know where you've been hit and you have to sit there a minute and feel around to find out just how seriously you've been hurt.

"One good thing," Gary said after a while. "Woody Held is over there. My old roommate."

He thought for a while, then he said, "We just bought a big TV. I'll have to call Nan and tell her to try to bring it back to the store. We sure as hell can't haul it clear across the country."

You worry about the damnedest things

It didn't come as any big shock. Gary hadn't been pitching well and the papers had a lot of rumors about a trade. But I felt particularly close to Gary, because we were roommates and because we spent time to-gether—our wives too—when we were at home. Another thing. Gary was my link to most of the other players. Despite my efforts to be one of the boys, the fact that I was Gary's roommate is what helped most. What-ever the reasons, I felt awkward, empty, not knowing what to say.

Gary took the bus to the ballpark with the team so he could pick up his equipment and say his goodbyes. There was a lot of kidding, of course. That's what you're supposed to do when a guy gets traded. There was a sort of stunned tension underneath, though, because, as Mike Hegan says, "Gary's the kind of guy who's good for a club even when he's not pitching well."

It was still before game time when Gary lifted his big equipment bag and walked down that long corridor from the visiting clubhouse in Baltimore to where the cabs unload. I watched him all the way. He didn't turn back once.

I asked Eddie O'Brien to catch me for a while tonight in the bullpen. Again he refused, and again I got pissed off. Ranew is developing a bone bruise on his hand. Also, I hit him on the knee the other night, so I hate to ask him to catch me. He had to for a while because I warmed up to go into the game. It was one of those safe games—we were behind 10–0. I pitched one inning, threw eight knuckleballs, seven of them for strikes. I struck Buford out on a beauty that went right over the plate, then broke outside. Got the next two guys on a pop-up and soft grounder. After the game no one came over and said I'd been throwing too much.

That was a lot of day today. I'm not sure I can take many like that.

JUNE

8

I grabbed myself by the seat of the pants this evening and marched myself into Joe Schultz' office. "I want to talk to you about my throwing program, Joe," I said. I didn't wait for him to say anything, but plunged ahead. I told him I knew Sal Maglie was telling him I was throwing too much, but that my arm didn't get tired throwing the knuckleball and the more I threw it the better it got.

"You mean I can use you every day?" Joe said.

I thought he knew that. "Hell yes," I said. "You can use me every day and twice on Sunday. But I'm not trying to tell you how to pitch me. All I'm saying is I need to throw."

"Listen, don't worry about Sal," Joe Schultz said. "I let a lot of the stuff Sal says go in one ear and out the other. Don't worry about it. Do whatever you have to do to get ready."

I could've kissed him. I mean there's a man who understands a lot better than I ever suspected. But then he said, "The problem with your knuckleball is that sometimes you can't get anybody out. You're not throwing it for strikes enough."

"Gee," I said boyishly, "I'm surprised to hear you say that. Since I came back from Vancouver there's only been one time I couldn't get anybody out. And that was the other day in Seattle. One bad outing, and I've had fifteen good ones. So far I've come in with fifteen runners on base and none of them have scored. And I'm not walking that many guys."

I think I convinced him.

"Well, you're doing a good job for us," Joe Schultz said. "If you weren't I'd have called you in here. You've helped the team. I'm pleased."

He wasn't going to let me off without some kind of lecture, however. About a week or so ago I'd been warming up for what seemed like an hour and finally put my jacket on and sat down. "Crissakes, don't sit down out there," Sal Maglie had told me. "It looks horseshit when you come into the game."

"But I was ready to pitch," I said. "I didn't have to throw any-more."

"That doesn't matter," Sal said. "Even if you just stand there with the ball in your hand it looks better."

Well, looks count, I decided. Now I was going to get it from Schultz anyway.

"Oh yeah," he said. "For crissakes, when you're warming up in the bullpen and it's in the middle of an inning you might get called in, don't sit down. Crissakes, it looks terrible. Real horseshit."

"Sal told me that," I said. "It was real horseshit. I won't do it any-more."

If I let it go now, I thought, this whole thing will have been wasted. He'll think of it as a time when he called in that joker Bouton to tell him not to sit down in the bullpen when he's supposed to be warming up. So I shifted gears. "About Eddie O'Brien," I said, then quickly explained to him that the catchers were beginning to hurt and that O'Brien seemed like a natural solution. Only he kept saying it wasn't his job.

"Can he catch the damn thing?" Joe Schultz asked.

I said he seemed to catch it okay when we played catch in the outfield. And what the hell, if he misses it, who cares? Wouldn't we rather have him get hurt than Ranew or Pagliaroni?

"All right. I'll talk to Eddie about it," Joe Schultz said.

I can't wait.

During batting practice the Orioles sneaked into our bullpen—word is that it was Eddie Watt and Pete Richert—and deposited three goldfish and a little black fish into our water cooler. They looked very pretty swimming around in our drinking water.

This was in retaliation for Brabender and O'Donoghue going into *their* bullpen the other night and depositing their benches on the roof of their weathershed.

Everybody thought this was all very funny except Eddie O'Brien. "Guess what he said to me," Talbot said. "He said we ought to protest this game to the Commissioner because how could we use the bullpen with fish in our water cooler?"

"He wasn't *serious,*" I said.

"Oh yes he was," Talbot said. "He was until he saw us all laughing. Then he tried to make out he was kidding. But he was serious as hell."

O'Donoghue told a story about the best pep talk a manager ever delivered. This was at Columbus in the International League and Don Hoak was the manager. "Boys, I'm just going to say one thing to you," he said at a clubhouse meeting. He held his thumb and forefinger about an inch apart and up where everybody could see them. "I want to remind everybody that you're just this far away from big-league pussy."

A young girl asked one of the guys in the bullpen if he was married. "Yeah," he said, "but I'm not a fanatic about it."

Mike Marshall said he learned something important tonight. He went to Curt Rayer, the trainer, and asked him to put some hot stuff on his arm. "I think it's a little tired," Marshall said.

It wasn't two minutes later that Rayer was in Schultz's office telling him that Marshall had a tired arm. It was good information. I mean, you know there's always a pipeline on a club. The trick is to find out who it is. When Johnny Keane was manager of the Yankees his spy was Vern Benson, the coach. We called him "Radar" because he always seemed to have an ear in our conversations. O'Donoghue says that in Cleveland it's George Strickland, the coach, who is called Pipeline.

And when I talked to my wife tonight she said the last time the wives got together one of the coach's wives (my wife insists we don't tell which) said some things she probably shouldn't have—namely that Curt Rayer was the guy on the club who was telling Milkes and Schultz which guys stay out late and which guys fool around and which guys spend a lot of time in the trainers room. She also said that there were a couple of deals on the fire, one of them involving Comer and the other Ray Oyler. Now I sort of understand how Milkes and Schultz feel. It's nice to have your own pipeline.

JUNE

9

Detroit

I asked Eddie O'Brien if he'd talked to Joe Schultz recently.

"Yeah," he said. "And I'm not going to be catching knuckleballs. It's not my job."

I was dumbfounded. "Did Joe say that?" I said. In moments of tension my voice has a tendency to rise. I must have sounded like a girl with a short skirt in a high wind.

"Well, I talked it over with the coaches and they agreed that I'm not going to be able to keep my head in the game and check on what's happening in the field and be able to answer the telephone in a split second if I'm spending all my time catching that goddam knuckleball."

"You didn't talk to Joe," I said.

"Well, for a minute. He said I could do whatever I wanted as long as I didn't let it interfere with my job. And I think catching knuckleballs would interfere with my job."

"What job is that?" I said gently. "You haven't *got* a job. All you do is go over to that ballbag and hand everybody a ball and then you sit there and watch the game. When the telephone rings you jump up and tell somebody to warm up. That's your whole goddam job. A monkey could do your job." And as I talked I got angrier. There was a corner of my mind that calmly told me to shut up, but I was able to ignore it. I was having too good a time. "You know what you do on this club?" I continued. "More harm than good. You get guys pissed off at you and you don't contribute a thing."

"We've got trained, professional catchers here," O'Brien said. "They're here to catch and that's their job. I've got my own job and I'm going to do it and that's the way it's going to be for as long as *you'll* be around."

"Oh boy, a threat," I said. "But I got news for you. You're not going to be here too long yourself. You just better hope one of these catchers doesn't get hurt. Because if he does, it's going to be your ass."

211

After the game Sal said, "Joe wants to see you in his office." He meant me.

"Oh, oh," said Brabender, who was standing next to me. "What do you think it is, J.B.?"

"I don't know, Bender," I said.

"I bet you O'Brien went in and told him," Talbot said. Fred was there during my talk with O'Brien, and I'd felt bad about that. Some things should be said in private, but baseball isn't a very private game.

When I walked into his office, Schultz gave me a dirty look.

"What's this about you getting on O'Brien?" he said.

"Joe," I said sincerely, "I've been trying for some time now to work out an arrangement so that the two catchers don't have to catch my knuckleball as often as I have to throw it. They don't like to catch it and I don't blame them. O'Brien should be catching it and he's trying to get out of it."

"Jim, you got to learn to get along with the coaches," Joe said. "If you got any problems with them, you come to me."

"I didn't want to bother you, Joe," I said. "That's why I tried to deal through Eddie. You got enough things on your mind without being bugged about who's supposed to warm up what pitcher."

It was at about this point that Joe Schultz started to smile. I couldn't tell whether he was smiling with me or laughing at me.

"You have to understand about Eddie," Joe said, smiling. "He's been out of baseball for a long time now."

I said I tried to make allowances, but he was exasperating the hell out of me and I still felt he was absolutely wrong, although I felt bad about blowing up.

"Well, we'll see what we can do," Joe said.

For some reason I felt he'd come around to see things my way. When I came out of Joe's office Fred Talbot said, "Did O'Brien tattle on you?"

"Yes." I said. "O'Brien tattled."

And one of these days he *is* going to catch me, and if we're all lucky the worst I'll do is fracture one of his knees.

The great story in the bullpen tonight was about having this chick up in the room and she's saying, "Tell me you like me, please tell me you like me, just tell me you like one thing about me, anything, just one thing you like about me."

"Like you?" the guy says. "I love you."

A pause. And the chick says, "How can you love me? You don't even know me."

Which reminded another guy of the girl in spring training who was stood up by one player, we'll call him Joe, and went out with another instead. At the end of the evening, he finally coaxed her into bed, but not until after she said, "I'm only doing this because I'm in love with Joe."

Which reminded yet another guy about something that happened to him. "Right next to the ball park there was this little gas station," the guy said, "and after the ball game this chick and I parked there in the dark. We were at it hammer and tongs, I guess you could call it, when all of a sudden I see these lights in the rear view mirror. Here comes this big electric utility truck and it pulls up side of us. The driver looks right in on us and says, 'Nice game tonight. Go get 'em tomorrow.' Jesus, I thought he was going to ask me for my autograph."

During the game a guy came down from the stands to the dugout and said to Mike Marshall, "Hey, is Mike Marshall in the dugout? I'm a good friend of his."

"No, he's not down here," Mike Marshall said. "Maybe he's in the bullpen."

The fellow went off to look.

This was the first of three games with the Detroit Tigers and Joe Schultz said, "Let's go get 'em. We're just as good as they are." Can he really believe that?

Joe asked Mincher when he was going to have a meeting to elect a player representative and alternate, and Mincher said we'd have an election for alternate tomorrow, which means he's decided he has inherited the job. Gary didn't work it that way, although he did sort of guide the election. But Mincher isn't taking any chances. I guess he really wants the car that goes with the job. It's a nice car.

Anyway, Kennedy said, "I nominate Bouton," and everybody laughed. I declined on the spot. I refuse to give them another chance not to vote for me.

During infield drill tonight Frank Crosetti yelled, "Thataway. That's the old Rufus Goofus."

Johnny Sain was working with a couple of Tiger pitchers on the sidelines and one of the catchers was Hal Naragon, the bullpen coach. I thought it might be a funny idea to ask Naragon if he had time to catch *me* for a while. On second thought, I don't see why Naragon should think it was funny.

We beat the Tigers 3–2 with two runs in the tenth. Maybe we *are* as good as they are. What happened was that Mayo Smith left a righthander in to pitch to Mincher with two on in the tenth and a lefthander warming up in the bullpen. Mincher knocked them both in with a single. When he got to first base Norm Cash was really boiling. "Crissakes," Cash said. "Mayo Smith has got to be the dumbest manager in baseball."

It was 3–1 when Diego Segui came in. He gave up two singles and a walk and had to be lifted. It was his third-straight bad outing. I think he might be getting a little tired. Gelnar came in with the bases loaded and one out, struck out Willie Horton on four pitches and got Tom Matchick on a grounder to end the game. It was a beautiful exhibition, especially for a guy who hasn't had that much time in the big leagues. Now he'll be the No. 1 righthanded short man while Segui rests up. It was interesting that O'Donoghue went in to face a lefthander and Gelnar came in against a righthander while at no time was I asked to warm up in a tough game. I wonder whether it's my knuckleball or arguing with coaches that counts most.

After the game Joe Schultz said, "Attaway to stomp on 'em, men. Pound that Budweiser into you and go get 'em tomorrow." Then he spotted Gelnar sucking out of a pop bottle. "For crissakes, Gelnar," Joe Schultz said, "You'll never get them out drinking Dr. Pepper."

JUNE
10

I'm pleased to note today that the New York Mets are 28–23 and in second place in their division, and that the New York Yankees are 28–29 and in fifth place in their division. Perhaps justice is about to triumph.

I also note with some puzzlement that the Yankees have bought veteran righthander Ken Johnson from the Atlanta Braves. Ken Johnson is thirty-six years old (I'm thirty) and throws a knuckleball. He has pitched 29 innings this season and so have I. He's 0–1 this season and I'm 1–0. His ERA is 4.9 and mine is 3.8. And I bet they paid more than $12,000 for him.

Bob Locker, who is called "Foot," or "Wall," for obvious reasons, and "Snot" because Mickey Mantle swore he personally had that kind of locker back home, was elected alternate player rep before the game. Mincher announced that as his first move as player rep he had gotten the Pilots to agree to move to a new hotel in Baltimore, from the Belvedere to the Statler Hilton. "A hell of an idea," one of the guys said. "Now my broad is going to be wandering around the wrong hotel."

It was suggested that as Mincher's next move, he arrange to get Marvin Milkes a room in whatever hotel we happen to be staying in. We're all convinced that Milkes never has a room, which is why he's in the lobby all the time, especially late at night.

Talking about his Chicago White Sox days, McNertney said that Eddie Stanky always insisted there was only one excuse for not being in the lineup—if there was a bone showing. Stanky was also responsible for storing the baseballs in a cool, damp place. McNertney: "You had to wipe the mildew off the balls before the game. First you'd take them out of the boxes, which were all rotted away anyway, wipe the mildew off and put them in new boxes. Then you gave them to the umpires and they never suspected a thing."

The idea, of course, is that cold, damp baseballs don't travel as far as warm, dry baseballs, and the White Sox were not exactly sluggers.

The game was lost 5–0. I could stand that. What I couldn't stand was pitching two-thirds of a miserable inning, giving up two runs and leaving the game with the bases loaded. (Fortunately, Bender got the third out without costing me any runs.) My knuckleball was so bad the only thing I could think of was suicide. This was no false sorrow. It was all I could do not to cry. Maybe I haven't been throwing it enough. Maybe I've been throwing too much. Maybe I'm going out of my mind.

I couldn't wait to get back to the hotel and call my wife so she could cheer me up. After I talked to her and the kids I felt better and agreed with her when she said that if I was going to allow myself to get this upset I wasn't getting paid enough. This did not change the nagging feeling that maybe I've lost it for good, that the knuckleball and I have gone our separate ways.

Milkes and Schultz just happened to be sitting in the lobby again around curfew time and Pagliaroni allowed as how he'd give us all the benefit of his experience. "If you're going to be late," he said, "be at least three hours late. Because if you're only an hour late they'll still be around trying to catch you."

At dinner Don Mincher, Marty Pattin and I discussed greenies. They came up because O'Donoghue had just received a season supply of 500. "They ought to last about a month," I said.

Mincher was a football player in high school and he said, "If I had greenies in those days I'd have been something else."

"Minch, how many major-league ballplayers do you think take greenies?" l asked. "Half? More?"

"Hell, a lot more than half," he said. "Just about the whole Balti-more team takes them. Most of the Tigers. Most of the guys on this club. And that's just what I know for sure."

11

In the bullpen it was can you top this on general managers. Bob Locker told this one about a contract argument with Ed Short, general manager of the White Sox. This was after Locker had had his best season in 1967—77 games, 125 innings and a 2.09 ERA. It was a year after Phil Regan of the Dodgers had had his super year—14–1 and a 1.62 ERA—in relief. Short had offered Locker $16,000 and he was asking for $18,000. Short said he was asking a lot and that what the hell, Regan had just signed a contract for $23,000. "If Regan is making only $23,000, then I'm asking too much," Locker said. "You check that. If he signed for $23,000, I'll sign for $16,000."

The next day Short called him and said, "I called Buzzie Bavasi (the Dodger GM) and he told me Regan was making $23,000 this year."

"All right," Locker said. "I'll take the $16,000."

After he signed he got to thinking about it and just for the hell of it he wrote Regan a letter. He asked if Regan would mind telling him about what he had signed for. And Regan wrote back saying he'd signed for $36,500.

"You know, you don't mind a guy deceiving you a little during contract negotiations," Locker said. "You get used to it. They all do it. But when a guy just outright lies right to your face, that's too much."

Brabender told about the generosity of Harry Dalton, the Baltimore general manager. When the minimum salary was raised from $7,000 to $10,000 he was making $8,000 and had a year-and-a-half in the majors. When he went to talk contract with Dalton he was told that he was getting a $4,000 raise to $12,000. He felt pretty good about it—for about a minute. Then he realized that no matter what, his salary would *have* to go to $10,000, so he was therefore getting only a $2,000 raise. Dalton didn't think he'd see it that way.

And O'Donoghue chipped in with the one about Eddie Lopat, when he was GM of the Kansas City A's. O'Donoghue agreed to terms with Lopat over the telephone and went down to spring training. When he got there he was offered a contract for a lot less money. "But you agreed to a different figure on the telephone," O'Donoghue said. By this time, who knows, he may have been crying.

Said Lopat: "Prove it."

This kind of stunt was pulled on several players. It cost Talbot $500. He offered to throw Lopat through a closed window, but it didn't do him any good.

In the end Lopat must have been hurt by all of that. Because now no one will ever forget that when Tony Oliva first came up Lopat's pronouncement was, "The kid will never hit in the big leagues."

Jim Gosger was sent back down to Vancouver. "You know, I didn't think I was that bad a ballplayer," he said. "But they're making a believer out of me."

Probably because we're going to be in New York soon, the conversation was about Whitey Ford and what great stuff he had when he was pitching for the Yankees. Fred Talbot, who came to the Yankees when Whitey was about through and looking for all the little edges he could find, said Ford could take advantage of every little nick on a ball and make it do something, dive or sail or hop or jump. "If Cronin's name wasn't stamped on the ball straight, he could make it drop."

For a long time Whitey got away with throwing a mud ball that was positively evil. Sometimes Ellie Howard would load it up for him by pretending to lose his balance and steadying himself with his hand— while the ball was in it. Ford could make a mud ball drop, sail, break in, break out and sing "When Irish Eyes Are Smiling." Eventually the opposition, particularly Bill Rigney, the manager of the Angels, got wise to him and he had to quit using the mudder.

Then he went to his wedding ring. He gouged such sharp edges into it that we used to kid him about having lost the diamond out of it. He'd scuff up the ball with the ring and make it do all the things the mud ball did, except maybe now the song was different. He got by with the ring for a couple of months until umpire John Stevens, I think it was, or John Rice (for some reason, every time Rice came onto the field, somebody would holler, "What comes out of a Chinaman's ass?") got wise. The ump could have caused real trouble, but he went out to the mound and said, "Whitey, go into the clubhouse. Your jock strap needs fixing. And when you come back, it better be without that ring."

After that, Ellie Howard sharpened up one of the buckles on his shin guard and everytime he threw the ball back to Whitey he'd rub it against the buckle. The buckle ball sang two arias from *Aida*.

JUNE
12

New York

Day off today and into New York for a three-game series starting tomorrow. There is always a flood of remembrances when I come back to New York. Like all the trouble I used to get into with the Yankees. One time nobody in the bullpen would talk to me for three days because I said I thought that Billy Graham was a dangerous character.

This was after he had said that Communists were behind the riots in the black ghettoes. I said that when a man of his power, a man with such a huge following, makes a statement like that, he is diverting attention from the real causes of riots in the ghettoes. As a result he delays solutions to those real problems, and this is dangerous. My heavens, you'd think I had insulted Ronald Reagan.

Another time, I recall, Crosetti and Jim Hegan were reading the paper and complaining about Father Groppi interfering in things he had no business getting involved in and I simply couldn't resist the temptation to let them know that I thought Groppi was doing a fine and courageous thing. As Mort Sahl says, you've got to fight the madness.

It's just the sort of thing I did when I went back to my old high school in Chicago Heights, Illinois, some years ago. I was invited to speak there as a returning hero. One of the things they wanted me to do was help calm some of the racial problems they were having. The principal asked me to speak from his office over the intercom that reaches the kids in all the rooms. I knew what I was expected to say; that students are here to learn and teachers are here to teach and that any feelings they might have, any grievances or problems, should be left outside the school. So let's all work together for a better education. Instead I sat down and wrote that I understood there were tensions within the school and that I recognized that they came about because of legitimate beefs that some of the kids had, and when the principal and the teachers who were there saw it they said, "No, Jim. Maybe you shouldn't, Jim. Why don't you just say hello to the kids and tell them you'll see them at the dinner tonight?" That's as far as I ever got. They told me politely and firmly that they didn't want me telling the kids any of that stuff.

And once at a father-and-son banquet, a kid with long hair got up and asked me what I thought about long hair and sideburns. The man sitting next to the kid was obviously his father and he just as obviously didn't like the long hair. So I said that the thing that disturbs me about long hair is not the fact that suddenly a whole lot of kids in this country decided to let their hair grow, but that a whole nation of adults would let it disturb them to the point where they were ready to expel otherwise excellent students from school simply because of their long hair. I got a big cheer from the kids. The parents sat there with clenched teeth resolving never to invite Jim Bouton again.

It turns out that Pagliaroni is a telescope buff. He has a 300-power telescope at home with which he not only explores the heavens but shoots a little beaver. The only problem shooting beaver with a 300-power telescope, he says, is that the image comes in upside down. He says it's very tough looking through the telescope while standing on your head.

JUNE
13

Getting on the bus to go from the Biltmore Hotel to Yankee Stadium, O'Donoghue said, "Well, boys, here we start our tour of the funny farm." He meant the streets of New York.

Ray Oyler shouted out of the bus to a long-haired guy on the street. "Don't you feel there's something itching you all over?" He got a very big laugh in the back of the bus.

Since we were in New York, the talk turned to sex (the talk also turns to sex in the eleven other American League cities). It was decided that the most interesting offbeat milieu for sex was a tubful of warm oatmeal. So Mike Hegan promptly leaned out of the bus and hollered to a girl walking by, "Hey, do you like oatmeal?"

Larry Haney read a selection from the *New York Post,* a story by Vic Ziegel. "Today Mel Stottlemyre goes after his seventh victory," Ziegel wrote, "and Gene Brabender goes after whatever the Gene Brabenders of the world go after."

Ray Oyler: "Hey Bender. That guy just shit all over you."

Brabender: "Will someone point out that fucker to me?"

Pagliaroni: "He must never have seen you in person, Rooms."

Footnote: Brabender beat Stottlemyre 2–1.

JUNE
14

Fifth inning and we're down 3–2. Bases loaded, nobody out. I'm warmed up. I get the signal. I climb into the golfcart that will take me to the mound. Yankee Stadium, and my heart is thumping under my warm-up jacket. It feels like a World Series. As the cart rolls along the clay track in left field I hear the fans saying, "Hey, that looks like Bouton." "Yeah, it is Bouton." My public.

They were out there before the game. When our bus pulled up there must have been 20 kids there chanting, "We want Bouton, we want Bouton." The guys on the bus said I must have been a big man in this town. I said yeah, modestly.

The infield is in as I start to pitch. The knuckleball is working. I get Ken Johnson, the pitcher, on a ground ball to Tommy Harper. But instead of going home with the ball, he goes to second and a run scores.

Roy White pops up. Jerry Kenney grounds out. End threat. None out, bases loaded and they got only one run. Not bad.

In the next inning there are three fly balls, by Bobby Murcer, Joe Pepitone and Horace Clark. Two innings, no runs charged to me. I rated it an excellent performance. Almost as good, we went on to win the game 5–4. Fritz Peterson said afterward I should have been given credit for the win because when the Yankees got only one run out of that situation, the game was turned around. Fritz Peterson is a nice man.

JUNE
15

Today in the visiting dugout at Yankee Stadium, Joe Schultz said to nobody in particular: "Up and at 'em. Fuck 'em all. Let it all hang out."

I pitched against one hitter in the game, Jimmy Lyttle. Struck him out on five knuckleballs. Nothing to it.

I wonder how the Yankees feel now about picking up Johnson.

On the plane from New York to Milwaukee, where we play the White Sox a game tomorrow, the stewardesses (we call them stews) were droning about fastening seatbelts. "Fasten your seatbelt," Fred Talbot said. "Fasten your seatbelt. All the time it's fasten your goddam seatbelt. But how come every time I read about one of those plane crashes, there's 180 people on board and all 180 die? Didn't any of them have their seatbelts fastened?"

People are always asking me if it's true about stewardesses. The answer is yes. You don't have to go out hunting for a stew. They stay in the same hotels we do. Open your door and you're liable to be invited to a party down the hall. They're on the road, same as we are, and probably just as lonely. Baseball players are young, reasonably attractive and have more money than most men their age. Not only that, baseball players often marry stews—and the stews know it.

Baseball players are not, by and large, the best dates. We prefer *wham, bam*, thank-you-ma'am affairs. In fact, if we're spotted taking a girl out to dinner we're accused of "wining and dining," which is bad form. It's not bad form to wine and dine an attractive stew, however. A stew can come under the heading of class stuff, or table pussy, in comparison with some of the other creatures who are camp followers or celebrity-fuckers, called Baseball Annies. It is permissible, in the scheme of things, to promise a Baseball Annie dinner and a show in return for certain quick services for a pair of roommates. And it is just as permissible, in the morality of the locker room, to refuse to pay off. The girls don't seem to mind very much when this happens. Indeed, they seem to expect it.

In Chicago there's Chicago Shirley who takes on every club as it gets to town. The first thing she does is call up the rookies for an orientation briefing. She asks them if there's anything she can do for them, and as the ballplayers say, "She can do it all." Chicago Shirley says that Chicago is a great place to live because teams in both leagues come through there. She doesn't like to miss anybody.

JUNE
16

Milwaukee

In the Milwaukee clubhouse there's a sign that reads: "What you say here, what you see here, what you do here and what you hear here, let it stay here." The same sign hangs in the clubhouse in Minneapolis. Also, I suppose, in the CIA offices in Washington. If I were a CIA man, could I write a book?

Steve Barber has been placed on the disabled list, although there's nothing wrong with his arm, just a little stiffness. The three weeks on the list will give him a chance to work it out.

Pitched an inning-and-two-thirds against the White Sox and gave up one hit, no runs, no walks. There was one strikeout. That's three good outings in a row since I last wanted to commit suicide. This might be a good time to ask Joe Schultz for a start again. He may not be much for the underprivileged, but I'll try anyway.

JUNE
17

Chicago

More examples of how easy it is for this veteran righthander to get into trouble. Yesterday a clubhouse meeting interrupted a chess game Mike Marshall and I were playing and during it we both stole glances at the board. Pretty soon, Ron Plaza was giving us some hard stares. Afterward I found out that when I didn't show up in the outfield quick enough for Crosetti after the meeting, he sent Plaza down to the clubhouse to see if I was still playing chess.

And today, I managed to let it slip my mind that we were playing a twi-night doubleheader. I strolled out to catch the bus at a quarter to five and no bus. Panic set in. All I could think was that we were playing another game in Milwaukee and how the hell would I get there in time. I dashed back to my room for my itinerary, and that, of course, explained it all. So I got to the park at five-thirty, a half-hour before gametime, and this time they weren't quite so friendly about it all. Hegan tried to help. "Quick, dress in your locker," he said, "and maybe they won't notice you're late." It didn't work, largely because when O'Donoghue spotted me in there he said in a loud voice, "Well, look who's here." Then Talbot, trying to be funny, stood in front of my locker with his hands on his hips and said, "Where in the hell have *you* been?" I made shushing motions at him but he said, "I'm telling." And he pranced down to where the coaches were sitting and said, "Hey, Sal, was Bouton out there during infield practice?" With friends like Fred Talbot I'm not sure you need any enemies.

Mike Marshall asked Merritt Ranew to catch him a while in the bullpen and in no time the phone was ringing. It was Sal Maglie telling him never, never, *never* to throw without permission. Later on Marshall heard Sal telling Ranew never to warm up any pitcher unless instructed to do so by Sal himself. Then Ranew must have said something about the way Marshall had been pitching, because Sal said, "He always looks good in the bullpen."

I'm not the only one who gets into trouble. But this business about asking permission to throw sounds ominous for the knuckleballer.

One of Marty Pattin's friends or relatives from downstate Illinois sent him a big box of cookies and he put them out on the table before the game. "Let's get to these cookies," Joe Schultz said. "They came all the way from southern Illinois."

Sitting at the table at the time was one of the young clubhouse boys, and he was reading a high school biology book. Joe peered over his shoulder for a while and then said, "Hey, Bouton, this is something that might interest you. A book about human tissues. Real scientific. Hey, look, they even got a picture of a cunt."

As we stood there, laughing helplessly, he added, "And don't forget, boys, pound those cookies into you."

John Kennedy flew into a rage at Emmett Ashford over a called strike and was tossed out of the game. Still raging, he kicked in the water cooler in the dugout, and threw the metal cover onto the field. Afterward we asked him what had gotten into him. He really isn't that type. And he said, "Just as I got called out on strikes, my greenie kicked in."

One of the guys asked Curt Rayer if he had any greenies available and he said no, he wasn't allowed to dispense them. "But I'd like to know who's taking them." This confirmed the feeling that Curt is selling information.

John McNamara, the equipment manager, is the sort who gets along well with ballplayers, but he's been told—warned in fact—not to hang out with us. I guess they think we can be easily corrupted, although I suspect we could corrupt Mac quicker than vice versa. Anyway Mac was standing in the hotel lobby the other night and Curt said, "Where you going, Mac?"

"To bed," Mac said.

Ten minutes later the phone rang in McNamara's room. It was Rayer. "Just wanted to see if you made it to your room all right," Rayer said.

The only thing that makes any sense, Mac said, is that Curt was checking up to see if he'd sneaked out with any players.

Also checking up on us, we're certain, is Marvin Milkes personally. The other night Talbot and Oyler came in a little while after curfew and there was Marvin in the lobby. "Good evening, Marvin," one of them said, cool.

"Good evening," said Marvin, just as cool. "See you in Seattle." Which means fine city.

Had dinner with Mike Marshall in a place called Cafe Bohemia. It's one of the few restaurants in America that serves what can accurately be called exotic food—like lion, tiger, hippopotamus and elephant steaks. Also buffaloburgers, which is what Mike had. I ordered elk steak. In the next room there were the coaches. Mike and I speculated on what Eddie O'Brien would order. I said a steak—beefsteak. Marshall said fried chicken. We were both right. He ordered lambchops.

JUNE
19

We got to talking about Marvin Miller. Pag said that when he was the player rep in Pittsburgh John Galbreath, the owner of the club, had a heart-to-heart talk with him about Miller. Galbreath said Miller would be bad for baseball.

"It just shows how out of touch these guys are," Pag said. "After his long heart-to-heart talk I had to tell him it was too late. Miller had already been signed."

There had been, by the way, a concerted effort to stop the players from hiring Miller. The St. Louis players were told by the front office, for example, that of all the candidates for the job Miller would be the worst choice. They voted for him unanimously.

My own mind was made up about Miller when Joe Reichler put his arm around me and solemnly warned me to be "very, very, *very* careful about this guy Miller."

Then there's this. Soon after Miller was elected to run the Players' Association, Joe Cronin, president of the American League, put his arm around him and said, very earnestly, "Young man (Marvin was forty-nine), I've been in this game a long time now, and I've learned something that I want you to think about. Players come and players go, but owners will be here forever, and don't forget it."

Locker said he understood very well why the owners get so mad at Miller. He said it was because Miller never lets up. "If he has a point he jumps on them with both feet and never gets off," Locker said.

I couldn't help saying that was fine with me. I told Locker that Miller isn't doing any more than any lawyer would do in the same situation and that the problem was not Miller, but the owners, who were so used to having things their way, getting away with technicalities, pushing things on us, that they were now affronted when all Miller was doing was his job. I'm not sure he understood.

Pag also said that he nurses a grudge against Bowie Kuhn, our new Commissioner. He remembers when Kuhn was the owners' rep and when we submitted a proposal to raise the minimum salary from $7,000 to $10,000, he waited six months before he answered. And then it was at a meeting and what he said was, "Oh yes, we've heard something about that. Just what are the details?"

Okay, so he was the owners' Marvin Miller. Now I'm glad *we* got one.

Broke bread with Gary Bell and he was feeling much down. He said he hadn't been able to find his rhythm and that he was afraid he'd lost it altogether. Gary said Ray Berres was a good pitching coach, but that nothing could help him anymore and he was terribly worried about his future. Not only that, his wife was still in Seattle and he hadn't been able to find a place in Chicago that wasn't crazy expensive, and all in all it was depressing.

Mike Marshall and I talked about the possibility of becoming room-mates, and he said he hesitated to because we'd probably have to take too much crap from the players and coaches—two kooks rooming together. And if there was crap, he said, he'd probably blow up. "I remember the time you were nominated for alternate player representative and got only one vote," he said. "If that happened to me I'd stand up and say, 'Fuck all you guys.' I mean, here you were obviously better qualified to do the job than anybody else and you get one vote. To me that's sheer stupidity and I couldn't let them get away with it."

All of which reminded him of a line Sal Maglie delivered tonight. Talbot was pitching and threw a slider that was nailed into the upper deck, just barely foul. So Sal hollers out, "Hey, watch the first pitch on this guy." Now, that's a classic second-guess, because there can no longer be a first pitch to this guy. It's now strike one.

Joe Schultz is not like Sal with the pitchers. Gelnar was telling us about this great conversation he had with Joe on the mound. There were a couple of guys on and Tom Matchick was up. "Any particular way you want me to pitch him, Joe?" Gelnar said.

"Nah, fuck him," Joe Schultz said. "Give him some low smoke and we'll go in and pound some Budweiser."

Seattle

At the meeting before the twi-nighter against Kansas City, Joe Schultz asked if anybody knew anything about John Martinez. Silence. "Well," said Joe Schultz, "we'll just zitz him. Up and at 'em men, and let's win two tonight." One of these days I'll find out how to "zitz" a guy. It sounds like a valuable pitching weapon.

Right after that I ran into Sal Maglie and, because I'd been pitching a lot lately, I felt I ought to tell him that I wasn't tired. Rather than just say I was ready to pitch, old stonehead here said, "Sal, I could pitch both ends of this doubleheader if you need me."

And Sal Maglie said, "Let's get one first."

I had broken a baseball taboo. You're not supposed to talk of winning two games. You should only be thinking of the first game, the big one, the one you play today after putting your pants on one leg at a time. If you're thinking about the second game, you can't be concentrating enough on the first game. Got it? Which is why I thought it sweet of Joe Schultz to tell us to go out there and win two—and pound some Budweiser.

Today the Seattle Pilots enjoyed one of their finest hours. We pulled off one of the great practical jokes of all time. The victim was Fred Talbot. Chief perpetrator, as the police like to say, was his roommate, Merritt Ranew. But we were all aiders and abettors.

When Talbot arrived at the ballpark a uniformed policeman handed him a letter. He sat down to read it in front of his locker. We all knew what it was; a legal document written by a local lawyer friend of Ranew's that announced a paternity suit against Talbot by an anonymous girl in New York. A paternity suit is only somewhat worse than being accused of murder. No matter how innocent you are, you lose. Who wants to win a paternity suit?

Business in the clubhouse seemed to be normal, but in fact everybody was watching Talbot. He opened the letter, looked at it, put his head down, looked at the floor for a while, gazed up into the air, shook his head slowly from side to side, started to read the letter again. Then he folded it, put it back in the envelope, tossed it onto the shelf in his locker, lit a cigarette and stared around the room. The expression on his face was one of shock and disbelief.

Meanwhile everyone in the clubhouse was biting his lips, trying not to laugh. Talbot stomped out his cigarette, reached up into his locker, opened the envelope and read the letter again, as though he was hoping it would say something different this time. Finally, after he'd devoured both pages, put them back in the envelope and thrown it on the floor of his locker, Brabender felt he had to tell him it was a joke. He might have slashed his wrists. "Some joke," Talbot said. "Why didn't you just send me a telegram telling me my kids had been burned to death?" While Talbot then looked around trying to figure out who would do such a terrible thing to him, there were, among others, the following remarks:

Tommy Davis: "I didn't think you caucasian guys could get any whiter."

Ray Oyler: "You couldn't have pulled a needle out of his ass with a tractor."

Finally Talbot decided that it was Marshall and I who had sent the letter. Of course. Fortunately we were able to convince him he was wrong. I wouldn't want to fight him. As far as he's concerned the Marquis of Queensberry is some fag hairdresser.

JUNE
21

Gene Brabender went all the way tonight and pitched a beautiful game. He had a no-hitter going for six innings. One of the nice things about it was that he gave the bullpen the rest it needed. I've pitched in four- or five-straight games now (my outings are beginning to blur together in my mind) and although I like the work, I liked the day off too. My earned-run average is down to 3.45. There are only four guys ahead of me in ERA. I wonder if anybody is thinking of giving me a start.

Another way Mike Marshall gets into trouble. He has conversations with Joe Schultz, such as:

"I went to him and said, 'Joe, what should I do in a situation like this? I started on Monday. On Tuesday I threw on my own. I pitched two innings in Wednesday's game. Then you had me warm up three times on Thursday. The first time I felt all right. The second time I felt a little tight. The third time my arm was tired and stiff and I wasn't effective.' All the time I'm talking, Joe doesn't look at me, only at the floor. Suddenly he looks up and says, 'You shouldn't have thrown on your own on Tuesday.'

"So I said, 'Well, yes. But the point is that I wasn't ready to pitch on Thursday. Now, what should I do in such a situation? Should I call down from the bullpen and tell you, or should I let you put me into the game knowing I wasn't going to be effective? It doesn't matter to me. I'll go out there and pitch no matter how tired my arm is. But I don't want to hurt our chances of winning. What do you think, Joe?'

"At that point Joe turned his back and walked away."

JUNE
22

In the rain the little Seattle clubhouse takes on an aura of great intimacy. The talk flows freely and takes in everybody. It's like sitting around in somebody's living room. Tonight we got into the Pilots' yearbook and we kidded each other about what it said in there about us.

Fred Talbot read out loud that when John Kennedy was in high school he was used for late-inning defense, which is funny because most guys in the big leagues were superstars in high school. Talbot then composed a last line for Kennedy's career. "Also has been known to pop a greenie." (Which reminded Wayne Comer that rainy days were sure tough on greenie-poppers. You never know whether to pop.)

Gene Brabender's biography noted that he was an outstanding athlete at Black Earth, Wisconsin. I wondered what the school song was there. "Black Earth, we love you, hurrah for the rocks and the dirt." Someone else suggested that Brabender had probably made the Future Farmers of America All-America football team.

Mike Hegan had made the All-Catholic High School baseball team and said that Jim Bouton had probably made the All-Agnostic High School team.

"Hey, Fred, how come you never went to college?" said Ray Oyler after reading that Talbot had received several football-scholarship offers.

"You ever hear of an entrance examination?" I said and was rewarded with a dirty look from Talbot.

And Hegan said, "Here's one for Oyler. Now taking correspondence courses for his high school diploma."

JUNE
24

For a while I was getting almost no work at all. Now I'm getting plenty. I've been in 29 games and about eight of our last ten. But I suddenly realized *I never get in at crucial times*. I'm never in there if it's close and we have a chance to win. No wonder I have 29 appearances and only one win and one save.

Today there was a perfect example of what I mean. We're playing a doubleheader against Chicago and in the first game Timberlake (even he gets a start) is taken out in the second inning, losing 4–0, bases loaded, two out. I come in and get the first hitter I face on a fly ball. I then get the next nine-straight hitters, three scoreless innings. Now we've tied it at 4-4 and I come out for a pinch-hitter. We end up losing 6–4.

In the second game we're losing 4–2 in the fifth and O'Donoghue's in there, pitching in relief of Talbot. They let O'Donoghue bat for himself in the fifth even though we're two runs down, which I don't understand at all. Anyway he's out. Somebody gets a base hit and Comer hits a home run. Now if somebody had batted for O'Donoghue, we might have gotten three runs instead of two. Instead we have a tie game and O'Donoghue is still pitching. Pretty soon they're ahead of him 5–4 and then 6–4. And when we tie it at 6–6, who goes into this critical situation? The knuckleball kid? Nah. Diego Segui. He's in trouble right away with a walk and a base hit, but he gets out of the inning. By this time I'm warming up. But do they take him out? Nope. So he gives up a home run. Do they take him out now? Nope. Not until he gives up a double in the ninth. *Then* I go in. I need one out, I get it. One third of an inning. And we lose 7–6. I never got a real chance to save either game, and if I had we might have won both. I think I'll go bite Sal Maglie on the leg.

JUNE
25

I read in the paper today that Richie Allen, who has left the Phillies, says he wants to be traded and will not play for them next year. Then I heard Van Patrick on the air complain that baseball ought to have some recourse against a player who simply walks out on a team during the season. Bullshit, I thought to myself, gently. Here's one of the few cases where a baseball player has enough courage or money or both to tell baseball to take its one-sided contract and shove it. How many times does a ballclub release a player without a thought to his future? The players have zero recourse, but Van Patrick wants to think up another weapon for baseball.

I've admired Richie Allen from afar ever since his second year in the majors when, after a great rookie season (.318, 125 runs, 13 triples, 29 home runs and 91 RBIs—I looked it up) he demanded a large salary, $50,000 or $60,000 and said he wouldn't play unless he got it. Philadelphia must have thought he meant it, because he got it. (I wonder if they told him there was a club rule against quadrupling salaries.)

The minute somebody refuses to work for somebody else at a particular wage, the onus, in the public mind, is on the person who chooses not to do the working. I'm not sure why this should be, but it is. Like the lady in my Wyckoff, N.J., bank who said to me during a plumbers' strike, "Well, they don't *have* to be plumbers if they don't like it." She probably thinks, well, Allen doesn't *have* to be a baseball player if he doesn't like it. Sure, he can always be vice-president of the Wyckoff, N.J., bank.

In the bullpen tonight Eddie O'Brien said he'd recommended me for a start if things get tight in the next week or so, especially with Timberlake going into the army for six months. Eddie O'Brien. How about that? Suppose he thinks that if I get a start I'll expose myself?

Hy Zimmerman, sportswriter, was around looking for a story and I said I had a good one for him.

"Of the 29 appearances I've made this year," I said, "how many times have I done well, and how many poorly?"

"Cheez, I don't know," Zimmerman said.

"I've done well 24 out of 29 times," I said. "I've had four bads and one fair. All the rest were either good or excellent."

"You know, cheez, I didn't realize that," Zimmerman said.

"Do you happen to know what my earned-run average is since I've come back from Vancouver?"

"No, I don't."

"I didn't think you did. It's approximately 2.6542."

"Cheez, is it that good?" he said, reaching for a notebook.

"Right. And do you know how many runners have been on base when I've come in and how many have scored?"

"No, I don't."

"There were 28 runners on when I came in and only 6 scored."

"Cheez, I didn't realize you were doing that good."

"I know you didn't. And as soon as I win a ballgame here you're going to come around and say, 'Hey, great. When did you put it all together?' I just want you to know that every day I'm putting it together a little bit more."

When all of that gets into the paper I hope the coaches and the manager don't think I said those things only for their benefit, although I really did.

I'm taking the family to Disneyland on our next trip to Anaheim and I asked Marvin Milkes if he minded if I stayed with them in a hotel next to Disneyland rather than the team hotel. Actually, the guys prefer that you don't bring your wife on road trips, and I thought this would be less awkward.

Milkes said I couldn't. "Nothing personal," he said. "You're doing a good job for us. If you weren't, you wouldn't be here. I wouldn't want you to misconscrue [sic! baseball fans] my meaning on this. It's just a club rule and it has to be followed."

The reason for the rule, he said, was that he remembered when he was with the Angels and the Yankees used to come into town and stay out all night at those Johnny Grant parties. (Grant is what they call a radio personality in Hollywood.)

"But Marvin," I said. "The way I remember it we would stay out all night and then beat you guys anyway. I remember having a particularly good time at a Johnny Grant party and then pitching a two-hitter against you."

In fact I remembered more than that. I remembered doing a strip to my underwear to the theme song of *Lawrence of Arabia* and then treading water in the swimming pool with a martini in each hand and *then* going out and beating the Angels the next night. In fact, every time I hear the *Lawrence of Arabia* music my mind still snaps.

"Yeah, well, maybe," Marvin said. "But I could always count on you guys keeping late hours and I want to crack down on it."

"I'm more likely to go to bed early if my family is here than if I'm with the guys in the team hotel."

"That may be true. But we're going to stick to this rule. As I said, don't misconscrue it. Nothing personal."

Having lost one argument, I brought up another. I had bought myself some Gatorade, which is supposed to restore the minerals and salts you lose through perspiration. I bought it because a lot of athletic teams use it and it's got to be better than Coca-Cola. I asked McNamara to buy some for the clubhouse. He said he didn't know where to get it so I volunteered and bought ten cases, which cost $50. When I asked McNamara for the money he suggested that since Gatorade was sort of medicinal, the club should pay for it. What do you say, Marvin old boy?

"I'll have to think about it," he said. "I'll taste it."

"Try it with vodka," I said.

In the bullpen tonight Jim Pagliaroni was telling us how Ted Williams, when he was still playing, would psyche himself up for a game during batting practice, usually early practice before the fans or reporters got there.

He'd go into the cage, wave his bat at the pitcher and start screaming at the top of his voice, "My name is Ted fucking Williams and I'm the greatest hitter in baseball."

He'd swing and hit a line drive.

"Jesus H. Christ Himself couldn't get me out."

And he'd hit another.

Then he'd say, "Here comes Jim Bunning, Jim fucking Bunning and that little shit slider of his."

Wham!

"He doesn't really think he's gonna get me out with that shit."

Blam!

"I'm Ted fucking Williams."

Sock!

Today Joe Schultz said, "Nice going out there today, Jim."

The only thing I'd done all day was warm up.

"Joe, I had a fantastic knuckleball today," I said. "Just fantastic."

"Did you?" Joe Schultz said. "Did you have the feel of it?"

"I sure did."

Whereupon Joe Schultz grabbed his crotch and said, "Well, feel this!"

JUNE
26

It's true that Joe Schultz does seem to have a firmer grip on reality than other baseball men. Example: Joe got into a terrible argument with an umpire at home plate about a checked swing and when it was over he stormed back to the dugout, still muttering. Just before stepping into the dugout, though, he spied a blonde sitting in the first row and said, "Hi ya, Blondie. How's your old tomato?"

O'Donoghue was saying in the bullpen today that he hopes he's not asked to pitch because he has this stiffness in his arm. It's not sore, just stiff. This is baseball newspeak. Nobody has a sore arm anymore, not O'Donoghue and not Steve Barber.

Another way kook Bouton convinces people he's a kook. When I come into the game in a bunt situation I like to check the turf around home plate to see how firm it is and whether I can field a bunt, stop, turn and make a throw without falling on my face. So I walk in and stomp around for a while, and a couple of times I've looked into the dugout and seen Joe and Sal giggling at each other. It's the exact same reaction Mike Marshall gets when he decides to trot in from the bullpen instead of walking in the way everybody else does. In baseball the only thing that's really changed in a hundred years is the attitude toward beards.

There was a meeting in the clubhouse on the new contract negotiations between the players and owners, which should be taking place soon but probably won't until after the season. I suggested that if you apply the standard-of-living index to the base of $7,000 that was set up 11 years ago, you come up with about $14,000 or $15,000 as a minimum instead of the present $10,000. So somebody said, "Why not $20,000, and everybody broke up laughing. But when you really think about it, $20,000 is not out of line at all. Consider how hard it is to make a big-league club. If only the same proportion of the population were accepted as lawyers, the going starting salary would be a lot higher. When you overcome odds of better than 10,000 to 1 you ought to collect big.

Steve Hovley has been called up. Old Tennis Ball Head hasn't had a haircut since he left. Which means Joe Schultz had four comments to him the very first day.

"Where's your barber?"

"Don't you need a haircut?"

"You're getting awfully mangy-looking."

"Are you sure you don't need a trim, Steve?"

Hovley explained to me why he had started out with such a tight crewcut and then let it grow. "In the spring I cut all my hair the same length—short." Hovley said. "After that I simply chose not to be selective against any of the hairs. Most people cut their hair around their ears and not on top. That doesn't seem fair. I want to let each hair do its own thing. Now everybody is upset—not about these hairs on top, just the ones around my ears and on the back of my neck. Those are the offending hairs. But they don't offend me."

Just before Hovley rejoined the club we were talking about him in the bullpen. I count him as one of the most intelligent men, the closest to a real intellectual, I've ever met in baseball. So I volunteered that he was a pretty bright fellow. "Yeah, but does he have any common sense?" Talbot said.

"I know just what you mean about not having any common sense," O'Donoghue said. "He doesn't."

I asked him what he meant by that.

"Well, one time we were sitting in a restaurant," O'Donoghue said, "and Hovley was walking down the street with a ski cap pulled down over his face and he came past the restaurant and stood outside on the sidewalk peering in at us."

Oh.

Another reason Hovley has no common sense is that he may wear the same shirt five days in a row and the same sportscoat and he doesn't dress the way most players do.

Sometimes I think that if people in this little world of baseball don't think you a little odd, a bit weird, you're in trouble. It would be rather like being considered normal in an insane asylum.

JUNE
27

Anaheim

During a radio interview before the game today, the manager was asked what the secret of the success of the Seattle Pilots had been so far and Joe Schultz said, "Well, we just come out and go to work and play ball. Use a little common sense, so to speak."

Going to Disneyland, I remembered going to the World's Fair in New York a few years back. Driving one of those little tour buses there was Dusty Rhodes, the guy who in 1954 helped win a pennant and a World Series pinch-hitting for the Giants. Dusty Rhodes, one of my heroes, wearing that blue uniform and driving a bus. I wondered how he'd feel if somebody hollered from in back of the bus, "Hey, bussy, there's a dog pissing on your rear wheel"—which is what we've said many times to a guy who wasn't driving the bus fast enough. Maybe Dusty said it too one day, a long time ago.

I am glad to note that Tommy Davis has become upset about our autograph rule. He has decided that to tell the kids that it's club policy not to give them is to alienate future fans. Which was my point when it first came up at a meeting. Hardly anybody listens when Bouton talks. But I hope they'll listen to Tommy Davis.

At our meeting tonight Joe Schultz said, "Now, this is for you new guys. The curfew is two-and-a-half hours after the ballgame is over at night and midnight after a day game. And watch yourself. The brass is here. They're all here this time."

"What about the night before an off-day?" I said. "Can we stay out later than twelve if we don't have a game the next day?"

Joe put his hands on his hips and smiled. "Jesus Christ, Bouton, you're always coming up with something tricky," he said.

Most of the guys laughed and I never did get an answer from Joe.

"I don't know why everyone laughed," Brabender said later. "I thought it was a good question."

"Yeah, but Jim asked it," Marshall said. "So we're all supposed to laugh. You should have asked it, Gene. Then we would have gotten an answer."

"Sorry, fellas," I said. "I didn't realize I was going to hurt our chances."

Steve Hovley got three hits tonight and nobody said a word about his hair. I suggested to him that the number of comments he gets will, from now on, vary inversely with the number of hits he gets. And if he ever stops hitting he may even have to get a haircut.

Mike was throwing in the bullpen and Eddie O'Brien asked Sal Maglie how much Mike should be throwing. Said Sal: "Tell him to throw until just before he comes."

JUNE
28

Lefty Phillips has replaced Bill Rigney as manager of the Angels. I wish Rocky Bridges, the coach, had gotten the job. He's familiar with the personnel over there and he was a great minor-league manager. He was successful, colorful, funny and the players loved him. A minor-leaguer named Ethan Allen Blackaby told me about the time Bridges gave the signs from third base while standing on his head. Blackaby promptly stood on his head in the batting box so he could get the sign properly.

I told the story to Pag. He said he'd love to see it but that baseball would consider it, well, sacrilegious. "Baseball wants color," he said. "But not that much."

"By 'color,'" I said, "they mean they want you to wear your cap at a jaunty angle."

Tonight we had a three-run lead in the fourth and the starting pitcher got into a little trouble, so Sal Maglie got on the telephone to the bullpen. "Anybody around here see a phone booth?" I said. "This looks like a job for Superknuck."

The call was for Segui. Good grief, how foolish can I be? How could it possibly have been me? We weren't behind.

I note today that the Topps Gum people have doubled their fee to players, from $125 to $250, for using their pictures on bubblegum cards. They explained that they were able to increase payments because of increased revenues. It had nothing to do with Marvin Miller and the players going to Topps and demanding the increase. Topps just happens to have a big heart. Yeah surrre.

And speaking of big hearts, a hearty mention here of Frank Scott, the player agent. During one of my big years with the Yankees, Scott called me and asked if I wanted to give a little talk before an IBM group for a fee of $300. "Delighted," I said. I made the speech and collected the fee from Scott. Then my brother Bob, who worked for IBM at the time, called me and said, "Congratulations."

"Thank you," I said. "What for?"

"Your speech to IBM."

"It was nothing."

"Well, $500 is good pay for nothing."

"Three hundred."

"Five hundred, babe. I got it from the guy who ran the dinner."

"Oh."

John McNamara is asking Don Minchet about Hovley. "Doesn't he need a haircut, Minch?" he says.

"I can't say anything about anyone's hair, needing a haircut like I do," Mincher says.

"Well, I think it looks horseshit," Marty Pattin says.

Moments later, perhaps feeling bad about his comment, or perhaps wishing to stick the needle in further, Pattin approaches Hovley and says, "I don't care how long you wear your hair, Hovley. You can wear it down to your ass as far as I'm concerned."

Nah. That would look horseshit.

JUNE
29

Today Joe Schultz said to Steve Hovley: "Don't you think you ought to at least get a *trim?*"

Hovley thought it over for a while and said, "I guess so."

Actually, Hovley said later that he hasn't made up his mind and doesn't feel he committed himself by what he said to Joe: "It's interesting," he said, "that no one really talks to me about the length of my hair. All they do is drop remarks. I guess that's because no one wants to get into a discussion."

If they do they have to listen to *your* position, consider it, come up with an answer. But by just dropping a remark they can get in and get out with no harm done.

On the other hand, there's the Plaza way, which also leads to no discussion. "You better get a haircut," Plaza said to Hovley.

JUNE
30

A note on the complicated life of a moonlighting author. I usually keep my notepaper in the back pocket of my uniform trousers and my pen in my jacket pocket. The reason is that I don't want to be separated from my notes and the jacket is often left on the bench. On the other hand, I don't want my pen with me when I'm pitching because I wouldn't want to fall on it. So today when I went out to the mound I discovered I had my pen in my pocket. I took it out and tossed it behind me on the mound. When the inning was over I went to sit on the bench and Ron Plaza, who coaches at third, handed me the pen. Without comment.

Bobbi and I went to San Francisco with Gus Gil and his wife and we got to talking about what fun it was to be on a baseball team and have the opportunity to listen to coaches and managers at work. Gus said that the other day on the bench they were looking for Mike Marshall, who was back in the clubhouse using the bathroom or something and someone said, "Where the hell is he?" And Joe Schultz said, "He's probably setting up the chessboard."

Another time Schultz said about Marshall, "Lookit. Brains is warming up out there."

Gus also said that when I was pitching, every time I threw a fastball that wasn't hit Sal would tell Joe how much of a help the fastball was. I'm a one-pitch pitcher now, just what I said I had to be and what Sal said I couldn't be. So he covers his early tracks with Joe every chance he gets.

Would you believe the talk in the bullpen was about pitching? At least the second-guessing of coaches and managers *about* pitching. One of the questions I asked was, "Has a good pitch *ever* been hit?" What I meant was that every single time a guy hits the ball it was in the wrong place, or the wrong pitch at the wrong time. Hitters almost never get credit for hitting good pitches. Every breaking ball that's hit "hung." It's a world of second-guessers.

McNertney told a story about Al Lopez when he was managing Chicago. Danny Cater of the A's was the hitter and Tommy John the pitcher. John threw a curve ball that was so low it was going to be in the dirt. He said he went down on his knees to dig it out and as he did Cater reached out with one hand and hit it into left field for a single. When he got back to the dugout McNertney was shaking his head and mumbling about Cater having hit a good pitch.

"It was a high pitch," Lopez said.

"No. If he doesn't swing, it's in the dirt," McNertney said.

"It was right there," Lopez said, holding his hand out thigh-high. End argument.

(Cater, by the way, has the reputation of being able to figure out his batting average to four decimal places on his way down to first base. He's almost as quick as I am figuring out my ERA.)

The second-guess is so ingrained in baseball that you can almost call it a first-guess second-guess. First a manager will say, "For crissakes, if a guy can't hit the curve ball, keep throwing the damn thing until he proves to you he can hit it." Of course, there's a logical converse. You keep throwing the curve ball to a guy and eventually he *will* hit it. And immediately you hear, "Jesus, you can't keep throwing a guy the same thing. He's bound to hit it."

Everybody has stories about that kind of thing. Jerry Stephenson says that over on the Red Sox when Billy Herman was the manager and there was a debate about how to pitch to a hitter, Herman would say, "Fuck him. Give him good stuff."

And that's the catch. You have to have it. And if you do, pitching isn't at all complicated.

Checking out of the hotel, Wayne Comer called for a bell captain to send up a bellhop to pick up his bag. There was no bellhop around, and no bell captain either. So Don Mincher, who happened to be standing there, picked up the phone. When he heard it was Comer, Mincher said, "Now wait a minute. It's about time you guys started carrying your own bags down. All you prima donna cocksuckers are alike, always wanting people to do things for you. Why the hell don't you carry them down yourself?"

Comer didn't even splutter. He slammed down the phone and carried his own bags.

JULY
2

Oakland
In the clubhouse meeting yesterday on the Oakland Athletics Sal Maglie said about Reggie Jackson, "Once in a while you can jam him."

I could just see the situation. Reggie Jackson up. Pitcher throws one high and inside, perfect jam pitch. Jackson leans back, swings and puts it into the right-field bleachers. And Sal screams from the bench, "Not now, goddammit, not now!"

Fred Talbot says that after listening to Sal in these meetings he's decided what kind of pitcher he must have been. "A mother," Talbot said. "A real mother."

Mother Maglie also said in the meeting that one way to handle Jackson was not to throw him any strikes. So Jackson hit three homers in the game, and after each one someone said, "There's one of those goddam strikes."

After Reggie Jackson's third home run, O'Donoghue said, "I'd have to plunk the man."

And I said, indignantly, "John, how the hell can you throw at the guy? He's just doing his job. He has no comeback at you if you get him out. So why should he have to risk getting injured just because he's successful?"

"I wouldn't mean to hurt the guy," O'Donoghue said. "I don't mean throw at his head. Just let him know that he should have some fear up there."

"What if you hit him in the kneecap or something?" I said. "You don't know how good your control is going to be. What if you hit him in the ankle? Or how do you know you're going to hit him just hard enough in the ribs so that you don't break something?"

John's jaw got tight. And he said, "Look, I don't want to argue about it. So we'll leave it at that."

How come nobody wants to argue with me? Can it be because I'm always so right?

Today I asked Joe Schultz for a start. I sat down with him on the bus and told him that I could help the team better if I started. I said I felt that being the ninth man on the pitching staff and being used as the mop-up man didn't help the team much. I reached into my pocket to show him my statistics and Joe Schultz said, "Aw shit. I don't want to see any statistics. I know what's going on out there just by watching the games."

"All right," I said. "I just wanted to show you that I've only walked one man in the last 16 innings and only three in the last 21."

"I know you've been getting it over."

"That's all I wanted to say."

"Well, okay, Jamesy," Joe Schultz said.

Steve Hovley broke up the clubhouse today when he undressed to get into his uniform and underneath his dress shirt he was wearing a Seattle Pilots T-shirt with his name and number on the back. Almost everybody just laughed, but some guys seemed upset—like Fred Talbot and Merritt Ranew.

Out in the bullpen Ranew said to me, "You think Hovley's a pretty smart guy?"

"Yes, I do," I said.

"Do you think wearing a Seattle Pilots T-shirt has anything to do with common sense or intelligence?"

"I don't think so," I said.

"Well, do you think it's very intelligent to wear something that isn't proper?" Ranew said.

"What's wrong with wearing a Seattle Pilots T-shirt?" I said.

At this point, I couldn't hold back and started to laugh.

Ranew sort of waved at me and walked away.

Another Hovley story. He was standing by the clubhouse man's tobacco shelf opening up a can of snuff. (Just wanted to try it, he said later.) Joe Schultz walked by wearing nothing but a towel around his waist and hollered out, "Hey, men, look who's dipping into the snuff." Then he grabbed a paperback book out of Hovley's pocket. It was Dostoyevsky's *The Possessed*. Schultz held the book up in the air and said, "Hey, men, look at this! What the shit kind of name is this?"

By this time there was a group of guys around him looking at the book like a group of monkeys might inspect a bright red rubber ball. Schultz read off the back cover—a sentence anyway—until he got to the word "nihilism." "Hey, Hy," Schultz said to Hy Zimmerman, "what the hell does 'nihilism' mean?"

"That's when you don't believe in nothing," Zimmerman said.

Whereupon Schultz, shaking his head and laughing, flung the book back at Hovley, hitched up his towel and strode off, amid much laughter.

If Hovley weren't 9 for 20 (.450) since he was called up I'd figure him to be back in Rochester in a matter of days.

Afterward Hovley said that this was, of course, anti-intellectualism at work, but that he didn't mind since he counted himself as anti-intellectual too—that is, if by "intellectual" we meant the academic community. Academic people bore him, Hovley said, and that while he wouldn't choose to spend all his free time with Joe Schultz, he rather enjoyed the company of players.

And Mike Marshall pointed out that Joe's act might have been more a tactic than an expression of his real feelings about college types. "You have to keep in mind that Joe's goal is to keep a loose clubhouse and that he uses this as a device to make people laugh," Marshall said. "I'd be careful not to put him down as merely a buffoon."

Well, I don't know. If it *is* an act, he's finding it awfully easy to play.

JULY

4

Kansas City

What could be better than a Fourth of July doubleheader in Kansas City? Anything up to and including a kick in the ass. Kansas City gets hot like few places get hot. The temperature was in the 90s and the humidity was in the 90s and most of us were in a blue funk. Fred Talbot, one of today's starters, was complaining louder than anybody about the heat on the bus, so when we got to the clubhouse a lot of guys came by to say a few words.

"Got to pace yourself today, Fred."

"Don't think about the heat, Fred. Just go out there and go as long as you can."

"Boy, it sure is a hot one today, Fred."

"Fred, why does it have to be you pitching on such a hot day?"

Finally Fred shook his head from side to side and said, "I knew I should have gone to college."

Joe Schultz announced that there were a lot of places in Kansas City that were off-limits because they were hangouts for gamblers. We expected to hear about three or four names. There must have been twenty-five. "Christ, you can save $900 just by drinking in the hotel bar," Ray Oyler said.

What he meant was that the hotel bar is forbidden to us at a penalty of $100. But if we got caught in one of those off-limit places, it would cost $1,000.

It came as no surprise today that Ron Plaza said, at least twice, "Good day to work, men."

It was a terrible day to work. With one pitch I undid all the good work I've been doing for weeks. I gave up five earned runs in a big one and one-third innings. I couldn't get my knuckleball over. I felt uncoordinated on the mound, and I threw one to Gene Oliver with the bases loaded that spun, and he knocked it over the center-field wall. On the bus some son of a bitch asked me if it was the longest home run I ever gave up.

It doesn't seem right that my ERA should have jumped back to 3.75 from 2.95 after only one and one-third innings. I felt so damn depressed after the game that I immediately forced it all out of my mind—all of it. What did you say my name was?

When Joe Schultz came to the mound to take me out of the game I was so angry with myself that all I could think to do was stand there and shout obscenities at the scoreboard. I still don't know if Joe said anything to me or not. I know he waved for a pitcher from the bullpen. The rest was all one dirty word.

Joe was cool enough not to get angry at me or think I was screaming at him. He knew I was just blowing off steam and let me go ahead and do it. There are managers who wouldn't have been so cool.

Mike Marshall and I started rooming together when we got to Kansas City, and in the room tonight we got to talking about the special pressures that are on ballplayers. We wondered what it's like for a guy when baseball is his whole life and he has nothing else, no financial security, no job or profession to fall back on, no real interests. We talked about Fred Talbot saying, "I should have gone to college," and decided that, yes, the pressures on him are worse than the pressures on us.

I know that a guy like Gary Bell felt that pressure all the time. He'd say things like, "Rooms, tomorrow we go to a bookstore and buy some of those real-estate books." Or, "Rooms, if you were in my shoes, what kind of job would you start looking for?" And then, sometimes, after a bad game, he'd sit in the back of the bus with five or six beers in him and he'd mumble to himself, "I don't give a shit. I don't give a shit."

But he did.

JULY
5

Steve Barber says he was watching me closely while I was pitching and thought I'd speeded up my motion too much and that my arm was dragging behind the rest of my body. He thought that if I slowed down I'd be able to get the proper release on the ball. As soon as I could I dashed out to the bullpen and asked Eddie O'Brien to catch a few knuckleballs. He said sure.

This is a new Eddie O'Brien. Since our big blow-up he's become a pussycat. He still doesn't warm me up during the game, but he's been great about catching me at other times and seems to be making an effort to do all the little extras. He even eats candy in the bullpen. No one has called him Mr. Small in a month.

Anyway I concentrated on a slow, easy motion—and, son of a gun, Barber was right. I threw about ten knuckleballs and every one of them jumped all over the place.

Then I got called into the game. The first thing that leaps into your head when you've been going bad is, oh Christ, here we go again. You have to lick this, get it out of your mind or you really *will* go again. Fortunately I was able to get two good innings in. At least now I won't be walking out to the mound with the taste of failure in my mouth.

Today Sal walked over to me, picked up a baseball and showed me the grip he remembered Hoyt Wilhelm using for his knuckleball when he was with the Giants. Here it is, midseason, and that was the first time Sal Maglie said anything constructive to me about pitching. In all this time he's never said anything about my grip, my motion or my release. Zero. Since he seemed interested, I suggested he keep an eye on me when I was pitching and if he thought I was speeding up my motion to let me know. He said he would.

JULY
6

Bat day in Kansas City. All the kids get free bats. Makes it very bad for beaver shooting because there are too many kids, too many bats and not enough beaver. John Gelnar brought a pair of binoculars out to the bullpen and we took turns looking into the stands. Then somebody said that we better not let the umpires catch us with binoculars in the bullpen—they're liable to think we're stealing signs. And I said, "No. If we explain we're shooting beaver, they'll understand." And they would. If there's a baseball universal, that's it.

Pagliaroni says that one of the great things about Gene Brabender as a pitcher is that he's big enough to intimidate hitters with his size. "He looks like if you got a hit off him," Pag said, "he'd crush your spleen."

Flying home from Kansas City we ran into a storm and were bouncing around in the air like a knuckleball. Pagliaroni and I started singing "The Lord's Prayer." "Our Father who art . . . " Suddenly Brabender, who was sitting in front of me, turned around, kneeled on his seat facing us, and, with neck flaming, shook a finger and said, "Now, look. No more of that. I don't go for that stuff, and I'm serious."

When Gene Brabender is serious, everybody is serious. We stopped singing.

After the storm Brabender turned around again and said, "Hey, J.B., I'm sorry I got mad. But that really scares me, especially when it's about the Big Man."

"Bender," I said, "it didn't scare you nearly as much as you scared me."

Right before the plane landed, the guys were telling stories about how much we'd been getting on the road. And as we were getting ready to leave the plane and dash into the loving arms of our waiting wives, Pagliaroni said, very loud, "Okay, all you guys, act horny."

JULY
7

Seattle

Mike Marshall was sent to Vancouver today. I'm having very bad luck with roommates.

I feel a little funny about him getting it because I know his wife warned him right from spring training about getting too closely associated with me. Not that she doesn't like me, but she knew my reputation and was worried about guilt by association. Now he rooms with me three days in Kansas City and gets cut.

Mike was concerned when one of the reporters wrote that he and I play chess on airplanes and sometimes carry the board out of the plane and into the bus without dropping a single piece. He didn't think it helped our images any.

Tonight my knuckleball was so good it was getting by the catcher in the bullpen and going out onto the field.

After the game I was shaving, as it happens, right beside Joe Schultz. "Looks like your knuckleball was jumping all over the place tonight," he said.

"It was a good one," I said. "As good as it was three weeks ago. Lately I haven't been able to throw it that good."

"Why not?" Joe said.

"Well, I kind of lost the feel of it in my hand, but tonight . . ."

At that point Joe Schultz turned his back and walked away.

Jerry Stephenson, who was also shaving, took note of this and said, "Boy, he was really interested."

"Yeah, that'll teach him to start a conversation with me."

It all reminded me of Charlie Maher, my baseball coach at Western Michigan. He was upset when I signed a professional contract and had to drop off the team. When I went back to school after my first season, I ran into him on campus and he said, heartily, "How are you doing, Jim? What kind of year did you have?"

"Not too good," I said. "I broke the thumb of my pitching hand and didn't get to throw all summer long."

And he said, "Good, good. Have a nice fall here in school," and walked away.

JULY
8

By threatening to quit, Mike Marshall has blackmailed the club into sending him to Toledo rather than Vancouver (Toledo is near his home, although not nearly as pretty as Vancouver). Mike willed us his secondhand English racing bike, so we've added it to our collection, which includes a Gary Bell bedroom lamp.

One nice thing about the whole business. Marshall's basic faith in the way the game is run remains unbroken. He gives this illustration. When Joe Schultz told him he was being sent to Vancouver, Mike said, "What about another major-league team? Isn't anybody interested in me?"

Schultz: "We asked waivers, and nobody wanted you."

So Marshall went to see Marvin Milkes and said he was quitting.

Milkes: "We just can't let you go like that. We paid $175,000 for you. We've got to get something for you. Isn't there something we can work out?"

Marshall: "Why don't you just sell me to some other club?"

Milkes: "Well, we've had feelers. But they haven't been for the right price. We couldn't let you go at the waiver price."

Now, some people would call that a contradiction. Others might call it a lie. Mike Marshall called it baseball.

One of our jocko things is to mince around like a fairy, which is pretty funny sometimes, especially while wearing baseball underwear. There is something hilarious about a lumpy, hairy guy trying to act like a queer while wearing the things we wear under a baseball uniform. Take my word.

After a while some of the guys began to walk up to each other and pretend to kiss on the lips. In fact one of them would put his hand on the other's face and kiss the back of it. If you did it fast, it looked like a real kiss.

Then it began to spread. As a gag, of course. You'd be walking down the aisle of a bus and all of a sudden a guy would clamp his hand over your mouth, kiss the back of his hand and continue on down the aisle. It was quite a game. And Gary Bell was a big one for it. So were Mike Hegan and Don Mincher.

Then we got a little drunk on a bus one night and the guys started kissing without bothering to put their hands up. And then *that* became a joke. We'd kid about how many guys had kissed other guys and then there was this little club, and only guys who had kissed and been kissed could be members. At one point I was standing in the clubhouse and John Kennedy came over and said, "Hey, c'mere, Jim, I got to tell you something. A secret." And he puts his face up close to mine and the next thing I knew, kiss! I was a club member. Everybody broke up. Eventually there were, I believe, at least a dozen guys in the club.

On our flight from Oakland to Kansas City, Wayne Comer, who had had a few beers, leaned down over Don Mincher, who was playing cards, and kissed him on the cheek. Wetly. Mincher whirled around and punched him on the jaw, knocking him down and into the aisle. It struck everybody as funny that Mincher, a member of the club, should suddenly get so uppity with a guy we all knew he was very friendly with.

"Wayne, I just had enough," Mincher said. "And I had to haul off and punch you."

Comer was still lying in the aisle feeling his jaw. "Well, that doesn't make you a bad person," he said.

Tonight Comer got his revenge. Mincher was on the postgame radio show because he was the hero of the game. He hit a three-run homer in the first inning, and we won 3–1. The moment Mincher came into the clubhouse, Comer, who by this time was wearing only a jock strap, dirt and no teeth, ran across the room with an insane gleam in his eye, leaped on Mincher's back and kissed him on the ear.

This time Mincher didn't punch him.

Had a spot of trouble with Ranew in the bullpen tonight. He warmed me up when Schultz ordered that I get up early in the game. But later on, when I got up to throw on my own, he let me know his heart wasn't in it. He stuck his glove up at every pitch and if the ball went into it, fine. Otherwise it bounced off and he had to go after it. And he took his time chasing it. If I have to wait a minute or more between pitches I'm not getting anything out of it, and he knows it.

Another gimmick he uses is to throw the ball back to me erratically so I have to scoop it out of the dirt or jump into the air. Or he'll steam it into me until my hand hurts.

The fact that I hurt Pagliaroni's thumb the other day, added to Ranew's obvious reluctance, makes it hard for me to ask anybody to catch me. It's part of the reason, probably, the knuckleball has been so in and out.

Studying my statistics today I note that in the last fifteen days, I've pitched a grand total of six-and-a-third innings. That's an even bigger reason for being in and out. My statistics scream out that I have to work to be effective. But I'm not getting the work. Not even in the bullpen.

Not only that, but Jerry Stephenson is getting a start. Now, I like Jerry, but he was just called up from Vancouver, where he had an 0–3 record and an ERA of 4.78. Here's a guy released by the Red Sox, picked up as a free agent, does poorly in the minors, gets called up and is handed a start. Who's going to get the *next* start? Ray Oyler?

JULY

9

There's a promotion they run here in Seattle called "Home Run for the Money." If a listener has his name drawn, he is assigned a certain hitter. If that hitter hits a home run in the right inning, the listener wins the jackpot. Sometimes there are several thousand dollars in it. And if the right hitter hits a grand-slam homer at the precise moment required, there is a $25,000 bonus.

It so happened that, *mirabile dictu*, Fred Talbot hit a home run with the bases loaded tonight. And thus a man named Donald Dubois, who lives in Gladstone, Oregon, won $27,000. The applause in the stands had not yet died down when it was decided in the bullpen that tomorrow morning Fred Talbot would receive a telegram from Donald Dubois of Gladstone, Oregon, thanking him for his Herculean efforts and telling him that a check for $5,000 was in the mail as a token of esteem and friendship. Since the telegram was my idea, I had to send it. We agreed that my identity would be revealed only under penalty of death.

I checked in with Marvin Milkes tonight and offered to go up to Vancouver and start a game there during the All-star break. I explained about how little I'd been pitching and said I'd like him to see what I could do as a starter, even if it was in the minors.

So Marvin Milkes said, "I don't know if we could guarantee about bringing you back."

I said the first thing that came to my mind. "What?"

"Your coming back would depend on a lot of things; how you did when you were down there and our situation here with this club at the time. We have roster problems. It's not always easy to get rid of a guy, to make room on the roster."

All of a sudden I got the feeling that I was being sent down, was asking to be brought back up and was being told, "Sorry, kid." And here I was *volunteering* to go to the minors so that I would, in the long run, help the club. I mean, if it worked, they'd have another starting pitcher. And all Milkes could think of was obstacles.

"Have you talked to Joe about starting?" Milkes said.

I was shocked. Milkes was here last year when I had such success starting. You'd think he would have remembered that, talked to Joe about it. Nothing. Nobody talks to anybody around here.

Another example. I went to Sal today and said, "Sal, I've only pitched six innings in fifteen days, and if possible I'd like a little extra time warming up. So if you think we're getting into a situation where you might need me, give me a quick call so I can get a head start."

And Sal said: "What if we need you in a hurry?"

With the Angels in town I took the opportunity to chat with Ed Fisher and Hoyt Wilhelm. I asked Fisher about the curse of inconsistency. "Everyone has the same problem," he said. "Hoyt has it and I have. I'll pitch for three weeks and it'll be going real good for me and then for ten days I can't throw one worth a damn and they hit me all over the place."

And Wilhelm said: "You know you can throw a bad one once in a while if you're throwing a lot of good ones. But you can't throw two or three bad ones in a row. Sometimes when I go out there I throw just about every one of them good. At other times it's just nothing. And I get hit. It takes a lot of work and a lot of concentration. It's that delicate a pitch."

Fisher came in to relieve tonight and got clobbered (in fact Talbot hit the grand-slam off him). And when I came in I pitched two scoreless innings, striking out three. Like Fisher said, that's the way it goes.

JULY
10

Freddy Talbot believes.

The telegram read: "Thank you very much for making our lives so happy, Mr. Talbert. We feel we must share our good fortune with you. A check for $5,000 will be sent to you when the money arrives." (I thought it was a clever touch to misspell his name.)

As soon as he read the telegram, Talbot called over his faithful roommate and asked him to step outside. "You know anything about this, Merritt?" he said. "You think it's a joke?"

"Looks legitimate to me," Ranew said, biting his lip to keep from laughing.

On the bus to the airport for our trip to Minnesota, Talbot showed the telegram to Ray Oyler. "You think it's for real?" Oyler said.

"Yeah, I think so," Talbot said. "If one of the guys had done it, he wouldn't have misspelled my name."

"That's right," Oyler said. "And what are you going to do with the money?"

"I think I'll buy that boat I always wanted, one with a 95-horse-power motor. I'll tell my wife I won it in a raffle. Otherwise she'll want me to put the whole $5,000 in the bank. And whatever you do, Ray, don't tell the writers about it. If they put it in the paper I'll have to pay income tax on it."

Ray promised he wouldn't tell.

Because we were rained out in Seattle, Jerry Stephenson did not get his start.

"How do you feel about missing your start tonight?" I asked.

"My one start?" he said. "You mean my one big chance?"

"Right. And how do you feel about the fact that you were going to get this one big chance with only one-third of an inning pitched in the last six weeks?"

"Oh, I've pitched more than that," Stephenson said. "Actually I have a total of two-and-two-thirds innings."

"Only two-and-two-thirds?" I said. "In six weeks? Has anybody said anything to you? Has this situation been discussed?"

"Nope," Stephenson said. "I'm just happy to be here. I'll take whatever they give me. If they took off my hat and shit in it, I'd put it right back on my head and say thanks."

I think he means it. I've felt that way myself.

But it can't be too good for Stephenson that they called up Dick Baney today. He's the righthanded pitcher who almost made the club this spring.

JULY
11

Minneapolis

There was a grave meeting before the game in Minnesota tonight. Joe Schultz had a clipping from the Los Angeles *Herald Examiner,* a story by Bud Furillo. The story said that the Seattle ballplayers, upset at the way Marvin Milkes sat in the lobby at around curfew time, checking bodies, had gotten together and had Milkes measured for a suit. Milkes was very pleased at the idea, until the suit arrived. It was a bellhop's uniform, with thirty-eight brass buttons. There were two pictures with the story: one of Milkes, the other of a bellhop.

It was a terrific story in every respect but one. It wasn't true. However, the possibility of fitting Milkes with such a suit *had* been discussed in the bullpen. And something like that gets around.

"Now this kind of thing is bad not only for the general manager," Joe Schultz said, "it's bad for the whole organization. This may sound funny, but things like this can get turned around. If Marvin Milkes has to sit in the lobby and check, the wives might start wondering who's staying out late and what they're doing."

"And that's bad," Ray Oyler said.

"We can all tell our wives it's McNertney he was checking on," Tommy Davis said.

Everyone laughed. McNertney is thirty-two, single, and rumor has it he's never been kissed. He spends all his spare time oiling his fishing rods and thinking about hunting in the winter. He hasn't got time to stay out late.

But Joe Schultz was serious. "Whoever gave out this story is a no-good cocksucker, I'll tell you that," Schultz said. "And I'm going to find out who it is."

At that point I felt a lot of eyes on me. Maybe I'm supersensitive, but it did seem that almost everybody checked me in case I was showing the white feather of guilt. And, of course, after the meeting, Fred Talbot said, loudly, as though he were kidding, "All right, Bouton, what'd you give them the story for?" In this kind of situation I'm always guilty until proven innocent.

That's what happened around the Yankees too. When Johnny Keane was manager and losing control of the ballclub, there was a story in the paper quoting an unnamed player as saying that Keane was a bad manager, that he was handling the club poorly, that none of the players liked him and that there was going to be a mutiny on the club any day now. And this all explained, of course, why the Yankees were losing.

Naturally there was a clubhouse meeting. Keane made a short speech asking who had said those things and what we could do about it? Elston Howard leaped to his feet in a rage, waving his arms and shouting. "How the hell could anyone do such a thing?" he demanded. "When are we going to learn not to talk to these writers? We shouldn't even let them into our clubhouse. And the guy who said those things, we ought to find him and fine him a thousand dollars." And so forth.

During this tirade I once again had that uneasy feeling that there were a lot of eyes on me. This was unfair. I never hid behind anonymous quotes. If I had anything to say to a newspaperman I said it. In fact, newspaper guys who considered themselves my friends sometimes wouldn't print things I said only on the grounds that they didn't want to hurt my career with the Yankees. Nevertheless, there were the eyes and all I could do was try to look as nonchalant as possible. I probably succeeded only in looking guilty.

The next day I asked the writer of the story to tell me who his source was. He said he'd tell me only if I promised never to reveal it. I promised. And I have never revealed it. Until now. It was Elston Howard.

Sometimes things just run away from a man. Take Pagliaroni. While Joe Schultz was making his speech about what a terrible thing for the ballclub the bellhop-uniform article was, Pag was a vociferous supporter.

"Damn right," he said. "Dammit, yes." And like that. But when the idea to do it first came up in the bullpen, Pagliaroni was one of its biggest boosters. I even thought he might run out and do it during the game.

Before the game Dick Baney and I were walking across the outfield grass to the bullpen, and the crowd was buzzing, and the organist was playing, and Baney looked around and said, "Hey, you know something? This is fun, walking across the outfield with all the people looking down at you."

And I thought, "It's true." You forget how much fun it is sometimes just to walk across the outfield. And then I remembered sitting up in the left-field stands in the Polo Grounds as a kid and thinking to myself, "Cheez, if I could only run out on the field and maybe go over and kick second base, or shag a fly ball—God, that would make my year. I'd never forget it as long as I lived if I could just run actoss that beautiful green outfield grass." And now, sometimes, I forget to tingle.

Baney asked me if I ever got nervous on the mound. I told him no, that you're nervous sometimes until you throw the first pitch, then everything seems to be all right. But I've been nervous. Like the first game I started in Yankee Stadium as a rookie in 1962. My first eight pitches were balls. Then, with two men on, I ran the count on the hitter to 3 and 1. My next pitch was ball four. I saw Houk step out of the dugout to come get me, not only out of the game, but to send me to the minors. Career over. Only the umpire called it a strike. Houk stepped back into the dugout. I got the hitter on a pop-up and went on to pitch the worst shutout in the history of the game. That's when I gave up seven walks and seven hits, stranded fourteen runners and won 8–0.

Then there was my first World Series game, 1963, against the Dodgers. It was the year Maury Wills stole all those bases. He was the first hitter and I stood there looking at him and thinking, "He's going to get on, he's going to steal second, we're going to throw the ball into center field and I'm going to be humiliated on national television." I remember being so nervous I could hardly throw the ball, and on the first pitch, Maury Wills, bless his heart, bunted the ball right back to me. Easy out. I've always been grateful to him for bunting that first pitch.

260

When Dick Baney went into the game to throw his first major-league pitch everybody in the bullpen moved out to the fence to watch him. We wanted to see how he'd do against the Brew, which is what we call Harmon Killebrew. Inside I still think of him as the Fat Kid, which is what Fritz Peterson over at the Yankees always called him. I'd say, "How'd you do, Fritz?" and he'd answer, "The Fat Kid hit a double with the bases loaded." Well, the first time the Fat Kid faced Dick Baney he hit the second pitch 407 feet into the left-field seats.

After the game I was shaving next to Baney. "Welcome to the club," I said. "You lost your virginity tonight."

"The only difference," he said, "is that all you guys will still be here tomorrow."

JULY
12

Today Baney, who's still here, asked me if I was throwing my knuckleball all the time now and I said that indeed I was. "Sal didn't like that pitch this spring," Baney said, "I guess he thought you were throwing it too much. I remember one time you gave up a homer on it and Sal said to Joe, 'Now you see? That's the pitch that's going to get him into trouble.'"

I said that was interesting.

"Well, if Sal didn't want you to throw it, and if you were getting hit, why did you keep throwing the knuckleball?" Baney said.

"My wife told me to," I said.

"And there's something I've always wondered about," Baney said. "When you go to spring training with a club, even a minor-league club, they always tell you to work on something. Then you get hit and they get mad, no matter what you're working on. So I still don't know what to do in the spring—work on something or try to get the hitters out."

Welcome to another club.

I made a terrible mistake today. I was chatting with Fred Talbot and said, "Hey, Fred, by the way, you ever hear from that guy you hit the home run for?"

Fred's eyes narrowed and he looked mean. "Were you the one who sent that telegram?" he said.

"What telegram?" I said, feeling my stupid face breaking up into a giveaway smile.

Now he was clenching his teeth. "I *knew* you sent the damn thing," he said, "and I'm going to get you back for that. I know you sent that paternity suit thing too."

"Fred, I did *not* send you the paternity thing," I said, all injured innocence. "I *may* have sent you a telegram. I don't know yet. What did the telegram say?"

And he said: "I'll get you back. I'm going to get you back on something, and when I do it's going to involve your wife, your whole family, your friends back home, everybody in the whole damn country."

After the game Talbot got back at me. It was still so hot that a lot of the guys didn't want to wait for the bus back to the hotel and grabbed air-conditioned cabs instead. We lined up for them, and when I started to get into one as the last man, Talbot, who was behind me in line, leaped in ahead of me and said, "Take the next cab, you Communist."

Got into the ballgame today. Pitched two-and-two-thirds innings and gave up two hits, one of them a tremendous double by a former teammate of mine at Western Michigan, Frank Quilici. We lost this one 11–1 and the Fat Kid hit another. The Seattle staff is impartial in the home-run race between Killebrew and Reggie Jackson. They *both* kill us.

Too bad McNertney didn't make the All-Star team instead of Bill Freehan of the Tigers. Freehan isn't having anywhere near the kind of year McNertney is. This shows that the players are voting on reputation rather than current performance.

Also, I think Mayo Smith should have had a manager from the Western Division as one of his coaches instead of three Eastern managers—Ted Williams, Earl Weaver and Alvin Dark. He could easily have picked Joe Schultz and left off Dark. Take a hike, son.

13

I've had the feeling for some time now that Wayne Comer and I don't get along. I can tell because every once in a while he says about me, "Get him the fuck out of here." An example. One night we were sitting around in Don Mincher's room waiting to look at some stag movies and Pagliaroni and I got into a conversation about a book we were both reading, *Psycho-cybernetics.* I had just launched into my expert opinion of it when Wayne Comer said, "Get him the fuck out of here." Anyway, we've now lost four straight to the Twins, having dropped a doubleheader, and we're waiting for the bus to leave for the airport. An elderly gentleman walks up to the bus looking for Garry Roggenburk. He wants to thank him for tickets that were left for him. He doesn't actually know Roggenburk, but he's a friend of Bob Locker, who left the tickets, and about fourteen others, in the names of various players. "I was with Locker's group and I just wanted to thank you for leaving the tickets," the old man said to Roggenburk. "I feel bad about how the afternoon went for you boys. It certainly was sad for . . ."

Just then Wayne Comer breaks in with his loud, "Get him the fuck out of here."

Somehow, at this moment, in this place, in front of this nice old gentleman, that seems obscene to me. So I say, "Hey, Wayne, knock it off. That's a friend of Locker's."

"I don't give a fuck," Comer says, with flashing wit.

"Take it easy," I say. "It's only a game, you know."

"Only a game, huh? Well, you want to do something about it?"

"Yeah, I do. I want you to knock it off."

"Why don't you do something about it with your fists then, instead of your mouth?"

"Just knock it off. You were wrong and you know it."

"Why don't you crawl all over my ass then? Jump up and crawl all over me."

"Yeah. That will solve it."

And it ends with that.

Except Comer keeps muttering, "Just a game, huh? Just a game."

After the bus left for the airport I was making notes on this brilliant repartee and Ray Oyler looked over my shoulder and tried to read them. "What are you writing?" he said as I covered the notes with my hand.

"None of your business," I answered, sweetly.

"Well, just keep my name out of it," he said.

Can't promise, kid. But it's tempting.

While we were losing the first game of the doubleheader—we were down 5–1 and it was going to be our third straight here—Joe Schultz called to John Gelnar, who was keeping the pitching chart. "C'mere a minute," he said, motioning Gelnar down to the other end of the dugout. Gelnar was sure he was going to get a big tip on pitching. And Joe Schultz, pointing up into the stands, said, "Up there near the Section 23 sign. Check the rack on that broad."

In the eighth inning, Joe Schultz said, "Well, boys, between games today we have a choice of roast beef, baked ham or tuna salad."

We were winning the second game 4–0 in the eighth when Fred Talbot, who had a beautiful three-hitter going, got tired. He came out with a runner on base and none out. Disaster set in promptly. First Joe Schultz used Locker. Then O'Donoghue, then Segui. Everybody in the Minnesota lineup got a hit. Rod Carew, just off the bus after coming back from his weekend in the army, ran into the stadium, threw on his uniform and, with his fly still unbuttoned, got a hit. I swear they pulled an usher out of the stands and *he* got a hit. We lost 5–4.

JULY
14

Seattle

I called Bud Furillo in Los Angeles today and asked him if he would tell me the name of his source for the bellhop-uniform story. Reporters, he told me, never disclose their sources. Too bad, I told him, because it was a lousy source. The story wasn't true. That shook him up nicely.

I explained to him that it was something we'd kidded about but hadn't actually done, and it turned out he got the story "from a very reliable Los Angeles writer," who got it from one of the Angels, which is about the way I figured it happened.

He said he'd call Milkes and apologize for printing an erroneous story. I also came away with the impression that he'd let Milkes know that no one on our club had given him the story. Not that I think Milkes doesn't know that. I think the whole point of that little meeting was to intimidate us into not telling things to the press in the future. Sneaky.

Jerry Stephenson was outrighted to Vancouver today just as he was moving into his new apartment. I know he lost a deposit and some rent money when he was called up from Vancouver, and I'm sure it will cost him again. Stephenson was here for seventeen days and pitched a total of three innings. He was on the road most of the time, and while he was away his wife had a miscarriage. Stephenson is all shook up. Now wait a minute. Bob Lasko lives in Vancouver and he's spending the summer in Toledo. Mike Marshall had to fight to get sent to Toledo instead of Vancouver. Why couldn't they just have been switched around? Because nobody thought of it. Because nobody cared. I agree with the title of a paper Mike Marshall wrote in college: "Baseball Is An Ass."

JULY
15

We have dropped out of third place into a tie for fifth with Chicago. And Kansas City, the other expansion team, is now ahead of us.

When I got to the clubhouse tonight, I found that my two pairs of new baseball shoes had been nailed to the clubhouse floor. Used for the operation were square cement nails. They tore huge ugly holes in the soles. Also the buttons were torn off my sweatshirts, my Yoo-Hoo T-shirts were ripped to shreds and several jockstraps were pulled permanently out of stretch. Talbot's revenge, I thought immediately. But he swore it was not him, and he convinced me. Ray Oyler and Gene Brabender admitted they were eyewitnesses, but they wouldn't tell me who did it. They assured me, though, that it wasn't Fred Talbot.

I asked Steve Hovley to find out for me, and he said, "If I can I will, but I doubt if they'll tell me."

The only other guy with a possible motive is Wayne Comer. Somehow I doubt it was him. In fact I can't imagine why anybody would want to do that. I think it was a prank. I think it was funny when I tried to pick up the shoes that were nailed down. I think it was *supposed* to be funny. I think.

Besides, I can still wear the shoes—as long as it doesn't rain.

Made my thirty-seventh appearance of the season tonight against Oakland and my super knuckleball showed up. I struck out the first three guys I faced. The third strike to Rick Monday broke so sharply McNertney never got a glove on it. It rolled between his legs to the backstop and Monday got to first base. Of course, this was after Diego Segui had come into the game at a crucial moment and given up a three-run homer and the game. Pitching in lost causes, my ERA is back down to 3.50. I still can't see how they can keep from starting me.

JULY
16

I should say something about all the injuries we've had. It will explain, at least to some extent, why we've been going so poorly. John Donaldson, our second baseman, has a fractured toe. John Kennedy wrenched his knee and is in a cast. Rich Rollins is having a knee operation that finishes him for the year. Steve Barber is still on the disabled list (his arm doesn't hurt, it's just a little stiff). Tommy Harper has a pulled thigh muscle and a bad sliding strawberry. Ray Oyler has been out with a hamstring pull. So has Mike Hegan.

You will also notice that while our infielders are dropping like flies, our starting pitchers remain disgustingly healthy, if not particularly effective.

I was chatting with Fred Talbot about contracts and keeping statistics to use as negotiating arguments and he said, "Aw hell, I don't keep statistics. Whatever they send me, I just sign and send it back. Of course, I call them a few names first."

JULY
17

Out for a most pleasant afternoon on my neighbor's boat, cruising through the locks from Lake Washington into Puget Sound with my wife and kids. Also Garry Roggenburk, Gordie Lund, utility infielder, and Steve Hovley, whom I invited along. Hovley wound up stealing my pants.

It was my fault. He was wearing Bermudas, and on the way into the ballpark I suggested he switch, that I'd get less static than he walking into the park in Bermudas. He agreed. But when he got out of the car, running, he had his Bermudas *and* my pants. So I had to walk into the clubhouse, late, wearing my bathing suit. And naturally Hovley was one of the people who said, "A *bathing suit!?*"

Tomorrow Diego Segui leaves the bullpen for a start. So I went over to Sal Maglie to chew on his leg for a while.

"Sal, what's the story?"

"About what?"

"About the fact that I'm not starting and Diego Segui is."

"Well, it has nothing to do with personalities."

Never occurred to me that it had. Well, hardly ever.

"You know something, Jim?" Pagliaroni said to me today. "I'm convinced that they think you're a character."

"What kind, Pag?" I said.

"Not your personality or anything," he said. "But that pitch. And the fact that you throw it all the time. As recently as two days ago I heard Sal telling Joe that he's told you time and time again that you're throwing too much in the outfield. I think Joe likes your knuckleball, I really do, but I don't think Sal does, and they think it's a little weird that you do all that throwing."

Jim Pagliaroni is one of the most perceptive Italian catchers in the big leagues.

Joe Schultz called a morale meeting tonight and did a good job of it. He said that we were losing because of injuries and that we shouldn't begin pressing to try to make up for them. He said that if we weren't big-league ballplayers we wouldn't be playing in the big leagues, and that we were just as good as any other club. "Sometimes things turn around all of a sudden and you start winning a whole lot of games. You can win them just as easy as lose them."

It was a good speech and made us all feel better, and I agreed with all of it. Except one small part. Minnesota is better.

Diego Segui pitched a marvelous ballgame. He was magnificent throughout and won it 2–1. As I watched the game I was torn between wanting him to get bombed and wanting him to do well, because we could use a win and because he's a good fellow. So there I was torn, and warming up in almost every inning. In the second game, same thing. And I never got into either game.

"You know something?" said Pagliaroni. "You looked great warming up."

I told him thanks.

Even winning we didn't do much to stop Rod Carew, who is now leading the league. He's the kind of hitter who puts the ball into a hole someplace, or bloops one, every time. "He can't miss," McNertney said. "If I were him I'd go looking for wallets."

Steve Hovley won the first game for us. It was a 1–l tie in the last of the ninth, bases loaded, Hovley up and Ron Perranoski, the old pro, pitching. It was a classic confrontation; the graybeard, wily pitcher against the upstart young slugger. In the end, Hovley beat the old man at his own game. He worked the count to 3 and 2 and then fouled off a couple of borderline pitches. It was exciting. Me, I ran all the way down to the dugout so I could be closer to what was happening. And as I watched Hovley struggling out there against the best reliever in the league, I thought, how can a guy with friends like Dostoyevsky be scared in this kind of situation? He wasn't. He hung in for another foul ball and then got the base on balls, forcing in the run.

As we walked down to the clubhouse I heard John Gelnar say, "You know, one good thing about having Hovley up there, he's too goony to be scared."

In the second game Hovley hit his second home run of the season. I'm the proud owner of the first ball he hit out. I bought it from the kid who caught it. Hovley said he didn't want it. He said he didn't think it was particularly important. The year he hits 62 it may be my most valuable possession.

I think the world should know that a girl one of my teammates goes out with is called "Rotorooter." Around the clubhouse, guys sing, "Tell Rotorooter I love her."

When I came in from the bullpen after we won the second game, Joe was patting everybody on the back, saying "Attaway to go" and "Nice job." When he got to me I said, "Joe, I really had it out there tonight in the bullpen."

"You did?" Joe said.

"Yup. Great knuckleball. Hellacious."

"Did you throw too much?"

"Hell no."

"Good. You're starting tomorrow night. Feel up to it?"

"Hell yes."

Well, what do you know? It's "put-up-or-shut-up" time for Jim Bouton.

Before I left the ballpark tonight, Sal Maglie said, "Get your sleep, Bouton."

And I said, "Right, Sal. And I want to have a catcher out there five hours before game time so I can start warming up."

Driving home I found myself doing a lot of worrying. Should I take a sleeping pill tonight? Should I sleep late or get up early and take a nap later? What should I eat? At what time? Then I thought, "What the hell am I worried about all this crap for? I've started a lot more important games. World Series games, pennant-race games. And here I am acting like a kid." Foolishness. I'm just going to be normal. I'm going to sleep tonight and not even think about it. When I start the game I'm going to pretend that I'm in there for relief, that I'm just going to pitch a few innings the way I do almost every day.

Look at it this way. In a couple of days two men are going to land on the moon. How the hell can I be nervous about starting a baseball game? Even if it is against the Fat Kid and his wrecking crew.

Part 6 Shut Up

JULY
19

I went over the hitters with McNertney before the game. For me the only thing this involves is deciding which hitters we're going to throw fastballs to on what particular count. We know we're going to start everyone off with a knuckleball and we're going with it until 3 and 0. On the big hitters, like Killebrew, we decided to throw the knuckleball even on 3 and 0. We'd also throw the 3-and-0 knuckleball to any guy who was hitting in a game-winning situation, even if we walked him. I mean, I'd rather give up a base on balls than a three-run homer.

My main concern was that Carew and Tovar would be stealing on my knuckleball, so we went over the pick-off signs carefully and hoped for the best.

It wasn't good enough.

In my first start of the year, on this day of July 19, 1969, A.D. I, James Alan Bouton, was creamed.

Five runs were scored off me before I was mercifully taken out of the game with two out in the fourth. There were two home runs, by Leo Cardenas and Ted Uhlaender. When Joe Schultz came out to get me I could only think of a line Fred Talbot delivered in similar circumstances: "What kept you?"

Not more than one out of every three knuckleballs I threw was doing its proper thing. Besides, my control was way off and I was behind on the hitters.

I started out in trouble and recovered. With two out, the Fat Kid got on base because of an error. A single and a walk loaded the bases, but I struck out Bob Allison on a 3-and-2 knuckleball.

After that, oblivion. I blocked it all almost as quickly as I could shower, dress and join my family in the stands. That's the easiest way for me to forget. I crawl back to my family and use them for a crutch. Some guys drink. I talk about the kids needing new shoes.

I was glad to have the chance to start, of course. Yet now that I've fouled everything up so royally I'm thinking of excuses. Why did they have to start me against Minnesota? Maybe if I knew a few days in advance I could have prepared myself better. Maybe I should have taken a greenie. That's just kidding myself, of course. I had a start and I didn't win, and now I can look forward to the All-Star break.

Now that I think of it, I didn't lose either. We were losing 5–0 when I left the game. We tied the game at 7–7 and went sixteen innings before stopping on account of curfew. I think I'll remind Sal and Joe that I'm still undefeated as a starter.

And I just remembered something else. When my boy Mike was still a baby and he cried, I'd say to him, "Harmon Killebrew's little boy doesn't cry." Now I wonder if Harmon Killebrew ever thinks of crying.

JULY
20

Poor John Gelnar. The game was picked up today in the seventeenth inning and he promptly lost it. Then he lost the regular game, which is two in one day and not, under most circumstances, easy to do.

And my record, as we go into the All-Star break, is 1–0. Not much to show for a half-season's work. Still, it's better than 1–1 . . . or 1–2, not to mention 1–3.

JULY
21

Kyong Jo has been with us for almost a year now and the rapidity with which he's learned English is amazing. Today he came to me with a complaint. "Dad, the kids call me John Jo, or King Jo," he said. "Why don't they call me Kyong Jo?"

I explained that Kyong Jo was a Korean name and difficult for American children to pronounce. And I asked him if he would like to have an American name.

This is something Bobbie and I had been talking about for some time. We didn't want to change his name right away. It was difficult enough for him to make the adjustment to a new country and new parents without, at the same time, robbing him of the only familiar thing he had left, his name. So we called him Kyong Jo. But we thought he'd want to change it eventually, and now was the time.

He said yes, he'd like an American name.

"How about David?" I said.

He thought about it for a moment, then said, "Yeah."

"Okay, we'll call you David. You'll be David Kyong Jo Bouton."

"Okay," he said.

And he ran out the front door shouting to the neighborhood kids, "Hey, everybody. I'm David. I'm *David!*"

JULY
22

I take this opportunity to present a lexicon of words and phrases encountered around baseball that are, more or less, unique to the game. There are a great many phrases having to do with a pitcher throwing at a batter. Among them are:

Chin music, as in "Let's hear a little chin music out there," this being a suggestion that the pitcher throw the baseball near the hitter's chin.

Purpose pitch, which is a pitch that knocks a batter down purposely, or perhaps may just

Spin his cap.

Keep him honest, which means, make the batter afraid if you can.

Loosen him up, meaning that if enough baseballs are thrown close to a hitter, he'll fall down easily.

Other phrases that often come up in conversation are:

Tweener, any ball hit not especially hard but directly between two outfielders, neither of whom can reach it in time.

Take him over the wall, hit a home run, as in "Horton took Bouton over the wall in the fifth."

Down the cock is the quintessence of the hitting zone. Any pitch like that is bound to be *Juiced,* with some kind of power.

Parts of the body also have special appellations:

Boiler, as in "he's got the bad boiler," or upset stomach.

Hose is arm.

Moss is hair.

Shoes are *kicks* and clothes are *vines,* and when the bases are loaded they're *drunk.* A good fielder can really *pick it,* and if you want to tell a guy to go sit down, it's *go grab some bench.* Organized baseball is *O.B.,* and a stupid player has the *worst head in O.B.* Wheels are legs, and an infielder has *the good hands* or *the bad hands* as girls have *the good wheels* or *the bad wheels.* For some reason the definite article is important there. An angry man has *the red ass* or *the R.A.*

Camp-followers, whether they're eleven or sixty-five or somewhere in between, are called *Baseball Annies.* And if a player, coach or manager should bring a girl with him to another city, she's called an *import.* If an import is a *mullion,* she may have to pay her own way.

A pimple or boil is called a *bolt,* as in "get a wrench for that bolt." A hard line drive is a *blue darter, frozen rope,* or an *ungodly shot.* To think is to *have an idea,* so that when a pitcher seems to be losing his cool a coach might shout at him, "Have an idea out there."

And a fellow who talks big but appears to lack courage is said to have an *alligator mouth* and a *hummingbird ass.*

Baseball is not without its charms.

JULY
23

Department of It's Not How You Play the Game, It's Whether You Win or Lose. I was at a pool watching my kids take their swimming lessons today and one of the women said to me, "Why aren't you watching the All-Star game?"

Somewhat abashed, I said, "Well, I'm getting some swimming lessons for my little boys."

And she said, "That's all right. You're really not missing much anyway. The American League's getting slaughtered."

JULY

24

Back to the salt mine. Once again I'm the forgotten man of the bullpen. Used three pitchers in the game, and even Fred Talbot, who's in the starting rotation, was asked to warm up. And I never got a call.

This gave me lots of time to chat with Pagliaroni. He told me about the first talk he had with Marvin Milkes when he came over from the Athletics. The last thing he did in Oakland was break a finger. So when he came to us he had to go on the disabled list. And Milkes said to him: "Now, Pag, I know you were a player representative over there and I know you worked on the salary problems we've had and I know you're going to have to be on the disabled list. But I want you to know you're still going to be receiving your full salary."

This is pretty funny, because they *had* to pay him, even though he was on the disabled list, maybe *especially* because he was on the disabled list.

It's like when the Yankees sent me to Syracuse. I remember Houk saying, "Now, you'll be getting the same salary," and I felt rather grateful until I discovered they *had* to pay me the same salary. It was in the contract.

If you want to know what aspect of the moon landing was discussed most, in the bullpen it was the sex life of the astronauts. We thought it a terrible arrangement that they should go three weeks or more without any sex life. Gelnar said that if those scientists were really on the ball they would have provided three germ-free broads for the astronauts.

JULY

25

Word is that Greg Goossen, who was with us in spring training, will be up to replace Mike Hegan when he goes into service for two weeks. Goossen is a burly guy with kinky blond hair and looks like a bouncer in an English pub. He also is a flake. And Ranew said to Pagliaroni, "Goossen ought to be assigned to Bouton." Okay, I'll take him.

Pag had a good story about Goossen. He remembered sitting in a bar with him and the Goose was putting them down pretty good. "Don't you have a game tomorrow?" Pag said.

"Yeah, we got a game," Goossen said.

"You're drinking a little heavy, aren't you?"

"You know something?" Goossen said. "I found I can't play if I feel good. I've got to have a little bit of a hangover to get the best out of me."

Got a letter from Jerry Stephenson. Says that God is alive and surfing in Waikiki. He also said that he had a marvelous final conversation with Milkes. He complained that he hadn't had an opportunity to pitch and Milkes said he'd blown two starting opportunities.

"When were those?" Jerry asked.

"You were going to start the night it rained," Milkes said.

"I know," Jerry said. "When was the other one?"

"When your wife had a miscarriage and you had to leave the club for three days."

The next best thing about the way things broke was that on the very day he was sent down, Jerry and his wife had moved into a new apartment. That afternoon they had to move out. "We felt groovy moving all that stuff," Jerry wrote. "By the end of the day we were working very well together as a team."

O'Donoghue was on the airplane flying east with Don Mincher and Joe Schultz, who were going to the All-Star game, and said Joe was feeling hardly any pain when he left the plane and was mumbling his two favorite words—shit and fuck—in all their possible combinations.

Tony Conigliaro was the subject for discussion at the pregame meeting.

"Curve him away," O'Donoghue said.

"Yeah, he's got a blind spot out there," Brabender said.

And Sal Maglie said, "Don't challenge him."

That's just the kind of thing Tommy Davis loves to pick up on. "Sal, what do you mean by 'Don't challenge him'?"

And Sal said, "Well, don't throw him a fastball down the middle. You got to spot it."

Like a great work of art, Sal Maglie is priceless.

JULY
26

It's still hard to get used to playing baseball again after the All-Star break. Three days off reminds you how much tension you live under playing baseball every day. During the break Harmon Killebrew can't get you. Reggie Jackson can't get you. It's peaceful. Like looking up at Mt. Rainier. That's the great thing about our ballpark. When a home run hit off you disappears over the fence, your eye catches a glimpse of the majesty of Mt. Rainier and some of that bad feeling goes away.

Great thing happened today. Police arrested a twenty-two-year-old blonde who had climbed a tree outside our clubhouse and was peeping in at us in the shower. A female beaver-shooter.

The game was great too, largely because J. Bouton recorded his second win of the season. I started warming up when the score was 3–0 against us. That's still too close to put me in. It was 5–0 with a runner on when I got the big call. I needed one hitter in that inning and got him, mowed them down 1-2-3 in the next inning and, of course, came out for a pinch-hitter. Only this time it was when we were in the process of scoring six runs. The big hit was a three-run homer by McNertney. The final score was 8–5. Locker got the save and I got a pat on the ass from Sal Maglie.

Another infielder got racked up during the game. Ron Clark collided with George Scott of the Red Sox and had thirteen stitches taken in his lip. Ron's a tough, gutty little ballplayer. He has a baby face, two tattoos on his arm (one says "Mother" and the other is of a black panther), smokes big cigars—and when he has thirteen stitches in his lip he drinks beer out of the side of his mouth.

Greg Goossen played his first game and went 3 for 3, including a tremendous line-drive home run into the left-field seats.

I love them, one and all.

We were talking about Bill Valentine, one of the umpires who was fired, ostensibly for being incompetent but actually, we all believe, because he was involved in trying to form an umpires' union. What we remembered about him is that he was one of the few umpires who would call Mickey Mantle out on borderline pitches. "Every umpire would give Mickey the benefit of the doubt," O'Donoghue said, "but every time I threw a pitch that nicked the corner on him, Valentine would call it a strike."

The whole Yankee team hated him for that.

The last time Marty Pattin had a bad game—and he's had about eight in a row now—he came charging up the runway to the clubhouse breaking things on the way. He kicked over a couple of garbage cans and crashed the door into the clubhouse. So today Talbot said to him, "Marty, what are your plans if you don't win tomorrow?"

JULY
27

Fred and I hung a hangman's noose in Pattin's locker, but he didn't need it. He pitched well, leaving the game after eight innings with the score 1–1. He didn't break up anything on the way back to the clubhouse.

We went twenty innings before losing it. I pitched two scoreless innings, the tenth and eleventh, which means I had another chance to win. It may also mean that I'll get into more games at crucial points. But if it takes twenty-inning games to do it, I'm still nowhere.

Talbot has finally been able to talk about that fellow Dubois who won that $27,000 on his home run. "Never made a nickel out of it," Talbot said. "They flew me out to Gladstone to go on four different radio shows. I went for the ballclub and they didn't pay anything either."

"Didn't Dubois offer you anything at all?" I said. "What did he say to you?"

"He asked for the bat," Talbot said. "He wanted to have the bat I hit the home run with as a souvenir. And when the whole thing was over it ended up costing me $2.75 for parking."

JULY
29

A bit of clever baseball strategy tonight by Joe Schultz. We're down 4–2 in the ninth against the Senators. Two out, man on second, Frank Howard is the hitter. Howard should be walked. But if Bob Locker, who's pitching, walks him he will now have to pitch to a lefthanded hitter, Mike Epstein. This won't do. So O'Donoghue, a lefthanded pitcher, will be brought in. In which case the Senators will pinch-hit for Epstein, bringing in a righthanded power-hitter, like Brant

Alyea, and we're stuck. O'Donoghue will have to pitch against him because the rules say he must pitch to at least one hitter. But Schultz was ahead of everybody. He brought in O'Donoghue just to walk Howard. Sure enough, they brought in Alyea to face O'Donoghue. So Joe took out O'Donoghue and brought me in. I struck Alyea out on three super knuckleballs.

As so often happens in this great game we play, all the strategy went for nothing. We lost 4–2 anyway. At least I was in a position to win a game, though, and Hegan could have tied it up in the ninth with a home run, but just missed.

At the pregame meeting, when Frank Howard's name came up, Joe Schultz said, "Look, whatever you do, don't let him beat you. Don't give him anything good to hit. Throw it outside to him. Christ, I don't mean on the corner, either. He'll hit that pitch right out of here. Throw it a foot outside. Hell, he'll swing at those. *Somebody's* been getting him out. The bastard's only hitting .305."

Joe looked around at the laughing faces, smiled and said, "So whatever you do, don't let him beat you. I'd rather walk him."

And Tommy Davis couldn't resist saying, "Skip, the last time we did that, Mike Epstein beat us."

Which is why I love Tommy Davis.

JULY
30

Dropped by to see Marvin Milkes about the Gatorade. I saw him sitting at his desk, but his secretary said he wasn't in. In that case, I told her, she better call the cops because there was a guy at his desk impersonating him. Not only that, he was wearing one of his sportscoats.

I was rewarded with a dirty look and an audience with himself. Milkes said he still hadn't made a decision about the Gatorade, hadn't even tasted it yet. But he wanted to talk to me about something else. He got up, closed the door and got very sincere. At first I couldn't imagine what he was getting at. "We've always had a good relationship," he said, turning on his big smile. Milkes has two faces he wears for players. He has this serious face and suddenly, as though he has remembered that he has to show he's your friend, he breaks into this dazzling smile. At first you think it's a real smile, then you realize that it's coming on at the wrong time, out of phase. He's not smiling because he's friendly. He's smiling the way he switches on his toaster. "Sometimes we have different points of view, but we've always gotten along fine and we've done a lot for you," he went on, wearing his sincere look now. "I stuck with you last year. I told Joe Adcock to use you and that I thought you had potential as a major-leaguer, and we paid you a major-league salary last year even though you were a minor-league ballplayer. I had confidence in you and you wouldn't be here now if it hadn't been for me. That's why I'm very upset to find out that you think that I've been a detective with this club, a gumshoe."

He looked so sincere and so sad I could feel a large tear welling up in my eye. How could I be so rotten?

"Now, you have to realize that a general manager's life is a lonely one, particularly when we're on the road," he continued. "I like to stay up at night and be around people. I don't like to sit in my room all night. Today, with the streets the way they are, you can't just walk around anymore. That's why I sit around the lobby and enjoy a cigar.

"But I don't check up on players. I don't fine players. That's not my job. I might tell the manager that somebody's staying out too late and it's making the club look bad, but I wouldn't fine a player myself. That's why I was disappointed to hear what you were saying about me."

"Who said I've been talking about you, Marvin?"

"I hear from people in Los Angeles and various writers. Through the grapevine. This kind of thing upsets me."

"Are you talking about the story in the Los Angeles *Examiner*?"

"Yeah," he said. "Now, that's a funny story. I read it myself and thought it was funny. And if the guy that told the story had come in and said to me, 'Marvin, I just meant that story as a joke,' I would have said, 'I enjoy a joke as much as anybody else,' and I would have forgotten about it. But I understand that you called a writer about it."

"Yes, I called Bud Furillo," I said. "But not to give him the story." I explained the purpose of my call and recounted what Furillo had said.

"Well, that's what he told me," Milkes said. "He called and said he would print a retraction because he knew it didn't happen. I said, 'Hell, don't print a retraction. It's not that important.' And as far as you're concerned in this thing, the only thing I care about is what you do out there between the lines. I know you do imitations and you give speeches and I've heard some of the people on the Yankees say you're kind of crazy and silly and I was told, 'You got stuck with one there.' But I tell them, 'As far as I'm concerned, if he gives me a hundred percent on the field, I'm going to use him. I'm judging him strictly as a ballplayer.' You hear all kinds of things through the grapevine. Bouton is this and Bouton is that. Hell, I don't even listen. I just got done reading a story by you in *Sport*. That's the kind of story I'm sure you could call controversial. [It was an account of the work I did in Mexico City during the Olympics. I went there for the American Committee on Africa, which was working to keep South Africa out of the Games.] If that's the way you feel, it's fine with me. That's completely apart from my judgment of you as a ballplayer. If you give me a hundred percent you can write or say anything you want."

I never believed that for a minute. Especially since I had found out that he'd fined Talbot and Oyler, possibly among others, for breaking curfew. But what I said was, "Well, I'm glad we've cleared it all up. And I hope it's clear to you that I did not call a writer to give him that story and that the only reason I called was so it would be understood that none of our players were responsible."

"Okay," he said. "It's all forgotten."

I didn't believe that either.

Before the game tonight pitchers were taking in extra bunting practice because we'd been having trouble moving the runner along. And Joe Schultz said, "Boys, bunting is like jacking off. Once you learn how you never forget."

Garry Roggenburk left the club. Gordie Lund, his roommate, said he woke up this morning, saw him packing and said, "Where you going?"

284

"I'm going home," Roggenburk said.

He marched in on Marvin Milkes, said that he had no interest in the game anymore, didn't enjoy it, was through with it and was going home. The next thing Gordie knew he was driving him to the airport. I know Roggenburk has his four years in on the pension and has a college degree and planned to go into teaching this fall. The trouble is, when you're a marginal player and you walk out, you can't come back. No one runs after you. You get marked down as a nut and it's all over. I don't know if Garry fully appreciated that fact when he left. Sometimes it's better not to act. Sometimes it's better just to sit around and grouse.

Greg Goossen hit two home runs and we won 4–3. I thought the outstanding play of the game was made by Wayne Comer, who bunted in a non-sacrifice situation, giving himself up just to move the runner along. He's that kind of player and recently Billy Martin, the Minnesota manager, was quoted as saying that he'd like to have Comer on his team, that he was his kind of ball player. It's true that he's a helluva player. And someday he'll make a pretty good coach.

JULY
31

A ten-year-old lad named Marvin Standifer wandered out of the stands and into the bullpen tonight and I grabbed him, put a warmup jacket and a hat on him and sat him on the bench. All his friends lined the fence and said things like, "Hey, is Marvin going to get into the game?" and "Does Marvin get to keep the hat?" and "How come you let Marvin into the bullpen?" And all the time Marvin had this giant grin on his face.

Of course, Eddie O'Brien said, "We have to get him out of here. We could get in trouble for that."

"Eddie, go sit down," I said. "This kid's got good stuff and we may need him later in the inning." Eddie sat down.

At the end of the inning I hoisted Marvin back into the stands. He'd had a big night.

The conversation turned to freezing people after they die and I said I'd like it to be done to me and then maybe I'd be thawed out in a couple of hundred years when they came up with a cure for whatever I'd died of. O'Donoghue was very angry at the idea. "How the hell are they going to thaw you out?" he said. "When you're dead, you should be dead. That's it."

O'Donoghue gets angry easily at what he considers flaky ideas.

Steve Barber pitched five innings of relief the other night and did quite well. I was surprised he went so long and asked him about it. "Joe asked me how I felt," he said, "and I felt all right, so I told him to leave me in there."

That's a tough spot for a ballplayer. What could Steve have said? "My arm doesn't hurt, but I don't think it would be a good idea to work anymore." No chance. So he stood out there risking two months of rehabilitation for one stinking ballgame, which we eventually lost anyway.

The Pilots have bought George Brunet from the Angels for something just over the waiver price. He'll fit right in on this ballclub. He's crazy.

I got in for two-thirds of an inning tonight and did well. Struck out Epstein on three pitches, all knuckleballs. I had Bernie Allen just about struck out, but he reached out and tapped one to the second baseman. Oh, Frank Howard got a single off me. He's liable to do that to anybody, isn't he?

I'm glad the knuckleball is in such happy shape. The Yankees arrive here tomorrow.

AUGUST

1

Another example of a general manager generously giving a ballplayer money that he is absolutely entitled to. Greg Goossen told the story. He lost $200 in rent when he was called up and Marvin Milkes put his hand on his shoulder and said, "We're picking up your rent check. [It's a rule that he has to.] And since you've signed a major-league contract, today you start on the pension plan."

"He made it sound like a special gift from him, a pot sweetener," Goossen said. "It was only after I left his office that I realized there was no way he could prevent me from starting on the pension plan today, even if he wanted to."

I talked to Fritz Peterson and Steve Hamilton in the outfield before the game and the pitchers' court fined me $5 for—in the words of Gene Brabender—"flagrantly flouting the rules." The court was in an ugly mood today.

"Before this season's over, Jim," Steve Hovley said, "we've got to steal the money, all $200 of it. We have to take it and keep it for a good long while."

I agreed that it had to be done.

Going over the Yankee hitters we came to Len Boehmer and Ron Plaza said, "Bad curve-ball hitter."

Dick Simpson, who'd played with Boehmer, said, "Hey, he hits the curve. He's a good curve-ball hitter."

"Well, I got it down on the card here," Plaza said. "Bad curve-ball hitter. Somebody must have said it."

And I remembered Gary Bell, and it struck me that somewhere in Plaza's files he's got a bunch of cards that say, "Smoke him inside."

Today Joe Schultz said, "Let's keep our minds on the game. And let's remember we're the same as everybody else. Let's go out there, kick the shit out of them and come back in and enjoy that beer."

We went out there, got two hits and lost 4–2. The beer was great.

AUGUST
2

Greg Goossen was doing his Casey Stengel imitation and he remembered the best thing the old man ever said about him. "We got a kid here named Goossen, twenty years old, and in ten years he's got a chance to be thirty."

There was a story in the paper about trades, and Milkes saying he was going to make some. He was reminded that the trade deadline was well past and that the only thing he could do was make waiver deals. And Milkes said, "Don't worry, I'll get waivers."

This is a typical attitude toward the rules that baseball itself makes. Waivers are not supposed to be used as trade vehicles. They are, partly at least, supposed to protect the players from front office capriciousness. But that doesn't faze the owners. They make the rules and they break them, and there's not a thing the players can do about it. Not yet anyway.

We got some forms to fill out from the Pilots' publicity department. One of the questions was, "Who is your baseball idol?" Mincher put down Mickey Mantle. Another question was, "What induced a major-league team to sign you to a professional contract?" And Mincher wrote, "Pretty fair country player." Finally there was this: "What's the most difficult thing about playing major-league baseball?" And Mike Hegan said, "Explaining to your wife why *she* needs a penicillin shot for *your* kidney infection."

Sibby Sisti is with us so that he can get in his fifteen years on the pension. And today Tommy Davis said, "I wonder if anybody will ever offer me a job like that?"

"All you'll get is a scouting job in Watts someplace," Tommy Harper said.

So I started doing a general-manager bit, giving scout Tommy Davis his instructions. "Now, Tom, you have to make sure to sign the right kind of colored guy. You know what I mean? None of that rabble-rousing."

"It's not 'colored' now, Marvin, it's 'black,'" Tommy said.

"Yeah, well, you know what I mean. I don't have to tell you. The right kind of kid. Can he laugh? Can he dance? Find out if he knows how to shuffle. We don't want any of that Vic Power shit."

"I know just what you mean," Davis said. "I know just what to look for. I won't give you any trouble."

Steve Hovley says the club wants him to play winter ball and he wanted to know what I thought about it. I said I didn't think it would be a very good idea. If you finish up a season well and leave a good impression you're not going to improve it playing winter ball. All you can do is hurt yourself by playing poorly.

"I know that," Hovley said. "But I've never been to a Spanish-speaking country, and I think I'd like that."

It's really just an afterthought to Hovley that he'd have to play baseball while there.

I find myself feeling sorry for Steve Barber. He had to get some shots in his arm today and he's scheduled to pitch against the Yankees tomorrow. He had those five good innings and now he's got trouble again. I asked him about it.

"No, it's nothing," he said. "Just a little tendinitis. It's not the trouble I had before. I'm just taking the shots as a precautionary measure."

Then we went to the outfield, the way we've been doing for the past weeks, and had a catch. He needs somebody to throw to and the price he pays is catching my knuckleball, which means every once in a while I bounce one off his foot. He doesn't complain.

AUGUST

3

"Boys, today it looks like Steve Barber and a cast of thousands." Bob Locker said it before the game and he was right. Steve never got by the first inning. He gave up five runs and we lost, 5–3. That was three in a row to the Yankees.

But it was a good weekend for me. I pitched five innings of relief Friday night and gave up one run, a home run by Pepitone. Saturday I pitched two scoreless innings. So now I've pitched about ten innings against the Yankees and given up only one run.

Ralph Houk has noticed. I was chatting with Fritz Peterson outside the Yankee clubhouse when Houk came out. We shook hands. "I've got to congratulate you," he said. "You're doing a helluva job. It just shows what can be done with a lot of hard work and guts. I knew you'd do it because you don't quit."

I said thanks. Then I said I'd been wanting to talk to him about something and would have called him. But since he was right there . . .

"There's going to come a time in my career, when the kids start going to school, and I have to make a decision about whether I'm going to continue to play baseball," I said. "It will be a lot easier for me to stay if I'm playing with a New York team. And I just wanted you to know that if you ever think you can use me, well, keep it in mind that I'd like to finish up my career near home."

"I'll do that," Houk said. "I'll definitely keep that in mind."

I did it, and I'm glad. I wonder what's going on inside his head, though. I wonder if he said to himself, "If that son of a bitch thinks he'll ever get back to Yankee Stadium while I'm there he's got another think coming." I also wonder if he said to himself, "You know, Bouton could be a help to us." Houk's a good manager and despite what's gone before I can still see myself pitching for him.

After the game I asked Barber how his arm felt and he said, "Oh, my arm felt fine. It was just that my rhythm was off, that's all."

Just then I noticed Fred Talbot packing his arm in ice because every time he pitches, his elbow gets sore and I TGFMK—Thank God For My Knuckleball. I can't describe how sweet it is not to have to go through all that.

AUGUST
5

Boston

Started a long road trip in Boston today and we talked in the bullpen about the same kind of thing we talked about in Seattle: Sibby Sisti. We decided that jobs as coaches were really a kind of political patronage. They're dispensed for former favors. There's not much to do. Being a coach requires only showing up at the ballpark, hollering clichés and being able to play false sorrow when you lose. It's a boring job. But people who become coaches are not easily bored. You ever see a baby play with a rattle for two hours?

So it's amusing that these jobs are often held out like a carrot on a stick. Like when a guy is in the middle of his career a general manager will say to him, "Someday we hope to have a place for you in our organization," or "Don't worry, we'll take care of you later on," or "We'll see that you stay in baseball." What he really means is, keep your mouth shut and be a good boy and do what we tell you. Sign a contract for this particular (low) figure and we'll reward you later with a coaching job.

Every once in a while there's a guy who doesn't fit into the coaching mold, a man with an original idea or two who's not afraid to express them, a guy who would like to have some influence on the club. I mean a guy like Johnny Sain. And what happens to him? He moves around a lot. He has to, because as soon as he asserts himself the manager wants to get rid of him, no matter how good a job he's doing.

At the start of this trip Joe Schultz called in Steve Hovley and said, "I want you to start dressing like a major-league ballplayer."

Joe only said that because Steve wears Levis to the park sometimes and thinks nothing of wearing his famous nondescript corduroy jacket seven days in a row (after all, what's a jacket for?). Steve said he thought that was pretty interesting, because when Joe says to dress like a major-league ballplayer he means there's a certain style of dress followed by baseball players and you're supposed to conform. In fact Hovley and I believe the style of the major-league player is not much style at all. Oh, they wear expensive sportscoats and turtleneck sweaters, and a lot of them started wearing Nehru jackets just as they were going out of style. But the mode is often *nouveau riche* jazzy. I consider it the same kind of taste that features plastic flamingoes on the front lawn or a bullfighter painted on black velvet in the living room.

Started the trip with Steve Hovley assigned to room with Greg Goossen and me with Steve Barber. I told Gabe Paul that Hovley and I wanted to room together and he said, "Marvin Milkes has to approve roommates. Why don't you stay where you are until we hear from Milkes?" I agreed to, reluctantly.

When we met at the hotel desk to pick up our keys, however, Hovley and I decided it was all very silly. It was silly for Milkes to worry about something like roommates and silly for us, as grown men, to care. So we switched, simply by having Steve Barber swap keys with Hovley.

Paul was furious. "I told you to wait until I had a chance to check with Milkes," he said.

I told him we thought it was too unimportant to wait.

"I tell you one thing," Paul said. "Don't ever ask me for any favors."

All right for you too.

Hovley and I were going to see *Midnight Cowboy* here but decided to wait until we got to Baltimore. We figured a good movie might just save Baltimore. On the other hand, probably nothing can.

Clubhouse speech by Joe Schultz. "Boys, I guess you know we're not drawing as well at home as we should. If we don't draw fans, we're not going to be making the old cabbage. I'm in this just as much as you are. We're all in it for the same thing. I'm going to lay it right out on the barrelhead. We got to win some games so we can draw some people.

292

"Oh yeah, and for you new guys, Brunet, it's two-and-a-half hours after a ballgame. That's curfew."

Tommy Davis started to giggle, and pretty soon everybody was laughing and looking at Brunet, and then he joined in and the whole thing became absurd. I mean, the idea of Brunet, coming in two-and-a-half hours after a game is ridiculous. *Nobody* gets in that fast, except maybe McNertney.

AUGUST
6

Carl Yastrzemski was recently fined $500 for loafing, and I've been keeping an eye on him. Sure enough, he hit a ball to second base today and loafed all the way to first. I'm afraid Yastrzemski has a bit of dog in him. Always did, and people around baseball knew it all the time. When things are going good, Yastrzemski will go all out. When things aren't going so well he'll give a half-ass effort. But he's got so much ability that the only thing you can do is put up with him.

I asked a few of the Red Sox if they thought he deserved the fine and I thought they would defend him. But they said, "He deserved it all the way."

We took the second-straight game from the Red Sox tonight. We were losing 4–2 when I came in with the bases loaded. I threw one pitch and we were out of the inning with a double play. Then we came from behind to win it. I enjoyed my contribution.

AUGUST
7

Today I didn't make any contribution and I was furious. We had a 4–2 lead going into the ninth and then came the trouble. Before it was over, O'Donoghue and Locker were bombed, the game was lost 5–4 and I, the very man who had gotten two out with a single pitch the day before, remained in the bullpen, warming up. *Warming up!* for goodness sakes.

Among the annoyed was Jim Pagliaroni. "If they're not going to use you in a situation like this," Pag said, "why the hell do they warm you up?"

I don't know. I honestly don't know.

Ray Oyler contributed a key ninth-inning error to the loss and spent a long time after the game facing his locker, drinking beer and playing genuine sorrow. The clubhouse was routine morgue and four sportswriters were trying to ask Oyler about the error—in hushed tones, of course. Newspapermen are required to play the sorrow game too, although why they should care, I can't imagine.

O'Donoghue, surveying the scene, said, "Goddam vultures. Hanging around waiting for the meat to dry." And Tommy Harper said, "What the hell do they need quotes for? They all saw the play." And Don Mincher said, "Miserable bastards." And Jim Bouton said, to himself, "Aw shitfuck."

On the bus from the airport to the Shoreham Hotel in Washington we passed a huge government building that had a bronze plaque on the front announcing it had been "erected in 1929." And Greg Goossen said, "That's quite an erection."

Hovley and Goossen were put in the same room again, so I assumed I'd been put in with Barber again and switched keys with Goossen. Then I went to Gabe Paul and told him Hovley and I wanted to room together again. And he said, "Well, I've got you in a room by yourself this trip."

It's interesting that they'd rather pay for a single room than have me room with Hovley. Just like the Yankees. They must think whatever it is I have that they don't like is catching.

I didn't tell Paul about the switch. Let him find out himself.

Hovley, Pagliaroni and I closed out the evening on the roof for a little beaver-shooting. We didn't get many good shots in but we kept trying. And Hovley said, "This is like fishing. All you need is a couple of nibbles to keep you trying."

O'Donoghue wound up his time in Boston screaming at the kids who lean out of the stands and throw things into the bullpen and at the mob of them that collects outside Fenway Park demanding autographs. O'Donoghue has a very low kid threshold.

He'd have hated me as a kid. I remember once at a Giant game in the Polo Grounds I took the top of a Dixie cup and scaled it down onto the field during the game. I couldn't believe how far it went—clear out to the infield. It landed halfway between the mound and home plate. I was scared when I saw it was actually going to drop onto the field and I looked around to see if anybody had noticed me throwing it. Johnny Antonelli, who was pitching for the Giants, walked off the mound, bent down, picked it up and put it in his back pocket. I got a huge kick out of that. Imagine, Johnny Antonelli picking up the cover of my Dixie cup.

One time my brothers and I and a friend decided that the way to catch foul balls in left field at the Polo Grounds was to have a net and stick it out over the stands at the proper moment. We constructed this big net, put a twelve-foot pole at the end of it and we were in business. We soon found, though, that we couldn't catch anything smaller than a flying barnyard in it. So we practiced and practiced and after a while we felt confident enough to take the net up to the Polo Grounds. On the train a lady asked us what we were going fishing for. We said baseballs. She gave us a funny look.

At the park we were refused admission. There was a rule they just made up: no nets. So we retreated to plot strategy. We decided to walk in one behind the other, net at our sides (away from the ticket taker, of course) and coats hiding the net and pole. It worked perfectly. Except for one thing. We didn't catch a single baseball.

AUGUST
8

Washington

Possibly because we finally all understood thoroughly by now that this club is going nowhere, the guys are very loose. Today, for example, everybody in the clubhouse is listening to Cal Tjader or somebody like him, keeping time by banging clothes hangers on chairs and John Donaldson, who is so skinny we call him Bones, puts two baseballs under his uniform shirt in order to get a set of shoulders, and towels around his middle so he has a belly, and he pulls his pants up so he looks like an old-time ballplayer, and he goes through the silent-film baseball-player routine in time to the music and everybody is having a great time.

"Hey, Mike," I say to Mike Hegan. "I wonder what this club would be like if we were fighting for a pennant."

Mike promptly puckers up his lips, sucks his cheeks in, pulls his legs together, presses his buttocks together with his hands and walks around the room as though he had been dipped in concrete. "Very tight," he says.

Eddie O'Brien continues working at being one of the boys. He didn't even call Marty Pattin for reading a magazine in the bullpen. And when I'm warming up in the bullpen he stands about fifteen feet behind the catcher in order to intercept any wayward knuckleballs. Come to think of it, everybody has been nice to me lately. Well, almost everybody. Plaza lets me take new baseballs out of his ballbag. Sal Maglie actually *smiles* at me. (Shudder. When the friendly undertaker starts smiling he may know more than you do.) I even get the feeling that if I talked to Joe Schultz he'd listen. Maybe (drool) I'll ask for another start.

That's what I say, and sometimes that's what I feel. Then there's a game like we had today. We lost it 10–3, which isn't the point. What is the point is that Brunet, who started, had a 2–0 lead, and as soon as he got into a little trouble, the phone rang in the bullpen. I grabbed my glove because I knew it had to be me. It was for Barber and Pattin.

They warmed up and Barber got called. Bang, we're losing 4–2. Then Pattin, and it's 6–2. Again the phone rang, and again I grabbed my glove. This time they wanted O'Donoghue. He got clobbered too. Now the score is 10–3 in the eighth and the phone rings again. This time I don't reach for my glove. But it's for me. So I warm up and pitch the ninth. One guy gets on with a single, another on an error. Nobody hits the ball good and I'm out of the inning. This doesn't change the score, which remains 10–3.

I'm saving up all my statistics for my next year's salary drive. I can just see Marvin Milkes when I whip them out. He'll say the same thing Charlie Brown said to Lucy.

"Charlie, I kept statistics on our team last season," Lucy says, "and they say something. There were 57 ballgames played, 57 ballgames lost; 3,000 runs scored by the opposition, 2 runs scored by our team, 900 walks given up by our team and . . ."

And after a while, Charlie Brown says, "Lucy, tell your statistics to shut up."

Steve Hovley and I spent the afternoon at the National Gallery of Art. Hovley said he had to check to see if Van Gogh's paintings were dry yet.

AUGUST
9

Took Hovley to my favorite Washington restaurant after the game, El Bodegon. He's been hitting the hell out of the ball and I thought we should celebrate. We had margaritas before dinner and Hovley remarked that before this year he'd *never* had a drink of any kind. But in Louisville he decided to do some testing. So he had a bourbon. Then he tried a Bloody Mary. Then a martini. Then a mint julep. All in the same evening. He said it was very interesting. He also said he had no hangover. I believe most of what Steve Hovley says.

Hovley was particularly interested in the flamenco guitarist at El Bodegon. He says he can't decide whether to play winter ball or stay home and learn to play the guitar.

Perhaps it was the heat. Or maybe just the stage of the season. Or the phase of the moon. No matter the cause, we got into an insane argument in the bullpen. It was a chicken-egg thing and it went like this: Can a pitcher get more strikeouts in a high-scoring game because he faces more hitters?

I said no. I said it didn't matter how many hitters you faced, that you could get only 27 outs in a nine-inning ballgame, and that the ratio between strikeouts and other kinds of outs would not change. Brabender and Pagliaroni thought differently. They said if you faced 100 hitters, you had a lot more chances to strike somebody out than if you faced only 27 or 28. And as he talked, Brabender got hot, and Brabender getting hot is like Old Faithful erupting. So I tried to cool him off. "Gene, you've got to learn that when you argue with somebody it's not a personal thing," I said. "I may disagree with you, but I still like you. I just think you're wrong. And that's no reason to get angry."

"I'm angry because you won't accept facts," he said.

"Well, I don't think it's a fact," I said. "I think what I say is a fact and that you won't accept it. But I'm not angry at you because of it."

"You know something?" Brabender said. "You're lucky. Where I come from we just talk for a little while. After that we start to hit."

I felt lucky indeed.

The whole argument seemed to irritate Marty Pattin. "Who wants to listen to all that stuff?" he said. "Why can't we just sit here and watch the ballgame?"

Poor Marty. It's not that he has no soul. It's just that he's been getting bombed lately.

Ran into Jack Mann, who is the author of *The Decline and Fall of the Yankees*. Vic Ziegel of the New York *Post* had asked me to review the book for his column, and when I did he refused to run it. He said I was so hard on the Yankees it would get me into trouble. As things turned out, it couldn't have done me any more harm.

Mann had recently written a piece for the Washington *Daily News* about being mugged by three young men in a park. He said that he believed he understood what motivated the kids and that he felt no hatred toward them. The young men were black, but Mann revealed this only under pressure. His point was that their color was irrelevant—that is, the point of the story was that it would be a better world if indeed it were.

I tell this story because it reminded me of something that happened to Mike Marshall in Cleveland. He was roughed up by a pack of about fifteen kids. When it was all over the police had great difficulty dragging out of him the fact that the kids were black. He didn't think it should make any difference either.

There was a difference, though—in Mike's pitching. The injuries he received fighting the kids off seemed superficial. Nevertheless, it was at precisely this point that he went from being our best pitcher to our worst.

Brant Alyea came up to me today and said that Ted Williams was asking about me.

"What was he asking?" I said. "About what kind of person I was?"

"Oh shit no," Alyea said. "What difference does it make what kind of person you are? We're all just merchandise anyway. He wanted to know whether you were in tight with the Pilots and whether they considered you in their plans for the future."

"It's obvious from the way they're using me that they don't consider me in their plans," I said. "So tell Williams I can probably be had right now for a song, maybe a short medley."

Right after that, Bob Short, the owner of the Washington club, came by and Alyea introduced me to him. I congratulated him on the fine job he was doing in Washington and he said that I was doing a pretty good job myself. I said I was glad he'd noticed.

What a beautiful day. Imagine playing for Teddy Ballgame. That's what he calls himself, in his autobiography too. What isn't generally known, except around the comfortable confines of the ballpark, is that he thinks of himself as "Teddy Ballgame of the MFL."

That's the Major Fucking Leagues.

Pagliaroni told a story about Joe Brown, the general manager of the Pittsburgh club. Brown called a meeting of the players and said, "Boys, we're fighting for the entertainment dollar. We have to learn to get along with the fans and get along with the writers. And we have to be more colorful as ballplayers."

That very night the Pirates got into an extra-inning game and Pagliaroni scored the winner in the fifteenth. "I come around and I touch home plate," Pag said, "and as I run toward our dugout I take a big slide, feet first, all the way into it."

The next morning there was a call from Joe Brown. "What the hell were you doing out there?," Brown said. "What are you, some kind of clown?"

And Pagliaroni said, "I was just competing for the entertainment dollar, Joe."

AUGUST
10

Talking about Yastrzemski not hustling recalled one of the great non-hustlers of all time, Roger Maris. Rodg always went to first base as though he had sore feet. If he hit a home run it didn't matter, of course. But every time he popped up or hit a routine grounder, it would take him a half-hour to get to first base—if he got there at all. He'd often just peel off halfway down and head for the dugout.

So Houk would call a meeting and he'd say, "Boys, it doesn't look good if we don't run the ball out. I want everybody to show some hustle out there."

And Maris would go out there and damned if he wouldn't do the same thing all over again. I could never believe Ralph's patience. I know Maris was sensitive to what was written about him in the papers, and I don't know why Houk didn't just blast him to the reporters. But he never did. And Maris continued to loaf.

Johnny Sain quit or was fired today. I'm amazed. Also not surprised.

Going into the last of the eighth we're ahead 5–4. O'Donoghue, who has relieved Brabender, has pitched three good innings. Now they get a couple of hits off him and he's lifted for John Gelnar. This isn't too bad a choice. Gelnar was knocked out in his last start, but his relief pitching hasn't been bad. Except he's hit this time and now the score is 5–5 and Gelnar's out.

Who comes in, Bouton? Nope. Steve Barber. We lose 7–5.

Because I have nobody else to talk to I ask Eddie O'Brien, "Eddie, what the hell is going on out there?"

"I don't know," Eddie O'Brien says. "I can't figure it out either."

Well, maybe I can. Maybe I'm about to be traded to the Senators. They can't finish first, but they can finish second. I still think I have a chance to be a hero someplace.

I try, but it remains most difficult to convey the quality of the banter in the back of the bus. There is zaniness to it, and earthiness, and often a quality of *non sequitur* that I find hilarious. Have an example from our trip to the Washington airport.

Greg Goossen: "Hey, does anybody here have any Aqua Velva?"

Fred Talbot: "No, but I gotta take a shit, if that'll help."

I've had some thoughts on what separates a professional athlete from other mortals. In a tight situation the amateur says, "I've failed in this situation many times. I'll probably do so again." In a tight situation the professional says (and means it), "I've failed in this situation and I've succeeded. Since each situation is a separate test of my abilities, there's no reason why I shouldn't succeed this time."

Then there is also the case of the professional player who is not professional enough. He goes on a fifteen-game hitting streak and says, "Nobody can keep this up." And as the streak progresses, his belief in his ability to keep it alive decreases to the point where it's almost impossible for him to get a hit.

The *real* professional—and by that I suppose I mean the exceptional professional—can convince himself that each time at bat is an individual performance and that there is no reason he can't go on hitting forever.

Is that clear? If it is, perhaps you ought to check with your doctor.

AUGUST
11

Cleveland

I'm still trying to decide why I haven't been in more ballgames in crucial situations and all I can do is agree with Hovley that it's because they think I'm weird and throw a weird pitch. I need a new image. What I ought to do is take up chewing tobacco and let the dark brown run down the front of my uniform and walk up and down the dugout with a slight, brave limp and tape on my wrist and say things like, "goddammit" and "shit" and "let's get these guys." Then, instead of being weird, I'd be rough and tough.

I think I'd do it, except I can't stand the thought of all that brown down the front of my uniform.

We may not be winning a lot of ballgames, but we've got a lot of spirit. In fact we might have the best "around the horn" in the league. You throw the ball around the horn—catcher to first baseman to short-stop to second baseman to third baseman—after an infield out, and you do it with a lot of élan. We get better at it all the time.

AUGUST
12

Pitched two more innings in another losing cause. We were down three runs when I came in and down three when I came out. The only problem I had was with Home Run Baker, a new Cleveland kid who's been hitting vicious line drives all over the place. This time he hit one right back at me and the only way I was able to avoid certain death was to perform a perfect veronica. Olé.

I also struck out Hawk Harrelson and Duke Simms. Double olé.

Called Mike Marshall. He's alive and well and pitching in Toledo. He's 3–1 and sticking to his no-plan plan, the one Sal Maglie said wouldn't do. Mike said that Bennie Borgmann, the scout, asked him what the problem was, that he had heard there was some personality difficulty. Mike said he didn't know of any. The next day Borgmann talked to Jack Tighe, the manager, and was told "Mike's fine. Gives me 100 percent. You just leave him alone and let him do it his way and he'll be all right."

Borgmann was impressed and asked Marshall if he wanted to go back with Seattle. He said no, not as long as there was no change in the situation there.

We go home after tomorrow night's game. It's commercial all the way with a lay-over in Chicago. Which means we'll get home at four-thirty in the morning local time, but actually about seven-thirty body time. This is done so we can spend all day with our families. It's also done to save a night of hotel expenses. Me, I'll be home with my family, but I'll be in bed all day, sleeping.

Steve Barber suggested to Sal Maglie that he send Brabender home a day early so that he wouldn't miss a night's sleep. Brabender opens for us against Baltimore. And Sal said, "The last time we did that the guy went only two-and-two-thirds innings. So we're not going to do it any-more."

I don't remember what that's called in logic, but the fallacy is: B follows A. Therefore A caused B.

Steve Hovley went down with an inside pitch tonight and took first base. I asked where the ball hit him and he said it didn't hit him at all.

"You sure went down to first like you'd been hit," I said.

"Yeah, that's what you have to do," Steve said. "You have to jump up, throw your bat aside and start down to first as if everybody in the ballpark could see the ball hit you. This intimidates the umpire."

Ray Oyler in the back of the bus: "Boys, I had all the ingredients for a great piece of ass last night—plenty of time, and a hard-on. All I lacked was a broad."

AUGUST

13

Beat Cleveland 5–3 and it was a struggle all the way. Brunet fell three runs behind early but managed to hold on. The reason he was able to hold on is that every time he had a couple of men on base, Fred Talbot yelled at him, "C'mon, fat boy, regroup out there."

There was a lot of grousing about the flight home. We had a three-hour wait after the game was over and then an hour-and-a-half wait in Chicago. If we had a charter flight we could have gotten in to Seattle at about twelve-thirty instead of four-thirty. The ballclub argues that it costs too much money to charter a plane and generally we just shrug and figure, well, it probably does.

There was a United Airlines man along on the trip, so I said to him, "Just out of curiosity, what does it cost to fly a team like this from Cleveland to Seattle on regularly scheduled flights?"

He said he couldn't give me an exact figure, but if he had to approximate, he'd say $5,200, give or take a few hundred. And what, I asked, would it cost to charter a jet to fly from Cleveland to Seattle?

"I couldn't give you an exact figure," he said. "But I can tell you that it costs $6,200 to charter a plane from New York to Seattle. So if you could get a plane out of Cleveland, it would be a little bit less, probably around $5,900."

Naturally I promptly told Mincher that the only difference between a charter flight and commercial was $700. Just as naturally, Mincher goes to Gabe Paul and says, "What's the story, Gabe? We found out that there's only a $700 difference between charter and commercial. And we don't think the ballclub should be stingy with that kind of money. They should get the guys home at a decent hour."

"I don't know where you got your figures," Paul said.

"Bouton got them from the United Airlines man," Mincher said. Just then the man came along down the aisle, and when Minch told him what the argument was about, he backed off. "I didn't give any exact figures," he said.

"You tell Mincher that there's a hell of a difference," Paul said. "Tell him."

"Oh yeah," the guy said. "The numbers are real big. I don't know exactly what they are, but there's a hell of a difference."

Mincher stalked off. Later on he came over to me and said, "What the hell are you trying to tell us about $700?"

I told him the way I got my information and said, "Why would I make those numbers up?"

"Well, somebody's lying in this deal," Mincher said.

"It's not me, Minch."

"No, I don't think it's you," Minch said. And he went away mad.

The country western music got a big workout in the clubhouse after the win. There are four or five different tape-players around and they make quite a racket. One of the favorites is "Dirty Old Egg-Sucking Dog." Gene Brabender knows all the words to that one. Another is, "Happy Birthday, Joe Beam." It starts out, "They're hanging Joe Beam today . . ." Seems that Joe Beam killed eleven guys before he was twelve and they said he was an "unruly boy." And right at the end, when they hang him, they break out into "Happy Birthday, Joe Beam."

Breaks us up.

Seattle

Today Joe Schultz said to John Kennedy, who just had the cast taken off his knee: "How's your old hinge, John?" Joe Schultz also said, "The starters here will be Brabender, Segui, Talbot and Brunet." When he said Talbot I winced, and Talbot caught it and said, "Eat your heart out, Bouton."

And when we were going over the hitters a lot of the comments consisted of: "He likes the ball over the plate."

Let's see, now. When the ball is over the plate isn't that what the umpires call a strike?

Also, there seemed to be a lot of first-ball hitters in the crowd. Brooks Robinson, Don Buford, Paul Blair, all first-ball hitters. One day I want to hear somebody say, "Good third-ball hitter. Likes to hit that third pitch." Then I'll have learned something.

At the end of the meeting Joe Schultz said, "Anybody got anything else to say about this club?" And in a very low voice, I said, "Pretty good ballclub."

And Joe Schultz said, "Well, hell, let's go beat the shit out of them. Fuck 'em. They ain't no different than anybody else."

He was right. They beat us too. The score was 2–1. Gene Brabender pitched a helluva game.

I was warming up in the bullpen when a fan leaned out and said, "Hey Jim, how do you pitch to Frank Robinson?" I told him the truth. "Reluctantly," I said.

Billy Williams just got called up. He was on the Seattle Angels club with me last year when it was Triple-A. He's played *eighteen* years of minor-league ball. He's a good-hitting outfielder. He should have had a better shot but I think he's one of those Negroes who wasn't quite good enough to be a star and wound up a good minor-leaguer.

The situation of the Negro in baseball is not as equitable as it seems. He still has to be better than his white counterparts to do as well. I recall a story Mike Marshall told about a guy in the Detroit Tiger organization named Ike Brown, who hit .300 for a number of years in Triple-A and was the International League All-Star third baseman for a couple of years. He drove in a lot of runs too, but he was never even invited to spring training by the Tigers. Mike says the fact that he was black must have had a lot to do with it. "How many Negroes on the Detroit club?" Mike said. "Earl Wilson, Gates Brown and Willie Horton. Two stars, and Brown is the best pinch-hitter in the business."

This brings up a point. There are a lot of Negro stars in the game. There aren't too many average Negro players. The obvious conclusion is that there is some kind of quota system. It stands to reason that if 19 of the top 30 hitters in the major leagues are black, as they were in 1968, then almost two thirds of all the hitters should be black. Obviously it's not that way. In the case of the Tigers, the fact that only three of their players are black is no less astonishing.

Joe Sparma and Al Kaline have a company that runs baseball clinics around the country. They line up the players to run the clinics and pay a thousand dollars for three mornings of work. It sounded like an unbelievable deal in the letter I got. They wanted me, Ray Oyler, Wayne Comer and two or three other guys. We wanted to know what the next step would be, so we asked Ray Oyler, because he'd played with the Tigers, to call Kaline or Sparma and check. This was about two weeks ago. Tonight I asked Oyler what he'd found out.

"I called Sparma twice," he said. "I wasn't able to get him."

"Oh," I said.

Consider this. There's quite a bit of money involved and Ray Oyler, one of the boys, the man everybody likes, the "in" infielder, makes two phone calls, and gives up. Zero. On the other hand, Mike Marshall arranges to have a railroad car to ship our automobiles from Tempe to Seattle. It takes a lot; phone calls, letters, a lot of organizing. But Oyler is okay and Marshall is a weirdo.

A good word about Sal Maglie. Lately he's been calling down to the bullpen to have me warm up even when I'm not going to get into the game. It makes it easier for me to get a catcher.

AUGUST
16

It's been nippy these last evenings and my fingers have felt a bit wooden. It's not freezing, of course, but the temperature gets down to about 55. So I've been using a handwarmer.

Talbot: "What the hell do you need a handwarmer for? Dammit, it's only 60 degrees."

Pattin: "Oh, he's just got to be different. You know him."

Bouton: "Marty, why don't you go feed your gopher?"

I was sorry I said that. Although Marty has been giving up a lot of home runs lately, it's not the kind of thing you mention. He got into the game and gave up two more, which made me feel bad. What made me feel worse was me getting into the game and giving up three runs in two innings. It was a terrible performance. I was wild as hell. I kept telling myself it was because I hadn't been pitching enough and I was angry at Joe, then I got angry hecause the score was 10–2 against us when he put me in, and when the ball would come back from the catcher I'd slap my glove at it. So instead of thinking about pitching and how to get the ball over the plate I was thinking about being angry. Did I say I loved this game?

AUGUST
18

The Orioles beat us for the fourth straight time. The score was 15–3. Said Fred Talbot: "We got no business scheduling these guys." Then, "This Baltimore outfit can sure fluff up your ERA."

Sure can. Especially mine. I came into the game in the second inning. George Brunet had had some bad luck; a few bleeders, a few shots, and the game was gone. I knew it was gone because I was in it. Second inning, bases loaded, one out. The first pitch was a good knuckleball that went by McNertney to the screen. A run scored. I walked the hitter, filling the bases again. I got the next guy on a strikeout, but then I got behind and had to come in with a couple of fastballs. Double; two runs. Now all three of poor Brunet's runs have scored and I've got runners on second and third. The pitcher comes up and hits the second pitch into left for a single and Sal Maglie comes out to the mound.

"We're going to have to take you out," Sal says.

"But, Sal," I say, "I need work. We're losing 10–0. What difference does it make now?"

"We brought you in with the bases loaded and you didn't do the job. We have to get you out of there."

So I turned around, walked off the mound and into the dugout. Since I hadn't really thrown much, I then ran out to the bullpen to get some more in. When I got there I picked up a ball and said, "I'd like to do a little throwing now. Who wants to catch?"

"I'm not catching," Ranew said.

"Pag, I'd like to do some throwing," I said.

"Why?" Pagliaroni said.

"Because I didn't get the right feel of the knuckleball and I think I have to do some throwing."

"I don't think you have to do any throwing," Pagliaroni said.

"Well, I think I have to. And I'm the one who decides when I throw and when I don't throw. Right?"

Nobody answered. I glared around the bullpen and no one would look me in the eye. So I sat down and sulked.

Eddie O'Brien had been listening to all of this, of course, but he wasn't going to get involved. He's only the bullpen coach. I decided to involve him. "Eddie, I need to do some throwing," I said. "Do you want to have somebody catch me, or what?"

"You better check with Sal," Eddie said.

"What for? Since I've been back from Vancouver I've had an agreement that I didn't have to check with Sal."

"You better check with Sal anyway," Eddie said. "Especially since you just came out of a ballgame. He might not want you to do any throwing."

So I got up and went down to the dugout. We're still not out of the inning and Pattin is getting pounded. I waited until the inning was over and went up to Maglie. "Sal, I'd like to do a little throwing in tbe bullpen. Is it all right?"

"No, no. It wouldn't look good. You just came out of a ballgame."

"It'll look okay. It'll look like I was working on something."

"Ah, crissakes. Ask Joe."

"Joe, do you mind if I get some throwing in the bullpen?"

"No. If you want to, go ahead."

Back in the bullpen I said to O'Brien, "Sal and Joe said it was all right if I do some throwing."

O'Brien didn't say a word. He just got up and walked all the way in to the bench. Meanwhile, no one was getting up to catch me. So I stood there, feeling awkward, and mad.

When O'Brien came back he gave Pagliaroni a nod. "It's okay," he said. "Joe said he could throw."

I could feel my neck flame. "I *told* you he said it was all right. What the hell are you going down there for?"

"I just wanted to check," O'Brien said.

"You mean you didn't believe me?" I said. "I have a bad outing or two, Eddie, and now suddenly my word isn't good anymore? Huh, Eddie? I'm not telling the truth, right?"

So Pag got up, very slowly put on his glove and mask and crouched down behind the plate. I started to get ready to throw when I heard John Gelnar say, "Come on, Merritt, I'd like to do some throwing myself." Merritt just laughed.

"Don't be a wise guy, Gelnar," I said. "This may be funny to you but it's not funny to me."

"If you're mad at us, don't take it out on John," Pagliaroni said.

"You didn't hear what he said," I told Pag. "He's trying to make fun of the fact that I need to do some throwing. This isn't a popularity contest. If it's between me doing my job or being one of the boys, it's going to be my job that comes first."

I started to throw, but it didn't make me feel any better. After about forty pitches, steaming all the time and thinking how wrong it was for O'Brien to check up on me, how mean it was of Pagliaroni and Ranew to just sit there, how unfair it was of Gelnar to try to make a joke of it, I marched down to the front of the bullpen and made a speech.

"You know something? There are going to be better days for me, but it's going to be hard to forget what people on this bench were like when things were bad. O'Brien, you've been nice to me lately and I thought it was because you were changing. Now I realize it was only because I was pitching well. You're really the same old guy just waiting for the right moment to come out and be yourself."

"You're making an ass out of yourself," Pagliaroni said.

"Well, maybe I'll apologize tomorrow," I said. "But I think I said something that needed to be said."

"Yeah, and how about the night you said, 'The hell with the rest of the guys. They don't pay my salary?' " Pagliaroni said.

I said I didn't know what the hell he was talking about.

"You know, the day we had that extra-inning game," Pagliaroni said. "You left in the ninth inning and when somebody asked you where you were going you said home, and he asked you what about team spirit, and you said, 'The hell with the rest of the guys. They don't pay my salary.' "

"Pag, I actually said that," I said. "But it was meant to be funny. I was smiling when I said it and it was supposed to be a joke. Anyway, it's unfair of you to bring that up now. You're just jumping on a guy when he's down. You're taking something you heard thirdhand and was misinterpreted in the first place and you're trying to tell me you're using that as an excuse not to catch me."

There must have been steam coming out of my ears by now, because Eddie O'Brien said, "Go take a shower."

"Okay, I'll take a shower," I said. "Only I want you guys to think about what I said."

"I'll think about it," Pagliaroni said. "My whole life revolves around Jim Bouton."

"I guess you won't think about it much at that," I said.

In the clubhouse I stomped around for a while and had a few beers, which I seldom do. I watched Brunet getting dressed and I nearly fell off my stool. "George, I got to know something," I said. "This is not a knock.

I don't mind guys who do things differently. But I got to know. *Did you forget to put on your undershorts?*"

"No, I never wear undershorts," Brunet said. "Hell, the only time you need them is if you get into a car wreck. Besides, this way I don't have to worry about losing them."

I guess that made me feel better, because I suddenly remembered something Mike Marshall once told me. "It doesn't hurt to say you're sorry," Marshall said, "even if you don't mean it."

All right, all right. I'll apologize. So I sat there eating spicy hot dogs and drinking beer and listening to the radio. When O'Donoghue came in—early, because he'd pitched—I stuck my hand out and said, "I want to apologize for losing my cool in the bullpen tonight."

"Okay, fine," O'Donoghue said.

Later on Gelnar said, "Sure, fine," and Ranew said, "Okay," and Pagliaroni smiled and said, "Likewise."

I didn't apologize to Eddie O'Brien. There are some things I just will not do.

McNertney stopped by my locker to—of all things—apologize. It was for the ball that went back to the screen. "Jesus, it just hit off my glove," he said. "It was a good knuckleball too."

The dear boy.

My wife says I was wrong. She says I blew my cool and that's not something I ought to do, especially if I plan to go into politics some day. She said she thought I was right, but that being right has nothing to do with it. "You won the battle," she said, "and you lost the war."

Maybe she's right. Maybe the only kind of politician I can be is the kind who sits on the sidelines and hollers. Take a guy like Ralph Nader. He's not a politician, I know, but how many politicians have contributed as much to American life as he has? So maybe I can find a way to be heard, to be effective without surrendering my right to pop off when I think I'm right.

In fact, though, I don't really think I did myself any good in the bullpen tonight. I mean what will get around about it is not that I said some tough things, but that I delivered a short speech in front of the bullpen. Nobody delivers short speeches in front of the bullpen. My trouble is I forgot one of baseball's most important axioms: "He's a helluva guy. Wouldn't say shit if he had a mouthful."

AUGUST
19

When I got to the clubhouse I was confronted by Pagliaroni. "Did you send me the check, Bouton?"

"Check? Me? Money?" I said. "How much did I owe you?"

"No. You don't owe me. I got a check for $100 from the guy who won $2700 on Home Run for the Money because I hit one. I just figured it might be a phony from you."

I bit the check and pronounced it genuine. "Nope, I didn't send it," I said.

It was then calculated that if Pagliaroni got $100 for winning his man $2700, Fred Talbot should have gotten a thousand from Donald Dubois. Did he ever get anything? "Nope," Talbot said.

Gee, wonder what old Dubois would do with all that money.

Said Talbot: "I hope he gets drunk on it, wrecks his car and kills himself."

George Brunet (who does not wear undershorts), was talking about the Negro in baseball, Tommy Harper in particular. "You know, for a colored player, he's not a bad hustler. Hell, he wants to play ball."

Before the father-and-son game Sunday, Pagliaroni said to Wayne Comer: "Now, no fair giving your son a greenie."

Greenie or no, the Comer boy stole the show. When he came to bat he took the handle and knocked some imaginary dirt off the bottom of his little sneakers, then he rubbed dirt on his hands, gripped the bat, tapped the plate with it and showed all the mannerisms of the big-league players. Said Fred Talbot: "Comer's kid has a little hot dog in him, doesn't he?"

The kids beat the fathers 40–0, and Sibby Sisti said, "Forty runs, for crissakes, and nobody gets knocked down." And McNertney said that he was standing next to Sal Maglie during the game and swore he heard Sal saying, "He's a first-ball hitter"—"a high-ball hitter"—"a fastball hitter"—and none of the kids was over four feet tall.

For some reason that reminded me of my manager in Amarillo, Sheriff Robinson, who used to say about every hitter, "Jam him." And then later on we talked with some old-timers who'd played with Robinson and they said, "He was a pretty good ballplayer. But we used to jam the hell out of him."

Max Soriano, one of the owners, had a party at his house for the players. It was supposed to be held on an off day except a lot of the players objected that it would ruin their day. So it was switched to Sunday night and, of course, it was a fine party, good food, bar, and the wives enjoyed getting dressed up.

The best line of the evening was delivered by Joe Schultz: "What are you drinking there, honey?" he said to Fred Talbot's wife.

"Coca-Cola," she said.

And Joe Schultz said: "You'll never make it on that, my dear."

This broke everybody up, and Bob Locker said, "You better write that down, Bouton."

My note-taking is beginning to make the natives restless.

A couple of guys have been needling me about it. Tossing fat on the fire, Steve Hovley my roommate, who knows, asks, "Hey, why are you writing down all those notes?"

"Yeah, what's he writing those notes for?" Fred Talbot adds.

So Hovley tells him. "When a guy smells the end of his career coming, he usually starts writing little notes to himself. You'll see. It will happen to you too."

Steve Hovley sauntered over to my locker and asked what was new on the Gatorade front. Not much, friend. Milkes snooped around to find out if I'd actually bought the Gatorade and if it had been drunk by the players. Everybody's checking up on me these days. Then he told Johnny McNamara that he wasn't going to pay for it.

What I ought to to about it, of course, is forget it. I never bothered about small things with ballclubs; things like cabfare if I did an appearance, or excess baggage. I'd much rather negotiate them out of $1,000 at contract time than bother about small sums. But things have been so petty around here I'm going to keep the pressure on in the case of the missing Gatorade money. May justice triumph.

Today, with the Orioles gone and the Detroit Tigers coming in, Joe Schultz said, "Well, boys, we got that other outfit out of here with all their bullshit. Fuck it. Let's go get 'em, let's start winning ballgames." We dashed out onto the field cheering. Some of us would run through a cheesecloth curtain for that man.

Bullpen humor:

The attendance at the Baltimore games was respectable, but we're back to not drawing much for the Tigers. It is decided in the bullpen that the people who came to see us play the Orioles are the same kind who went to see the lions eat Christians.

There's going to be a Day soon for Tommy Harper, so John O'Donoghue is reminded of the Day that was given to him in Kansas City. "All my family and friends were there," O'Donoghue says. "And they gave me a Legionnaire's cap, a *used* Legionnaire's cap. They also gave me honorary memberships to all the drinking clubs in town. They gave me two plaques. And then they gave me a wallet, a brand-new wallet. I practically tore that damn thing apart looking for the money. I know there *had* to be something more than a used Legionnaire's cap and a wallet. But there wasn't."

"Hey, Merritt," Fred Talbot says to Merritt Ranew. "Tell Bouton to his face what you said about him last night."

Merritt's face gets red and he says, "I didn't say a thing." And I say, "What'd he say, Fred? You can tell me."

And Fred says: "I didn't get it all. Something about your mother."

I'm telling Talbot and Comer about El Bodegon in Washington and Talbot says, "If Bouton recommends a restaurant, you can be pretty sure they got some good Communist dishes."

Talbot says to Hovley: "Hey Hovley, some of the guys are starting to talk about your hair." He pauses. "And I'm one of them."

Then he turns to me. "You know, writing notes like that, Bouton, it's worse than whispering."

Talbot and Ranew get into a deep discussion about the South.

Ranew is from Georgia and Talbot is from Virginia. Talbot started it because he said that all the guys from the South are dumb.

"Well, where the hell are you from?" Ranew says, because he knows the answer.

"I'm from the north part of the South," Talbot says.

"It's better down where I live than it is where you are," Ranew says.

"Everything but the people," Talbot says. "The people are dumb."

I can't resist. I get into the discussion. "It's true, Merritt," I say. "What other state in the union has a governor that never even finished high school?"

"The reason they got this guy Lester Maddox," says Talbot, "is because he's so dumb. That's what they need to talk to all the dummies they got down there. They'd never understand a guy from Yale or Harvard or one of them colleges."

Ranew scratches his head. "I still think the South is better where I live."

"How can you compare which part of the country is better?" Talbot says. "I say mine, you say yours. How can you compare?"

"Why doesn't Bouton do some research on it tomorrow in the library and come back with some figures for us?" Ranew says.

"Nah, let's do it right here," Talbot says. "All right, let's start. How many dummies you got down there?"

By this time there is a lot of general laughter. I'm not prepared to explain why.

"I tell you one thing," Ranew says. "We got better-looking guys down where I am."

Talbot is shocked. "Better *looking?*" he says. "For crissakes, look at yourself. You've got hair like a sissy."

It's not a felicitous description. Ranew has his hair styled in the modern mode. It is not unattractive. Talbot wears his in an oldfashioned crew cut.

"Look at you," Talbot says, moving in for the kill. "You use hair spray and go to a goddam beauty parlor."

"With that hair *you've* got," Ranew says, "you could use a little beauty parlor yourself."

"I'll tell you one thing," Talbot says. "I don't walk around with hair spray and I don't look like a goddam sissy and I don't squat to piss, either."

Now the laughter has turned against Ranew and he is searching desperately for a counter. One can almost hear the file cards in his head fluttering.

"You know what you look like, Talbot?" Ranew says. "You look like a perch, a goddam perch."

"A *perch?*" Talbot says. "What the hell do you mean, a perch?"

"Well, you look like a perch," Ranew says. "Your head is square, you have bardly any nose at all, your eyes bulge out and you look like some kind of fish."

Now the laughter has turned on Talbot.

"But I don't look like a goddam sissy," he says.

I am afraid he is defeated.

That's not the funniest. The funniest is what happened to Ray Oyler. He was warming up Locker and caught a sinker right on the cup. It didn't even hit the ground first. Ding-dong! He went down on all fours and crawled around that way for a while. Then he limped into the dugout and vomited.

The boys were hysterical. We were getting beat a ballgame and we were *laughing.* Joe Schultz laughed so hard he had to take off his glasses, dry his eyes and hide his head in a warm-up jacket.

AUGUST
20

Big meeting before the game to discuss proposed items for negotiations in the player contract after the season. Mincher started it by saying, "Listen up, everybody." I once had a sergeant who said, "Listen up, everybody."

And Talbot said, "Hey, Bouton, no notes during the player-representative meeting."

I started jotting down some notes anyway in the hope that someone would confiscate them: "One bunch of carrots, loaf of bread, half-dozen eggs." No one tried. Foiled again.

The big topic was the reserve clause. There is some thought that we should try to eliminate it, or at least limit it. Joe Schultz led off the discussion by saying: "Boys, the reserve clause is the one thing you can't fool with. It's the foundation of this game. If you get rid of it we're all out of business. And I'm serious."

Contrary to popular belief the reserve clause is not a single paragraph (although its single intent is to bind a player to one club for as long as he lives or until his contract is disposed of). There is a whole set of rules which covers things like options, waivers, severance pay, moving allowance, etc. Many of these rules could be amended without upsetting the structure of the game.

It has been suggested that baseball adopt an option rule like pro football's. Instead, I propose that we keep the one-way contract we currently play under and use it as a public relations lever to change some of the more repugnant aspects of the clause.

The football option rule gives only the illusion of freedom. A footoall player is required to sign a two-year contract, that is, one year plus an option for the next. At the end of the first year of his contract, he may elect to announce that he is playing out his option. In which case he is required to play only one more season, and the team may, if it wishes, cut his salary by twenty-five percent. At the end of the option year he theoretically becomes a free agent and can sell his services to the highest bidder. Except that there is a rule which requires his new team to give his old team "equal value." What this amounts to then, is a trade. So the only right a football player has is to demand to be traded. We can do that too. Only it's not a demand, it's a plea.

One rule change I suggested was to have a player receive some kind of bonus when he got traded so that the owners wouldn't feel free to trade guys just to give them a change of scenery. Make it expensive to trade and they'll only do it when they have to.

Another thing that should be done, I said, is to take into consideration the amount of time a man has spent in the minors. If he's had only two years or so in the minors, $10,000 isn't bad to start with. But if a guy has been in the minors for five, seven, ten years or more, a guy who's in his 30s and has a wife and kids, it's unconscionable to start him at $10,000. What made me think of this was talking to Billy Williams the other day. I said he didn't have to tell me if he didn't want to, but I was curious about the kind of money he'd been making in the minors.

"I was making $1,300 a month," he said. That's for a five-month season.

"What did you make last year?"

"Last year I made $1,100 a month, and the year before I was under a thousand."

And this was his eighteenth season in the minors. "Did they sweeten up that $1,300 when they called you up?" I asked.

"Oh yeah, they sweetened it."

"How much?"

"I'm making $10,000." (That's a *rate*, or $1,666 a month.)

"What's so sweet about that? They *have* to pay you that."

"Yeah, that's true. I guess they have to."

It made me sad, and mad.

Finally there was a debate about severance pay. If a player is released in the middle of the season he gets thirty days pay. But if he gets released in spring training, actually at the end of it, he gets nothing. I suggested he get ninety days pay, on the grounds that he should get paid for spring training, plus severance. I was voted down. The other guys said we should ask for only thirty days after spring training and sixty days during the season. And what I say is, it doesn't hurt to ask for more than you expect to get. Don't be afraid to climb those golden stairs.

Sitting in the bullpen tonight it seemed as if I'd never given my little bullpen lecture. The guys were coming over to tell me stories and I felt right back in the swing of things. I guess Mike Marshall was right. It doesn't hurt to apologize.

We scored a run in the ninth, which meant we had just enough runs to lose 4–3. I think that's six in a row now and we're in fifth place. Nobody talks about it, except Joe Schultz.

AUGUST

21

Gene Brabender sometimes walks around bellowing "cowabunga!" So I threw some trivia at him. "Bender, who first said 'cowabunga?'"

This upset Marty Pattin. He's never understood the importance of trivia. "Who the hell cares who said 'cowabunga,' for crissakes?" Pattin said.

"This is vital stuff, Marty," I said.

I gave Bender time, but he actually didn't know who said 'cowabunga'—even after I told him the line was "Cowabunga, Buffalo Bob." Poor fellow. It was, as almost everyone knows, Chief Thunder Thud on the "Howdy Doody" show.

It cost me a dollar to the pitchers' fund because I didn't back up third base the other night. The play was at second, so the fine wasn't altogether fair. I think they enjoy taking my money. The play got the talk around to how we backed up plays in high school, and I remembered that when I was a kid I didn't trust anybody else to make a play. I used to run into the outfield for relays and throw the ball home. Sometimes I'd even call the shortstop off a pop fly if I didn't think he was a very good fielder. Which reminded Talbot that high school was great. "In those days I'd pitch, bat fourth and hit .400," he said.

Not me. Even in high school I batted ninth. I knew at an early age I'd never be a hitter. Like I said, pitching's easier.

During the ballgame last night, Brunet was watching carefully as Mickey Lolich warmed up. "Hey, you know something?" Brunet announced. "Lolich is fatter than I am." He then proceeded to shout the things that have been used to put him down over the years: "Hey, fatso" and "One man to a pair of pants out there." Fat man's revenge.

It seems awfully late in the season to be learning things about my knuckleball, or rather, my pattern of knuckleball pitching, but the process goes on. Sometimes I'm a little slow.

I got into the game in the eighth inning with the score tied 6–6. *Tied!* I took the count to 3 and 1 on Mickey Stanley, then got a fastball by him for 3 and 2. Full of overconfidence now, I gave him another super Bouton fastball, with smoke on it, and he hit it out of the park with fire on it. *Pow.*

The rest went fairly well. Tresh tried to bunt on me. I made the play myself and when I went to put the tag on him, he decided to knock the ball out of my hand. So I decided to tag him in the face. We both went down and I was left with a good deal of satisfaction and a stiffening leg. Baseball is a strenuous game for men my age. However, I was pleased when Tresh had to leave the game because his back was bothering him.

No hard feelings, understand. If I'd said to him as he was getting up, "How are Cherie and the kids?" he'd have said, "Fine, and how's Bobbie?"

Anyway, after Tresh I struck out Willie Horton and Al Kaline—and what I learned on this late August day was that I should not have thrown Stanley any fastballs. Even if I'd walked him, so what? All season long I've been telling myself, "If you're going to get beat, don't get beat throwing a fastball." And I did it again. My definition of a knucklehead is a man who doesn't learn from experience. So just call me knucklehead. Not only that, my record is now 2 and 1.

AUGUST

22

Pep talk by Joe Schultz before today's game with the Indians. "I know you guys have been reading in the paper that we're supposed to finish third this year. If this is putting pressure on anybody, forget it. I don't want to put any extra pressure on anybody."

He also talked about the possibility of geting fired. "I try to manage the best way I know how. I don't know who's going to be managing this club next year. I don't know if I'll be hired or fired or what. There's been rumors in the papers that I'm not going to be back, and I know one thing—whatever happens I'm going to be boss to the end of this year. Some of you may not like me. It doesn't matter. You're out there to do a job when your name's on that lineup card. You go out there and do the job because you got to do it for yourself. I don't expect you guys to do anything for me. Hell, whoever heard of everybody liking a manager anyway? Think of some of the managers you've known. There's damn few of them that everyone liked, and if they did, sometimes they all go down the drain together. As far as next year goes, I don't know what it's going to hold, but we're all in this together and I'm going to be boss right down to the end of the season."

Actually, I've heard no complaints about Joe. I think he's the kind of manager everybody likes. And we're all going down the drain together.

This was Tommy Harper Night and Joe made him rehearse his speech for us before the game. Tommy got up and said, "'Preciate it. Thanks."

Tommy needs only two more stolen bases to break the American League record and on his Night only 6,000 fans showed up. It's not a good sign for the future of baseball in Seattle. We draw a little better when we're winning, which means the fans have taken this third-place finish talk seriously. We'd all be better off if they came to see us because we played exciting baseball—like tonight. It was damned exciting, especially for me. We were down 8–4 when I went into the game in the ninth. I throw two knuckleballs to Tony Horton and he misses them both by a foot. The third one spins a bit, so he knocks it out of the park, so it's 9–4 instead of 8–4. I strike out the next two guys on six knuckleballs and get the third on a pop-up, so I'm feeling pretty good about the whole thing. And what happens? So we score four runs in the last of the ninth and have two runners on before losing 9–8. So if I don't give up the home run it's a tie ballgame. And so it goes.

The best gift Tommy Harper got on his Night was from Dewey Soriano: a trip to Hawaii for him and his wife. Greg Goossen said he didn't think that was much. "Soriano sent me to Hawaii, too," he said. "Of course, I went there as a Vancouver Mountie."

Tommy said they wanted to surprise him by having his mother fly up from Oakland. It would have been a great surprise, except for one thing. United Airlines sent the bill to his house the day before.

"With my luck I'd probably have gotten a season pass to the opera," Fred Talbot said.

We talk a lot about not drawing fans. At the same time most of the players are still telling the fans they'll be fined $50 if they sign any autographs. If some of the guys spent as much time signing autographs as they do shooing kids we'd have a lot more friends around here. Chief kid-shooer is O'Donoghue. He enjoys the work. One of these days he's going to make another Frank Crosetti.

The Cleveland trainer is called Wally "It'll Get Better" Bock. That's because if you come to him with a hangnail or a broken bone, he says the same thing, "It'll get better."

AUGUST
23

Two great putdown lines by Talbot: Before the game the pitchers were running in the outfield and an old, fat guy with two missing front teeth was giving us the business from the stands. "You guys are gonna get murdered in Baltimore," he yelled. Then there was this sudden silence, and Talbot yelled up at him, "Nice teeth ya got there." It put the old guy away for the rest of the night. The other line had to do with John Donaldson's body. Donaldson is the winner of the First Annual Sal Maglie Death Warmed Over Award. Sibby Sisti says he could take a shower in the barrel of a .22. In other words, he's fairly scrawny. And so is Ray Oyler. "Know something about Oyler?" Talbot said. "He's the only guy on the club who's physically afraid of his wife."

Funny thing about the Billy Martin fight with his pitcher Dave Boswell. The guy who sort of caused the whole thing was Art Fowler, the pitching coach. He complained to Martin that Boswell wasn't doing his running. Fowler, when he was a pitcher, was a notorious non-runner (not to mention several other things he was notorious for). In fact Fowler once put it this way: "The only reason I don't like to run is that it makes me tired."

We picnicked with the Steve Hovleys this afternoon but had to leave early because Steve had an audience with Marvin. It turned out that Milkes wanted to know what Hovley's plans were. He said the Pilots didn't want to increase their investment in him if he wasn't going to continue playing baseball. I couldn't think of anything more delicious. Here baseball is shoving around uncounted thousands of human beings who need baseball more than baseball needs them. And here's Hovley, who needs baseball less, and he's got them uptight. Beautiful. Steve told Milkes he wasn't sure, that he'd just have to play it by ear. Which is exactly what baseball tells a player who wants to know what *his* future is.

After that, Milkes said, "Steve, how are you doing financially? Is everything all right?"

"Yes, I'm all right financially," Steve said. "Why do you ask?"

"Well, I just wondered if you had enough money to buy the same kind of clothes the other players wear."

"Look, on the road you told me to wear a sportscoat and a tie, and I have been. Are you referring to clothes I wear to the ballpark here?"

"Yes. As you know, one of the problems we're having in this country is a lack of heroes and the improper image that some of our heroes have. We think our players should be clean-cut and well-dressed. It means a lot for the image of baseball, the image of the Seattle Pilots and the image of the country as a whole for the young kids to be able to look up to well-dressed athletes. Don't you agree?"

Steve didn't hesitate. "I consider that nonsense," he said. "The clothing I wear has to do with my preference. I don't see how the Seattle

Pilots' image can be threatened in the time it takes to leave my car and enter the clubhouse. Besides, I prefer to have people judge me by what I say and do, not by what I wear."

Hovley hitched up his blue jeans and left.

It's interesting that no one even mentioned his hair. Steve hasn't had a haircut since before spring training and it was six weeks ago that his manager in the minors was getting upset about the length of Sleve's hair. But no one says anything here any more. Could it be because Steve is hitting so well? Hitting over hair? Ridiculous.

Joe Schultz threatened Bones Donaldson, an ordinary lefthanded hitter, that he was going to put him in the lineup against super lefthander Sam McDowell. Donaldson sniffed. "Hell, put me in," he said. "I faced him before. The son of a bitch wouldn't throw me a strike."

Joe Schultz was being remarkably cheerful considering that we'd lost eight in a row now. I think he's doing a little in-the-dark whistling, trying to keep us loose. Didn't do any good tonight. Marty Pattin got knocked out in the fourth. Sam McDowell hit a bases-loaded double and we were off again. Number nine.

It doesn't seem to me that there's any complicated formula to building an expansion team. We all know how it's done—the way Kansas City is doing it. You go for young players and understand it's going to take time. Seattle didn't, and it shows. Kansas City, which was getting its brains beat out early in the season, is doing fine now. We're struggling with Chicago to stay out of last. It looks like a losing battle. One question: Who will be blamed for this lack of foresight, Schultz or Milkes? Answer: Can Schultz fire Milkes?

AUGUST

24

        "If we get a lead tonight, boys," Fred Talbot said, "let's call time out."

We did get a lead, 3–0. And Fred called time out. Didn't do a bit of good. Pretty soon we were down 4–3. Greg Goossen tied it with a home run, but they got two off Talbot to make it 6–4. In the ninth we scored a run and had two runners on—again—and lost it 6–5. Ten in a row.

One of the reasons the team has been doing so poorly is that we don't make many double plays. And we don't make many because, what with injuries, we've had a lot of different infielders out there. We did manage to work one today and I couldn't resist asking the bullpen a trivia question. "What's it called when you get two out with one ground ball?"

"Wait a minute," Pagliaroni said. "I remember from some of the other clubs I used to be with. I think they called it a double play."

A fan wrote a letter to one of the newspapers the other day about attendance at Sicks' Stadium. He said that the team was playing interesting, exciting baseball, but he thought the blame for low attendance lay with the front office, which priced tickets so high. (Six dollar top.) I think he's partly right. I also don't think this is a town that will ever draw 25, or 30,000 regularly. It's a town that's much more concerned with culture than athletics.

Hy Zimmerman complained in print recently that there was always tax money available for some cultural thing, but there was no money for sports, which is why there was no air-conditioning in the pressbox and the showers in the clubhouse often didn't work.

My feeling is that Seattle is the kind of cosmopolitan city that may never be good for baseball. People *are* interested in cultural events. They're interested in boating. They're interested in a great variety of outdoor sports. I don't think they're very interested in sitting and watching a baseball game. I guess to really like baseball as a fan you've got to have some Richard Nixon in you.

My wife's been having some pains in her stomach and decided it was an ulcer. "Why would you be getting an ulcer?" I said.

"Well, I get nervous when you pitch and you've been getting into so many games this year," she said. "I get nervous every day."

"Why should you get nervous? I don't. Except once in a while."

"I don't know, but I do. And every time they hit a home run off you, I just get sick to my stomach. I worry about how you feel, too, because I want you to be happy."

"Aw, come on," I said. "When they hit a home run off me I have a little switch on the side of my head. I turn it and immediately forget about the home run. Instead I start thinking about the next hitter. Most of the time, anyway. Sometimes I think about Mt. Rainier. Besides, you can't get upset about an individual performance. It's the long view of things that really matters. Hell, even if I got bombed every day, when you take the long view, as far as our life is concerned, why, we've got everything in the world to be happy about. Baseball doesn't really matter that much to us."

"I know," she said. "I know. But I still get upset when they hit those home runs off you."

AUGUST
25

We can now look forward to snapping our losing streak on the road against such weak sisters as Baltimore and Detroit. Maybe something nice will happen in New York.

Part 7 Honey, Meet Me in Houston

AUGUST
26

Baltimore-St. Louis

Maybe it will. But it won't happen to me. At nine this morning while I was asleep in my room at the Statler Hilton in Baltimore the phone rang. I picked it up and Joe Schultz said: "Jim, you've been traded to the Houston Astros."

There were two things I wanted to know. The first was, where was I? You travel as much as we do and somebody wakes you up in the morning, you don't know where you are. The second thing was, who for? You like to hear a big name on the other end. It's good for your morale.

"Who for?" I said to Schultz.

"Dooley Womack," he said.

Dooley Womack? Holy mackerel. The same Dooley Womack whose great spring I almost matched with the Yankees? Oh Lord! I hope there was a lot of undisclosed cash involved. I hope a hundred thousand, at least. Maybe it's me for a hundred thousand and Dooley Womack is just a throw-in. I'd hate to think that at this stage of my career I was being traded even-up for Dooley Womack.

Joe sounded as down as I felt. I know he's in trouble. All kinds of rumors in the papers about his being fired. So I tried to cheer him up. After all, he wasn't going to the Astros, I was. I told him I thought he was a helluva man and that I was sorry I couldn't do more for him. I told him that even though I disagreed with the way he used me, that looking back I think he did the right thing.

I was only lying a little.

I wouldn't say I was excited, but as soon as I hung up on Schultz I called Gabe Paul to arrange a flight to St. Louis where Houston was playing a twi-night double-header. "Jim Bouton here," I said. "Listen, I've been traded to the Houston Astros and I got to go to . . ." I must have talked for three minutes without pausing. When I finally did, this voice on the other end said, "I think you've got the wrong party. My name is Dave Walker. I'm with Kimberly-Clark. But what you've told me is very interesting. I'll keep it to myself."

"Hey, Steve, wake up, wake up!" I said to Hovley. "Wake up. I've been traded to Houston."

And he sort of rolled over a little and said, "Ah, the dreams, the dreams." Then he said, sitting up, "You can't go to St. Louis today."

"Why not?"

"Because you're supposed to go to the Museum of Art this afternoon. You promised."

We speculated why Milkes would make a deal like that and Hovley said, "He's building a team for the future, and how long can a knuckleball pitcher last?"

It is possible to laugh at nine in the morning in Baltimore.

I thought of calling my wife right away but realized it was only 6 A.M. in Seattle, so I went down to breakfast instead and ran into Mike Hegan, who was just rejoining the club after two weeks in service. Opposite us was Curt Rayer, the trainer. They started talking about how tough it probably was in Houston, since they were only two-and-a-half games out of first place in a five-team race.

"Now you'll be with a real ball-club," Hegan said.

"Think of it, imagine the pressure on those guys," Rayer said.

"Hey, knock it off," I said. "I'm one of them now. I hope they have plenty of Titralac for my stomach."

And I thought, Jesus, the Houston Astros, a pennant race, my first since 1964. Pinocchio, you're a real boy now.

"The end of an era," Mike Hegan said, "and there goes the Seattle dynasty, slowly crumbling."

When I went back to my room to pack I started to feel a knot in my belly. What if I don't have the feel of the knuckleball when I get there? Christ, they'll kill me in that league. Well, I'm just going to have to tell the Astros that I'm still learning the pitch and they'll have to be patient and not expect any miracles. Lord, wouldn't it be awful if I couldn't get the feel of it? If it happened in Seattle, nobody would notice. But here the whole country is watching a pennant race, and I'm in it, and suppose I can't pitch? I took a Titralac and started to pack.

Now about those waivers. I wondered how I happened to be waived out of the American League. I know Williams was interested in me in Washington. What happened? The waiver price is only $25,000. If waivers are supposed to protect players, they're not working. *Somebody* in the American League had to want me. All you can think is that some sort of deal has been made. No wonder Milkes said, "Don't worry, I'll get those waivers." You don't claim my waiver, I won't claim yours. You scratch my back, I scratch yours. One hand washes the other. It takes two to tango. And the player gets the dirty end of the stick.

Not that I mind going to Houston. How much did you say a World Series share would be?

I was supposed to call Spec Richardson, the Houston general manager, first chance I got, so I called him from the room. He seemed pleasant enough for a general manager. I asked him if they had anyone who could catch the knuckleball and he said, "Well, we have Johnny Edwards. He's our catcher. I talked to Johnny and he said he'd give it a battle."

Sudden thought. Could Milkes have traded me because he doesn't want to pay for the Gatorade?

I checked into the Chase Hotel in St. Louis, which brought back memories of staying there with the Yankees for the World Series. I remembered the inside of the hotel very well, because I had spent the night before my first Series game looking at the walls and memorizing the carpet and the potted plants and eating about a dozen times in the coffee shop. It was a good feeling of nervousness, and now I felt it again. I went up to Spec Richardson's room to get a schedule before calling Bobbie. He asked me to sit down. Then he said, "Are you a bad actor? You know what I mean?"

Now, let's see. What's a bad actor? Whose definition should I use? Steve Hovley's? Frank Crosetti's? Jim Turner's? Elston Howard's? The Motion Picture Academy's? So I said, "If I get work, I'll be a happy man here." I thought it was pretty snappy.

He said I'd get plenty of work. Then he began talking about the team, and how it was so young, and that they thought they could win the whole thing, and that I could be a big help because Gladding had 26 saves and needed someone to back him up. "Listen," he said, "if you get your nose out of joint, don't go popping off. You know what I mean? You just come to me first."

Another thing Spec Richardson said was, "Now I want to be honest with you." As soon as a general manager says that, check your wallet. It's like Marvin Milkes telling you, "We've always had a nice relationship." The truth is general managers aren't honest with their players, and they have no relationship with them except a business one.

I called home, but nobody was there. The bus to the ballpark left at three, and when I got there the equipment man told me my number would be 44. I asked if there was any chance I could get 56. He said he didn't think so, that all our pitchers have numbers in the 30s and 40s. He said I'd have to talk to Richardson or manager Harry Walker if I wanted to change the rule. I said I was sure they wouldn't want to be bothered with something so small, and he said, "Oh, you'd be surprised."

Oh no I wouldn't.

I hadn't been on the bus two minutes when the players started warning me about Harry Walker, Harry the Hat. Before the day was over, half the club had whispered into my ear.

"Don't let Harry bother you."

"Harry is really a beauty."

"Harry's going to scream. He screams all the time. He's going to scream at you. Try to keep from laughing if you can."

"Half a dozen guys have wanted to punch him."

"When he starts shouting at you, restrain yourself and be patient. After a while you'll learn to understand him and live with him."

"We've all adjusted to him, and you can, too."

After I put my uniform on, Harry Walker motioned me to his office, Harry Walker sat me down, and—for the next half-hour, solid—Harry Walker talked.

He said the way you recover from a sore arm is to throw in the outfield as he'd done a long time ago when he used to throw the ball 400 feet and stand at thc foul line in Pittsburgh and throw the ball over the roof of the right-field stands. And he said that he came back twice after hurting his arm and now he knew that people have to learn to reach a little bit further back and try harder. And he knew I had a sore arm and there was no reason why I couldn't come back and have a great, whole new career, first getting my slider back, then my fastball.

This reminded him that he was the manager when Jim Owens had a whole new career and that baseball had given him—Harry Walker—everything he's got and baseball can be a wonderful thing and he'd rather be a manager than President of the United States because he doesn't have all the President's worries and he gets to travel first-class just like the President does.

He said he has twenty-five guys to worry about, and they have only one guy to worry about. He said that everybody tries to get along and we all have our bad days and we just have to pull together and this team has the best spirit he's ever seen and this is good experience for them to go through a pennant race because next spring they'll all go to spring training together.

Etc.

Etc.

Etc.

All the time I was itching for him to get around to talking about the knuckleball. I know I've got to tell him I'm going to throw it 100 percent, and I figure maybe I'll get an argument. So finally he stops long enough for me to bring it up and I tell him that I throw it all the time, no matter what the situation is, unless a pitcher's up and I'm 3 and 0 on him.

"I'd hate to see you throw a knuckleball 3 and 2 to a guy like Maxvill, if the bases are loaded and a walk means your ballgame," he said.

I agreed. "In a situation like that, if the winning run was on third base I'd make him hit the ball. What I want to get across is that I'm not throwing curves and sliders and fastballs and changes, not only because I can't throw them, but because I can't spend time on them and pay proper attention to my knuckleball too."

I told him I was still learning this pitch and that there were going to be some days when it wouldn't be any good. But I had to throw it a lot, before and during games. He said that was fine with him, I could do whatever I wanted.

It looks like I'll be able to get along with Harry the Hat. Even if I'm the only one.

There are rules on this club too. Harry said it's $100 if you're out more than two-and-a-half-hours after the bus gets back to the hotel. Some players say they were hit for $499, a dollar below the figure that is classified as a grievance a player can take to the Commissioner. Also, the word is that Harry doesn't like to see you walking through the lobby with a young woman, even if she's your cousin or aunt or sister. I'll have to check out about good-looking moms. I have one.

Coach Mel McGaha told me first off that as soon as I get on the field I'm to take five windsprints across the outfield, just to loosen up. Everybody does it, not only pitchers. After *that,* the pitchers run. Hoo

335

boy. In Seattle six sprints across the outfield was it for the pitchers. I'm going to have to start building up my legs. Maybe Johnny Sain was wrong. Maybe I *can* run those pitches over the plate.

I asked Harry Walker if I could watch the first inning from the dugout to get a look at the hitters and he said, hell, I didn't have to go down to the bullpen until the fifth. I'm the long man, but they don't plan on needing me until then. In Seattle the long man had to be in the bullpen when the game started.

Larry Dierker, who pitched the first game, has tremendous stuff. I can't believe how young he looks, like a high-school kid. He made me want to look in a mirror for wrinkles. Doug Rader, the third baseman, has an interesting face: curly red hair, big smile, looks half-Jewish, half-Italian. You look at him once and you figure he's your friend. Wade Blasingame, pitcher, is the mod dresser on the club. He looks like a Latin lover and smokes a long thin cigar. Norm Miller is one of the club characters. He's called Jew, and doesn't mind. Before the game, Miller was doing the radio-broadcaster bit, interviewing Ron Willis, relief pitcher. "How does the team look to you this year, Ron? How about Gary Geiger? He's doing a fine job this year in right field, isn't he?" Geiger is sitting right there. "No," Willis says. "No, no, no. He's doing a brutal job. Just brutal."

"Thank you, Ron. Now tell us about the pitching situation."

"No, I won't tell you about the pitching situation."

"Then to what do you attribute the success of the team this year?"

And Willis says, in a voice loud enough to carry the whole bench, "Oh, of course, Harry Walker. No doubt about it. Harry Walker is the reason for the success of this team."

Harry never turned a hair.

It was exciting to sit out in the bullpen in an Astro uniform in beautiful Busch Stadium with people, real live people, 27,000 of them, in the stands. It was like a goddam World Series. Dierker was losing 1–0 in the eighth when Harry called down and told me to loosen up. Me and Fred Gladding. I guessed Gladding was going in if we tied it or went ahead, and I'd go in if we remained behind, which we did. I went in to pitch the last of the eighth. The knuckleball was a doll. An easy one-hopper back to me, a pop fly to first base, then I struck Del Maxvill out on a 3-and-2 knuckleball. Edwards did a fine job catching it. He dropped a few, but none of them got by him to the screen.

When I sat down on the bench, Leon McFadden, the infielder, sat down next to me and said, "A 3-and-2 knuckleball? Man, you were giving those guys some *shit* out there." I told him I'd pay him later.

Jim Owens, the pitching coach, wanted to know how come I threw a 3-and-2 knuckleball. I told him that first time around I want to earn a little respect. I want everyone to know that I'm liable to throw that pitch in any situation—3 and 2 or 3 and 0. And I want to do it right off in situations that aren't too crucial. It wouldn't have hurt much to walk Maxvill. But I want them to know that they can't count on getting the fastball.

Still, we lost 1–0.

I still haven't talked to Bobbie. I had tried to call before the game and got the babysitter. She said Bobbie had taken Mike and Dave to see *The Sound of Music.* I told the sitter not to tell her I'd been traded, that I'd call between games. And then I thought, "Good grief, she'll put on the Seattle game and hear it on the radio." As it turned out, she didn't. She read it in the paper when she got home. "Oh good," she said to herself. "A picture of Jim." That's how she found out.

She said she was excited and happy for me and we arranged to talk on the phone again and make plans for her to join me. She was happy to hear that I'd already pitched my first successful inning for the pennant-contending Houston Astros.

We won the second game 4–2 with two runs in the ninth. Julio Gotay got a pinch single with the bases loaded. After what I'd been watching and playing with, this looks like a super team, especially the double-play combo—Joe Morgan and Denis Menke are only great.

It was hard for me to feel part of it. It was weird sitting there trying to cheer for guys I didn't know. Hey, come on, let's get a hit, No. 14; you, the tall fellow, what say you get on base for us; lean into one, there No. 7.

I got to learn the names of these guys.

On the bus back to the hotel I was treated to several stanzas of "Proud to Be an Astro." There's a printed songsheet and all rookies get a copy. The song is sung with great gusto—to the tune of Tom Lehrer's "It Makes a Fellow Proud to Be a Soldier"—in the back of the bus and Harry Walker doesn't seem to notice. Sample verses:

"Now, the Astros are a team that likes to go out on the town,
We like to drink and fight and fuck till curfew comes around.
Then it's time to make the trek,
We better be back to Buddy's check,
It makes a fellow proud to be an Astro.

Now, Edwards is our catcher and he's really number one,
Dave Bristol said he drinks too much and calls some long home runs,
But we think John will be all right,
If we keep him in his room at night,
It makes a fellow proud to be an Astro.

Now, our pitching staff's composed of guys who think they're 'pretty cool',
With a case of Scotch, a greenie and an old beat-up whirlpool,
We'll make the other hitters laugh,
Then calmly break their bats in half,
It makes a fellow proud to be an Astro.

Now, Harry Walker is the one that manages this crew,
He doesn't like it when we drink and fight and smoke and screw,
But when we win our game each day,
Then what the fuck can Harry say?
It makes a fellow proud to be an Astro.

Johnny Edwards says that the most popular verse is the last one.

Back at the hotel I ran into Dooley Womack. He'd sent out his laundry and was waiting for it to come back before he joined the Seattle club. He made me feel a little better about the deal. He said the Astros

338

gave up a minor leaguer in addition to him, and he understood the Pilots were expecting some cash too. He didn't know how much.

Dooley told me he was making $25,000. So here I am making $22,000 and I'm traded for a guy making three thousand more, another player and cash. By rights I should be able to go in and demand at least $3,000 on the spot. Fat chance. But I'm going to think about it.

Curt Blefary invited me up to Jimmy Wynn's room, where some of the guys were sitting around, talking about the games and having a few drinks. Blefary, Wynn, Don Wilson and I. A few of the other guys drifted by and left. At two-fifteen the phone rang and Wynn answered. It was Mel McGaha, the coach, and Wynn said, "Mel, I'll tell you who's here, so you don't have to bother calling their rooms."

And McGaha said, "I don't want to know who's there. Tell them to go back to their rooms right now.

"That's it, men," Wynn said. "Curfew. It's not Mel's fault. He's got a job to do."

AUGUST
27

Plans. Bobbie and the kids are flying to Houston to join me on Sunday, the thirty-first. We'll live in a hotel for the ten-day home stand and then she'll fly to Chicago to go to her brother's wedding in Allegan, Michigan. She'll stay with her folks until the end of the season, except she may be able to join me for a few days in Cincinnati near the end of September. We're having our car driven from Seattle to Michigan by a schoolteacher and his wife who advertised in the paper. It will only cost us about $75 for gas. The air fares are murder, but what the hell, it's only money.

Today Don Blasingame was wearing a blue bellbottom suit, blue shirt, a blue scarf at his throat and was smoking a long thin cigar, brown.

"Little boy blue," Fred Gladding said, "come blow my horn." And everybody on the bus went "Oooooh." Blasingame feigned indifference.

Back-of-the-bus story about spring training: A lot of times during the exhibition season you change your clothes in the hotel because there are no clubhouse facilities. So you go down to the lobby in your shower slippers, carrying your spikes in your hand. On this day, we're told Joe Torre of the Cardinals swears, his roommate, already leaving with his spikes in his hand, picked up a girl in the corridor and in a matter of moments, had talked her into his bed. The quote from Torre: "The last thing I remember seeing was my roommate screwing this broad and all he had on was his baseball socks and shower slippers."

The Astro game is mock anger. It's a teasing humor that can be quite funny even if it's directed at you. It goes like this:

Tom Griffin pitched a gutsy game. He'd been having trouble with his arm and at the start of the game he looked like he was just pushing the ball up there. Bob Gibson was firing seeds for the Cards, and I thought, "Forget it. It's all over." The first two Cards got on base and I covered my eyes. But Griffin hung in there and wasn't taken out until the tenth—and then for a pinch-hitter—with the score 1–1. He was sore when Harry took him out. "I'm trying to win a ballgame here," Harry said.

We scored four runs in the tenth and won 5–1. Now the guys gave Griffin the business.

"Who the hell you think you are, Griffin?"

"You know, by getting mad at Harry taking you out, you reflected on Fred Gladding. Whatsamatter, don't you trust Gladding?"

And Gladding said, "That's right. You just showed you have no confidence in me at all."

"Now, wait a minute, Fred," Griffin said. "I've got confidence in you."

"Bullshit," Gladding said. "You don't have any confidence at all. You don't think I can do the job."

On the bus, while Blefary, Dierker, Edwards, Wynn and a few other guys sang a couple of choruses from "Proud to Be an Astro," Gladding apologized to Griffin. "I was just kidding," he said, patting him on the shoulder. "Nice game, bubble ass."

And Blasingame immediately jumped in. "Did you hear what he called you, Tom? Bubble ass? Jesus, that's absolutely uncalled for."

And so on.

There's a different relationship between whites and blacks on this club than there is in Seattle. Although there was no trouble in Seattle, there was a certain distance. Generally Davis and Simpson and Harper went their separate way. Pagliaroni and Segui were quite friendly and had dinner at each other's homes and there were no strained relations, Yet there was not a lot of—what else to call it?—segregation. Here it's obviously different. It's as though the blacks go out of their way to join with whites and the whites try extra hard to join in with the blacks. Blefary and Don Wilson room together on the road, and this is probably unique in baseball. In Jimmy Wynn's room the other night, the group was thoroughly mixed. Tonight Miller and I were having milkshakes and Joe Morgan and Jimmy Wynn came over and sat down with us. It doesn't seem forced, and I think it's worth a lot to the ballclub.

Of course, the humor sometimes gets self-consciously heavyhanded. Like one time Norm was supposed to play in a game against some tough pitcher, but he had a bad ankle and at the last minute Harry Walker decided to let him rest another night. Naturally the word went right out that Miller had asked out of the lineup, which everybody knew wasn't true. And soon there was a song called "Jew the Jake" sung to the tune of Hava Nagilla.

It just struck me that I'm playing for a team that has beaten the St. Louis Cardinals two out of three and we've got Don Wilson, one of our aces, going tomorrow, and we're in a pennant race, and we won tonight because their shortstop made an error in the tenth inning and opened the door and we stepped in, just like the old Yankees used to. I think I'm going to cry.

When I got back to the hotel, Harry Walker was standing in the lobby with Jim Owens and a couple of the other coaches. They asked me to join them, and Owens asked me what my longest stretch in a game was this season.

"About five innings," I said. "But I could have pitched longer."

"We were just thinking," Harry said.

"I know he likes to run those long sprints," Owens said. "So his legs are in shape."

"Yeah, he just might be able to give them fits," Harry said. "Niekro stopped them 1–0 tonight."

And I think, "What the hell is going on here?"

"We're just thinking about it," Harry said. "There's a possibility we may start you against Pittsburgh on Friday. "

"Oh well, hell, sure," I stammered. "I think I can do it." Of course, after facing Niekro's knuckleball they might not think much of mine.

"Well, shit, if you can throw it like you did the other night, that jumps around good enough," Owens said. "You'd give them fits. The knuckleball screws up the mind."

"We're just thinking about it," Harry said again. "We wanted to know how far you'd gone with it."

"I'm ready," I said. "But don't hesitate to use me before in relief if you need me. I can pitch in relief, then start the next night."

I walked away, my head buzzing. Here the Seattle Pilots, fighting to stay out of last place, wouldn't take another chance on starting me and the Houston Astros, in the middle of a pennant race, may just do it. Beautiful.

The Pilots ended their losing streak with a 2–1 win against Baltimore. Brabender pitched. I felt happy for them. I found I wasn't rooting against them the way I rooted against the Yankees. I guess I'd like Joe Schultz to keep his job. But I wonder what the guys think about getting Dooley Womack. I hope Dooley gets hammered. That way maybe somebody will wise up to Marvin Milkes.

We lost a 2–1 heartbreaker in extra innings. It was tough to take. On the other hand, President Nixon today nominated Judge Haynsworth for the Supreme Court. I think that will turn out to be a more famous defeat.

Houston

I start tonight against Pittsburgh. I decided I wasn't going to be nervous. I wasn't going to let my stomach churn over. It was the Bard or Johnny Sain or somebody who said, "He who would be calm must take on the appearance of being calm." So that's what I did. I tried to look relaxed, and after a while I felt relaxed. Shakespeare or somebody would have been a helluva pitching coach.

I don't think Bobbie would have been very good at it, though.

I called to tell her about the start and she said, "You? Why you?"

Lovely girl.

Why me, at that? I guessed because of Niekro's success against the Pirates. I also guessed because of doubleheaders, which have jammed up the pitching staff. And I guessed because Harry Walker likes to take chances.

The trouble for me in a pressure situation is that the knuckleball isn't like other pitches. Throwing conventional stuff in a tight situation, I'd just throw harder. It didn't take any thinking, just more muscle. Whitey Ford once said to me during a World Series game, "Kid, you're throwing nervous hard out there." But with a knuckleball, if you start cutting loose, it starts spinning and you spend a lot of time watching baseballs fly over fences.

Still, the pressure, I think, is one of the most exciting things about athletics, and it's one of the reasons I have so much fun playing. I remember sitting on the bench before my game in the 1963 Series. I was to pitch against Don Drysdale. Houk was sitting about five feet away from me on the bench and for some reason we were all alone. And I said, "You know something, Ralph? Whether I win today or lose, this sure is a helluva lot of fun, isn't it?"

Houk understood. I could tell because he didn't say, "Whaddaya mean lose? We're gonna win," the way a lot of other managers would have. All he said was, "It sure is. I know just what you mean."

I'm getting a big kick out of Blefary. He's called "Buff," short for Buffalo, because he works so hard. If I had to be in a foxhole I'd like him in there with me. He's the kind who picks up hand grenades and throws them back. He's a perfect Marine, yet he doesn't seem to have the Marine mentality. One winter he spent his time, not selling mutual funds, but working with retarded children. Blefary on the pickoff play: "Now if you see me reaching for my throat—like this—that means you go into your stretch position, take your set, don't even look over. As soon as you get to your set, turn around and fire over there, hard and low, between the runner and the bag. I'll be there."

"And if you see me going for *my* throat," I said, "it means I'm choking to death."

Which reminds me of Joe Pepitone's pick-off play. In the 1964 World Series with Lou Brock on first base, I gave the pick-off sign to Pepi and when I took my stretch position and looked over toward first, he was standing there shaking his head, tiny shakes because he didn't want anybody to see. It was the first time I ever saw anybody shake off a pick-off sign. It was in the 1963 Series that he lost a throw from third base in the shirts of the crowd and was the goat of the game. Now he didn't want to handle the ball any more than he had to. Just for the hell of it, I gave him the sign again a few pitches later. I wanted to see if he'd shake me off again. He did.

One day Joe Pepitone inserted a piece of popcorn under his foreskin and went to the trainer claiming a new venereal disease. "Jesus Christ, Joe, what the hell have you done?" the doctor said. Pepitone didn't start laughing until the doctor had carefully used a forceps to liberate the popcorn.

The Marvin Milkes bellhop story has finally hit *The Sporting News*. It quotes Brabender as saying that Milkes spends more time in the lobby than the bell captain. I wonder if Milkes will call him in for a grilling like I got. Doubt it. Brabender just won his tenth game. Besides, if Brabender gets angry he's liable to crush his spleen.

"Bulldog," said Curt Blefary, "if we get back to the Dome no more than four games out, we're going to win it. We don't get beat in the Dome."

Then Don Wilson came over and said, "When we get back home, we're going to win this thing. We just don't lose in that motherfucking Dome."

The idea is that I'm not supposed to lose there either. I'm willing not to.

Spec Richardson got on the bus to the ballpark last night and there were five Latin players talking Spanish. He stood listening for a while, his eyes shifting back and forth, as if he understood what they were saying. Finally he said, "Abbadabba dabbadabba."

When we got into Houston last night we stopped off at the Astrodome so the players could pick up their cars. I went inside to look at it. I'd been there once, with the Yankees, when it first opened. The only thing I remembered was this huge band that played seven songs during the evening, five of them "Dixie."

Also last night, I was standing in the skin part of the infield before the game and Miller came over and said, "Hey, you're not allowed to stand on the infield dirt." I asked why. "Because Jimmy Wynn was fooling around in the infield and he's an outfielder and he got hit on the finger and couldn't play, so Harry made a rule. Every time something happens, we have a new rule."

It shouldn't matter that much what happens to me tonight. If I win, I'll be all the way back from the basement. On the other hand, if I lose, it will still have been a pretty good season. Still, I've been having all kinds of insane thoughts. On the airplane last night I thought, "Damn, if this plane goes down I hope the newspapers at least have me listed in the probable starting pitchers."

Here it is, my dream. I'm pitching for a pennant contender in August. I really am lucky.

That's what I thought about when I went out to the mound. This is fun, this is kicks. Stay cool. Be calm and try to get the feel of that good

345

knuckleball with the first pitch. Find that tricky abstract thought, the one that makes you feel so competent and smooth. I tried to recall the last few warm-up pitches I threw and I remember thinking, "Why are they playing the National Anthem so slowly?"

I walked the first hitter on four pitches. The first two pitches to the next hitter were balls. Christ, am I ever going to throw one over? Fortunately the runner tried to steal second and Edwards threw him out. Edwards is a great catcher. He catches the knuckleball better than McNertney, and he doesn't have the big glove. Edwards ought to be President.

That enabled me to walk the second hitter. But somehow I got by the inning. I felt a great surge of nervousness, and while I couldn't throw hard, I think I was able to use it, make it work for me.

I just kept throwing the knuckleball, and after a while I looked up at the scoreboard and we were in the fifth inning, leading 1–0. Gravy. After this it's all gravy. I've done it for five innings and nobody could ask for more.

There was a lot of scraping and scrounging after that, hanging tough with men on base, the way it was back in the old days. Each inning I came back to the dugout and I could see a little more respect in the eyes of my teammates. I wasn't with them from the beginning, when they were four and twenty, when they battled back into the pennant race. I'm a newcomer, and I have to prove myself, and I was doing it. I could see new appreciation in their eyes and sense an excitement as they realized how much help I could be.

The game went ten innings. I was ahead 2–1 in the ninth. All I needed was three outs. I got them, but not before a few things happened. Like I bounced a knuckleball off the first batter's kneecap. The next batter conspired with heaven and Astroturf to hit a chopper that took so long coming down it went for a base hit. Two outs later I've got runners on second and third. Now a base hit to center field ends the ball game. I mean it's *over*. Except Jimmy Wynn and Leon McFadden make a blurry fast relay that nails the second runner at the plate and I'm out of it with a 2–2 tie.

Now here I am in the tenth inning, the tenth unbelievable inning, and I swear I expect Joe Schultz or Sal Maglie or Merritt Ranew or somebody to come out and tell me I'm throwing too goddam much. Instead, all I got to do is pitch to Matty Alou. He strikes out. On a passed ball. And reaches first base. It happens.

Then Gene Alley moves him to second on a ground ball and I strike out Willie Stargell. With first base open we walk Roberto Clemente intentionally. Here comes Al Oliver, a lefthanded hitter. I fool him on a knuckleball, outside. Somehow, though, he puts his bat on it and pokes it into left field, on the line. Who'd want to play him there? Nobody. So it goes for a double. Two runs. The ballgame. We lose 4–2.

I could've cried. There wasn't a tear in me, though. Just joy, elation, satisfaction, vindication, a great sense of accomplishment. The knuckleball *worked.* In the National League. For ten innings. I struck out eleven, walked only four. A bounce, a bit of luck, I could have won. No matter. For the first time, for the first time in what seemed eons, I went all the way through a ballgame getting the hitters out on my stuff, my very own personal, natural stuff.

If I cried, it would have been for joy.

I called my wife, and then my mom and dad and brothers. Then I was alone in the Astroworld Hotel, with nobody to talk to but my tape recorder. I was still talking to the machine at 2:30 A.M., knowing it would be hours before I could fall asleep.

AUGUST
30

Norm Miller said he wanted to room with me and I said sure, but wouldn't I be coming between him and somebody else? "Nah," he said, "I've already filed papers on my former roommate."

My note-taking has quickly attracted attention. Dierker got on me pretty good, and since I was going so good I told him flat out I was writing a book. Now he keeps coming around with good stories. "Write this down," he says.

Watching the ballgame today someone broke off a real good curve and I said, "That was a real yellow hammer."

Dierker agreed.

"Hey, Dierk, you ever hear 'yellow hammer' before?" I asked.

Jim Owens jumped to his defense. "Of course he did," Owens said. "You think he came into town on a load of watermelons?"

Then Owens got on me. He insisted I show him my notes. There was nothing much in them, so I did.

"You going to write a book?" he said.

"Yeah," I said. "Someday I might get to be President and want to write a book about my life."

Owens sniffed. "We haven't had any flaky Presidents so far, and I doubt if we'll have any in the future."

Owens may not be much on Presidents, but I think I'll like him as a pitching coach. He thinks rather like Johnny Sain.

"You just can't tell some guy he has to throw a slider," Owens says. "That's what they did to me. I had a helluva overhand curve when I first came up and they told me I had to throw a slider. So I worked on the slider until I lost my overhand curve. That taught me never to take a young pitcher and force him to come up with a new pitch. I give them their own head."

That's just fine with me, Jim baby, especially since every time I try to throw a slider my elbow feels like an alligator is biting it.

Drinking rules: They're different on the Astros. You're allowed to drink at the hotel bar. With the Pilots you were not allowed to. I suppose this goes back to Casey Stengel, who said, "You can't drink at the hotel bar, because that's where *I* drink." Billy Martin and Dave Boswell can tell you what happens when managers and players drink in the same bars. Still, it seems more adult to be able to have a beer at the bar of your own hotel.

The other difference is airplanes. With the Astros you're allowed the same two drinks as all the other people aboard. With Seattle you could drink only beer. You could have 143 beers and get sloshed out of your skull, but you were not allowed to enjoy a cocktail before your meal.

AUGUST
31

The football season is almost upon us, so I got to thinking about some basic differences in the two games for the players. Baseball players play so many games it's impossible to get emotionally high for any one of them. Football players get all gung-ho in the locker room. They chant and shout and jump up and down and take pills and hit each other on the helmet and shoulderpads and spit and kick and swear and they're ready to go out and bust some heads. If a baseball player got that emotional, he'd go out swinging hard—and miss. I think baseball is more of a skill sport than any other. Hitting is the single most difficult feat in sports. Second most difficult is preventing hitting. That's why Milkes bugged me when he'd say things like, "If some players don't perform the way they're supposed to, there's going to be some changes." I think we did perform the way we were supposed to. It was Milkes who missed. He's the one who chose the ballplayers. Did you ever hear a general manager say, "It looks like I'm not as good at picking talent as I thought I was. I guess I'll take a $10,000 cut"?

Yes, Virginia, baseball players watch the scoreboard. Is Cincinnati changing pitchers? Is Seaver really shutting out San Francisco? Who's No. 37 for St. Louis? It's really exciting. Today Atlanta got beat, San Francisco got beat, Cincinnati won and we could have been no worse than four games out of first and only two behind Los Angeles and San Francisco. But we blew the ballgame. We had a 4–2 lead going into the ninth and we wound up losing 6–4. I can see why this club was desperate for another relief pitcher.

So I play an interesting game. I try to project my performance with Seattle onto this club. Those 24 games I came into without so much as giving up a hit. Not one *hit!* Suppose I'd done it here? Suppose my mother and father had never met?

No false sorrow in the clubhouse after that one. Only real sorrow, and a lot of it. Losing a ballgame so suddenly is like being punched in the stomach. You've counted it as a win and you've subtracted a full game from the teams that have lost—then *poof,* it's gone. So there was no food right away in the clubhouse, and when I asked why I was told that once, after a game like that Harry came in and tipped the table over and threw food all over the place. So after tough games, there's a cooling-off period before the food arrives.

Okay, so we're in fifth place and there are four teams that have a better chance. But we're not out of it. That's the way you have to look at it. Especially when it's true.

Trade: Tommy Davis to Houston Astros for Sandy Valdespino. Welcome, Tommy. It makes a fellow proud to be an Astro.

SEPTEMBER
1

Old Timers' Day today and naturally Harry Walker got into the game. For the Astros it was both hilarious and chastening. It was hilarious because the guys gave Harry the business. Everything he'd ever yelled at them, they yelled at him.

While he was at bat:

"Take a shot at left field, Harry."

"Just stroke it up the middle, Harry."

"Go to right field, Harry."

He takes a strike. "Jesus Christ, right down the middle, Harry."

"Just punch at it, Harry."

"Make sure you get your pitch, Harry."

"Step out on him, Harry."

Of course, Harry hung in there, stroked it up the middle and got a base hit, just as he tells everybody else to.

While he was on first base:

"You got to break up two, Harry."

"Make sure you get a good jump, Harry."

"Don't get too far off the bag, Harry."

"Watch out for the pick-off, Harry."

Sure enough, there's a ground ball to the infield and Harry flies into the shortstop and breaks up the double play, a perfect slide.

"Son of a bitch," said Doug Rader, "every time we have an Old Timers' game Harry gets a hit up the middle and breaks up the double play."

We lost again. Jesus Christ, *we lost again*. That's eleven out of seventeen. It doesn't seem possible to have it all slip away so fast.

Harry didn't throw anything. Instead he told Don Wilson what a helluva game he'd pitched. "Go get 'em tomorrow, boys," he said. "We'll be all right."

He sounded just like Joe Schultz.

Norm Miller was doing the broadcast bit in the fourth inning when Joe Morgan came back to the dugout after missing a big curve ball for strike three.

"Joe, Joe Morgan, may I have a word with you?"

"Sure, Norm, how's it going?"

"Fine, Joe, fine. We wanted to ask you about that pitch you missed. What was it?"

"Norm, that was a motherfucking curve."

"Can you tell our listeners, Joe, what's the difference between a regular curve and a motherfucking curve?"

"Well, Norm, your regular curve has a lot of spin on it and you can recognize it real early. It breaks down a little bit, and out. Now, your motherfucker, that's different. It comes in harder, looks like a fastball. Then all of a sudden it rolls off the top of the table and before you know it, it's motherfucking strike three."

"Thank you very much, Joe Morgan."

Tommy Davis says that the day I left, Joe Schultz had a meeting in the clubhouse to discuss the rumors that he would not be back next season and he broke down and cried. "It was a sad and touching scene," Tommy said.

Davis also said that the talk around the club was that I wasn't traded just to get two players, but because Marvin Milkes wanted to get me off the ballclub. The rumor did not explain why.

Gatorade?

Upon a promise from me that I'd never tell, Tommy Davis revealed that the man who had nailed my shoes to the clubhouse floor, tore the buttons off my sweatshirts and pulled my jockstraps out of shape was Gene Brabender. I have kept my word. I have not told a soul. Until now.

My wife watched her first game in the Astrodome and found the fans oddly reserved. They sit there very quietly unless the scoreboard tells them to say something, like "Charge!" or "Go! Go! Go!" So when Mike and Dave started yelling, "We want a hit," people turned around to look at them.

SEPTEMBER

2

I thought I'd climb a few golden stairs today, so I dropped in on Spec Richardson and, speaking over the blare of Billy Graham pouring out of the office radio, I told him my tale of woe. I told him I'd lost a lot of money on the deal—at least $1,000 moving my family, etc.—and that when I signed a contract for $22,000 with Seattle it was on the basis of not knowing whether I'd be able to pitch in the majors. I said I accepted the $22,000 with the thought that if I stayed in the big league for the whole season I would go in and ask for an increase. I was just about to do that, I said, when I was traded and wound up having to *spend* money. I also said I knew that Spec would want to be fair.

Yes, indeed, he said, he wanted to be fair. He said that he certainly would help me with my hotel bill here and that he'd see if anything else could be done. He said if I did the job for him I wouldn't have to worry.

So right away I started worrying.

We're staying in the motel section of the Astroworld Hotel, paying $20 a day for $40 worth of rooms. Both rooms are filled with doublebeds, which doesn't give us much running-around room. But there's a swimming pool right outside the door and a nice playground nearby. In order to cut down on the high price of room service we've rented a little refrigerator and have breakfast and lunch in, simple things like cold cereal and sandwiches. I know a lot of the players would laugh at the idea of a refrigerator, but there's a matter of values involved. Like one spring in Ft. Lauderdale I hired a car for a dollar a day. It was a terrible car, with no muffler and a missing door, and I took some abuse because of it. But it's not a matter of being cheap; it's a matter of what you want to spend your money on. In Florida we stayed at a great hotel rather than some crummy apartment. I'd rather pay for that than for a fancy rented car.

Good ballgame tonight. Justice and the Houston Astros triumphed 7–6 in eleven innings. It was a team effort all the way because we were down 5–0 almost before the game started. My own contribution was one scoreless inning followed by one near-disaster. Vic Davalillo led off the inning with a double off a fastball that I shouldn't have thrown. Joe Torre walked. Mike Shannon hit a line drive off a knuckleball that would without doubt have separated me from my head if I hadn't deflected it with my arm, a matter of blind, instinctive self-preservation. It not only raised a big welt on my wrist, it knocked in a run and me out of the game. I told Harry I wanted to stay in, but he said, "No, no. If this was a close game I'd leave you in. But I want to save you for the future."

I think Harry was just trying to be nice.

SEPTEMBER
3

Some more thoughts on getting along with baseball players. The other night after the game we had our usual great spread of food: spaghetti and meatballs, fried chicken, steaks. It really does make a fellow proud to be an Astro. I had a steak in one hand and a glass of milk in the other and Curt Blefary said, "Hey, Bulldog, what's with the milk? Why aren't you drinking beer?"

Rather than tell him the truth—that I'd rather drink milk—I said I had a bad stomach and had to drink milk. Now, why would I do that? Because I want to be one of the boys. I really do, just the way I did in Seattle. I think I failed there, but that doesn't mean I have to fail here. I feel embarrassed at telling a lie. But me drinking milk in the clubhouse is like a guy walking into a western saloon, pounding on the bar and demanding a sarsaparilla.

SEPTEMBER
4

A $37 C.O.D. package arrived today from a photographer in Detroit. In it were 100 color photographs of me in a Seattle Pilots uniform. Just what I needed. Anybody who wrote a letter requesting an autograph prior to my being traded to Houston will get one of those marvelous photos. Also, anyone else who wants one, just send a stamped self-addressed envelope.

Today there was a clubhouse meeting. The guys wanted to get together without Harry and the coaches. Johnny Edwards, one of the team leaders, told us that we had to keep busting ass. Edwards said he was disturbed to hear guys talking about next year. He said that's bad. He said we shouldn't write ourselves off. He said we got to win it this year. The consensus was that we weren't going to let Harry Walker bug us; if necessary we could finish two games ahead of the manager.

Me, I think the reason the club has done as well as it has is Harry Walker. I'm told he can be a pain, but a ballclub like this needs a Harry Walker. It's a club that probably didn't believe in itself, having finished so poorly last year and having started out 4 and 20 this year. So Harry drives and harasses, reminds everyone how to run the bases, how to hit the ball, to watch for this, watch for that, and keeps everybody agitated and playing better baseball.

Right after the meeting I asked Tommy Davis how come he hadn't said anything. "Look, you and I have been through this kind of thing before," he said. "And maybe we could have said something that would have been helpful. But I feel that before I say anything I should do something to help the team."

Interesting that even a Tommy Davis should hesitate to say anything until he's proved himself with a new team. It seems like a nice, modest thing. What it means, really, is that nobody wants to say anything until he's going good. And when he's going good, nobody wants to tell him he's wrong. So we have a tendency to substitute batting average or ERA for brains. The converse is also true. When you're going bad there is no dearth of guys waiting to jump on you with both feet, even if you're right.

On September 1, rosters can be expanded from twenty-five to forty players. This means there are a lot of eager young players around. Mine is named Bob Watson. He's a young catcher who thinks it will help his career if he learns to catch the knuckleball. "Yeah, put that knuckleball on me," he says.

Heh, heh, heh.

SEPTEMBER
5

Willie Mays was standing at the batting cage. I stuck my hand out, "I'm Jim Bouton."

"Oh sure," he said. "Jim Bouton. I know you."

"You've always been one of my heroes," I said. "When I was a kid, my brother and I always used to go up to the Polo Grounds to watch you play."

"Now, why'd you have to go and say you came to see me when you were a kid?" Willie Mays said, his voice squeaky with mock anger.

"And you know something, Willie?" Tommy Davis said. "He's only thirty-five years old."

Mays groaned. "Why couldn't you just come over and say 'Hi'?" he said. "Now I feel like an old man."

Funny, he doesn't look like an old man. Especially when he plays baseball.

We beat the Giants 2–0 on a home run by Denis Menke. Larry Dierker pitched a marvelous game. This kid has everything. He's twenty-three years old and he's been in the big leagues five years, having spent only two weeks in the minors. He has a great fastball, great slider, great overhand curve, great control—and he makes me sound like Leo Durocher. Great! He's a smart pitcher too, knows what he's doing out there, and as Jim Owens says, "He has the balls of a burglar."

Watching him pitch I remembered that after pitching a two-hit shutout or something, just completely dominating the game, I'd think, "How in the hell could anybody possibly throw a better ballgame than that?" Dierker showed me how. Just watching him throw his hard slider made my shoulder hurt, and I had to convince my arm, after a short discussion, that we wouldn't go back to that stuff anymore.

Another insight. Between innings of this great ballgame he pitched, Dierker sat on the bench and sang "Rocky Raccoon."

SEPTEMBER
6

There ought to be a third column in the baseball standings: GAT, for games almost tied. Seattle would be leading the American League and Houston would be way up there in the National. We were down 7–1 going into the ninth and lost 7–6. I contributed three scoreless innings and got my hero, Willie Mays, on a pop-up.

What baseball players do to each other is punch each other in the groin and say "cup check." Norm Miller pulled it on me today. Fortunately I was wearing it. When I was in the minors I got caught short a couple of times. The cup is uncomfortable, and on days when I wasn't pitching I wouldn't bother to put it on. This one time the manager said, "Bouton, loosen up. You pitch the next inning."

Now, the last thing you want to tell a manager is that you're not ready. So I warmed up and went in to pitch, scared. I threw every pitch inside, so they'd pull it. The last thing I wanted was any one-bounce comebackers. Ugh.

The clubhouse in the Astrodome is so big you could almost have infield practice in it. I noticed because the Seattle clubhouse was too small for chess.

Niekro pitched a one-hitter against Cincinnati, and that's good, because I'm supposed to pitch against them next time. The idea is that they have a bunch of free-swingers on the club. They also have a lot of .300 hitters. Does that worry me? Yes.

Johnny Edwards was quoted in the paper here today saying that my knuckleball is better than Niekro's. That's progress. When I started out with it last year it was only better than Bob Tiefenauer's.

The Astros have an Exergenie. It's an exercise contraption involving ropes and tension. You lay on your back, put your feet in stirrups and work like hell. Denis Menke says he hadn't had any leg trouble in two years and gives credit to the Exergenie. I haven't had any leg trouble for two years either, and I never even heard of the Exergenie. Still, I'll use it. The word is out that if you do, you make Spec Richardson happy. I like to make general managers happy.

SEPTEMBER

7

Quote from Larry Dierker, whose ERA is so low everybody listens when he talks: "You know a ballclub I can't see? I just can't see Atlanta. They just don't seem to have the depth. You know another club I can't see? Ours."

Fred Gladding, called Fred Flintstone, doesn't look like a baseball player. He doesn't even look like a pitcher. He looks like a grocer who's been eating up a good bit of his profits. The other day Blefary told him, "For crissakes, Fred, put your shirt on. You embarrass the whole ballclub."

Norm Miller is stomping around asking to be traded because he's not playing regularly. He really is too young to be sitting around and he does have a lot of ability. He also has a sense of humor about it all. Today he was watching me squeeze two baseballs with one hand and asked me what for. "To stretch my fingers," I said.

"Yeah, I know what you mean," he said. "I have the same problem. When I wake up in the morning I'm 5–4. I hang on the closet door while my wife makes breakfast and by the time I leave for the ballpark I'm 5–10 again."

Warming up before the game today Wilson didn't seem to have a thing, and it was obvious his arm hurt. But after visiting the clubhouse he came out throwing BB's. "What the hell got into Don?" I said.

"Four greenies," somebody said.

"I'll tell you what makes him throw like that," Blefary said. "Guts. Sheer guts."

He pitched well until the fourth, when he walked four straight batters and they brought me in with the Giants leading 2–1 and the bases loaded. It wasn't my day. The first hitter bounces one over the first baseman's head for two runs. After an out Ron Hunt hits a 3-and-2 knuckleball into right-center for two more runs. Now I face Willie Mays again. There we are, me and my hero, nose to nose. He hits a single up the middle. Another run. I was glad to escape alive. Still, we came back to beat Mike McCormick in the ninth. That's two out of three. If we can beat the contenders two out of three while they play .500 against each other there will be a five-way tie for first place. That's what I'm rooting for. What a playoff!

There was a rumor abroad in the land that the Astros were going to get Richie Allen from the Phillies and some of the Astros were against it. They said he's a bad guy to have on a ballclub. *Humph.* I wonder what the Astros would give to have him come to bat just 15 times for us this season. It might mean a pennant.

If I could get Allen I'd grab him and tell everybody that he marches to a different drummer and that there are rules for him and different rules for everybody else. I mean what's the good of a .220 hitter who obeys the curfew? Richie Allen doesn't obey the rules, hits 35 home runs and knocks in over 100. I'll take him.

There was a National League questionnaire around asking for our outstanding accomplishments in school, and I had a few. I hold the record, as far as I know, for eating two large pizza pies with everything —peppers, onions, anchovies, the works—in an hour. At the time it was for the championship of Western Michigan, and possibly the world. And when I finished there were about ten guys in the dorm who were willing to put up $16.37 that I couldn't follow the two pizzas with 100 sit-ups. Now I knew I could do 650 sit-ups, because I once set a record in high school with that many. A mere 100 seemed like child's play. And it was. In addition to the two free pies, I picked up the $16.37 and a knack for walking doubled over. It was two days before I could straighten up. I also grew a set of boils on my stomach. But to this day, my name is legend in the dorm.

One of the ways the guys relieve the tensions of the pennant race, and there are some, is by their own version of the Dozens, the insult game. They remind each other of failures on the field of battle.

Blasingame: "That sure was a hell of a performance by you yesterday, Billingham. Three walks in a row. You were so tight you couldn't drive a pin up your ass."

Billingham: "I haven't seen you do anything lately, Blasingame. What's *your* record?"

Blasingame: "I've won some games in the big leagues, sonny. How many have you won in the bigs?"

Billingham: "We can't be talking about ancient history. What have you done this year? Go ahead. Tell me."

Blasingame: "I haven't won a goddam game."

Billingham: "Okay. So you're no one to talk."

Gladding: "Well, maybe not. But he was right about those three walks, Billingham. That was a disgrace."

Billingham: "Oh sure. Listen to you, with your 5.6 earned run average. Some relief pitcher you are."

And like that.

SEPTEMBER

8

We beat San Diego 9–2 tonight and I felt sort of sorry for Mike Corkins, their starting pitcher. It was his first start in the majors and on his very first pitch Joe Morgan hit a triple to right field, and on his second pitch Jesus Alou hit another one to right-center. His third pitch was wild and Alou scored. So on three pitches the kid had given up two runs. And Marty Martinez yelled out to him, "Welcome to the National League, kid."

Before the game one of the clubhouse men asked Fred Gladding, who has the locker next to mine, if he had a spare pair of size-9 spikes. Tom Dukes, a righthanded pitcher who used to be in the Yankee organization and was now with San Diego, had been caught short. Gladding said he didn't have any. So I reached into my bag and pulled out a pair of size 9s. "Only one thing wrong with them," I said. "They have some nail holes in the soles. But it never rains in the Astrodome."

Sure enough, Tom Dukes got into the game. He'll never know what he owes to Gene Brabender.

Some of the guys were on Nate Colbert, the San Diego first baseman, formerly of the Astros. They kept yelling that he was ugly and calling him "Mullion" and other nice things. Blefary said to cut it out, that the last time they got on him Colbert hit a couple of home runs and beat us. Well, we jumped out to a 4–0 lead, and the first time Colbert got up, sure enough he jolted one into the left-field seats. Next time up, Colbert jolts another home run. I figured if the game lasts long enough he's bound to beat us. Actually, he's not that bad looking.

I saw Blefary's name on the lineup card and said, "Hey, Buff, go get 'em."
"You know why I'm playing tonight?" he said. "Two reasons. One is that a righthander is pitching. Two is that he's very weak."

Universal beaver-shooting note:
Norm Miller drilled a small hole in the back of the dugout. We can now beaver-shoot any woman who sits in a certain seat in the first row. Not only that, if you blow through the hole you get some interesting reactions. Miller is being acclaimed as a genius.

I have just ordered up a strawberry sundae (for my wife) and three scoops of chocolate ice cream (for me) here at the Astroworld Hotel. The bill came to $3.06, plus tip. Outrageous.

I have this theory that the reason prices are so high in hotels is that no one objects. Thus prices no longer have any relation to reality. We are charged, higgledy-piggledy, whatever number that seems to be wildly high enough.

Example. Checking out of the Sheraton Cadillac in Detroit not long ago, there was a $9 bill for valet. I was shocked. All I had sent out were three pairs of pants and three Banlon shirts. It was $1.50 each to clean the pants and, get this, $1.50 for each shirt.

"How could that be?" I said to the cashier.

"Well, they classify those shirts as sweaters."

"But they're just shirts," I said. "What's more, I'm not paying."

"Oh, but you have to pay it," she said. "It's on your bill."

"Like hell," I said. "Just because somebody puts a number on a piece of paper that doesn't mean I have to pay it."

She wound up calling the manager and he said, yes, I would have to pay only one dollar per shirt, so I saved a buck and a half. Now if everybody did that, the savings would add up to millions. Millions, I tell you.

Odd thing about being an Astro. When I got to the ballpark one of the coaches told me, "You don't have to be on the field for batting practice tonight. But be ready to run over at Colt Stadium at five-fifteen." I thought he was kidding. Shows what I know. At five-fifteen I was running over at Colt Stadium, which is about ten minutes away from the Astrodome by Astrotram. It's a little-used field, overgrown and dismal. And look out for snakes.

Now hear this. The reason we ran at Colt Stadium—about fifteen of us pitchers—is that just before we go on a road trip, Harry Walker likes to have his pitchers run outside the dome so they get used to hot weather.

Harry Walker thinks of everything.

After the ballgame, Buddy Hancken, one of the coaches, sidled up to me and said, "Look, we could be using you almost any night. So would you do me a favor, please. Stay out of the swimming pool there at the Astroworld. You're liable to stay in that pool a couple of hours and there's no telling how much it takes out of you."

"Sure, I'll stay out," I said, wondering all the time how the hell he knew I was swimming. Then I remembered. There's been a helicopter hovering around the Astroworld. I bet Harry Walker was in it.

"I like him," I was saying to Blasingame about Harry Walker. "Maybe it's because I haven't been here long, but I like him."

"I do too," Blasingame said. "You know, he gets on guys and he's always talking and you can't turn him off. But everything he says, he's right. He always makes a point and he's always right."

I agreed. The other night, for example, there was a foul ball hit out near the bullpen and the fielder pulled up well in front of the fence and let it drop. Bang, the phone was ringing in the bullpen. It was Harry telling us not to sit dead-assed out there in the bullpen, to do some yelling, tell the fielder how much room he had. We felt like kids being scolded and didn't like it a bit. In fact, though, Harry was absolutely right.

Jim Owens' famous remark about the Astrodome: "It isn't much, but we call it home."

SEPTEMBER
9

Before the game today, Doug Rader was kidding Nate Colbert. "Hey, Nate, I think you're cute," he said. "Not ugly—cute. Cute like an iguana."

Little old star-maker me was at work tonight. I was talking to Tommy Davis about his injured leg and it wasn't hard to tell he wanted to sit down instead of play. "Why don't you tell Harry?" I said.

"I haven't been here that long," Davis said. "I'd feel funny about it."

"But Harry isn't like most managers," I said. "He'd appreciate the information and he wouldn't hold it against you."

"Well, maybe I'll talk to him," Davis said.

Sure enough, he walked into Harry's office and pretty soon he was scratched from the lineup. Harry put Norm Miller in and he went 3 for 4, knocking in four runs. It was a great evening.

After Miller got his third-straight hit, Davis hollered down to Walker, "Hey, Harry, that leg isn't nearly as bad as I thought it was."

Davis is now being called Wally Pipp. That's the fellow who had a minor injury and was replaced by Lou Gehrig. It was ten years before Gehrig missed a game.

I'm in normal weird shape. In the middle of the night I got up, rummaged around until I found that ball I work with and made throwing motions for a half-hour or so, just to get the feel of it. Considering I never released the ball, I did great. My wife never even noticed.

Fantasy time. The Houston Astros are playing the New York Mets for the league championship. I come in to relieve in Shea Stadium with a one-run lead and the bases loaded in the last of the ninth. I get behind 2 and 0 on the first hitter and it looks like we're dead. Of course, I come back and strike him out. I strike out the next guy too, but the ball gets away from Edwards, who goes back to the screen, picks it up and fires it to me at the plate. The throw's a bit late, but I've blocked the plate and I tag him out for the final out. How fabulous are my dreams?

Conversation with Tommy Davis while he's got a hot pad on his leg in the trainer's room:

"Tell me about the attitude toward me on the Pilots," I said. "Don't worry about my feelings. Lay it on the line."

"If you promise not to tell anybody . . ."

"Not a soul. Not a single soul."

"Well, my feeling was that the manager contributed to the guys thinking you were a weirdo. For instance, Joe would watch things that you did out on the field and he'd start laughing and making fun and naturally all the players took the lead from Joe. They laughed at you.

"I didn't see anything funny. I thought, 'Well, here's a guy who's got his own ideas. Some of them are certainly different, but hell, I respect him.' That's what Joe should have said. Joe could have said, 'He's always thinking, anyway. And boy, look at how hard he works.' Instead he sort of smirked and laughed, and you know how players are. They smirked and laughed too."

I suspected as much. Hovley. Marshall. Bouton. And another guy, real early on, Lou Piniella. Joe Schultz would have been a better manager if he understood more. Of course, if he understood more, he might not have been a manager.

I don't want to be that harsh on Joe Schultz. I rather liked him and still do. And I thought he had the most character of anyone on the staff—and in the front office.

Don Wilson was sitting on the other side of Tommy Davis, so Tommy got to saying that it would be great to be young like Wilson, and I said, "Don, did you ever think that someday you'd be sitting on the bench with Tommy Davis? I mean *the* Tommy Davis, just talking to him as though, well as though he were some regular person? Did you ever think that?"

"I thought about it," Wilson said. "I didn't ever think It would be a big deal, though, and I was right."

Turned out Wilson was from Los Angeles too, and he'd once tried to get Tommy Davis' autograph. "He was too good to sign it," Wilson said. "Ever since I never looked forward to sitting with him on a bench."

"You really resent him, huh?" I said, adding eggbeater to troubled waters.

"Well, yeah," Wilson said. "It's been kind of a thing with me. In fact, right now it's no big deal sitting here with him. If he's too good to sign autographs, the hell with him."

"You see how smart these young guys are?" Davis said. "Boy, if I ever said that when I was a kid, that would have been something. Imagine me saying that to Roy Campanella. Boy, for young guys these kids really talk a lot."

And I said, "That's good, too, isn't it Tom? They should be allowed to say whatever they feel, don't you think?"

"Well, that's *your* idea," Davis said. "I know that's what *you* think."

Generation gap revisited. I loved it.

There was a happy, funny clubhouse after the game, which we won 9–2. Nate Colbert was no threat.

Whitey Diskin, the clubhouse man who prepares all that great food every night, an elderly stooped-over gentleman with glasses who looks something like Henry the Chicken Hawk, had this great big pot of chicken á la king. It was fine chicken á la king. It was *great* chicken á la king. But we hadn't been having chicken á la king, so the guys got on it.

"Jesus Christ, Whitey, what the hell is this stuff?"

"What have you done here, Whitey?"

And each guy comes over, takes a taste, spits into garbage. Well, not everybody. Me, I had two big plates of it.

"Look at that stuff. Whitey, this is fifth-place food."

"Christ, here we are fighting for a pennant and you serve us this shit."

I couldn't resist calling Jim Ewell, the trainer, in on it. "Doc, you better come in here and examine this stuff," I said. "Maybe you better take its temperature."

So the trainer comes marching in, ceremoniously, with a tongue depressor in one hand, thermometer in the other. He sticks the thermometer into the chicken á la king, reads it, sticks the tongue depressor in, tastes it, shakes his head sadly, says, "No chance," and walks out.

"Holy Budweiser," I yelled, "get the names of the guys who've been pounding that shit into them."

After a while, nobody could think of anything more to say, so Blasingame looked at Whitey with contempt and said, "And that's a horseshit shirt you're wearing, too, Whitey."

When I got back to the hotel, I found the kids had been eating potato chips on my bed. So Bobbie and I took the spread outside to shake it out. And there we were in full view of a patio full of people having a cocktail party. The Beverly Hillbillies eating in their room at a swank hotel.

In the last few weeks, little Mike has become more aware that his father has a special occupation. That's because other kids come up to him and say, "Hey, does your dad pitch for the Astros?"

We've tried to get it across to him that what I do is just another job, that it's not special. But it gets a little difficult here, and as his awareness grows, the braggadocio emerges. So now he walks up to people, strangers, and says, "You know something? My dad plays for the Houston Astros." The other day I heard him tell a kid at the swimming pool. "My dad's Jim Bouton of the Houston Astros. I'm not kidding you." And sometimes we'll just be sitting around and he'll say, "Hey, Dad, go over and tell those people who you are."

Pardon me, sir. My name is Jim Bouton. I used to be with the Seattle Pilots. No, not a ferry captain. That's a baseball team. You know, baseball. B-a-s-e-b-a-l-l.

Little David is making a good adjustment. His English is fine, and I think he feels like a part of the family. I believe he's starting to think about the future now and where he fits into the scheme of things. The other day he asked, "Dad, are you going to die?"

"Yes, David. Everybody dies sooner or later."

And he said, "I don't want you to die."

The Mets are beautiful.

Here they are virtually tied with the Cubs and the panic is on in Chicago. Leo Durocher is not talking to the press, and I don't have to be there to know that their clubhouse is like a morgue. And here's the funny thing. The Mets have virtually the same record and they're going crazy with joy. The players are happy, the manager is happy, the fans are happy. Now what's the difference? It's that the Mets won their games at a different stage of the season. The point is that right now they both have an equal chance to win the pennant, yet the Mets are up and the Cubs are down. And the Cubs are down because they think they should be down. Why? If they were as happy as the Mets they'd win more games.

SEPTEMBER

10

Up the golden stairs. I'd been itching about it for days. "Spec, I've been thinking about the conversation we had the other day and I really feel I deserve an increase in salary. Not only do I deserve it, I need it, because of the traveling expenses. What I want you to do is tear up my contract and give me a new one calling for $3,000 more. I wouldn't be asking for this if I didn't think I'd earned it."

"No, Jim. We can't do that."

"I know ballclubs have torn up contracts and given guys more money in the middle of the season when they've done a lot better than expected. So I know it can be done."

"You haven't done anything for me yet."

"I realize that. But you traded for me because you thought I was more valuable than Dooley Womack, and you gave up another player for me besides. So why don't you pay me what Womack was getting?"

"I don't know what Womack was getting."

"He told me he was getting $25,000."

"He was kidding you. He's not getting that much."

"Maybe not. But how many major-leaguers do you know who've been up seven years and have had the kind of year I've had who are getting only $22,000?"

"You signed a contract. If you didn't want to sign it, you shouldn't have."

"I signed as a minor-leaguer. There was a good possibility I'd spend the season in the minors working on my knuckleball. I figured I'd stay in one place and travel wouldn't cost me all that much. Hell, I've had to make three moves."

"Well, I told you I'd help with your hotel bill if you wanted me to."

"I've already made arrangements to send my family to Michigan. Most of our expenses are behind us. And I don't feel it's asking too much if I ask you to give me a $3,000 increase."

"If you want a loan, we can work that out. But we can't give you an increase."

"A loan won't help me any. It would just cut down on my credit possibilities. No, I need the increase."

"You haven't done anything for me yet. As soon as you do something I'll take care of you."

"But Spec, I can't go back to Seattle and ask *them* for money. And if everybody took your attitude, all you'd have to do is trade a guy toward the end of every season and no one would feel obligated to give him a raise."

"How bad do you need this money?"

"I wanted to get this straightened out before I go on the road trip."

"Well, you're not going to. And if you don't want to go on the road trip, that's your business. If you don't want to suit up for the game tonight, you can pack your stuff and go on home."

"Now wait a minute. I didn't mean I wasn't going to play. I just wanted to get things squared away before my wife left so we'd be able to pay some of our expenses."

"You're not going to get it, and that's all there is to it."

"Well, why not?" They don't call me Bulldog for nothing.

"I don't have to tell you why. I'm the general manager. I'm in charge here. I don't have to give you a reason for anything I do."

"Tell you what. Why can't you give me $3,000 now and we'll just take it out of next year's salary?"

"I can't do that. That would give you a $3,000 head start in the bargaining."

"Well, look. What are we talking about in terms of contract next year? What do you think the kind of season I had is worth? By the time the season is over I'll have been in more than seventy games and say I continue pitching the way I have, which is pretty good, and we finish where we are now, fifth. What would I be worth to you?"

"A lot of general managers would tell you $2,000 more, hoping that they could get you at around $5- or $6,000. But I'm going to tell you the truth right out. I think your salary should be increased about $7,000 or $7,500."

"Well, hell, Spec. We're not going to have any problem at all. All we do now is add $7,500 to $22,000. Call it $30,000. I'll tell you what I'll do. I'll sign a contract right now for $27,000 if you give me the other $3,000."

"All right. All right. That's what we'll do. You come in tomorrow and the papers will be ready."

Now that's what I call a fair and reasonable general manager.

Putting my baseball cap on today, I remembered an odd conversation with Mike Marshall. He watched me put on my cap and noticed that I put it on back first, then smoothed the front of it over my forehead. He said that in the minors he had a manager who told him that only colored players put their hats on that way; that white players put their caps on front first and smoothed them in the back. Marshall said that from then on he put his cap on back first and was glad to see I did it that way too.

As I dictated this, my wife said, "How does Joe Pepitone put on *his* cap?"

And I said, "Very carefully."

What a lovely pennant race. Today the Mets beat the Cubs twice, the Pirates lost two to St. Louis, San Diego beat Cincinnati, Atlanta beat San Francisco and we beat Los Angeles. So now we're only two games on the loss side out of first place. It's closer than the Astros have ever been to first place since they were expanded into existence. It is now almost possible to go from first place to fifth in a single afternoon. And vice versa.

SEPTEMBER
11

Claude Osteen, who looks like a white rat, beat us 1–0 tonight. He pitched a great game. Wilson pitched an even better game because his control was off and he had to keep battling out of jams.

In the ninth Tommy Davis came up with two out and two on and Osteen struck him out on three pitches—two fastballs on the outside corner and a curve ball that broke about two feet and bounced on the plate. No one was mad at Tommy. Don Wilson came over and said, "Hang in there. He threw you three bastard pitches."

Road trip starts tomorrow. The family goes to Michigan and I'll have to tell David that I won't be seeing him for four weeks. The other kids don't seem to mind much, but David gets upset. I guess it goes back to when he first arrived from Korea, forlorn and scared, and we developed a special closeness that he still feels. I'll say to him, "Now, David, I won't be seeing you for four weeks. That's this many days." I hold up ten fingers and flash them three times.

Invariably, he says, "I don't like that many days."

SEPTEMBER

12

Atlanta

Blefary was giving me the business tonight. The first time he played in the big leagues he hit against me. It was after my arm trouble had started, and I must say I wasn't throwing very well. Anyway, it was great for Blefary. "Bulldog," he said, "you made my big-league debut a success. There I was in Yankee Stadium, on national television, with all my friends and relatives looking on, and I hit that blooper pitch of yours into the upper deck with two dudes on base. Thank you, Bulldog."

No scoreboard action tonight because everybody was playing in the West and I had to sit and watch us lose to Atlanta 4–3. But as Harry Walker said on the bench, if we can take two out of three here we'll be in good shape.

It sure has been a long time since I've taken baseball games this seriously.

SEPTEMBER

13

It's been more than two weeks since I was traded, and I still haven't received my $900 travel allowance from Seattle. I understand that Valdespino and Dooley Womack both got their money here before they left. It's interesting that when I owed the club $6.48 in incidental expenses at one of the hotels, I got two reminders in four days and then it was taken out of my paycheck.

My joke these days is about Julio Gotay, who scrounges about a dozen passes to every game. His friends are legion all over. The line is that as soon as Joe Schultz hung up in Baltimore after telling me I was traded, the phone rang and it was Gotay. He wanted to know if he could use my passes in St. Louis that night.

Larry Dierker vs. Phil Niekro. Second of this crucial three-game series. My first crucial series in years. It turned into one of those mean, tough ballgames that you try to win even while you're sitting on the bench. At one point I was standing in the dugout when Harry put the pitchout sign on and I thought, damn, if they look over here and see all of us standing up, they'll know there's a play on. So even though I was dying to watch, I turned around and sat down on the bench. It was more neurotic than sensible.

I can't stand the tension of these games. Poor Larry Dierker had a no-hitter going into the ninth inning and hung in there until the top of the thirteenth. We pinch-hit for him, scored two runs and then Gladding came in. They belted him all over the lot, so Blasingame came in and walked in the winning run. Heartbreaker.

I felt terrible for Dierker. Every inning he got up he knew he not only had to get them out in the bottom of the inning, he had to get them out the *next* inning too. It's like climbing a mountain, struggling to the top, then realizing there are two more peaks to climb. And then we go and lose.

It was a tremendous performance by Dierker, and at the end he never said a word. After pitching like that and getting zero for it, he just sat there in the locker room, listened to the game go down the drain and never once so much as flinched. Which is why Paul Richards, when he was with Houston, said of Dierker: "He's a cold-blooded, fish-eyed son of a bitch." He said it with approval.

Me watching Niekro pitch was like a young artist inspecting his first Picasso. I examined him very closely. His knuckleball seems to wobble up there, moving three or four times in a small pattern. Wilhelm's swishes up to the plate in swinging arcs. My knuckleball gets up there in a bigger hurry and breaks more sharply and erratically, but only once. When it's working, I mean.

I think my knuckler has more potential. Nevertheless, I can see why he's more successful than I am. For one thing, he has the knuckleball down to where he can count on it always jumping around. He throws very few that spin on him. This gives him time to concentrate on other aspects of his game. He has a pretty good fastball, and a great pick-off move. Me, I still get real wild with the knuckleball, my fastball isn't that good, and never will be, and I have a lousy pick-off move. I like to think, though, that I'm at a stage where Niekro was two or three years ago. All I need is a little time.

Game was over about eleven-thirty and we got back to the hotel an hour later. There's a day game tomorrow and we were in bed when the phone rang at 2:15 A.M. It was Buddy Hancken, the coach.

"Norm, are you in?" he says to Miller again.

Norm, in his pajamas, said, "Yes, but I'm getting ready to go out again."

"You better not. Spec's on a tear."

At 2:45 A.M. the phone rang again. Now we're trying to fall asleep.

"Norm, who's your roommate?" It's Hancken again.

He knows, and Miller knows he knows. But he tells him anyway. "Bouton."

"Is he in?"

"Of course. Do you want to talk to him?"

"No, I'll take your word for it."

Big of him. I mean, a lot of guys would have insisted on talking to me, checking me out, asking me something personal, like my social security number.

"What's going on?" Miller said. "You know you already called me once."

"The shit's hit the fan."

Anyway, because of the two phone calls we decided to stay up an extra fifteen minutes. One small step for freedom.

SEPTEMBER
14

Norm Miller has announced to all the people in our room that he will not play baseball on Jewish holidays. "But Norm," I said, "just last week you were telling me that you look down on organized religion and that you don't observe any of the religious holidays. What makes you suddenly religious?"

"I play on a Jewish holiday and go 0 for 5 against Niekro and the next day I go 0 for 4 and that's it," Miller said. "I'll never play on Jewish holidays again."

The guys were laughing about last night's phone calls. Like when Hancken asked Tommy Davis if he was in, Tommy said, "No. I'm out chasing broads."

Ron Willis was in the coffee shop at 2:15. According to club rules he didn't have to be in his room until 2:30, but Richardson walked over to him and said, "What are you doing here?"

"Waiting to order," Willis said alertly.

"Go to your room," Richardson said. "I'm going to call you on the telephone."

He went to his room and sure enough, the phone rings.

"You're suspended," Spec tells him. "Don't suit up. Call Harry in the morning. He'll tell you what to do."

Willis had some trouble sleeping. In the morning he called Harry.

"Don't know anything about it," Harry says. "I'll see you at the ballpark."

So in the clubhouse later, there was Willis, sitting with his baseball shirt on and no pants. "The manager told me to dress," he said, "and the general manager told me I was suspended. I don't know what the hell to do. So I'll stay halfway until I get further instructions."

The other day Wade Blasingame's girlfriend visited him in his room. He's single, of course. Soon Spec called him on the telephone and told him to get that girl out of his room. Fifteen minutes later he was down there in person, telling the girl she ought to be ashamed of herself and to get the hell out of the room.

Later, Blasingame was told he'd been fined $500. I can't believe it. But I do.

I'll tell you why I believe it. Because Blasingame hasn't won any games this year and because he walked in the winning run the other night. And the baseball tradition is if you're going bad on the field you're in trouble all over.

Dierker tells this story. Last year he and Danny Coombs, pitcher, were three hours late for curfew in New York and staggered into the hotel holding each other up. Spec Richardson was in the lobby. As they listed by him, Dierker slurred, "How're you doing, Spec baby?"

The next day Coombs was fined $100 for blowing the curfew and Dierker was fined $200 for being drunk. The premise was that Dierker was the only one who said anything, so he was the only one who could be accused of being drunk.

The payoff is that the $100 was taken out of Coombs' pay, but the $200 was never deducted from Dierker. It must have been that they felt the threat alone was enough punishment for Dierker. It couldn't have had anything to do with the fact that Dierker is a twenty-game winner and Coombs is a marginal relief man. Could it?

Fines and suspensions don't change the score. We lost again today, 3–2, a sweep. Denny Lemaster was the loser. Rico Carty hit two home runs off him. One of them was a two-run job in the last of the eighth and wiped out our 2–1 lead.

Note about Rico Carty. He doesn't trust banks. He also doesn't trust the clubhouse valuables box. So that big lump you see in his back pocket during baseball games is his wallet.

I looked up Niekro before the game tonight and asked if he usually threw so many fastballs. He said he didn't, but that his arm felt too strong when he started pitching and that when his arm is strong he's unable to throw a good knuckleball. So he threw more fastballs to tire his arm out.

They have bedsheet banners in Atlanta too. They say REBEL. Sometimes the bedsheet is a Confederate flag. I wonder how the Negro players

375

feel about them. The worst part is that these things are hung by kids. Why the hell couldn't they let that stuff die with their grandfathers? These are not rebels who want something new. These are rebels who want to bring back the old.

Doug Rader, the third baseman, may be a good-looking cat, but I'm afraid he might be too tight for a pennant race like this. Right after he hit a soft pop-up that sent the second baseman back on the grass, he came into the dugout and said to me, "How far did that last one go?"

"All the way out behind second base," I said.

"It's all in the wrists," he said.

SEPTEMBER
15

San Diego

On our trip from Atlanta to San Diego we had a stopover in Dallas at Love Field. There's a huge statue of a Texas Ranger in the terminal and it's inscribed: "One Riot, One Ranger."

It reminded me of an incident when I was playing baseball in Amarillo. There were about five or six players having a drink at a table in the middle of this large, well-lit bar, all of us over twenty-one. Suddenly, through the swinging doors Old West fashion—come these four big Texans, ten-gallon hats, boots, spurs, six-shooters holstered at their sides, the works. They stopped and looked around and all of a sudden everybody in the place stopped talking. I wouldn't have been surprised if one of them said, "All right, draw!"

They spotted us ballplayers and sauntered over, all four of them, spurs jangling, boots creaking, all eyes on them.

"Let me see your IDs, boys," one of them says.

I don't know what got into me, but I had to say—I *had* to after that entrance—to these obvious Texas Rangers, "First I'd like to see *your* identification." I said it loud.

He rolled his eyes up into his head in exasperation and very slowly and reluctantly he reached for his wallet, opened it and showed me his badge and identification card. I gave them a good going over. I mean a 20-second check, looking at the photo and then up at him. Then I said, "He's okay, men."

Then, of course, we all whipped out our IDs, which showed we were all over twenty-one, and the Texas Rangers turned around and walked out, creaking and jangling.

We laughed about that for weeks.

I find it curious that of all the things Dallas could have chosen to glorify in the airport, it chose law enforcement. The only thing I know about Dallas law enforcement is that its police department allowed a lynching to occur on national television. Maybe the statue should have been of a group of policemen at headquarters, with an inscription that read: "One Police Department, One Lynching."

SEPTEMBER

15

On the bus from the airport to the hotel in San Diego it was a dark and tired time, and all you could see was the lighted ends of cigarettes. It was quiet, except for a few mumbled conversations. Then suddenly there was this loud scuffling in the back. A fight between Jimmy Ray, called Stinger (of course), and Blasingame. Foolishness. The Stinger was pretending he was talking a girl into coming up to his room and the Blazer took exception. What he's really upset about is the way he's pitching and that $500 fine and he decided to take the Stinger's monologue personally.

We broke them up quickly enough. What impressed me, though, was the way the guys reacted when a coach tried to get into it. Buddy Hancken started to move toward the back but Curt Blefary, Jimmy Wynn and Joe Morgan stood up and blocked his way and his vision. So the coaches and manager don't know who's involved. "Get the hell up to the front of the bus where you belong," Lemaster said to Hancken. "Stay out of this thing."

Hancken is the kind of coach who enjoys his work. He's always the one who asks on the bus, "What time tonight, Harry? What time?" He's also the guy who checks the Exergenie list and your pockets for baseballs you might be accidentally taking off the field.

A lot of coaches would make very good prison guards.

Jim Owens: "Hey, are you going to use names in that thing you're writing?"

"Once in a while."

"Christ, be careful. I remember the story *Sports Illustrated* did on the Dalton Gang. [This was a group of high-flying Philadelphia Phillies. Owens was a member in good standing.] We thought it was going to be a real nice spread. They took pictures and everything. Then they did a hatchet job on us."

"Weren't you the guys who sued?"

"Yeah, and we'd have gotten a helluva lot more money if one of the guys hadn't attacked a maid a week before the trial."

There was a play in yesterday's game that would have been funny if it weren't so bad. We were leading 2–1 at the time and Jimmy Wynn's on second. With two out Blefary hits a clean single to right, certain to score Wynn except that Wynn rounds third, gets halfway home, then realizes that he hasn't touched third. So back he goes, tags it and again sets sail for home. Naturally he's thrown out at the plate. All we have on Blefary's perfect scoring single is a third out. So today Blefary was grousing to Joe Morgan about the RBI he lost on the play. "For crissakes, Helen Keller could have scored from second base on that hit. If I was a black man he'd have scored."

"If you were a black, it would've been a home run," Morgan said.

I found the plane ride from Atlanta to San Diego interesting because of a long discussion I got into with Leon McFadden, infielder, black, Doug Rader, infielder, white, and Scipio Spinx (now, there's a name), pitcher, black. McFadden was talking about the first time he ever ran into prejudice. He'd grown up in Los Angeles in a mixed neighborhood and never had a single racial encounter until he was a baseball player in Georgia. The team bus stopped at a restaurant and all the players piled in. The man behind the counter asked McFadden if he'd like to come back and eat in the kitchen.

"I really didn't think anything about it at first," McFadden said. "I thought maybe they had another room in the back, someplace more comfortable. It just didn't register. So I said, 'No thanks, I'll sit here.'"

He was soon enlightened by the manager.

"I was angry. I had a package of crackers in my hand and I just threw them down, walked out and sat in the bus."

After a while his teammates came out, bringing him food, and he got angry at them for that. "I realized later that they were just trying to be nice to me. But when that kind of thing happens, you don't think straight. I was so hurt and so angry I could feel the tears in my eyes. I didn't know whether to cry or punch somebody."

McFadden said that incident marked him. For the first time in his life he began to view white people with anger and suspicion. And as he grew older he saw more and more things. Even on this team. "We'll be riding on the bus and we'll pass a couple of Negro girls in the street and one of the white players will say, 'Hey, Mac, there's a soul sister for you.' Now, why do I have to have any special interest in a black girl? And why can't *he* be just as interested in the black girl? And why can't I be interested in a white girl?"

Another thing he resents is the way ballplayers describe other players. They'll say, "He's that colored first baseman, or the colored catcher." They never say, "He's that *white* first baseman."

My own thinking on that is that black is certainly an identifying characteristic, and that no one should be upset to be identified as black. But McFadden is quite right to be annoyed that no one is ever identified as white.

Then Doug Rader had some interesting comments on Curt Blefary. Curt has a good relationship with at least three of the Negro players. He rooms with Wilson and he's always playing cards with him and Morgan. Because of that, McFadden said, there are guys on the club who are afraid *not* to like him. "It would be healthy if you could say, 'Curt's just not my kind of guy,' without having to be afraid that you'll be considered racist," Rader said.

Nothing works that way, of course. Around baseball you are what people think you are. Like Doug Rader said that white players often call him "nigger lover" as a result of his friendship with McFadden. Or they say, "You're just like one of them," whatever that means.

McFadden said he frequently runs into players who are friendly, pat-on-the-back types but who, as soon as they're in a group of white players will start throwing "n's" around. "N" is black code for "nigger." "You realize they're only putting up a facade when they're around you," McFadden said. "As soon as they think there are no black guys around they start dropping "n's" all over the place.

Doug Rader said it happened to him all the time. Even though white players know how he feels, they drop "n's" on him and all he can do is get up and walk out.

Maybe the best attitude to have is Dick Gregory's. He called his autobiography *Nigger,* dedicated it to his mother and reminded her that when people said "nigger" now, they were just promoting his book.

My wife suggested that I might save some money at the Astroworld after she left if I had a roommate. She had noticed that Tommy Davis was living at the hotel alone and thought maybe he would like to save some money too. So I asked him. He said he'd think about it.

Even though we're friends, there was this moment of awkwardness. Maybe Tommy Davis doesn't want to room with *anybody.* Maybe he doesn't want to room with me, but wouldn't mind a different white guy. And he might have wondered if I was trying to prove something. I wondered if he wondered. The tiny tension was there. Too bad.

I think I should explain here that I too have gone through a difficult learning process. When I was in high school I was certain—with all the snobbish certainty of youth—that I would never let my daughter marry a Negro, nor would I like to live next door to a Negro family. What I know now is that life is a lot more complicated than that.

Lost our fifth straight game today 5–3 to the San Diego Padres. I pitched two scoreless innings, but the game was gone by that time.

If you could disappear from embarrassment I wouldn't have been available.

Coming out to the bullpen just before the game began, in front of thousands of empty seats, I took off my hat, made a deep bow and generally behaved as though I was being acclaimed by millions. Then I looked up and all I could see was San Diego uniforms. "What are you guys doing in our bullpen?" I said. Of course I had it all wrong. I was in *their* bullpen, act and all. I felt like a goddam clown.

SEPTEMBER
16

Doug Rader and I agreed over breakfast that Harry Walker is a good man. One of the things Doug gets a kick out of is when Harry strikes a batting pose in the coffee shop or some other unlikely place to explain how he used to get base hits all the time. He's always giving out useful information. And how many managers are able to go over to a player and say, "Listen, I handled it wrong. I'm sorry"? Harry is.

Another impressive thing about Harry is this blazer he wears. It has his family crest on the breast pocket. Contrary to rumor, it's not an open mouth emblazoned on a field of wild verbiage. I know because I checked.

I had a chat with Spec Richardson about how the club came to make a deal for me. He said he'd been talking to Seattle about Tommy Davis and mentioned he could use some pitching. And Milkes said, "How about Bouton?" Spec said he hadn't had any reports on me, but he took a chance.

Anonymity is pitching in fifty-seven ballgames and finding out that no one knows.

Norm Miller says that it has long been his ambition to sit in a laundry bag. He thinks if he did, and pulled the string tight over his head, it would be very quiet and peaceful.

Norm and I came down to the lobby and spotted Ron Willis sitting in a lobby chair. At the same time we noticed a most attractive young girl standing nearby. So naturally we walked over to have a chat with Willis.

"How come the only time someone comes over to talk to me is when there's a pretty girl around?" Willis said.

"Ron, you're getting a complex," Miller said. "You didn't even give us a chance to speak to you."

"No, it's no complex," Willis said. "Bill Henry is the only one who actually sat down here and talked to me. Everybody else is here to check that girl out."

"Listen, Ron," Miller said. "I'm your friend. I'm trying to help you. You're a sick person. You need help."

I couldn't help thinking that Norm would be a sick person too if he were traded from St. Louis in mid-season and did nothing since but pitch batting practice and be threatened with a suspension for sitting in the coffee shop.

Has anybody noticed that we haven't won a game since we ate that chicken á la king?

Jim Owens says he'd like to see me in the starting rotation. He agrees that the knuckleball is far from ideal for short relief. But so far Harry still thinks he needs me more to relieve than to start. "I'm still plugging for you," Owens said. Bless him.

A friend of mine named Lou Kramberg is friendly with a scout in the Chicago Cubs organization. It was still early in the year when Kramberg called this scout and told him about me: that I was getting in a lot of ballgames, pitching effectively, but not accumulating much of a record. He said I was a hard worker, a good battler, that I field my position well and could pitch under pressure. Just what the Cubs needed. The scout told him no, that the word on me is that I'm a clubhouse lawyer.

Two losses to San Diego makes it six in a row, and Rader decided to do something about it. "Can you drown yourself in the shower?" he asked.

He went up on his toes and put his mouth to the shower nozzle. It looked as though the water was coming out of his ears. Some guys just can't take this pennant pressure.

SEPTEMBER
17

San Francisco

Curt Blefary doesn't like being platooned. So this is him on Harry Walker. "Look, he doesn't drink and he doesn't smoke. He's not my kind of man."

It was great coming back to Candlestick Park. I hadn't been there since the World Series of 1962. The odor of the clubhouse was strangely familiar, and I remembered where all the guys had their lockers and the table in the middle of the room loaded with ten dozen baseballs for us to autograph.

This was my rookie year and I remember Whitey Ford hurt his arm and I was going to have to pitch the seventh game, except that it rained for five days in a row and Ralph Terry was able to come back and win the final game 1–0 when Willie McCovey hit a screaming line drive off him and Bobby Richardson caught it for the final out. And I remember the police escorts we had wherever we went, sirens screaming. Great year for a rookie.

"It was a terrible year," Tommy Davis said. "The Dodgers should have been in that Series, not the Giants."

Except that they lost to them in a playoff. Can't be a great year for everybody, I guess.

Maybe we're not out of this thing yet. We beat the Giants 2–1. Larry Dierker won his twentieth and I saved it with two innings of hitless relief. I shook everybody up by walking a couple of guys right away, but they hit only one ball out of the infield on me, a pop-up that Norm Miller made a nice running catch on. It was a good game because we stopped our losing streak and we beat Gaylord Perry. When I came off the mound, Harry threw his arms around me and said, "Attaboy, this was a real big win."

I felt good about the whole thing until twelve-fifteen, which is when I came into the hotel. Buddy Hancken was in the lobby.

"Go to your room," he said.

"What?" I said, thinking fast.

"Curfew," he said. "Twelve-o'clock curfew."

When I got up to the room Norm Miller said, "They called, they called."

"What time?"

"Well, they called at eleven."

"But the curfew is twelve."

"I know. They called at eleven and asked if you were here. I said you weren't. Then they called again at twelve and I told them you were in the bathroom. I asked if they wanted to talk to you and they said no, they'd take my word."

"Who called?"

"Buddy Hancken."

Poor Norm. I wonder if they'll fine him for lying.

SEPTEMBER
18

The Giants clobbered us 9–3. Denny Lemaster got knocked out in the first inning and that was it. We have only fourteen games left and we'd have to win all of them to accomplish very much. It's not possible. We're out of it now. Ah, shitfuck.

The game depressed me, and coming back to the Astroworld Hotel with Bobbie gone depressed me even further. (Tommy Davis, by the way, has decided against having a roommate. I'm sure it's not because I'm white.) Besides, my stomach has been bothering me and Jim Owens didn't win any fights, so Jimmy Ray, who is called "Ultraviolent Ray" since his scuffle with Blasingame, will be starting against Cincinnati and not me.

Another thing that's depressing. I finally got the traveling-expense check from Seattle and $88.68 was deducted from the $900. That's what Marvin Milkes says is what it cost to repair a clubhouse door I, little old Jim Bouton, pulled off its hinges in a fit of anger. Now, wait a minute. It's true enough that I kicked a door. It was such a minor matter I never even mentioned it in this little diary. All I did was kick it a little bit after one of my frustrating appearances and broke loose a bit of molding. Johnny McNamara said not to worry about it, it was a small deal. And now this stupid bill.

As soon as I think up something awful enough to do about it I will.

A group of terrorized pitchers stood around the batting cage watching Willie McCovey belt some tremendous line drives over the right-field fence. Everytime a ball bounced into the seats we'd all make little whimpering animal sounds. "Hey, Willie," I said. "Can you do that whenever you want to?"

He didn't crack a smile.

"Just about," he said, and he hit another one.

More animal sounds.

One of the Houston radio announcers, Loel Passe, interviewed me and a few of the guys were on the earie, so I thought I'd entertain them. "Congratulations are certainly in order for the job you did last night," Loel said.

And I said, "Loel, I couldn't agree with you more. I was absolutely fabulous out there."

Broke the lads up.

I learned that from Mickey Mantle. He'd be interviewed by some announcer about a home run he hit, with the wind blowing from left to right and the ball had been curving into the wind and thus was saved from going foul. "That's right," Mickey said. "When I noticed the wind blowing like that—I always check, you know—I put the proper English on the ball, left or right, up or down, depending upon which way the wind is blowing."

And the poor guy just said, "Uhuh, uhuh, uhuh."

Most interviewers don't listen to the answers; they're too busy thinking of the next question. I've often been tempted, when I notice a guy's eyes all glazed over, when I'm answering a question to say something like, "I believe you know that there were over 20,000 tons of iron ore shipped from Yugoslavia in 1948." And I'm sure he'd say, "Uhuh, uhuh."

Bob Watson's name was on the lineup card but he couldn't play. Seems he was catching some weirdo knuckleball pitcher the other day and the ball took a strange hop in the air and hit him on the finger. He's been taking whirlpool treatments, but the finger is still fat and he can't grip a bat. Sorry about that. I wish it had been Eddie O'Brien instead.

SEPTEMBER
19

Houston

Larry Dierker and I much prefer the Beatles to country-western music. As a protest against the amount of country-western we have to listen to, we have composed what we consider a typical song of the genre. It took us about two innings.

"I want my baby back again,
She done left town with my best friend,
And now I lie here all alone,
I'm just awaitin' by the phone.
Her lips were sweet as summer wine,
And when I held her hand in mine,

I thought she'd never be untrue,
But now she's broke my heart in two.
The mailman let me down today,
And so I made that mother pay,
And now I'm locked in this old jail,
And my dog died and there's no bail.
My teardrops fall like pouring rain,
The bottle doesn't ease my pain,
And no one gives a hoot for me,
Since Billy Joe took my Marie,
And ran away to Tennessee.
I wish I had someone to tell,
'Bout how I'm locked up in this cell,
And all my kinfolk dead and gone,
But with the Lord I'll carry on.

Major difference between the National and American Leagues. In the American League part of the scouting report on a player is, "Watch out, he takes a big turn at first base and may go to second on you if you're not careful." Maybe one or two players on a team do that. In the National League everybody does it. It's a hustling league.

I pitched two scoreless innings against the Reds, striking out the side in the eighth—Alex Johnson, Tony Perez and Johnny Bench, .300 hitters all. On the second strikeout, the game was stopped to announce that the Astros had broken the league record for strikeouts in a season, 1,123. And there were pictures of me with the ball and me with the manager, and I felt foolish. I mean, here are Dierker, Wilson and Griffin with about 200 strikeouts each, and me with 23, and I happen to be pitching when the record is broken. I feel as awkward about that as I feel about moving in as No. 1 relief man ahead of Fred Gladding. That's why I was pleased that Gladding wound up getting credit for the win tonight, even though if I'd been left in the game I might have picked it up. Gladding has had a helluva year, no matter what's happening right now. Me, all I had was a year with Sal Maglie and Joe Schultz.

Harry Walker was absolutely right. In the ninth inning we were down 2–0 and had a man on base.

So he reached down to his bag of tricks and pinch-hit Keith Lampard, a rookie outfielder, for Curt Blefary.

A natural move. They're both lefthanded hitters. Lampard won the game for Gladding with a big two-run homer and all the writers crowded around him after the game. And I said to Tommy Davis, "Do you remember the first time you did something big like that in the big leagues?"

He said he did. He said he also remembered when he was a rookie with the Dodgers and made his first trip back to New York to play in front of his home-town fans and friends. "I get a single my first time at bat and I'm going crazy," Tommy said. "The first thing you know, I steal second and I'm out there with a big grin on my face, really having fun. I look up in the stands where my friends are and I shoot them a little bit of a wave and a big smile and I get picked off second base. Boy, did I feel terrible."

He said another big thrill was the 1963 World Series. "Drysdale was the pitcher for us, Willie Davis was on second base, the score was nothing to nothing and I hit a hard smash off Bobby Richardson's knee and we won 1–0. I forget who was pitching for them. Somebody named Button or Bontown or something."

By this time I'd walked away and was in the shower room. I don't have to listen to that stuff. And I yelled back from the shower, "Hard smash, my left clavicle. It was a goddam ground ball that bounced twenty-five times and took a bad hop off a pebble."

I was happy for Lampard and could see he was having a lot of fun talking to the reporters. And I remembered when that would happen to me with the Yankees, the reporters would be all around me and several of the players would walk by making mouth-moving motions with their hands, meaning I was talking too much. I just don't understand what goes through a man's mind to make him behave that way. Hell, you got to live it up a little when you have a good day.

SEPTEMBER
20

I'm pitching with a runner on third base, and Bob Tolan, a lefthanded hitter with a good average, is up. Ted Savage, a righthanded hitter with a batting average of around .220, is the next hitter. Harry Walker motions to Johnny Edwards to see if we want to walk Tolan and pitch to Savage. And I, big thinker that I am, indicate that I want to pitch to Tolan. So Harry gives me an okay wave.

Tolan promptly swats my second pitch into right-center for a triple. Savage I strike out on three pitches. In the dugout, Harry says, "Look, you've got a guy hitting .220 as opposed to a guy hitting .320."

"I was afraid if we walked Tolan he'd steal second base," Edwards said.

"Okay, so Tolan gets on and steals second," Harry said. "Savage gets a hit and drives both of them in. The score is 5–0 instead of 4–0, the way it is now. But as far as I'm concerned I want to hold them at three. Once they get over three that extra run doesn't mean much because we're in the eighth inning. Besides, Tolan's very fast. Even if he tops the bat he can beat it out and you've got a man on third who's going to score. Me, I walk him and pitch to Savage."

Harry was absolutely right. Harry always is. It's why he's considered such a pain.

We were taking physical exams today, and I was glad. I think I need some help. I've lost about seven pounds in the last few weeks and my stomach has been telling me sad stories. Acid indigestion is my constant companion, heartburn keeps me awake. I don't know if it's because of missing my family or pitching every day of this damn pennant race, but I'm suffering.

I was waiting my turn, sitting next to Johnny Edwards, and somehow Jim Turner was mentioned. Maybe it was the talk of heartburn. At any rate, Turner was pitching coach in Cincinnati when Edwards was there. "Boy, that son of a bitch," said Edwards. "I remember when Sammy Ellis won twenty games, Turner was with him every day. He knows how to take a winner and ride him to his next job. But when Ellis started going bad, Turner wouldn't even talk to him. He got a sore arm and Turner didn't say three words to him all season. The funny part was that the guys would kid Turner about being such a front-runner, but he couldn't stop." Front-running was in his blood.

Curt Blefary is a big, rough, physical man. He likes to slap people on the back too hard, jab you in the ribs, squeeze your arm black and blue. He also likes to charge Robert, our twenty-five-year-old clubhouse assistant, throw him to the floor and choke him until he starts to turn blue. Robert laughs about it and pretends he loves every minute of it. But when he sees Blefary, he runs the other way.

On the hospital elevator, Blefary said to Larry Dierker, "C'mon, Rock Pile, get on."

"Curtis, what are you calling him 'Rock Pile' for?" I said. "He's one of the more intelligent guys on this club."

And Blefary said, "When I was in to see that eye doctor today he told me that with my eyes I should be hitting .450."

It's easier to ignore a question, sometimes, than try to answer it.

Johnny Edwards drove some of the players to the hospital, and when we got there he pulled his car into a spot marked "Doctors Only." That's baseball player all the way. We get used to special privileges and come to expect them. In the minor leagues a baseball player can tear up a bar or impregnate the mayor's daughter and he'll be asked please not to let it happen again. I'm certain that if they'd towed Edwards' car away he wouldn't have had to pay a fine. He'd have said we were with the Houston Astros and somebody would have said, "Oh, the Houston Astros. Okay. Sorry we had to tow you away. Please try to be more careful next time."

I've seen guys get into bar fights and when the cops come the ballplayers are sneaked out the back way. Even if you get stopped for speeding you can usually get away with it if you let the cop know you're a ballplayer. "Jim Bouton of the *Astros?* Hiya Jim, glad to see you. Suppose you can get me a couple of passes to the ballgame?"

SEPTEMBER
21

We have a day off between Cincinnati and our trip to Los Angeles. I'm going to see if I can get permission to stop off and see my family. I need some emotional refueling. So does the family. My wife tells me that when I'm not around for a long time the kids get restless and hard to handle.

I told Tommy Davis about being charged for a broken door and he said that the only man on the club who had strength enough to rip that door off its hinges was Brabender. "I hope you *will* call the man and get your money back," Davis said.

I said I had, but somehow couldn't get through to him. I also left word for him to call me, but somehow he hasn't. I get the strange feeling he's trying to avoid me. Just for that, it's going to cost him. He's responsible for the expenses of my moving to Vancouver, which I hadn't planned to bill him for. It's a small deal, but if he can take $88 from me, I can bill him for $97. Does he think he's playing with kids?

SEPTEMBER
22

Harry Walker called the pitchers and catchers in for a meeting and made several good points. He thinks that the pitchers should practice their pick-off moves during games. Just keep trying to pick guys off, even if it's not necessary. Then, when you really need it in a close game, maybe you'll have it.

He also suggested we take an Exergenie home over the winter. He says it makes sense to keep your arm stretched. He also thinks we should work on some aspect of our pitching over the winter. We don't have to do any actual pitching, he said, just practice our motion or pick-off move. You can do that in your bedroom, he said. (Our wives will love it.)

Finally he reminded us that you're just as strong at thirty-five as you are at twenty-five. He said doctors have proven it. And he said the strongest time of your life is when you're thirty. I hope Harry Walker's right again.

The Houston Astros do not give paychecks to their players. The money is deposited in Judge Roy Hofheinz' bank and the players write personal checks for the money. This does two things. It gives the bank an opportunity to hold onto your money for a while. And it gets you into the habit of banking with the Judge's bank. The Judge never misses a trick.

SEPTEMBER

23

Called Gary Bell just to chat and find out how he was doing. He said he'd just been clipped for $100 by the White Sox for not meeting a curfew and it was the night before an off day. He said about ten guys got caught. But he personally was getting even "In the last eight days I've taken twenty-five baseballs home and I'm not going to stop until I have $100 worth."

Then this: "What time is it there, Jim?" "Two o'clock."

"Don't you have a game today?" "Yes, but it's a night game."

"Are you sure?"

The rat.

Bell also said that things are going so bad he's working on the knuckleball. He throws it in the outfield and gets pretty good movement on the ball about half the time.

Lots of luck.

I also called Steve Hovley, partly to see if he knew where I could find Marvin Milkes. In this modern time it's impossible not to be able to reach a man by telephone, yet with Marvin Milkes, that seems to be the case. A lesser man than I would become suspicious.

Hovley said the pitchers had their party with the pitchers' fund money (a good deal of it mine) and it was a good one. They had $500, spent it all and did it up brown: posh hotel suite, whiskey, champagne, caviar, the works. He said everybody said to tell me thanks.

Steve asked me how things were over here with Houston. I told him how closely they checked us into our rooms, and he said, "Right now baseball is about twenty years behind the most puritanical of freshman girl dormitories."

Which reminded me of something Tommy Harper once said: "In the winter I have a beard, a mustache and wear my hair long and natural. But before I come to spring training I have to shave off my beard and mustache and cut my hair. I feel like I'm going to boot camp."

With Jimmy Ray pitching, the Braves had runners on first and second and Clete Boyer was the hitter. Ray threw a curve ball and Boyer, attempting to bunt, fouled it back and there was a loud moan in the dugout. "What's it all about, Don?" I said to Don Wilson. "We had our bastard play on," he said. "And you're not supposed to throw a curve ball on the bastard play."

"What's the bastard play?" I said.

"It's where, in a bunt situation, the third baseman and the first baseman charge in for the bunt. The shortstop sneaks over and covers third and the second baseman sneaks over and covers first. Then, whomever fields the ball, fires it to third base. The guy on third fires to first and maybe we get a double play. If we don't, we at least get the lead runner."

"But why is it called the bastard play?"

"Well, if the play works, it's a real bastard for the other team," Don said. "And if the hitter decides to swing away instead of bunt he's got three big targets to hit, pitcher, first baseman and third baseman. All of them are charging in. If he swings it can be a real bastard for them."

And the reason Ray should not have thrown the curve is that when the play is on you *want* the guy to bunt, and it's harder to bunt a curve ball than a fastball. The idea, Harry said, is to just lay it in there and let him bunt. Once again, Harry was right.

My super knuck is gone. And I got racked. No innings pitched; four earned runs on three hits and a walk. Actually the knuckler was fair, but I had no control over it. In fact a couple of balls got away from Marty Martinez and Harry took him out with a count of 2 and 0 and the poor fellow was embarrassed, angry at himself, and angry at Harry for taking him out.

I was embarrassed myself. With the count 3 and 1 on Rico Carty I threw him a fastball that had nothing on it, just trying to get it over for a strike, and he hit a line drive that almost tore my head off. With first base open, I should have thrown him a low knuckler and taken my chances of walking him. Harry was pretty good about taking me out of that shambles. He just waved for the new pitcher and said, "Hang in there. Once in a while you have days like that." So I trudged off the mound to a smattering of applause, tipped my cap to show my class and, well, now Jim Owens knows what I mean when I say there are days when I just don't have it. He's been telling me that he doesn't know what I'm talking about.

After the game Marty Martinez came over and apologized for missing so many and I told him to forget it. I'm hell on catchers. Found out tonight that Watson's finger is broken. All those whirlpool treatments and it only got worse. I feel bad about that.

A terrible night. All alone and I just got my ass kicked. To top it all off I was the losing pitcher. What a year. It will go into the books as Jim Bouton: 2–3. It will look like nothing happened. Perhaps there ought to be a suffering quotient (SQ) added to the pitching statistics.

24

Curt Blefary is one of the players who thinks baseball games last too long. I mean, when a pitcher is having control trouble he's yelling over from first base, "C'mon, now, get the ball over. Get it over." The man sounds positively irritated. I do believe he has the potential to be a coach.

Tried to get Marvin Milkes again. No soap. Next time I'm going to make it a collect call and say that Bowie Kuhn is on the line.

Well, one more time. And this time his secretary took the call and said she knew all about the problem and that there were two doors involved and I had not been billed for the door that was pulled off its hinges, just the door I'd broken.

So I explained that there was no way I could have caused $88 worth of damage, because all I did was pull a bit of molding away from the door and the clubhouse man said he fixed it and it didn't cost anything.

She said she'd tell Mr. Milkes.

Lost another close one to the Braves tonight 2–1. Tom Griffin was the loser. On the airplane to Cincinnati I asked him what he thinks when he's out there on the mound struggling through a rough inning. "I think to myself, 'If I can just get out of this inning, if I can just get away alive, I'll be all right.' "

Which is about what I do. Particularly this year, when I don't have a good knuckleball and am at their mercy. I think to myself, "I know you're going to nail this next one. Please hit a line drive at somebody. Please." All I want to do is get back into the dugout and get myself together.

Harry gave it to us after this one. He waved all of us into a corner of the clubhouse so he could be sure he had our attention and lit into us. "You guys aren't bearing down," he said. "You say you are, but I don't buy that bullshit. You can't be as horseshit as you look out there. You guys look like Tom Thumb."

This fractured us. I had to bite my lip to keep from laughing straight out. We've been called things in the clubhouse before. A lot of managers say their players look like Molly Putz out there. But never Tom Thumb.

"You couldn't knock anybody's hat off," Harry said. "You look like you're going downhill on a scooter." By then it was almost impossible to hold back. Shoulders were shaking, heads were disappearing under sweatshirts, no one could look at anybody else. "And I don't want any bullshit on that airplane tonight. I don't want anybody playing the fool. If you're going to play like you're down, you better act like it."

Then he said, "You used to have some pride in yourselves, but it's gone."

The guys say this was a fairly mild Harry Walker exhibition. He didn't throw any food or kick over any stools and, said Blasingame, "When he's really pissed there are a lot more 'fucks' in there."

Larry Dierker said that when Harry had these meetings at the beginning of the season the guys would huddle together in a corner, really scared. After a while, though, all they could do was giggle.

Dick Williams has been fired as manager of the Red Sox. I think that when a team wins a pennant the tendency is to give too much credit to the manager and when a team loses the tendency is to blame him too much. I don't think Dick Williams was that good a manager when the Red Sox won the pennant. I think there was a right combination—a lot of things falling into place at once. I don't believe that Gil Hodges is as bad as Hawk Harrelson makes him out to be in his book, nor do I think he's as great as he seems to be with the Mets right now. The Mets are putting it all together this year and Hodges just happens to be there at the right moment.

In the dark of the airplane Doug Rader was saying that he feels he's living out of time and out of place. He thinks he would have been much happier as a Tahitian war lord, or even a pirate. And Norm Miller said, "I think I would have made a good pirate too. I wonder if there have ever been any good Jewish pirates?"

We also talked about the expressions we used in high school. Things like "Get bent," which was meant to put a guy down. Or if somebody said, "Are you taking Louise to the dance," you had to say, "Fuckin' ay I am." Doug had one I never heard: "You 'bout a cool sucker, Bill." I guess that meant you were cool. But "eat a hodgy" must have been nationwide, because Norm was saying "eat a hodgy" out on the coast while I was saying it in Bloom Township High in Chicago Heights.

John Wilson, the sportswriter, was pretty loose on the plane tonight and we got to talking about Don Wilson.

"What's the matter with Wilson?" he said.

"His arm is bothering him."

"No, no, no," Wilson said. "You've seen him pitch. How can your arm be bothering you if you can go five, six innings? It's only after that that he blows up. How can that be his arm?"

"He's out there on guts," I said. "It hurts him, hurts like hell, but he's doing the best he can."

"No, that's not it," Wilson said.

"Then, what is it?"

Wilson pointed to his head. "Maybe it's all up here," he said. "Maybe he's a mental case."

"Are you kidding?" I said. "After all the games Wilson has been in, suddenly he's a mental case? Here's a guy that has over 200 strikeouts, a guy who pitched a no-hitter against the Cincinnati Reds, a proven big-league pitcher, and suddenly he's a mental case? Suddenly he's afraid to pitch against the San Diego Padres?"

That's the same kind of thinking I ran into on the Yankees. This was in '65. My arm hurt and I tried to throw through it. I thought that if I kept throwing, it might strengthen and the pain would go away. And people would ask, "If your arm hurts, how can you go out there and throw?" Dammit, you *can* throw. It's just a question of how much it's going to hurt and how effective you're going to be. Granted I shouldn't have been out there. But I didn't realize that until later. I thought I could work it out by pitching. And people began to say after a while that I had a mental problem. Hell, I had a sore arm. It's hard for people to understand how your arm can hurt when it doesn't hurt them to watch you throw.

Baseball player's description of Cincinnati: "Horseshit park, horseshit clubhouse, horseshit hotel, lots of movies, nice place to eat after the game, tough town to get laid in."

We had to wait for an hour-and-a-half at the airport because there were no taxis and our bus didn't arrive on time. It was three in the morning, but that's no excuse. And do you know that all you can hear at the Cincinnati airport at three in the morning are crickets? Goddam *crickets?* While we were standing there Larry Dierker said, "This city isn't a completely lost cause. Look, they've got one of those computer IQ games." So we walked over, dropped a couple of quarters in and discovered the machine was broken.

SEPTEMBER
25

Cincinnati

I got into my seventieth ballgame tonight. We were ahead 3–1 in the seventh and I got called in with two out and runners on first and second. Pete Rose up. Real clutch situation. I throw two knuckleballs for balls. Edwards calls for a fastball and I shake him off. Rose is just going to rip my fastball. I know it. So I throw a knuckleball for a strike, another knuckleball for a foul ball, a third for strike three and strut off the mound.

Then we have a long inning and I hate it. I feel like I ought to go down to the bullpen and get some throwing in. I'm not throwing my super knuckler. Sure enough, I go out there and give up three straight singles. They don't splash me against the fences but they hit sharp grounders. So Harry takes me out and says, "Well, you can't get them all the time."

I know, I know.

Fred Gladding came in, stopped them cold, and we won. He's been having his problems for the last month or so, but tonight we all called him "Ace."

After the game Pete Rose told a reporter that he never expected a knuckleball on 2 and 0. I think I'm wising up.

SEPTEMBER
26

Persistence is its own reward. I called Marvin Milkes' secretary again. She said the whole thing had been straightened out. Milkes had put a check in the mail for $88. Oh boy. Wonder what caused the change of heart. Could it be that Milkes read Larry Merchant's column in the New York *Post* the other day, which was the first public revelation of the fact that I'm writing a book about this season? Could it?

Norm Miller, who is married to an Italian girl, says he likes the idea of the bar mitzvah. He said he didn't have one. His brother did and Norm was jealous. "A bar mitzvah," he said, "is like signing for a bonus."

I looked like Tom Thumb on my first pitch in the game tonight. Tony Perez hit a knuckleball over Norm Miller's head and Norm could have caught it if he'd climbed over the fence and ran across the street. The fact that I struck out the next two guys didn't ease the pain.

It was a painful evening all around, especially for Jack Billingham. He and Dierker were scheduled to pitch the doubleheader and he asked Jim Owens which game he was pitching. "You pitch against Maloney," Owens told him.

"But he's their best pitcher," Billingham said, figuring that honor should go to Dierker.

"I know, I know," Owens said. "That's why you're pitching against him."

The idea is to win three more games and finish over .500. So you throw Billingham up as a sacrifice to Maloney, a guy you've got to figure on shutting out to beat, and let Dierker win his game. Sure enough, Maloney beat Billingham 3–0 with a one-hitter. We got three runs for

Dierker in the second game. Unfortunately they scored four off him and we lost 4–3. Nice doubleheader.

We were kidding in the bullpen about how many greenies the Reds must have been taking during this pennant race and just then there was a ball hit into short right that Pete Rose made a great diving run at and caught on a short hop. "Five more milligrams and he'd have had it," Tom Griffin said.

At this time of year, unless you're in a pennant race, what you really think about most is going home. So the story was told in the bullpen about Umpire Ed Runge and Frank Lary, pitcher. It was the last game of the season, probably 1960, and Frank Lary had booked a three-o'clock flight although it was a two-o'clock game. Of course, he wasn't sched-uled to pitch. Right before the game started Lary said to Runge, "Hey, Ed, I've got a three o'clock plane to catch home. See what you can do about getting me out of this ballgame." Runge said he would.

On the first pitch of the game Runge calls a strike and Lary, stand-ing on the top step of the dugout, yells, "Hey, Runge, what the hell kind of call is that? You trying to make a quick getaway?"

And Runge points a finger at him and says, "You're out of the game."

"Thanks," Lary said. And he left.

The other thing you talk about in the bullpen this time of year is sex. You talk about sex at all other times of the year too. Ballplayers don't exactly admire the sex habits of the human baseball player. They say things like, "If I ever catch my daughter hanging around ballplayers . . ." or, "I'll tell you one thing. I'm never going to let my daughter go to a ballgame."

Anyway, this is about something that happened last year here in Cincinnati. Rader and Miller were out strolling one evening and noticed in the window of a cosmetic shop a vibrating device called, as they recall, a "Personal Vibrator." To their twisted, sex-wracked minds it looked, of course, like nothing but a vibrating phallus.

The next morning they were at the store bright and early, only to discover that Blasingame and Lemaster were already there. "I'll take all of them," Blasingame said, leering evilly at the salesgirl and pointing to the vibrators.

"Now, wait a minute," Rader said. "You can't have them all. Norm and I have got to have at least one each."

Out of the kindness of his heart, Blasingame let them each buy one. And he bought the rest.

That night he called a clubhouse meeting. "Pay attention, men," he said, "especially you married men." And he proceeded to make a speech describing graphically the marvelous uses to which these vibrators could be put. "You married men," he said, "this little device will revitalize your sex life at home."

And he sold every single vibrator, purchased at $4.98, for $10. The demand was greater than the supply.

"Say, Norm," I said. "You happen to remember where that cosmetic shop is?"

SEPTEMBER
27

We had the pleasure today of knocking the Reds out of the race. We beat them 4–3 and they were mathematically eliminated. Tough. A newspaper guy here wrote that Houston always knocks off Cincinnati and then rolls over and plays dead for Atlanta. Silly, of course. We try to win all our games. Against some teams trying isn't enough.

Instead of our usual running in the outfield we were running pass patterns, Jim Owens at quarterback, against pass defenders. The idea was to see who could work the most intricate patterns and who could fake who out of whose jock strap. Harry Walker made us stop. "I hate to spoil your fun, boys," he said. "But we better knock it off. Crissakes, if Dierker gets hurt, we're all out of a job."

Harry was probably right. There is a pecking order in the major leagues which goes like this: owner, general manager, super star, manager, established player, coaches, traveling secretary, trainer, clubhouse man, marginal player. That's Harry down there under super-star Dierker. In Seattle that was me down there under the clubhouse man.

I was warming up late in the ballgame when Jim Owens came out and said, "It doesn't look like it's breaking real good."

"No, it isn't," I said.

"Okay," he said. "I'll get Gladding up."

Now this makes sense. I tried to get the idea across in Seattle that there should be some sort of relationship between how a guy looks in the bullpen and how he does on the mound. The conundrum is that often there is *no* relationship. Except that with the knuckleball, if I haven't got it in the bullpen I'm not likely to when I get out on the mound.

I'm reminded of Mike Marshall asking Joe Schultz what to do if he didn't have it in the bullpen and Schultz just walking away.

Bedcheck—with four games left in the season? I suppose that at the end of the season they'll hand out chastity belts for use at home over the winter.

SEPTEMBER
28

Although we'd lost again I was lighthearted as I set off to spend a day with my family in Michigan on the way out to Los Angeles for the final series of the season. No bedcheck tonight.

Sudden thought. Suppose somebody told Johnny Sain to conduct a bedcheck. He'd tell them to take the phone and stick it up their receivers.

SEPTEMBER
30

Los Angeles

When I landed at Los Angeles after flying in from Michigan, I promptly took the limousine for Anaheim. I got out at the Grand Hotel and couldn't figure out why none of the guys were around the lobby. Suddenly there was this little click in my head. The Houston Astros do not play the Los Angeles Angels. They play the Dodgers. So it was into a taxicab to Chavez Ravine, and I barely got there in time for batting practice. The whole thing cost me $17 and some nasty comments from my teammates about the size of my brainpan.

We beat the Dodgers and now have an 81–79 record with two games to go. Can't go below .500, and if we beat them twice we'll tie them for fourth. It could have been worse.

OCTOBER
1

We played bocci with my iron ball in the bullpen during the game, and stickball, and I beat Dierker in a word game, which I consider an accomplishment. The kid has a helluva vocabulary. The most interesting part of the baseball game came when Norm Miller threw his helmet in the dugout and it bounced up and hit Hector Torres in the eye and Harry fined Miller $50 on the spot. Next time up Norm hit a home run.

Johnny Edwards asked me if I planned to bring my family to spring training. I said sure, why?

"If you don't you have to stay in the barracks and they padlock the doors at midnight," he said. "If you don't make it in, you have to pound on the door and that's the way they catch you."

OCTOBER
2

The New York *Post* has asked me to cover the World Series for them if the Mets get into it. They said they couldn't pay me for the articles, but might, just might, be able to pay some, only *some*, of my expenses—like, maybe hotel, but not travel. That's very similar to the arrangement that Tom Sawyer had with his friends on painting the fence. The more they painted, the more it cost them. I guess they figured I'd enjoy it because I'd get to watch some baseball games for free.

I said no, thanks.

The last day of the season and I'm looking forward to being home again. It's convenient to travel with a ballclub. Your suitcases are picked up at the hotel and your equipment at the ballpark and you never see anything again until you get to the next hotel, the next ballpark. On the last day you carry your own suitcase, and you carry your equipment bag and somehow the weight feels good. On the bus out to the airport I thought about my season; 73 outings, and I graded 50 of them either good or excellent, and for the first time since 1964 I felt no gnawing emptiness at the end of a season. Only quiet fulfillment, the cool of the evening.

It's good that the season is over. And let's see, spring training should start about February 22.

WINTER, 1969/70

In the winter I always find myself remembering more good things than bad. And in many ways 1969 was a great season. I began it as a minor-leaguer trying a new style and a new pitch and finished as a genuine gold-plated, guaranteed-not-to-tarnish-major-leaguer again. My 73 appearances for Seattle and Houston were fifth in the majors, and my two wins, three losses and two saves say something—although I'm not sure what.

The pettiness and stupidity were exasperating, sometimes damaging. And it's going to be a long winter before I can enjoy having had my shoes nailed to the clubhouse floor. New levels of noncommunication were reached. Still, there were rewards. There were enough laughs in the bullpen and in the back of the bus to make me eager for a new season. I met a lot of people I'll feel warmly toward for the rest of my life. Observing and recording my experiences for this book taught me a great deal not only about others but about myself. (I'm not sure I liked everything I learned, but learning is often a painful experience.)

I lucked out with five great roommates: Gary Bell, Bob Lasko, Mike Marshall, Steve Hovley and Norm Miller. I went the whole season without an injury. I traveled the country in both leagues. And I saw the look in my son Mike's face when I came back from a road trip and he turned his big eyes up at me and said shyly, "Hey Dad, you're Jim Bouton, aren't you?"

I enjoyed living in the Great Northwest for most of a season and I'm sad that Seattle didn't keep its franchise. A city that seems to care more for its art museums than its ballpark can't be all bad.

The team will play in Milwaukee next season and it will be a new team in every respect. Even before the franchise could be shifted, Marvin Milkes, operating on the theory that when you make a mistake you make a change, made a lot of changes. Joe Schultz was fired and signed on as a coach in Kansas City, moving in considerably below Lou Piniella in the team's pecking order. Piniella, groomed for oblivion in the first weeks of spring training with Seattle, became rookie of the year in Kansas City, hitting .282. Sal Maglie, Ron Plaza, Eddie O'Brien and Frank Crosetti were also fired. As this is written only Crosetti has hooked on—with Minnesota.

Fred Talbot, Diego Segui, Ray Oyler, George Brunet, Don Mincher and Ron Clark were all traded to Oakland for some warm bodies. Dooley Womack was released, Merritt Ranew was sent to the minors and Mike Marshall, sold to Houston, will be back with me this spring. Gary Bell, released by the White Sox, was signed by Hawaii. Hope he can handle *mai tais*.

Houston traded Curt Blefary to the Yankees for Joe Pepitone, and we will have all spring to practice Joe's pick-off sign. Wade Blasingame was sent to the minors. Ted Williams of the MFL was Manager of the Year and the Fat Kid won Most Valuable Player.

I did not win Comeback of the Year, but I went to a local sports banquet the other night and took a bow from the audience. As I watched the trophies being handed out, my mind wandered and I saw myself being called up to the dais and accepting the Fireman of the Year award for 1970.

And then I thought of Jim O'Toole and I felt both strange and sad. When I took the cab to the airport in Cincinnati I got into a conversation with the driver and he said he'd played ball that summer against Jim O'Toole. He said O'Toole was pitching for the Ross Eversoles in the Kentucky Industrial League. He said O'Toole is all washed up. He doesn't have his fastball anymore but his control seems better than when he was with Cincinnati. I had to laugh at that. O'Toole won't be trying to sneak one over the corner on Willie Mays in the Kentucky Industrial League.

Jim O'Toole and I started out even in the spring. He wound up with the Ross Eversoles and I with a new lease on life. And as I day-dreamed of being Fireman of the Year in 1970 I wondered what the dreams of Jim O'Toole are like these days. Then I thought, would I do that? When it's over for me, would I be hanging on with the Ross Eversoles? I went down deep and the answer I came up with was yes.

Yes, I would. You see, you spend a good piece of your life gripping a baseball and in the end it turns out that it was the other way around all the time.

TELL YOUR STATISTICS TO SHUT UP

APPEARANCE	HOME OR AWAY	DATE	TEAM	INNINGS PITCHED	HITS	RUNS	EARNED RUNS	WALKS	STRIKEOUTS	RUNNERS ON	RUNNERS SCORED	DECISION	TOTAL INNINGS	TOTAL HITS	TOTAL EARNED RUNS	TOTAL WALKS	TOTAL STRIKEOUTS	EARNED RUN AVERAGE	EVALUATION
1.	A.	4/9	L.A.	1/3	0	0	0	1	0	1	0		1/3	0	0	1	0		Good
2.	H.	4/13	Chi.	1	3	3	3	1	0	1	0		1 1/3	3	3	2	0		Bad
SENT TO MINOR LEAGUES																			
	A.	4/19	Tacoma	1	0	0	0	0	2			—							Excellent
	A.	4/20	Tacoma	2 1/3	2	1	0	0	0			L							Fair
	A.	4/21	Hawaii	1	0	0	0	0	1			—							Excellent
	A.	4/22	Hawaii	2 1/3	1	0	0	1	1			—							Excellent
	A.	4/23	Hawaii	1	0	0	0	1	1			S							Excellent
	A.	4/24	Hawaii	1	0	0	0	2	0			S							Excellent
	A.	4/25	Hawaii	1 1/3	0	0	0	1	0			S							Excellent
	A.	4/27	Hawaii	1 1/3	1	1	1	2	1			S							Excellent
RECALLED FROM MINORS																			
3.	A.	4/30	Minn.	2	0	0	0	1	1	0	0	—	3 2/3	3	3	2	1		Excellent
4.	A.	5/1	Minn.	2 2/3	5	1	1	2	2	3	0	—	6 1/3	8	4	4	3		Good
5.	A.	5/2	Oak.	3	4	2	2	0	2	0	0	—	9 1/3	12	6	4	5		Bad
6.	A.	5/4	Oak.	1 1/3	1	3	3	3	0	1	0	—	10 2/3	13	9	7	5		Bad
7.	H.	5/6	Bost.	1 1/3	0	0	0	0	1	2	0	—	12	13	9	7	6		Excellent
8.	H.	5/10	Wash.	1	1	1	1	0	1	2	0	—	13	14	9	8	8		Good
9.	H.	5/14	N.Y.	1	1	0	0	0	0	0	0	—	14	15	9	8	8		Excellent
10.	A.	5/16	Bost.	3	0	0	0	1	1	0	0	W	17	15	9	9	9		Excellent
11.	A.	5/22	Wash.	1/3	0	0	0	0	0	2	0	—	17 1/3	15	9	9	9		Excellent
12.	A.	5/23	Cleve.	2 2/3	3	2	1	0	2	3	0	—	20	18	10	9	11		Good
13.	A.	5/25	Cleve.	1/3	0	0	0	1	0	0	0	—	20 1/3	18	10	10	11		Good
14.	H.	5/28	Balt.	1	0	0	0	0	2	0	0	—	21 1/3	18	10	10	13		Excellent
15.	H.	6/1	Det.	1/3	0	0	0	0	0	1	0	—	21 2/3	18	10	10	13		Excellent
16.	H.	6/2	Cleve.	4	2	1	1	1	3	0	0	S	25 2/3	20	11	11	16	3.90	Excellent
17.	H.	6/4	Cleve.	1 1/3	5	4	2	1	1	0	0	—	27	25	13	12	17		Bad
18.	A.	6/6	Balt.	1/3	0	0	0	0	0	1	0	—	27 1/3	25	13	12	17		Good
19.	A-	6/7	Balt.	0	0	0	0	0	1	0	0	—	28 1/3	25	13	12	18		Excellent
20.	A.	6/10	Det.	2/3	2	2	2	3	2	0	0	—	29	27	15	15	20		Bad
21.	A.	6/14	N.Y.	2	0	0	0	0	0	3	1	—	31	27	15	15	20		Excellent
22.	A.	6/15	N.Y.	1/3	0	0	0	0	1	1	0	—	31 1/3	27	15	15	21		Excellent
23.	A.	6/16	Chi.	1 2/3	1	0	0	0	1	3	3	—	33	28	15	15	22	4.13	Bad
24.	A.	6/18	Chi.	1	0	0	0	0	1	0	0	—	34	28	15	15	23		Excellent
25.	A.	6/18	Chi.	1	0	0	0	0	0	0	0	—	35	28	15	15	23	3.89	Excellent
26,	A.	6/19	Chi.	4	3	2	0	2	3	2	2	—	39	31	15	17	26		Fair
27.	H.	6/20	K.C.	3	3	1	1	0	0	0	0	—	42	34	16	17	26		Good
28.	H.	6/23	Chi.	3 1/3	0	0	0	0	1	3	0	—	45 1/3	34	16	17	27		Excellent
29.	H.	6/23	Chi.	1/3	0	0	0	0	0	1	0	—	45 2/3	34	16	17	27	3.18	Excellent
30.	A.	6/27	L.A.	2 2/3	2	0	0	1	2	2	0	—	48 1/3	36	16	18	29		Excellent
31.	A.	6/29	L.A.	1/3	0	0	0	0	0	3	0	—	48 2/3	36	16	18	29		Excellent
32.	A.	7/3	Oak.	1/3	0	0	0	3	0	3	3	—	49	36	16	21	29	2.93	Bad
33.	A.	7/4	K.C.	1 1/3	4	5	5	2	0	2	2	—	50 1/3	40	21	23	29	3.78	Bad

APPEARANCE	HOME OR AWAY	DATE	TEAM	INNINGS PITCHED	HITS	RUNS	EARNED RUNS	WALKS	STRIKEOUTS	RUNNERS ON	RUNNERS SCORED	DECISION	TOTAL INNINGS	TOTAL HITS	TOTAL EARNED RUNS	TOTAL WALKS	TOTAL STRIKEOUTS	EARNED RUN AVERAGE	EVALUATION
34.	A.	7/6	K.C.	2	1	0	0	1	0	0	0	—	52 1/3	41	21	24	29		Excellent
35.	H.	7/9	L.A.	2	2	0	0	0	3	0	0	—	54 1/3	43	21	24	32		Excellent
36.	A.	7/12	Minn.	2 2/3	5	2	2	0	2	3	2	—	57	48	23	24	34		Bad
37.	H.	7/15	Oak.	2	1	1	0	1	3	0	0	—	59	49	23	25	37	3.51	Excellent
38.	H.	7/17	Oak.	2 2/3	2	0	0	0	3	2	0	—	61 2/3	51	23	25	40		Excellent
39.	H.	7/19	Minn.	3 2/3	6	5	5	2	2	0	0	—	65 1/3	57	28	27	42		Bad
40.	H.	7/20	Minn.	2/3	1	1	0	1	0	1	1	—	66	58	28	28	42		Bad
41.	H.	7/25	Bost.	1	0	0	0	1	1	0	0	—	67	58	28	29	43		Excellent
42.	H.	7/26	Bost.	1 1/3	0	0	0	0	0	1	0	W	68 1/3	58	28	29	43		Excellent
43.	H.	7/27	Bost.	2	1	0	0	0	3	0	0	—	70 1/3	59	28	29	46		Excellent
44.	H.	7/29	Wash.	1/3	0	0	0	0	1	2	0	—	70 2/3	59	28	29	47		Excellent
45.	H.	7/31	Wash.	2/3	1	0	0	0	1	2	2	—	71 1/3	60	28	29	48		Bad
46.	H.	8/1	N.Y.	5	5	1	1	1	4	0	0	—	76 1/3	65	29	30	52	3.41	Excellent
47.	H.	8/2	N.Y.	2	1	0	0	2	1	0	0	—	78 1/3	66	29	32	53		Excellent
48.	A.	8/6	Bost.	2/3	0	0	0	0	0	3	0	—	79	66	29	32	53		Excellent
49.	A.	8/8	Wash.	1	0	0	0	1	0	0	0	—	80	66	29	33	52		Excellent
50.	A.	8/9	Wash.	2	1	1	1	0	2	0	0	—	82	67	30	33	55		Good
51.	A.	8/12	Cleve.	2	1	0	0	0	2	0	0	—	85	68	30	33	57		Excellent
52.	H.	8/16	Balt.	2	4	3	3	3	1	0	0	—	86	72	33	36	58	3.45	Bad
53.	H.	8/18	Balt.	1/3	2	2	2	1	1	3	3	—	86 1/3	74	35	37	59		Bad
54.	H.	8/19	Det.	1	0	0	0	0	0	0	0	—	87 1/3	74	35	37	59		Excellent
55.	H.	8/21	Det.	1	1	1	1	0	2	0	0	L	88 1/3	75	36	37	61		Fair
56.	H.	8/22	Cleve.	1	1	1	1	0	2	0	0	—	89 1/3	76	37	37	63		Fair
57.	H.	8/23	Cleve.	2 2/3	2	1	1	0	4	0	0	—	92	78	38	37	67	3.71	Good

TRADED TO HOUSTON ASTROS   *2 Wins, 1 Loss, 1 Save, 40 Good or Excellent, 17 Bad or Fair*

APPEARANCE	HOME OR AWAY	DATE	TEAM	INNINGS PITCHED	HITS	RUNS	EARNED RUNS	WALKS	STRIKEOUTS	RUNNERS ON	RUNNERS SCORED	DECISION	TOTAL INNINGS	TOTAL HITS	TOTAL EARNED RUNS	TOTAL WALKS	TOTAL STRIKEOUTS	EARNED RUN AVERAGE	EVALUATION
58.	A.	8/26	St. L.	1	0	0	0	0	1	0	0	—							Excellent
59.	H.	8/29	Pitt.	10	9	4	2	4	11	0	0	L	11	9	2	4	12		Excellent
60.	H.	9/2	St. L.	1	2	1	1	1	0	3	3	—	12	11	3	5	12		Bad
61.	H.	9/6	S.F.	3	2	0	0	1	1	0	0	—	15	13	3	6	13		Excellent
62.	H.	9/7	S.F.	1 2/3	4	1	1	1	1	0	0	—	16 2/3	17	4	7	14		Fair
63.	A.	9/14	Atl.	1/3	0	0	0	0	1	2	0	—	17	17	4	7	15		Excellent
64.	A.	9/15	S.D.	2	1	0	0	1	2	0	0	—	19	18	4	8	17		Excellent
65.	A.	9/16	S.D.	2	0	0	0	0	2	0	0	—	21	18	4	8	19		Excellent
66.	A.	9/17	S.F.	2	0	0	0	2	0	0	0	S	23	20	4	10	19		Excellent
67.	H.	9/19	Cinn.	2	1	0	0	0	4	0	0	—	25	21	4	10	23	1.44	Excellent
68.	H.	9/21	Cinn.	2	3	1	1	0	3	0	0	—	27	24	5	10	26		Good
69.	H.	9/23	Atl.	0	3	4	4	1	0	0	0	L	27	27	9	11	26		Bad
70.	A.	9/25	Cinn.	1/3	3	1	1	0	1	2	0	—	27 1/3	30	10	11	27		Fair
71.	A.	9/26	Cinn.	1	1	1	1	0	2	0	0	—	28 1/3	31	11	11	29		Fair
72.	A.	9/27	Cinn.	1/3	2	2	2	0	0	0	0	—	28 2/3	32	13	11	29		Bad
73.	A.	10/2	L.A.	2	1	1	1	1	2	0	0	—	30 2/3	33	14	12	31	4.11	Good

2 Losses, 1 Save, 10 Good or Excellent, 6 Bad or Fair

TOTALS FOR SEATTLE & HOUSTON   **122 2/3** **111** **52** **49** **98** **3.81**

2 Wins, 3 Losses, 2 Saves, 50 Good or Excellent, 23 Bad or Fair

408

Ten Years Later . . . . .

BALL FIVE

THE BOYS OF BALL FOUR

A lot has happened in ten years. The Seattle Pilots have become the Milwaukee Brewers and Sicks Stadium is now a parking lot. Only one member of the Pilots, Marty Pattin (Kansas City), is still playing in the major leagues. From the Houston Astros, only Tom Griffin (Giants), Bob Watson (Yankees), and Joe Morgan (free agent) are still active.

The wisdom and foresight of the Seattle Pilot management has been reconfirmed several times. That hot tempered rookie who was sent to the minors because Joe Schultz didn't like him became "sweet" Lou

Piniella. And Mike Marshall, who would "never make it" with his screwball, made it as a Cy Young award winner and one of the game's greatest pitchers.

The lot of all players has improved dramatically under the leadership of Marvin Miller. Since winning their free agency, many players have become millionaires, and they all have agents, more security, and some control over their destinies.

On the personal side, my editor and best friend, Lenny Shecter, passed away. Former teammates Elston Howard and Don Wilson have died. And I'm divorced.

I still keep in touch with some of the guys, like Gary "Ding Dong" Bell. I call him on the phone once in awhile and he sends me letters addressed to "Ass Eyes." One year Gary sent me a note saying that since *Ball Four* nobody in baseball would give him a coaching job. He figures they didn't want a coach who's only advice would be to "smoke 'em inside."

Instead, Gary became a restaurateur near his home in Phoenix, Arizona. Actually he was a short order cook at his own fast food joint called the Chinese Paisan (I'm not kidding). It catered to people who wanted a choice between Italian and Chinese food. I invested a few thousand dollars and the place promptly went bankrupt. Gary said it failed because the customers could never make up their minds. I told him he should have read some of those real estate books.

A few years after he left baseball Gary got divorced from Nan. Theirs had been a true baseball marriage. Once the road trips ended it couldn't withstand all that togetherness. Gary is remarried now and very happy working in a sporting goods store. I wonder if he says "ding dong" everytime he sells someone a protective cup.

I still exchange Christmas cards with Steve Hovley. After the Brewers let him go, old "tennis-ball head" was picked up by Kansas City where he had good years in 1972 and '73. In '74 he was sold to Baltimore, missed six weeks with an injury and was released. Now living in Ojai, California, Hovley says he has no interest in baseball whatsoever. "It wouldn't be a part of my life at all," he explains, "except that people keep bringing it up."

Hovley says he doesn't understand why he was portrayed in *Ball Four* as an intellectual and somehow different from other players. He insists he was just one of the boys. After he left baseball, Hovley chose to work as a janitor at his daughter's grade school and then became a plumber, just like any other former major leaguer who went to Stanford and read Dostoyevsky in the clubhouse.

I speak to Mike Marshall once in awhile. He tells me about his latest battles with the establishment. Marshall is always interesting to watch, whether he's suing the Michigan State Athletic Department (and winning), or filing a grievance against baseball for unfair labor practices. Marshall was the Minnesota Twins player representative before he was released last year with two years remaining on his contract. Why would the Twins release a guy they still had to pay for two more years, who had won or saved 31 games for them as recently as 1978? And why hasn't any other team signed this 39-year-old physical fitness expert who could probably pitch for another five years?

Well, because baseball hasn't changed *that* much. Everybody but the Baseball Commissioner suspects the owners want to keep Marshall, a militant leader, out of the Players Association. His release keeps him off the very important joint study committee working on the question of free agent compensation. Also, Marshall has been heard to say that when Marvin Miller retires, he would like a shot at Marvin's job. If there's anyone the owners fear more than Marvin, it's Mike.

It's interesting that Mike went from a clubhouse weirdo to a clubhouse leader in the time it took to become a great pitcher. There's another thing that hasn't changed about baseball; you're still just as smart as your earned run average.

Another roommate of mine, Norm Miller, is alive and well in Houston, Texas. I had lunch with Norm a few years ago when I came into town during my comeback with the Atlanta Braves in 1978. Norm recalled those hectic days we spent together right after *Ball Four* came out. "Howard Cosell came banging on the door at seven in the morning screaming, 'Let me in, let me in!' You were on the phone doing one of your hundred interviews," he reminded me. "I was buck naked as Cosell shoved his way in the door, grabbed the phone out of your hand and

said into it, 'This interview is terminated!' I couldn't believe this guy."
Norm said it was exciting being my secretary for a couple of weeks.

Today, when he's not pitching batting practice for the Houston
Astros, Norm is an executive with Monterey House restaurants. It's better than being a Jewish pirate or sitting all alone in a laundry bag.

Right after the book came out I heard from a few old teammates.
Tommy Davis sent me a note which started off with, "Hello, Big Mouth."
Tommy said that he was offered four movie contracts. "After reading
your book, everybody thinks I'm some kind of actor."

Jim Pagliaroni dropped me a line saying that he loved the book
and if they ever made a movie out of *Ball Four* he wanted to play himself. Pag said he would be perfect for the part of a "deranged, perverted,
moral degenerate, iconoclastic, loving husband and father."

They never made a movie from *Ball Four* but it did become a TV
situation comedy. It was on the CBS network in the fall of '76 before it
was mercifully cancelled after five weeks. The show was created by me
and a couple of friends: television critic Marvin Kitman and sportswriter Vic Ziegel. We wanted "Ball Four," the TV show, to be like
"M.A.S.H.," only in a locker room. Instead it turned out more like
"Gilligan's Island" in baseball suits. The story was all about a mythical
team called the Washington Americans. We were first in the American
League and last in the hearts of our countrymen, according to the Nielsen
ratings.

The characters for the sitcom were loosely drawn from people in
Ball Four. We had a tightfisted general manager and a pain-in-the-ass
coach. We also had a big strong guy named Rhino who couldn't wear
contact lenses "because if he blinked he'd break them." Rhino was from
a small town in Wisconsin where, "we only talk for awhile, then we start
to hit." To make the show as realistic as possible I suggested we get the
guy who inspired the character, Gene Brabender. After a few calls we
located Bender in Sturgeon Bay, Wisconsin, where he was fishing. I felt
sorry for the fish.

So Bender flew into New York and it was good to see him again. I
assured him it was a small speaking part and all he had to do was look
big. He did a good job, too, but surprisingly, he didn't look right for the
part. It's funny, but on stage in front of the cameras, Bender looked

smaller and somehow vulnerable, not as fearsome as I remembered him in the Seattle Pilot clubhouse.

The part went instead to former Oakland Raider football player Ben Davidson, who turned out to be the best character in the show. Brabender flew back to Wisconsin where he owns a dairy farm. Unfortunately, Bender was in and out of New York so fast we didn't have time to talk about anything. I wanted to kid him about the time he nailed my shoes to the floor.

A few years after the book came out I had lunch with Marvin Milkes, of all people. Not only that, but Marvin invited *me*—and *he* paid! This was when I was a sportscaster and he was the general manager for a hockey team called the New Jersey Golden Blades. Marvin told me he liked the book because it helped open a few doors for him. He said wherever he goes, people ask him if he's the Marvin Milkes in *Ball Four.*

Then, believe it or not, Marvin offered to pay me the $50 for that Gatorade I bought years ago. Of course I didn't accept, but we had a good laugh about it. The last I heard Marvin was working for a soccer team in Los Angeles. I made no connection between Marvin's recent generosity and the fact that the Golden Blades went bankrupt.

What about the rest of my teammates, I wondered. What were they doing now? To find out, I hired a researcher to help me track them down. Locating the Seattle Pilots, in particular, was not an easy task. The team had existed for only one year and, it turns out, nobody wants to claim them. The Milwaukee Brewers disdain their Seattle origins and the people in Seattle only care about the new Mariners. The old Pilots are orphans, a team without a city.

One of the Pilots, John O'Donaghue, was impossible to find. We reached his mother by telephone, and she said he was in another country on business but she didn't know what country or what business. Sounds like old John might be working for the CIA. Like the team he once played for, he just disappeared without leaving a forwarding address.

The Pilots left town but Ray Oyler didn't. Made to feel welcome for the first time in his career by the existence of the Ray Oyler fan club,

Oyler bought a home in Seattle. Today he works in town as a salesman, a local hero without a team.

I got a chuckle out of Steve Barber's new job. He owns a car care center in Las Vegas. He has a bunch of cars all lined up getting cortisone shots, whirlpool massage, and diathermy treatment.

Dooley Womack, for whom I was once traded, is a carpet salesman in Columbia, South Carolina. I got a funny letter about Dooley just the other day. It seems that an all-night disc jockey in Syracuse, New York, asked his listeners recently, "Who or what was, or is, a Dooley Womack?" Some of the more interesting responses were: a guided missile, a computer, a famous sunken ship, a mixed drink, a New Wave rock 'n' roll band, the first Polish astronaut, an old car like the Edsel, a former Miss America, one of Captain Hook's pirates, a comic strip character, a type of dance, a CB term, a gospel singer, or one of Howard Hughes' airplanes. After about 30 minutes somebody called in to say he was a ballplayer. I like to think that *Ball Four* added to Dooley's fame.

THE DEVIANT

The aftermath of the book hasn't all been fun. I got a hint that some players might not like it shortly after it came out. Someone calling himself an ex-teammate sent me a newspaper clipping critical of *Ball Four*. There was a note scrawled across it which said that my writing would, "gag a maggot." I can't be sure, but I think it may have been Fred Talbot. Who else could have come up with the maggot line?

And there have been a few unpleasant encounters, like the one with my main man, Joe Schultz. A year after the book came out I was a sportscaster from New York covering spring training in Florida. Before a game one day I spotted Joe Schultz, then a Detroit Tiger coach, hitting fungos to some infielders. I hadn't spoken to Joe in almost two years. Naturally, I had to go over and say hello.

I half expected him to tell me I was throwing too much out in the bullpen. Instead, he said he didn't want to talk to me, that he hadn't read my book, but he'd heard about it. When I tried to tell Joe that he came off as a good guy, Billy Martin, the Tiger manager at the time, who's a bad guy, came running across the field hollering for me to get the hell out (this was before Martin wrote *his* tell-all book). Because I've grown accustomed to the shape of my nose, I got the hell out. The sad part is that I never had a chance to invite Joe to go out and pound the ol' Budweiser.

Billy Martin probably never read the book, either, but like Joe and many others, he believed the book was somehow a bad thing. The most incredible thing to me about the book has been the overwhelming negative reaction by so many players and coaches. What's more, they're still angry, even though the books that have come after mine make *Ball Four,* as an exposé, read like *The Bobbsey Twins Go To The Seashore.*

Why so much anger? It couldn't have been that I said Mickey Mantle hung out in bars. Last time I flipped on the TV there was Mantle, in a bar, bragging about how much beer he used to drink. He can't even make up his mind which beer he likes best.

It couldn't be that I said Whitey Ford used to scuff up the baseballs to make them do tricks on the way to the plate. In his own book, Whitey recently went into even greater detail about how he used to doctor the balls. Maybe these guys are mad because they wanted the stories for *their* books.

There had to be some explanation for the intensity and longevity of baseball's collective anger toward me. And I think I know now what the answer is; a behavioral scientist explained it to me.

In any human group, family, tribe, (or baseball team), there are norms—shared expectations of behavior. Any member who deviates from these norms calls into question the basic values of the group. And groups don't like to have their basic values questioned. It makes them *nervous.*

A famous rule of major league baseball is posted on every clubhouse wall: "What you say here, what you do here, let it stay here, when you leave here." I broke that rule, which makes me a deviant, sociologically speaking. Studies have shown that in order for rules to exist, deviant members must be punished by the group. This is usually done according to the following criteria: The more primary a group is felt to be by its members, the more violent the punishment will be. (Many players think of baseball as family.) The less status a deviant member has, the less tolerant the group will be toward him. (If Mickey Mantle had written *Ball Four* he would have gotten away with it. A relief pitcher on the Seattle Pilots has no business being a deviant.) In addition, the more authoritarian a group's personality is, the less tolerant it will be toward a deviant. (This explains about the Commissioner and the owners.)

However, I am happy to report that while the deviant shakes everybody up, he performs valuable functions for the group. For one thing, the deviant relieves tensions by acting as an acceptable outlet for group frustrations (very helpful in baseball where only a few can play at the top, and of those, only half do well at the other half's expense). Second, the deviant helps the group unite in times of uncertainty and change. If group members can't agree on important issues (salaries, contracts, free agency, etc.), at least they can be united against the deviant. Third, uniting against the deviant by asserting common ideals gives group members the reassurance of a solid front and strengthens their sense of worthiness (especially important to men making large sums of money playing a game).

Of course, I didn't plan to be baseball's resident deviant but I'm glad to help out. It's the least I can do for a game which has given me so much pleasure. I still serve in that capacity, probably because I'm doing such a good job. Somehow though, I don't think I'll get a plaque from the Commissioner.

THE COMMISSIONER

Bowie Kuhn still hasn't forgiven me for not apologizing when *Ball Four* first came out. I remember he called me into his office, which was decorated in Early Authority—paneled walls with pictures of presidents and a large desk between two American flags. The Commissioner said he was going to do me a big favor. He said he knew that I realized I had made a terrible mistake and all I had to do was simply sign a statement he had prepared. The statement said, in effect, that the book was a bunch of lies and it blamed everything on my editor, Lenny Shecter.

When I politely told the Commissioner what he could do with his statement, he turned a color which went very nicely with the wood paneling. He then spent the next three hours extracting a promise that I would never reveal what went on at our meeting. The sanctity of the clubhouse is exceeded only by the sanctity of the Commissioner's office.

Observers of the Commissioner, over the years, may wonder where he gets his arrogance. I think the problem lies with his title "Commissioner of Baseball." The guy thinks he's the ruler of an entire sport. But since he is hired and paid by the owners and not the players or the fans, he should more accurately be described as the Person in Charge of Protecting the Financial Interests of the Twenty-Six Business Groups Which Make Profits from Baseball.

And speaking of money, you may be wondering what I think about these enormous salaries being paid to players today. Aside from thinking I was born too soon, here's how I feel: a million dollars a year is a lot of money to get paid for hitting a ball with a stick. Based on contribution to society, ballplayers are grossly overpaid. Teachers, policemen, and firemen should get more money. But we live in a society that says a man is worth what someone else is willing to pay him. Is Robert Redford worth three million dollars a picture? Is Barbra Streisand worth five million dollars a song? Evidently somebody thinks so. In baseball, the income is there, the only question is who's going to get it. My position is that while the players don't deserve all that money, the owners don't deserve it even more.

The irony is that if the owners hadn't abused the players so badly, we wouldn't have gone out and hired Marvin Miller and the players wouldn't be free agents today. If the owners had just doubled the minimum salary, say to $14,000, and given us some extra meal money, we would have been more than content to let things ride. Most ballplayers had no idea what kind of money they could be making. I remember sitting in the Yankee clubhouse while the player representative asked each of us what we thought the minimum salary should be. This was when it was $7,000. The players were all saying numbers like $8,000, $9,000, or $10,000. When it came to me I said $25,000 and everybody just laughed.

Now, thanks to Marvin Miller, the laugh is on the owners. Marvin showed the players how to become free agents and the owners are showing the players how much they're worth.

Since they can't use the reserve clause anymore, the owners are looking for the next best way to hold down salaries. (What good is having a monopoly if you can't make enormous profits?) That's what the "compensation" issue is really about. If a team that signs a free agent is required to compensate the team he came from, free agents won't be worth much. That's why there is likely to be a strike over the issue and if there is a strike, public opinion will be important.

Which is where the Baseball Commissioner comes in. Besides censoring books, it's the Commissioner's job to go around telling the fans, the media, the Congress, and anyone who will listen that the owners are losing money and that free agency will destroy "competitive balance" leading to bankruptcy, cancer, jock itch, and the end of the Free World as we know it.

The Commissioner has forgotten his humble beginnings. Twelve years ago, when the owners were looking for a new Commissioner, they met at an airport hotel near Chicago so they could fly in and out in a few hours. But instead of taking a few hours, the meeting lasted all day and half the night because different cliques of owners promoted their own man, each of whom was viewed as a threat by the other owners. After about a thousand cups of coffee, and maybe half as many ballots, they gave up and went home without selecting a Commissioner.

During all this time, sitting there unnoticed, was Bowie Kuhn, the lawyer for the National League—in charge of yellow pads. It wasn't until about ten days later that it dawned on somebody, probably Walter O'Malley, that the next baseball commissioner had been right under their noses all along. Bowie Kuhn, it was heartily agreed at their next meeting, represented no threat to any of them.

And that is how Kuhn came to be elected unanimously after not having been mentioned on any previous ballots. It was as if the Democratic convention couldn't decide between Carter and Kennedy and chose a page instead. Maybe it is the shadow of his past which frightens Kuhn into acting like a dictator. At any rate, I'm sure I would have been forgiven for writing *Ball Four* if I had just signed his statement, stood in the corner for awhile, and kept my mouth shut.

THE SPORTSCASTER

Instead, I went on television. Why not? I was learning I could make a living in the deviant business. A nervous living maybe, but a living. Baseball had cast me in this role and so I might as well play it as well as I could. In truth, I found it rested comfortably upon my shoulders. Not that I was looking to be an oddball, nor that I relished the role, because it sometimes gets lonely. Whenever I go near a locker room, players will say, "here he comes, watch what you say." I feel like I have a dread disease. Sometimes I'm nervous about how people will respond to me. When my Yankee teammate Elston Howard died recently, I wanted to pay my respects at his funeral, but I was afraid to go. I knew he'd been upset by *Ball Four* and I wanted to avoid the possibility of one of the players making a scene.

Just when I'm asking myself if it's worth it to rock the boat and wondering if I should compromise, something will happen to keep me going. Like one year I got an award from a women's group for, "exposing the jockocratic values of society." Then there was the time that John Lennon told me he enjoyed my work, and said I was "the Marjoe of sports." And every once in a while some stranger will come up to me and say he likes what I stand for.

I wouldn't call what I do "telling it like it is" because nobody knows how it is, including Howard Cosell. It's telling it like you see it, and for some reason I seem to see things differently.

Take sportscasting, for example, which is what I did in New York for six years after I left baseball in 1970. One of my ideas about sports is that it's something you play yourself, not just watch others do on television. So I did stories about girls' basketball teams or old men lifting weights in their basement. One year I followed a high school football team that hadn't won a game in five years. I'd cover the hopeful pep rallys on Fridays and the losing games on Saturday. (When the team finally won, they couldn't understand why I stopped following them since they were just getting hot.) The best part was that the coach let me into the locker room for his halftime speeches where he tried to get the players to believe in themselves. Television viewers saw muddy, tired faces of teenage kids trying to believe. This was an inside view of sports that professional teams would never allow. What's more, surveys showed that viewers liked these kinds of stories.

The Jets and Giants, however, did not. They wanted you to comeout and interview right tackle Joe Doaks about his sore left toe and whether or not he'd be ready for the big game on Sunday. Professional teams have come to expect this form of free advertising (two minutes' worth could otherwise cost $10,000), which is even more effective than a commercial because it's presented as news. They get all upset when you don't interview the coach about how great the club looks.

These kinds of stories are very boring but sometimes you have to do them anyway. Once our weekend reporter Sal Marchiano did an interview with Giants' coach Alex Webster who explained why the Giants had won only four and lost nine. Alex gave all the reasons coaches always give: l. injuries, 2. bad breaks, 3. more injuries, 4. all of the above. (Just once I'd like to hear a coach say maybe he's not such a good coach, or the team isn't so hot.)

My producer suggested I use a piece of the interview in my broadcast since I hadn't done much on the Giants lately. I reluctantly agreed. In the process of screening the interview to select the portion I would use, the editor ran the film backwards in order to show it a second time. Suddenly I heard Alex saying, "seirujni rof neeb tndah . . ." That's it, I told the editor! Ten seconds of Alex Webster talking backwards would make a good commentary on coaches explaining a lousy season.

When I played it on the air, however, there was a technical difficulty and no sound came out of Alex's mouth. This did not prevent the Giants from becoming irate. How they even knew I played the film backwards, since there was no sound, I'm not sure, but I have my suspicions. I relate this story to show the lengths to which professional sports will go to intimidate a reporter who fails to show the proper reverence. The Giants used this ten seconds of silence as an excuse to sue me and WABC–TV for a million-and-a-half dollars. Of course the case was eventually thrown out of court, but not before my employers were forced to conduct an inquiry, give depositions, and pay for expensive lawyers. You can be sure it became part of my file.

In television the greatest pressures come from within. Station executives don't like it when their sports guy isn't chummy with the local teams. It makes the news director uncomfortable when he calls up and asks for tickets to a ballgame. When I worked at WCBS in New York in 1979, Yankee tickets were used as currency in the newsroom for favors. In the sports reporting business, more phone calls are made to team press offices to arrange tickets than to arrange stories.

A reporter who makes waves creates problems for the station's general manager, too. It puts him in a bad bargaining position if he wants to televise a team's games. It's no fun trying to hammer out a contract with disgruntled team officials.

Then there is the thunder from above. At the network they already have contracts to televise games; multi-million dollar contracts with entire leagues which make the networks, in effect, partners with professional sports. There are big bucks riding on these games and they need to be hyped, not ignored, and certainly not criticized. This could explain why my comment that, instead of watching three hours of super bowl hype, viewers should play touch football in their backyards, was not wildly hailed in the newsroom.

With network sports, of course, there are no real reporters. Although there are a few who pretend to be, like Howard Cosell. Howard will criticize the relevance of a particular boxing match, for example, while at the same time he will lead the pre-fight hype, announce the fight, and do the post fight analysis. Cosell is always lecturing about the absurd overemphasis on sports in our society and yet nobody gets more excited about week-old football highlights than Cosell.

Many years ago, when he was outside the establishment, Cosell used to question everything. But now that he is personal friends with people like football Commissioner Pete Rozelle, he is reduced to criticizing coaches for poor strategy and athletes for not hustling.

Cosell does deserve credit for a past willingness to take unpopular positions, like the time he stood up for Muhammad Ali during Ali's persecution for draft evasion. Unfortunately, Howard has become so unpopular himself that today his occasional criticisms of the establishment produce the opposite effect. Viewers figure that if Howard dislikes something, it can't be all bad. So that a knock from Howard becomes a boost in the same way that if Idi Amin knocked Ayatollah Khomeini, we'd have to give Khomeini another look. This may, in fact, be the secret of Cosell's longevity on the air. He serves a real purpose for the establishment—as an unwitting agent provocateur.

Of course, most announcers don't even try to be reporters. Their idea of objectivity is to avoid rooting openly for a particular team. That announcers are approved by the various league Commissioners is a fact which the FCC now requires the stations to mention. This is not a knock on announcers. They are hired as salesmen and some of them do a very good job. It's just that with everyone involved in sales, who's doing the reporting?

On television today, what announcer is going to suggest that the college draft and the four-year rule are probably unconstitutional? Or that the rule forbidding college athletes to have agents is unfair? Or that tax write-offs for professional teams make no sense? Or that scholarships should go to underprivileged scholars and not athletes? Or that sports commissioners don't truly represent a sport since two thirds of the interested parties (players and fans) have no say in their selection? In short, who is questioning the basic values of college and professional sports? Not anybody you're likely to see on network television.

Nor on any other kind of program. Frank Deford, a marvelous writer at *Sports Illustrated,* was recently commissioned by ABC television to do a movie script. It was about a college football coach who gave pep talks with his fists, a la Woody Hayes. The head of programming loved it and pushed it upstairs to Roone Arledge. Since the script conflicted with ABC's college football contract, Roone Arledge pushed it out the window. So much for editorial balance.

As if it weren't enough that television has become partners with sports, they are now inventing sports—the propriety of which may be as questionable as the events themselves. Take Evel Knievel's leap across the Snake River, which was hyped to a fare-thee-well. "Would this motorcycle daredevil make it alive across the Snake River in a rocketship?" the nation's viewers were continuously asked. My opinion was yes, on the grounds that if we could get a man to the moon and back we could probably get him across the Snake River.

The key to an event like this is the hype, without which there would be no event. Even ABC's distinguished science editor, Jules Bergman, was brought in for an analysis of Knievel's chances. When an event must be sold, everybody's gotta get into the act.

In 1973, Wide World of Sports bought the rights to televise a "Battle of the Sexes" tennis match between Billy Jean King and Bobby Riggs. Then they began hyping the event as only a network can do. Part of that hype, they figured, should come from me as the local sportscaster for "Eyewitness News," ABC's flagship station in New York.

Except that I saw myself as a reporter for an autonomous (albeit affiliated) station, not as a salesman for the network. My producer and news director agreed with me. So when the network sent me a very dull three minute interview between King and Riggs the Friday before the match, I didn't use it. Instead, during my three minutes, I gave the match a 30 second plug, which was more than it deserved. Before you could say "network apoplexy," our producer received a nasty telephone call. In the control room. While the news was still on the air. It was Roone Arledge calling from home, screaming into the phone that "Eyewitness News" will never get any cooperation from *Wide World of Sports* as long as Jim Bouton is doing the news." A short while later, my contract was not renewed. It came as no surprise to this reporter.

I don't want you to think that I didn't enjoy being a sportscaster. On the contrary, when I wasn't being fired, I was having a wonderful time. I was an original member of the "Eyewitness News" team (WABC, channel 7 in New York), the first of the Happy Talk news programs, a concept which swept the country in the 1970s. It was developed by a very bright guy named Al Primo, who was a news director before he left to set up his own television consulting business. The idea was that viewers liked our news team because we liked each other. And we did, mostly.

We got to be great friends not by covering the news, but by making commercials showing us having fun together. All hell could be breaking loose in New York City and seven of our station's crack reporters would be across town somewhere in a studio decorated to look like a Puerto Rican wedding hall or a birthday party. The fun came during the breaks between scenes when they brought in the catered lunch and the booze. Sometimes if we didn't get our lines right we'd get back to the station just in time to go on the air, slightly looped.

Occasionally it would affect the news. One afternoon we all came back feeling pretty good and our weatherman, Tex Antoine (the most popular member of our team), had to lean on his weathermap for support. Problem was, he accidently rubbed off a low pressure area with his elbow and when he went to point it out, the mark was gone.

Mostly, we did a lot of good work. Our anchormen, Roger Grimsby and Bill Beutel, were, and still are, excellent newsmen. Geraldo Rivera exposed the mistreatment of our mentally retarded in a way that brought real changes in their lives. (Give Arledge credit for making Rivera a national reporter on ABC's 20/20.) And Melba Tolliver has won numerous awards over the years for her journalism.

The only member of the team nobody liked was our 6 o'clock sports guy, a fellow named Howard Cosell. "Monday Night Football" was just getting started and Howard was annoyed at having to be on the same news with mere local personalities, whom he would attack on the air. This was a mistake in the case of Roger Grimsby who was a lot sharper and even more devastating than Cosell, in his own way. I remember one night, at the end of his report, Howard went into a sarcastic putdown of Grimsby that lasted for what seemed like two minutes. Finally, when Howard was finished, the camera switched to Grimsby who was sitting there with his eyes closed, snoring.

At WABC I learned to cover stories from different perspectives. My favorite was the one on the Yankee tryout camp. Each summer the Yankees would hold open tryouts for anybody who thought they could play for the Yankees someday. Butchers, bakers, lawyers, and garage mechanics would show up wearing the strangest assortment of uniforms you ever saw. Out of about sixty players only one or two actually had a chance but everybody got a look.

I thought it would be fun to show what a tryout camp was like from the point of view of the player. So I put on a disguise and a wireless microphone and went as Andy Lawson, twenty-one-year-old righthanded pheenom. I was able to direct my camera crew by whispering to them through the microphone hidden under my shirt.

When it came time to pitch I almost forgot who I really was. The scouts were getting excited by the fact that I had excellent control over six pitches including a knuckleball. My undoing came when they called me over for another look. "You've got surprisingly good stuff for a young kid, Lawson," they said. "What year were you born?" I knew I was supposed to be twenty-one but I hadn't memorized the year of my birth. Not being able to subtract quickly under pressure I blurted out the first date that came to my mind and seemed reasonable. 1961. This indicated I was twelve years old.

After WABC let me go I worked for WCBS from 1973 to 1975 and again briefly in 1979. There I had the privilege of working with top newsmen like Jim Jensen, Rolland Smith, and Dave Marash, who's now with Geraldo over on ABC's 20/20.

I also had a lot of respect for our intrepid consumer reporter John Stossel who exposed rip-offs in the marketplace. I particularly remember one of John's rip-off stories that never got on the air. John was doing an exposé on the fast food industry and one Sunday he bought a pizza for $400. The reason it cost $400 was not because of restaurant business practices but because of television labor practices. John needed a pizza for a prop but because of union rules he couldn't get it himself. A set decorator had to get it. Then a prop man had to hold it. Then a stagehand had to give it to him. By the time they figured out the overtime and holiday pay, it came to something like $400. Of course, if John had tried to expose the cost of the television pizza he might have had to finish his story in a suddenly darkened newsroom.

In my six years as a sportscaster I discovered a few things about television news. I learned that the integrity of the programs comes basically from the reporters. They have to battle constantly to cover stories of substance, against management's impulse to go for sensation and high ratings. I remember when Stossel was offered a job by a competing station, he asked how much his researchers would be paid. "Researchers?" asked the station manager. "What do you need them for?"

In television, the news tends to be whatever happens that's visual in the vicinity of the station when a camera crew is available. If a senator or a congressman dies, it might rate 30 seconds on the news. But if a camera crew happens to catch some anonymous person jumping off the World Trade Center, you'll see all 110 floors plus the splat for at least two minutes worth.

Controversy is also a big seller, although when it involves a local team it can put the station management in a bind. How can you have controversy yet maintain good relations with the teams? Usually, they try to do both.

Take the Thurman Munson incident a few years ago. I was covering spring training for WCBS in New York and an interview with the Yankee captain seemed logical. When Munson brushed me off, I couldn't tell if it was me, my book (which was then eight years old), or the fact that he didn't like reporters. Players and teams will often resort to this form of censorship: "You will say or write what we like or we won't cooperate with you." (One year the Yankees barred me from spring training so I did an interview with my old roommate Fritz Peterson through a wire fence.)

On the grounds that a professional athlete has some obligation to cooperate with reporters who speak for the fans who pay the salaries, I thought Munson should have to explain himself. When I approached him a second time with the cameras rolling, Munson grabbed the microphone and suggested I perform a physical impossibility. If Munson's response had been out of character I would not have allowed it to go on the air. In fact, it was rare television: A ballplayer had been caught in the act of being himself.

The station's response to all this was very interesting. The first thing they did was privately apologize to Munson and the Yankees. The second thing they did was to send the piece out on the network feed. This confirms Newton's (or somebody's) Law that every action has an equal and opposite reaction.

Several months later, however, the station had no ambivalence about how to handle Munson's untimely death. They embraced it with a fervor reserved for heads of state. In fact there seemed to be a contest among the media to see who could out-eulogize the other. The New York *Post* won the newspaper competition (single day) by promoting Munson death stories on pages 1, 4, 5, 21, 66, 67, 70, 71, and 72.

When I heard of Munson's death, I got a sick feeling in my stomach. Besides the fact that no one likes to hear of someone's death, I was particularly uncomfortable because our only meeting had been unpleasant and I wished it had been otherwise. I said this on the air and talked about what a great hustling ballplayer Munson had been. Although I said nothing negative, I couldn't bring myself to say things about Thurman Munson the man that I didn't believe were true.

Because I didn't weep openly for Munson as some of my colleagues in the media were doing, I was considered disrespectful by the WCBS management. I told the news director that, aside from my differences with Munson, I objected to indiscriminate hero-making. To which he replied, "So what's wrong with doing that." All I could think of to say at the time was that it was dishonest.

But beyond that there is an even greater danger in the deification of athletes who are ordinary men aside from their ability to star on a ballfield. And it is this: It diminishes that which is truly valuable. Contrast the media's handling of the Munson death with the way they cover the death of someone like Margaret Mead, say, or a Nobel Prize winner and you get an idea of how the media tells us what's important.

That spring and summer of '79 I wasn't happy with WCBS and they weren't happy with me. I was in the middle of the aftershock of the breakup of my marriage and the pain of dealing with the kids. My disorientation showed on the air. The light touch I used to have was missing too much of the time. Things I used to laugh about in the past now frustrated me, like when I'd be doing the ballscores and they'd flash up a picture of Golda Meir.

And they tried to save money on the damnedest things. There weren't enough tape machines to edit all the news stories and the promos, so they'd sacrifice the news. Then there was the great typewriter shortage. Every day there would be eight to ten broken typewriters lined up waiting to be fixed, and everybody had to scramble for the few that worked. Producer John Reilly said they should have a fulltime repairman sleeping on a cot in the newsroom. They probably didn't want to spend for the cot.

I prefer to remember the old days at WCBS when General Manager Tom Leahy and News Director Ed Joyce ran a really professional operation that also happened to get the highest ratings. Sad to say, Leahy and Joyce are no longer there, having been replaced by two guys from out of town, which seems to be the latest trend in New York television. Stations are hiring anybody who's not a New Yorker. Even the reporters, who ought to know the city, are being imported from places like Texas and Ohio. An assignment editor will tell a reporter to hurry out and cover a fire in the Bronx and two minutes later the reporter will come running back into the newsroom screaming, "Where's the Bronx?"

Maybe out-of-town news directors figure they'll get less lip from reporters who don't know enough to argue about which stories they should cover. Or the news could be getting like baseball, where players on another team's roster always look better than your own.

I remember when stations used to groom their own talent. Before they became television reporters, Geraldo Rivera was a lawyer for the Young Lords and Melba Tolliver was a nurse. They would be the first to admit that, beyond a halfway decent face and an inquiring mind, television doesn't require much skill. Before my first night on the air I was told by the News Director to come in a day early to get some practice. But when I showed up, a story was breaking and instead of practicing I had to go cover it. I protested that I didn't even know how to hold a microphone. "Don't worry about a thing," they told me. "Just make sure the station logo is facing the camera."

Being on television led to some wonderful opportunities. Possibly because of my expertise at handling microphones, I was elected as a delegate to the Democratic Convention in 1972 in Miami. I was vice-chairman of the New Jersey delegation which meant that I was in charge of going out for cheeseburgers during the floor debates. You may have seen me on television at four o'clock in the morning announcing that the great and sovereign state of New Jersey, boycotter of non-union lettuce, was casting its votes for George McGovern.

And I got to meet a lot of interesting people. Like Elliott Gould. He called me one time at three o'clock in the morning to tell me I was going to be in a movie with him called *The Long Goodbye,* directed by Robert Altman and I should catch the next plane to California. As a method of being discovered it sure beats sitting at a drug store soda fountain in a tight-fitting sweater.

My audition consisted of shaking hands with Altman at the airport. He took one look at me and said I would be perfect for the part of a playboy killer. I didn't know whether to take that as a compliment or not. Altman must be a great judge of talent because Vincent Canby of *The New York Times* said I was "excellent." The entire movie got good reviews. Elliott Gould is such a good actor that in the middle of our first scene together he was being so natural I asked if the cameras were rolling. The answer was yes.

It's true what they say about Altman being easy to work with. He told me not to worry about the script, I could say anything that came to mind, as long as I said the few lines that were necessary to carry the story along. Still, out of fear, I had memorized the script. I think Elliott knew this and decided to have some fun with me. Just before they rolled the cameras for my first scene he came over and asked, very seriously, "Did you get the script changes?"

THE SITCOM

And then there was that sitcom adventure I mentioned earlier, with my co-creators Marvin Kitman and Vic Ziegel. I spent a year-and-a-half working on that project and my sides still hurt from laughing so much. Not at the scripts, of course, but at the whole process of making a prime time network television show.

In the spring of 1975 Marvin and Vic and I submitted an idea to the CBS network for a half hour situation comedy based on *Ball Four*. We had written an 89-page proposal (called a "treatment") which described the show, sketched a few characters, and outlined possible episodes. First we listed a few disadvantages to our idea: It contained no lawyers, doctors, policewomen, or animals. Then we listed all the advantages: A locker room is a freewheeling place where anything goes, offering more flexibility than a living room or a class room. It's like an army barracks where people expect put-down humor, ethnic jokes, gross sarcasm, and insults. The partial nudity and male cheesecake potential should attract a large female audience. Players from every ethnic group, economic level, and educational background are thrown together naturally in an occupation which causes constant tension. And, the best part of all, if an actor demands a bigger contract, he can simply be traded.

We figured CBS would buy our idea and when the show became a big hit we'd get royalty checks for the rest of our lives. Instead, the CBS programming executives told us they would buy our idea only if we wrote the pilot script. We protested that we'd never written a script before, we were just creators. We wanted them to go out and hire professionals who really knew how to write scripts. They told us we could probably write a script as well as most people in television. Unfortunately, they were right.

Because we were new at script writing, they explained the rules. Every story has to have a beginning, a middle, and an end, they said. "And a tag," said Marvin, the television critic. There has to be a problem which gets stated in the first 30 seconds (so the viewer gets absorbed before he switches the channel). Then the hero (there has to be a hero) solves the problem after a climax which must have a happy ending (because viewers don't like sad endings). "All day long they lose," said a network vice-president, "and when they watch television they want to win."

Scriptwriting is not easy. The story line, the character development, and the jokes all have to come out of somebody's mouth. In spite of our inexperience the three of us wrote a "wonderful" script. "We love it," the network executives said, "it just needs a little rewrite." It turned out they "loved" our script so much we only had to change 98 percent of it.

In televisionland no script is ever good enough the first time. Or the second, third, or fourth time. The script always needs "a little rewrite." This process continues until you run out of time. I remember that even the night they shot the pilot they wanted us to change one more line. We said that since it was the only line that remained from the original script, we wanted to leave it in for sentimental reasons.

It's hard to get upset by this process, because the programming executives are always so nice about it. You're on their team and they're rooting very hard for you. And they do the same thing to every writer. Television executives would want to rewrite *Gone With The Wind*. If they had *The Old Man and The Sea,* they'd say to the author, "Ernie, we love it. But the part about the fish is boring. And the man is too old. He should have a girlfriend."

The writing is crucial since "if it ain't on the page, it ain't on the stage," as they say. The problem with the writing is that there are half a dozen executives supervising the project and a line that one executive likes, another one won't. They always pop their heads in from time to time to see how you're coming. It's like writing by committee, and the committee is out to lunch.

Writing sessions consist of a bunch of fairly funny men sitting around bouncing lines off one another—very few of which may actually be usable in the script. The funniest guy in our group was sportswriter Vic Ziegel. Unfortunately, all his hilarious lines had to do with things like the wallpaper or ordering lunch.

The rewrite sessions last all day and late into the night. The later it gets, the funnier the lines are. By two o'clock in the morning you laugh at anything just to get out of there. And the writing is always done in a room without windows. That's so you don't catch a glimpse of a tree or a bird, or something that might remind you there are other things in life. In California, we were told, they write scripts in a swimming pool. They hold your head under water until you think of a funny line.

We were lucky to have a great producer like Don Segall. He's a chubby little bald guy with a moustache and a goatee, who went around like Joe Schultz saying funny things to keep people loose. Don's favorite expression was "in the toilet," as in, "if you guys don't hurry up and write something funny, this show is going in the toilet."

We had some very productive writing sessions. Here is one that actually took place. Don walks in and says, "OK, if you guys don't behave yourselves today I have three writers waiting outside in the trunk of my car." A network vice-president stops by to say there is a need for a put-down line we can use all the time like the one on "Welcome Back Kotter": "up your nose with a rubber hose."

"Well, we can't have 'up your nose with a bat'," says Don Segall. Vic remembers that during rehearsals that day, one of the actors had forgotten a line and substituted the word "doodah" and everybody on the set had laughed.

"Since nobody knows what 'doodah' means," Marvin said, "how about 'up your doodah with a bat.' If Standards and Practices (the CBS censor) objects, we'll tell them doodah is a baseball term meaning nose."

"We can't use that," Don said. "Standards and Practices will think it means ass."

Vic: "We can have another line in the script where somebody says, 'this guy sure has a doodah for news.'"

Don: "They're still going to think it means ass."

Me: "We can have somebody wearing glasses and a fake doodah."

Marvin: "Keep your doodah to the grindstone."

Don: "Marvin, keep your doodah out of other people's business. That's enough! It can't go in the script."

Vic: "How about that old favorite, 'Camptown races five miles long, nose, nose! . . .'"

Don: "I can see it now. Dr. Jones: eye, ear, doodah, and throat. Listen to me. I'm laughing and I'm going in the toilet."

Which is where the show eventually wound up in spite of all that brilliance. Our main problem with the show was a difficulty in conveying reality. The CBS censor wouldn't let anybody spit, burp, swear, or chew tobacco. Any similarity between the characters in the show and real ballplayers was purely coincidental. Even our real ballplayer didn't seem like a real ballplayer. I had tried out for the lead character even though I didn't expect to get the part and was half hoping I wouldn't. As I told Don Segall, I didn't want to be part of a show that would have me as an actor.

I discovered that television acting is a lot different from movie acting. In the movies, you get to do a scene over and over again until you get it right. And you can talk in a normal tone of voice and the camera comes in and makes you larger than life. In television you only get to do it twice, on tape. And you do it in front of a live audience so you have to project your voice and have lots of energy. I'm normally a low key guy and suddenly I'm on stage with a bunch of actors who all sound like they're on some kind of uppers. In spite of that I didn't do a bad job. My performance is often compared to Paul Newman. A wooden statue of Paul Newman.

The show was cancelled in November of '76, after five episodes, and we never did make a lot of money. In fact, when the three of us figured out how much time we spent writing and rewriting scripts, the money came to $1.48 an hour, each. Still, we were in exclusive company for awhile. Every year a network gets about 2,000 ideas for sitcoms, from which they commission about 150 scripts and from that they make about 30 pilots of which only three or four ever get on the air. That means we beat 500 to 1 odds. We just couldn't make it happen on the stage.

After our sitcom experience, the three creators were so dizzy that Vic went into seclusion, Marvin went into shock, and I went back into baseball.

THE PROBLEM

I first noticed it about six years ago although it may have existed before that and I just refused to admit it to myself. Something was wrong with my marriage. Things were not the same anymore between Bobbie and me. It was hard to put my finger on it then. I only knew that daily living had become extraordinarily difficult. I was so unhappy that I talked out loud about leaving someday but actually doing it seemed unthinkable. In spite of outward appearances I was very old fashioned. I came from a background in which divorce was something that only happened to other people.

This was all complicated by the inner struggle I was having with myself. Somehow my past successes hadn't made me feel secure. There were all these thoughts racing through my mind, fragments of this and that. It was like listening to twelve radio stations at the same time. And I had trouble breathing. Sometimes I'd get this tightness in my chest and it felt as if I was buried ten feet underground breathing through a straw, terrified that someone would kick dirt into it. Even the memory of it frightens me. I felt I needed to get away from the noise in my head and find someplace I could breathe. The illusion was always that it would come with the next achievement, the next success. If I could just find that ultimate accomplishment I'd be safe.

THE COMEBACK

I began throwing a ball against the garage. I had always joked about making a baseball comeback. What if I actually tried it? I could be back on the road and have time to figure things out. I was convinced I needed a challenge in my life and it would be a blast if I could make it all the way. Maybe I could recapture that happier, simpler time in our lives that I wrote about in *Ball Four*.

Our friends all laughed, of course. I was 37 years old, there were good job offers in television, I hadn't played professionally for seven years and baseball didn't want me. The whole thing just didn't make sense. That's probably why it felt right to me.

I wasn't completely out of shape because I had been playing in a beer league over the summers. At various times I'd been the ace pitcher for the Ridgewood-Paramus Barons, the Teaneck Blues, the Englewood Rangers, and the Clifton Tigers. I was like Jim O'Toole, hanging on with the Ross Eversoles in the Kentucky Industrial League. I threw a mediocre fastball which I had no trouble getting over the plate. I just had trouble keeping it in New Jersey. To make it in the pros I'd have to resurrect my old knuckleball. Maybe "Superknuck" would make a reappearance.

My comeback did not get off to a rousing start. In the spring of '77, White Sox owner Bill Veeck gave me a shot with his AA farm team in Knoxville, Tennessee. I was released after six weeks but I didn't take it personally. My pitching record was 0 and 5. Then after a couple dozen phone calls I ended up pitching in Durango, Mexico. Only a foreign country would have me. I brought the family with me as I had always done years ago. Partly because I needed to be with Michael, David, and Laurie (between road trips), and partly because sometimes people pull closer to ignore the truth.

After five weeks of 26 hour bus rides, galloping "tourista," and a 2 and 5 record, I was released by Durango. At that point, any sane man would have quit. Naturally, I packed my spikes and headed for Portland, Oregon, home of the independent Portland Mavericks in the Class A Northwest League. They would give anybody a chance.

The Mavericks were the dirty dozen of baseball, a collection of players nobody else wanted, owned by actor Bing Russell. The team motto could have been "Give me your tired, your poor, your wretched pitchers yearning to breathe free." In a league stocked with high-priced bonus babies, Maverick players made only $300 per month and had to double as the ground crew. Revenge being a strong motivator, the Mavs had the best team in the league.

The soul of the Mavericks was an old red school bus which was used for transportation. In addition to a seatless interior with mattresses on the floor, it featured a loudspeaker on the roof from which important announcements could be made via a microphone inside the bus. The Mavs had a unique way of attracting crowds to the ballparks. The afternoon before a game, we'd drive through the streets of whatever town we were playing in and insult the citizens over the loudspeaker. "You there, in the blue shirt," one of the players would broadcast while the bus stopped at a light. "Pull in that gut, it looks disgusting." No insult was too outrageous. "Hey, Lady, that sure is an ugly baby you got there." And so on. Needless to say, that night the stands would be filled with hundreds of irate fans rooting passionately for our defeat.

And the Mav manners weren't any better at the ballpark. Whenever the opposing pitcher got knocked out of the game (which was often), the Mavericks, resplendent in red uniforms with black trim, would stand in front of the dugout and serenade the departing player. It was always the same tune, a loud chorus of Gene Autry's closing theme, sung with a smirk. "Happy trailllls to youuuu, until we meet againnn. Happy trailllls to youuuu, keep smiling until thennn."

One night an umpire came over to our dugout (umpires were always coming over to our dugout) and said we should knock it off because we had too much class for that. To which one of our players responded, "Oh yeah! Who says?" I'm embarrassed to say I enjoyed every tasteless minute of it. It was just the sort of slapstick humor I needed to cover the pain.

On the surface it seemed like a good summer for the family. We saw the Smokey Mountains in Tennessee, the Sierra Madre Mountains in Mexico, and Mount Hood in Oregon. We traveled any distance necessary to avoid seeing the problems nearby. Looking back, I realize that it had always been our pattern. We would go places and we would talk, but we never went places *together* and we never talked about *us*. As good as I was at observing others, I had always been blind to myself.

Bobbie and I had gotten married after I became a ballplayer. Our life had been built around separations and homecomings. Yet it's hard to believe ours was a baseball marriage, like Gary Bell's. We had always liked baseball and we enjoyed traveling. If we couldn't be happy during a baseball season, we couldn't be happy together.

That summer I realized we couldn't be happy together. But could I live alone and still be close to the kids? I still didn't know what I wanted, only what I didn't want.

It was the worst of winters. Bobbie and I grew further apart and our life together became unbearable. After my 6 and 13 season there were no teams willing to give me a chance. Still, I worked out three nights a week in a gymnasium until two o'clock in the morning. Some nights I stayed out later than that.

And it was the best of winters. I got to meet Ted Turner when he came to New York to accept the Yachtsman of the Year award for winning the America's Cup. Ted said, "Sure, what the hell, why not?" He'd give me a chance to make one of his minor league teams. So what if I was 39 years old. He was 39 and *he* wasn't washed up. Ted said he believed in the American way, that everyone should get his chance, and let the best man win.

THE MAGIC LADY

And I met somebody else. It was at Bloomingdale's department store in Hackensack, New Jersey, at an evening fund raiser for a local hospital. I spotted her across a crowded room. She was very beautiful. Our eyes first met in the furniture department and we smiled. We saw each other in notions and we stared. We crossed paths again near the luggage and we smiled and stared. When we saw each other back in furniture we stared and smiled and laughed. Then to my astonishment she walked over and said, "I think we're destined to meet."

I told her I was Jim Bouton. She said, "What's a Jim Bouton?" I said I was a former baseball player with the Yankees. She said she knew nothing about baseball. Her name was Dr. Paula Kurman and she was a behavioral scientist. I said, "What's a behavioral scientist?" She replied that she was a college professor and she also helped people with relationship problems. I told her I had a few relationship problems that needed help and asked for her telephone number. She handed me her business card.

This was October. The next day I called and got a recording. Since I didn't want to talk to a machine I hung up. For the next three months everytime I called I got the machine. After awhile, I wasn't even sure why I was still calling, except that there was something about this woman. And things were falling apart at home.

Finally, in January I left a message, she called back, and we had lunch. She was just as lovely as I had remembered her. This was a college professor? I had this silly nervous grin on my face and her hand trembled when she drank her sherry. The next time we had a longer lunch. I told her my story and she told me hers. "My God," she said, "I think we're going to be catalysts for each other." I didn't know what the hell she meant but I liked watching her say it. In two weeks I would be leaving to play baseball. I gave her the address of the Braves minor league camp in Florida.

Ah, spring training. I needed to run in the sunshine and clear my head. The pitching mound was my isolation booth and the locker room was my sanctuary. And I could use some laughs. These are not hard to find around baseball players. Especially if they're 19 years old and you're 39. In my first exhibition game I was winding up for my first pitch when my shortstop hollered, "C'mon, Mr. Bouton!" I had to call time out to laugh. Actually, the players were very kind to me. They called me Dad. Or Oldtimer.

After the workouts we'd go out and have a few beers together. I felt a little out of it whenever they'd be trying to pick up 19-year-old girls. Then one day somebody walked in and the players all started screaming, "Hey Jim, here comes one for you." It was a little old lady with blue hair.

In the beginning I was a real curiosity. The players would sneak glances at me and whisper a lot. But they seemed to respect me. Maybe that's because I was old enough to be their father. They knew I was the guy who wrote *Ball Four,* but they didn't dislike me for it. In fact, they liked me *because* I wrote it. A few players said it sounded like so much fun, they were inspired to play harder so they would be sure to make it. They told me if I was writing another book I should be sure to spell their names right.

It was an incredible spring. I was in terrific shape, worked harder than anybody in camp, pitched 13 scoreless innings—and was *released!* I had suspected things might be difficult back on the first day when farm director Henry Aaron told the press I was there only because the owner invited me. Henry hasn't been a fan of mine since we were on the Dick Cavett show together and he attacked my book and then admitted he hadn't read it.

Strangely, after I was cut, I didn't panic or get angry as I might have in the past. Instead, I felt calm and somehow in control. What's hard to believe is that I was feeling this way because of what I was getting in the mail. Every other day I'd receive a letter from Paula which contained, among other things, some fables and poems she would make up. Her letters were not only warm, but very educational. The stories were simple but their effect on me was profound. And she seemed to sense exactly what I needed to know.

One of her fables was about a group of people watching three men challenged by the ocean waves. The first man angrily tried to stop the waves with his fists, flailing about until he drowned. The second man stubbornly built elaborate barricades which the water eventually demolished. The third man sat and thought for a while. Then he carved a wooden board which he took into the ocean and used to ride the waves, dipping and swaying, using the force of the water to his advantage. The people thought this was remarkably clever and elected him their king.

And this was *before* I got released. When Aaron gave me the bad news I didn't argue or complain. I told him very nicely that I respected his judgment but if he didn't mind I was flying to Atlanta that afternoon to speak with Ted Turner. After a friendly chat, in which I compared the baseball establishment to the yachting establishment, Ted smiled and said he would find a place for me.

Let me say a word here about Ted Turner, the maverick baseball owner who gives other mavericks a chance. In person, this guy is hard to believe. For one thing he doesn't act like a millionaire yachtsman who owns two sports teams and the world's first 24-hour cable news television network. He's a regular guy who you're likely to catch walking down the hall wearing jeans and a work shirt and a railroad engineer's hat.

And Ted will talk to anybody. At the ballpark, instead of sitting in some sky box like the other owners, Ted sits down by the dugout and shoots the bull with the fans. In this high pitched voice that sounds like Rhett Butler with a head cold, he'll talk about any subject from military preparedness (he's for it) to the high cost of third basemen (he's against it). But he listens to people and he remembers their names. If a fan or an usher comes by with a good idea Ted will write it down and promise to do something about it. And he will.

The only other baseball man who comes close to Turner in imagination and spirit is former White Sox owner Bill Veeck, the original maverick who sat with the fans in the bleachers. And their rustic personal styles are also similar. When Veeck told me I had earned a shot at his Knoxville farm team he was sitting on the grass in spring training massaging the stump of his peg leg. "If you dust off old junk sometimes you come up with a gem," he told me as he squashed a lighted cigarette butt into a knothole on the wooden peg.

The Braves decided I could pitch batting practice for their AAA farm team in Richmond, Virginia. This was like Br'er Rabbit getting thrown into the briar patch. The Richmond pitching coach was my old friend Johnny Sain, who also happens to be the best teacher in baseball. (Astute readers will not be surprised to learn that John is in the minors. In the coaching business, loyalty to the manager is more important than ability. The best qualification a coach can have is to be the manager's drinking buddy. John drinks milk shakes and is loyal to pitchers.)

For five weeks I threw batting practice waiting for somebody to get a sore arm, but it never happened. What did happen was that the Atlanta Braves came to town for an exhibition game against their top farm team. And Ted Turner said I should pitch for Richmond. This generated considerable laughter among the Richmond players, including myself. I hadn't pitched in a game since spring training and the Braves were a month into their season with four guys batting over .300. Not only that, but my pitching arsenal consisted of an uncertain knuckleball and a little sinker that was only two weeks old.

But I had a few things going for me that nobody knew about. Like, I understood how to get out of my own way. It's hard to explain but as it applies to pitching, it means that instead of thinking about the mechanics of the knuckleball, as I had been doing, I thought about nothing and just let it happen. I had forgotten that my unconscious knew a lot more about pitching than my conscious.

I got this strange idea about pitching from a book about archery sent to me by someone who knew nothing about either sport. Along with her letters, Paula was now sending me books, one of which was *Zen and the Art of Archery*. This was a helluva pen pal. She wrote me letters and I called her on the telephone. We were starting to have some long conversations.

On May 10, 1978, in front of the second largest crowd in the history of Parker Field (they were standing in roped off sections of the outfield), I got out of the way and let my knuckleball do its thing against the Atlanta Braves. In the seventh inning I left the game to a standing ovation with a 3-1 lead, having struck out seven of the big boys, including Jeff Burroughs (.416), the National League's hottest hitter. It was my greatest night ever in a baseball uniform. My reward was a contract with their AA farm team in Savannah, Georgia. I had made it to the next plateau.

Mesmerizing the Atlanta Braves was unexpected, but it was nothing compared to what was happening with the rest of my life. I was feeling happy and peaceful for the first time in longer than I could remember.

Was it possible to fall in love through the mail with a college professor you met at a department store? I wouldn't believe a movie like that. Maybe I'm old fashioned but it seemed to me that before a guy fell in love he ought to have spent at least three days with that person. Which is how it happened that Paula Kurman, Ph.D., came to be sitting in the wooden bleachers in Charlotte, North Carolina, wearing basic silk and pearls. That was the weekend my teammates stopped kidding me about blue-haired old ladies.

Being a trained observer, it did not take Paula very long to grasp the significance of baseball. "Obviously," she said, "one of the cardinal rules is: When in doubt, spit. Everybody spits. It's like punctuation." She was also very adept at picking up the signs. "I'm not sure what it means," she said, "but whenever the ball is not in play, somebody grabs his crotch."

And she made some other fascinating discoveries. Because she didn't know enough about baseball to watch the game as a fan, Paula watched the things she did know about, like nonverbal behavior. She noticed that each pitcher went through his own series of mannerisms before every windup and, what's more, that minute differences in this routine appeared to be connected to the success or failure of the pitch. In any case, she said, it was clear that the totality of a pitch began many moments before the windup. Of course, it may be a few years before baseball takes advantage of this information. I can just hear pitching coaches saying, "O.K., men, let's go to work on those mannerisms."

I was learning new ways to win games without even picking up a ball and new ways to feel about myself as a person. It was a very enlightening summer.

And it was a lot of fun. The Savannah Braves were the youngest team in the league but I felt more at home with them than I ever had with the Yankees, the Pilots, or the Astros. Once the players got used to me I became the team guru. I was the fountain of wisdom on everything from pitching and finances to careers and love lives. I'd sit around my room at night with guys like Roger Alexander and Stu Livingstone, we'd make some popcorn on my hotplate, and have a few beers and shoot the bull. It was a kind of closeness which had been impossible for me to achieve years ago. At age 39 I was finally one of the boys. It was late in coming but it was sufficient.

We had a great manager named Bobby Dews. Bobby also happened to be 39 years old and going through a few changes of his own. He used to be a wild man. The players told stories about the time he got ejected from a game and took third base with him on the way out. Which made a lot more sense than the time he kicked dirt on home plate and broke his toe. When I played for Dews at Savannah he had calmed down a lot. I asked him why. "I finally got to the point where I felt confident and didn't have to bluff anybody anymore," he said. "Then I got to know some umpires and found out that a couple of them were actually human." At the end of that summer Bobby got called up to the major leagues. It couldn't have happened to a nicer guy.

It was a helluva ballclub, too. What the Savannah Braves lacked in ability we made up in spirit. One night we lost a game in Knoxville, Tennessee, 17-1, got on a bus and drove all night to Montgomery, Alabama, and kicked their ass 10-2. The memories of those bus rides will be with me forever. We'd play poker by flashlight on the back of the bus 'till three o'clock in the morning and then stagger into a truck stop four hours later for breakfast.

It was a wonderful summer but it was not without a great deal of pain. My wife and I decided to separate.

This was a major and frightening step into the unknown for both of us. Aside from the hurt of ending a 15-year relationship, there were

441

all those questions. What would it do to the kids? Would they think they were from a broken home, or would this be called a rearranged family network? What would our family and friends think? We hardly talked about our problems to each other much less discussed them with others. And we had this public image of togetherness, reinforced by *Ball Four*, which increased the pressure to keep up a facade. And finally, was this the right decision for the two of us? Should we stay and try to work it out and maybe settle for some compromise, or would a clean break heal quicker? Whether we had guessed right or wrong, only the future would tell.

My life was changing and I felt somehow older, without feeling old. Whatever was happening inside my head produced terrific results on the mound. I pitched a one-hitter, a two-hitter, and a thirteen-inning shutout, pitching in a hundred degree heat after all-night bus rides and with two days' rest. In three months I had won twelve games and pitched the league's least experienced team to a division championship. In September the Atlanta Braves called me up to the major leagues. I had made it to Emerald City.

THE BIG LEAGUES

When I walked into Atlanta's Fulton County Stadium, I was floating as if in a dream. How large it was compared to the tiny stadiums I'd been playing in for two years. When I got into my uniform with my old No. 56 on it and went out to the field, I could feel my heart pounding under my shirt. And what a feeling it was standing on the mound listening to the national anthem, waiting to pitch my first game. I felt like I was standing on top of Mount Everest. I thought to myself how lucky I was to experience this twice in the same lifetime.

My first pitch to Dodger second baseman Davey Lopes was a called strike and the crowd cheered. Four pitches later, with a full count, Lopes struck out swinging on a dancing knuckler and the crowd roared. I felt like Rocky. After I got the next two hitters on easy outs, I ran to the dugout and threw my arms up in a victory salute. In the fourth inning the Dodgers broke up my perfect game, my no hitter, and my ballgame by scoring five runs. But the day was more important than the game and it had been extraordinary fun. I laughed a lot—until I read the newspapers the next day.

"He showed me nothing," said Lopes. "Nothing." "It was a circus," said Reggie Smith. "It was like batting against Bozo the Clown," said Rick Monday. "The Commissioner should investigate this," said Cincinnati manager Sparky Anderson. "We're in a pennant race. Bouton should have to pitch against the Giants and Reds, too."

Incredible! Sparky was losing a pennant, so I understood about him but why were the Dodgers so angry? My phone was ringing off the hook from reporters wanting to know what I thought. I didn't know what to say except that I felt sorry for the Dodgers who were obviously suffering from sun stroke.

In his next game, Bozo the Clown beat the San Francisco Giants, 4-1. The pennant-contending San Francisco Giants. It would have been 4-0, but I threw a double play ball into centerfield. After the game, reporters asked me if I won because it was windy. I said that was it. The wind blew hot dog wrappers around the field and the batters couldn't see the ball. I had won my first major league game since July 11, 1970. I couldn't wait for the reviews.

"Next time I'm going to bring up my little boy to bat against him," said Bill Madlock, who was hitless in two at bats. "It was the most humiliating experience of my life," said Darrell Evans, who had a pop fly double in three at bats. "He was terrible," said Mike Ivie, who was hitless in three at bats. I almost forgot who won the game.

Johnny Sain told me later I had revolutionized the sport by inventing a new way to judge baseball ability. Results in a game didn't count anymore. You just ask the opposition what they think.

Maybe the hitters were confused by how I got them out. Players today don't mind being outmuscled, but they hate being outsmarted. It's a macho thing. When Atlanta relief pitcher Gene Garber ended Pete Rose's hitting streak in 1979 by getting him out with a change-up, Rose got mad. He said Garber should have "challenged" him with a fastball. I used to challenge the hitters when I was young. Now I couldn't, of course, but more significantly, I didn't have to. That summer I felt more in control on a pitcher's mound than I ever have in my life. All the stuff I needed was inside my head.

It wasn't my lack of speed which threw them off, as the hitters claimed. All season long these guys clobber batting practice pitchers (usually old coaches) who throw the ball even slower than I do. No, what mostly did them in was their own conviction that they ought to be knocking this old sportscaster out of the box in the first inning. I understood that the duel between pitcher and hitter was a relationship and I was able to use their anger to my advantage. By feeling instead of thinking, my body chose the proper pitch, speed, and location. All I had to do was execute. It's like bullfighting, where the bull knows the fighter is out there but he can't quite get ahold of him.

After I beat the Giants, I pitched a few more games. My next start came against my old team, the Houston Astros. Returning to the Astrodome brought back a flood of memories. When I walked out onto the familiar artificial turf I thought I heard Harry Walker calling to me from across the field. And I remembered the night I struck out eleven Pittsburgh Pirates a long long time ago.

This time I only struck out one but I pitched seven innings. My opponent, J. Rodney Richard, maybe the hardest thrower in baseball, chose the occasion to break the modern league strikeout record for righthanders. The young flamethrower and the old junkballer were each taken out for pinch hitters in the eighth inning with the score tied 2-2. A standoff. I loved the contrast. There was no criticism this time, just silence.

Then Sparky Anderson of the Reds got his wish. I pitched against Cincinnati, and they did beat me, but only 2-1. I allowed just five hits. Reds centerfielder Ken Griffey swung so hard at a third strike he actually fell down on home plate. After the game Anderson said, "We didn't even hit the ball hard off him and we got two runs we shouldn't have gotten." Sparky Anderson is a gentleman.

It's interesting that the response from the baseball establishment to what I had done was a resounding silence. A two-year odyssey through the minor leagues by a 39-year-old man who finally makes it, may be one of the best testimonials baseball has ever had. Yet the Commissioner of the sport never uttered a peep, never even sent the congratulatory telegram. And at the New York Baseball Writers Dinner that winter after my comeback, only one player was not announced as being in attendance. It was yours truly, the deviant.

THE EPILOGUE

During my comeback, I had been telling people that Hoyt Wilhelm threw knuckleballs in the big leagues until he was 48, which meant I had about ten years left. Actually, I thought I'd play about five years but by the time I got called up, I knew I wouldn't even stay around that long. In an article I wrote for *Sports Illustrated* two years ago, I explained my reasons for not going back. (I had thought of saying it was because baseball didn't deserve me but that sounded a little too arrogant, even for me.) What I said was that being there was not as much fun as getting there. That the real experience of baseball was the bus rides and the country ballparks and the chile at 3 A.M. with a bunch of guys chasing a dream. And it was true enough.

But there was another reason for not going back. And it had to do with why I attempted a comeback in the first place. When I started out with Bill Veeck's Knoxville White Sox some people said it was a publicity stunt. Publicity for what, they didn't say. They never explained why I would leave a New York television station five nights a week to get my name in a Knoxville newspaper once a week.

Other people said I was doing it to gather material for another book. Not a bad guess, although it would have to be a hellava book to justify the sacrifice in income. A few people said I just loved baseball and that certainly was true but that was only part of it. The ones who said I was crazy were probably the closest. Johnny Sain hit it right on the nose when he said I wanted to do something nobody had ever done before.

Making it to the major leagues a second time was going to be the ultimate achievement that would finally do it for me. Do what? I wasn't sure. I only knew that I didn't feel right about myself and it had something to do with acceptance and recognition. The funny part is that what did it for me happened off the ballfield and it happened long before I ever made it back to the majors.

It began when a magic lady had this strange idea that I was somebody special. This was a view of me I wasn't used to. In spite of the

445

public recognition I had received, I privately held a different view—one I had always had—which was that I was not quite good enough no matter what I did and anything I had achieved was somehow a lucky accident.

For a long while I didn't trust Paula's feelings about me. I kept expecting she would change her mind once she got to know me. I used to say to her, "you don't really know me." It was when she persisted in her view of me as special, that the summer took on a new meaning for me. The challenge of making it to the majors became secondary to the challenge of changing the way I thought about myself. This change business was a whole different ballgame.

A negative self-image is hard to shake in a world which confirms that image by reflecting back what we feel about ourselves. What's more, when you've lived with something all your life you can't see it easily. Comedian Buddy Hackett tells a funny story about how he didn't know what heartburn was until one day he didn't have it. He had just joined the army and for the first time in his life he wasn't eating his mother's cooking. When he woke up the next morning he was terrified. He ran into the infirmary hollering, "Help me, I'm dying. The fire went out." Which just goes to show what you can get used to. And it also shows that new feelings, even if they're an improvement on old ones, can be scary.

On the baseball field I had a chance to try out the "new" me and I discovered a kind of power I'd never had before. What a relief it was to be free of the feeling that I needed to invent a cure for cancer or be the first person to jump off a building and fly. The irony is that losing the feeling that I had to top myself gave me the strength and the freedom to do just that. Making the big leagues a second time seemed almost easy. And instead of it elevating me to some new level, it didn't seem like that big a deal.

Paula had called it way back in her second letter to me, which I hadn't understood at the time. She had said that one day I would finally come to know myself as worthy and strong and it would no longer be necessary to prove it, or to pick up burdens unnecessarily just to convince myself I could carry them.

Having found what I was looking for, I was able to stop running. It was no longer necessary to play baseball, nor was it even possible. I needed to stay around and build a new life for myself and the kids. I'd been a part-time father for too long and I wanted to organize a new family.

And some family it is. There are seven of us now. Besides Paula and me there are her two kids: Lee (20) and Hollis (18), plus my three: Michael (now 17), David (16), and Laurie, (15), who stays half the time with her mother. We all live in a small Tudor house we call "Teen City." Or "the Zoo." When the stereos are all going at the same time (which is too often) it feels like we're living inside the speakers at a rock concert. And when everybody's home the front of the house looks like a used car lot. That's a good feeling.

Things haven't always felt that good. Like the day I told Michael, David, and Laurie that their mother and I were actually going to split. I took them to a local park and we sat on the grass. Then I told them I loved them very much and that I wanted all three of them to live with me all of the time. I said I was sure their mother wanted the same thing and so they had some choices to make. They could live with either one of us full time, part time, two days a week, every other week, go back and forth, whatever. And they could always change their minds whenever they wanted to. I told them they were old enough to make their own decisions and I felt certain that no judge would tell them where they had to live. It would always be up to them. And that's the way it's been.

What's really nice is how well the kids from both families have blended together, contributing their own special talents and interests.

Lee, a sophomore at the University of Pennsylvania, is the new adult in the family reporting back from the outside world. He's the one the others look up to, partly because he's six foot two. Lee has decided to study law because of his cool logic and natural aptitude and as he says, "because it seemed like the thing to do at the time."

Hollis, a high-school senior, is perceptive and sensitive like her mother and a natural born comedienne. She does expert imitations of everything from her French teacher to a dead cockroach and performs impromptu skits which Laurie enters into with great gusto. Hollis is also thinking of law but for slightly different reasons. She wants to "wheel and deal and make big bucks."

Michael, whom you last saw at age six, is now shaving and taking driving lessons from Dad. Talk about time warp. These days Mike is into filmmaking and politics. He cares passionately about things and shows up at no-nuke rallys and worked hard for John Anderson. Mike is also very good with young children and could make a terrific teacher some day. A high-school senior like Hollis, he too is sending out college applications. Except he's a little nervous about it. To cover all contingencies, he's applied to every college east of the Mississippi.

David (a.k.a. Kyong Jo), now sixteen and a junior, leads the family in nicknames. Besides "the mean Korean," which Hollis tagged him with after watching him play hockey, there is "Kato" because he creeps up on silent feet and "Pookie" because he's so cute. David is not sure what he wants to do yet, or even who he is. Looking among some old papers recently, we found the name and address of his mother in Korea. He's debating about whether he wants to write to her and try to find his roots. He hasn't seen her since he was four and there may be some pain involved. On the other hand, it's a pain not knowing certain things. As David says, "the trouble with being adopted is that you don't know whether you're going to be short, or bald, or gray, or what."

Laurie, "The Unsinkable Molly Brown," is still unsinkable. And it's a good thing because it's tough being the only one living in two houses. One of the benefits, of course, is having two sets of friends and going to twice as many parties. Laurie has a number of interests but her main goal is to become famous. She's at that stage now where she will suddenly appear in a doorway wearing earrings and highheels while carrying a stuffed animal. She can't seem to make up her mind, but just in case adulthood wins out, she's practicing walking and sitting glamorously. Recently Laurie walked into a beauty parlor where Paula was taking her for a haircut and the hairdresser, who didn't know the connection, took one look at her and said, "this has got to be Jim Bouton's kid." In spite of the fact that Laurie looks exactly like me, she's very pretty and getting beautiful. Until she becomes famous she's working as a candy striper at a nearby hospital and is one of the world's great babysitters.

Meanwhile, the "Professor and the Jock," as we are sometimes referred to around the house, are working separately and together on a variety of things. In addition to writing and lecturing, we both do industrial consulting which, as a friend of ours said recently, is better than working for a living.

Paula also gives seminars and is the behavioral director for a chain of weight control clinics. She's presently working on a dietless weight control book which explains how existing weight control programs maintain the system which keeps people fat. I told her that after the book comes out, the people in the weight control business probably won't talk to her anymore.

One of my favorite things to do these days is to video tape corporate conventions. I tape everything from the business meeting and the president's speech to the golf tournament and the cocktail party. Then I edit a ten minute cassette that they can use as an image builder, a performance incentive, or a recruiting tool. Ever since my years as a TV reporter I've enjoyed the challenge of putting a story together creatively. The great thing is that these guys never refuse to be interviewed. And if you play something backwards, they love it.

You may also see me promoting something called Big League Chew. It's shredded bubblegum in a tobacco style pouch, designed for ballplayers and other kids. My partner, Rob Nelson, and I dreamed it up out in the Portland Maverick bullpen while we were sitting around one day drowning bugs in tobacco juice.

Rob, a lefthanded pitcher and thinker, decided there needed to be a substitute for that terrible tasting stuff which was so necessary for a ballplayer's image. So we sent away for some gum base, mixed it up in a saucepan, colored it brown with molasses, and sliced it up like chewing tobacco. Then we put it into some pouches we designed ourselves and shopped it around to the different gum companies. The Topps company, of bubblegum card fame, turned us down on the grounds that mothers wouldn't want their kids spitting brown stuff all over the place. Finally, a guy named A. G. Atwater at Amurol Products, a division of Wrigley's, bought the idea and now Big League Chew is the hottest selling bubblegum in the country.

I'm a little concerned about promoting a product with sugar in it but I figure I'm morally covered. Our original idea called for brown sugarless wheatgerm gum. It just didn't test well.

Things don't always work out the way you plan them, which is one of the lessons I've learned along the way. As the song says, "life is what happens to you while you're busy making other plans." That's why I have no idea what I'll be doing ten years from now or even one year from now. Except I know I'll be doing something because I've got three college educations to pay for.

With a new family, a new home, and a new set of careers, I hardly recognize myself these days. I look in the mirror and wonder who that is, but I notice he's happy. I don't even play sandlot ball on Sundays anymore. My arm is so out of shape it took me four shots the other day to hit a telephone pole with a snowball.

Once in awhile I take the family to a ballgame. It's a strange feeling to sit there and watch from the stands. The game looks easier than it really is. Fans can't see the up close grunting and straining. Or when someone hits a home run you can't hear the pitcher making little whimpering sounds. And it all looks so much more serious than it really is. You can't see any of the nonsense and the fun going on out there. When the manager goes out to talk to the pitcher it looks very scientific.

Which is another reason I'm glad I wrote *Ball Four*. I don't ever want to forget what they're really saying. If it weren't written somewhere that a manager named Joe Schultz advised pitchers to "zitz 'em and go pound Budweiser" I might not believe it myself anymore—and I was there.

Ball Four has changed my life. But going back even earlier than that, my life was changed when I first picked up a baseball. And it was changed again after I put it away.

Twenty Years Later . . . . .

BALL SIX

"How ya doin' Dickhead?"

Just great, I replied. It was Gary Bell on the phone from his home in San Antonio, Texas.

"I saw your old buddy, Mickey Mantle, the other day at a golf tournament. Heh heh heh."

Was any beer consumed out on the golf course? I asked.

"I set an all-time record on the front nine."

Gary runs his own sporting goods business in San Antonio, selling uniforms and equipment to local schools and teams. Gary says his other job is defending me for having written *Ball Four*. "I have to go around telling everybody that you're not fuckin' Adolf Hitler."

"But, to be honest with you," said Gary, "I loved the book. People remember me more for *Ball Four* than for pitching. Guys come up to me and say, 'Gary Bell, right? *Ball Four*.' "

Gary says his wife is feeling a little left out. "Rhonda says *she* wants to be in the book this time," said Gary. "But don't get her mixed up with all the others."

Gary said that he ran into Dick Radatz recently at a Red Sox fantasy camp and Radatz wants me to print a retraction about a story I told in I'm Glad You Didn't Take It Personally (the sequel to *Ball Four,* published in 1971). This was right after *Ball Four* came out, and Radatz and I had been comparing bizarre baseball stories. Radatz told me that some guy once paid him $100 to throw oranges at his bare ass. "And this was when I could really bring it," said Radatz.

Gary said Radatz now claims it wasn't him, but Mickey McDermott who threw the oranges. I said I believed Radatz the first time because it sounded like something he'd do. "Hell, for 100 bucks, I would too," said Gary. "Wouldn't you? Maybe we could get somebody out for a change."

"Hey, did you hear about Darrell Brandon?" said Gary. "He's going down to play in that damn Seniors League in Florida. He's like a new man again now, with all those road trips."

I asked Gary why he didn't go down there and give it a shot.

" 'Cause my shit's a little weak."

We spoke for a while longer and made tentative plans to get together in the spring. I told Gary it would be great to see him. "Yeah," said Gary, "and we can talk about beyond the universe again."

Talking to Gary brought back memories of the Seattle Pilots. It's been twenty years and we've never had an Oldtimers' Day. The problem is, where would we play it? As Gary says, "We're a team without a damn city." Still, it seems that we ought to do something on our twentieth anniversary.

"We should celebrate," said Tommy Davis. "You can't forget that group. They were unreal."

Tommy was speaking from his home in Los Angeles. He said he's not coaching for the Dodgers anymore because they went with young guys. "I'm working for myself now. I sell premiums, give batting clinics. I'm going to open up my own batting cage. I wear several hats. You know, hustling."

We got to talking about the old Pilots. Tommy recalled how big Gene Brabender would scare guys to death by shooting a dart into the wall above their heads with a homemade blowgun. "Oh, Brabender, would you please stop that?" we'd ask politely in deference to Brabender's size.

Tommy said he recently spoke to Steve Hovley on the phone. "It was great to hear his voice again," said Tommy. "He . . . still . . . talks . . . two . . . miles . . . an . . . hour."

Then Tommy remembered Steve Hovley's travel gear. "All he had was a paper bag with a shirt and a pair of pants, a toothbrush and toothpaste," remembered Tommy. "And this was for a two-week roadtrip!"

Speaking of Hovley, he's still living in Ojai, California, and he's still in the plumbing business. I can understand that. Hovley is one of the few people left in America who still gets pleasure and satisfaction from doing a good day's work, apart from the title that comes with it.

"I keep getting these calls from writers asking me about the Pilots," said Hovley. "It's all your fault."

"They always ask me whether you should have written the book or not. I give them a different answer each time to make it interesting."

"The other thing is," said Hovley, "I got a call from Tommy Davis. Some guy I played ball with in high school is working on this development in Oxnard; you know, we're not just another pretty name. Anyway, they got Tommy Davis as a celebrity promoter for this development. And they're all drunk one night, so they call me.

"What Tommy said was, there's a new league in Florida and it's a chance for a comeback. But I told him I was retired."

Hovley asked what I was doing these days. I told him about Big League Chew, that shredded bubble gum invented in the bullpen during my comeback in '78. It's still selling pretty well. And I just invented something called Collect-A-Books, which are little books the size of baseball cards, coming out in 1990. There's also a picnic plate I invented called Table-To-Go.

"You see how you continue to piss these people off," said Hovley: "by taking all the opportunities and running with them yourself?"

Then I asked Hovley how he feels about having been a member of one of the most forlorn teams in baseball history.

"The way I like to think about the Pilots," said Hovley, "it's like the upside-down postage stamp. The most important one is the one they screwed up."

And what's become of my other roommate, Mike Marshall?

"I'm still pitching," said Mike. "I'm an associate professor and head baseball coach down here in Arkadelphia, Arkansas."

Arkadelphia? Sounds like a happenin' place.

"I love it down here, even though they don't understand a bleeding-heart liberal. I enjoy coaching. You wouldn't believe what I've learned about the mechanics of pitching. I've sent fifteen pitchers into pro baseball so far. And I personally am throwing the dog doo-doo out of the baseball."

So why don't you go down and play in that Seniors League?

"I might if they get their act together," said Mike.

I reminded Mike that this was the anniversary or our wonderful year together in Seattle. And did he have any thoughts on the old Pilots or that book that guy wrote?

"The Pilots were a joke," said Mike. "*Ball Four* was funny because it was true. And, baseball hasn't changed that much. There are still guys drilling holes in doors and fighting to get laid. I thought it was an excellent book."

The truth is, however, that not many Pilots liked *Ball Four*. Sad to say, a lot of them are still pretty angry about it. A Seattle newspaper did a big article recently and called players to get their reactions. Here's what they said:

"If you're going to do a story about that book, I'd just as soon you leave me out of it," said Don Mincher, who now runs a sporting goods store in Huntsville, Alabama.

"I don't want to talk about him," said Frank Crosetti, who is retired and living in Stockton, California. "It's terrible to write a thing like that."

"What offended me more than anything was that no one was aware what he was writing," said Rich Rollins, now an executive with the Cleveland Cavaliers basketball team.

"Even today you won't find many guys who would cross the street for him," said Mike Hegan, who broadcasts road games for the Cleveland Indians.

And the saddest quote of all came from my main man, Joe Schultz. "Roger Maris told me that with the Yankees, when Bouton was taken out of the game he'd dress and go in the stands behind third base. He'd then holler at (Yankee) coach Frank Crosetti until everyone was booing him. Then he'd leave."

Now, just imagine me up there in section 23 rallying a bunch of Yankee fans to boo Frank Crosetti. Boo him for what? For giving a batter the wrong sign? Say it ain't so, Joe.

I must admit that it pains me to hear that some former teammates are still angry about *Ball Four.* But I'm not surprised. They see the book as an invasion of their privacy. And maybe they're embarrassed by something they said or did.

What those players don't realize is that nobody thinks badly of them, no matter what they said or did, especially after twenty years. But they just don't have that perspective.

And it's not because they're ballplayers. Last year the state of Kansas refused to join the rest of the country in celebrating the fiftieth anniversary of *The Wizard of Oz.* The people out there are still pretty upset about the movie, which showed Kansas as a place Dorothy dreams of escaping. As Dick Busby, publisher of *The Hutchison News,* wrote: "All the nasty things that happen to Dorothy are in Kansas. The moment she gets out of Kansas she's in color." Welcome to Munchkin Land.

And then there are the Houston Astros. Last winter I got a call from the team's public relations director, actually inviting me to write a story for their yearbook. It would be a look back at the '69 Astros on their twentieth anniversary. They gave me a bunch of phone numbers and I started calling.

It was wonderful to hear those familiar voices again. Especially my old roommate, Norm Miller, who now works for the Astros in TV spot sales. Norm said he enjoys being back in baseball again, but he doesn't understand the modern players.

"These guys are very religious," said Norm. "They don't cut up like we did. They actually have Bible readings in the clubhouse before games. I don't know how they can relax."

I spoke to Larry Dierker, the ace of the staff that set a National League record for strikeouts (1221) that still stands today. Dierker, who's been a radio and TV broadcaster for the Astros during the past thirteen years, remarked on his two careers. "It's strange," said Dierker. "More people know me today as the TV announcer than the guy who pitched for the Astros." Pretty degrading for the legendary songwriter who penned the immortal "Proud to Be an Astro."

Music fans will be glad to hear that Dierker's talents have not withered with time. Larry revealed a few of his latest songs to me, which include such epics as "Home Run King," "The Manager," "Baseball Wives," "Utility Man," and my personal favorite, "Lost on the Road."

A couple of other pitchers, Fred Gladding and Jack Billingham, worked for the Astros last year as coaches. And they still rag on each other today, except in a different way. Billingham, who was skinny, used to belittle Gladding, whose ample girth contributed to his nickname of "Fred Flintstone." Today Gladding gets on Billingham, who weighs 250 pounds.

According to Dierker, Gladding almost looks trim today. "You know how he always had an old man's body?" says Dierker. "Well, it's still the same body but he's aged into it."

It was good to talk to Johnny Edwards again. He still has that reassuring quality in his voice that I remembered from those meetings on the mound. John is the operations manager for Cameron Oil and Gas Supply Company in Houston. "I got completely out of baseball," said John. "I try to make my way as an engineer rather than an ex-ballplayer. "

This did not prevent John from having a few memories. Like the time Doug Rader slugged a game warden in spring training the year after *Ball Four*. "He was fishing in the middle of some river without a license," said Edwards, "and they came after him in one of those airboats. So Rader threw his fishing stuff in the bushes, dove underwater and breathed through a reed. And he might have made it too, but he kept hearing the boat getting closer ancl closer and he didn't want to get Osterized by the propeller. He came right to training camp from jail," said Edwards. "No shoes. Hadn't changed his clothes in three days. He looked like hell."

Dierker and Norm Miller remembered how Rader liked to use the Astros locker room as a driving range. "He'd tee up a golf ball while guys would dive for cover in their lockers, behind trunks and under the whirlpool," says Dierker. "Then he'd hit the ball—real hard too—and it would ricochet around the room while the players prayed it wouldn't hit them."

At this writing, Rader is the manager of the California Angels and he tries to play down his image as a wild man. Rader said recently that he only teed off in the clubhouse when nobody was in there. Yeah, surrre! He probably doesn't want any of his California Angels players pulling that same stunt today.

However, Rader does remember a TV interview where he gave advice to Little Leaguers. "They should eat bubble gum cards," said Rader. "When I was a kid I accidently ate a bubble gum card, but unfortunately, it wasn't a very good player. Kids should make sure they eat the bubble gum card of a good player, like Willie Mays."

Norm Miller says the strange thing about Rader is that he's really smart. "It's dangerous to have someone like him have a brain," says Norm. "He has no fear. He's like the Tasmanian devil."

Speaking of characters, Dierker recalled the Astros' best Dominican utilityman, Julio Gotay. It was Gotay who provided the service of carrying a dead fish on plane trips to ward off evil spirits. Don't laugh, the team never crashed.

Gotay was also famous for having a cheese sandwich fall out of his back pocket. While he was sliding into second base.

And I enjoyed speaking with Bob Watson again. He was the rookie who was never afraid to catch my knuckleball. Right up until the time I broke his finger with a real beauty. Watson was also a kid who couldn't believe the lifestyle of a major league ballplayer. He was always going around saying, "Gee whiz." Today, Watson's finger and his mind are still permanently bent.

Watson is now the Astros assistant general manager. We got to talking about Spec Richardson, the old Astros GM who threw nickels around like manhole covers. Spec once offered Watson a $1,000 raise to $11,000. "But the minimum salary just went up from $10,000 to $11,000," Watson pointed out. "That's your raise," said Spec.

The best part about writing that story for the Astros yearbook was discovering that most of the guys aren't upset about *Ball Four*. Here's what some of them had to say:

Larry Dierker: "As a writer myself, I understand what you had to do."

Johnny Edwards: "My son David read it. He kids me about it once in a while."

Jack Billingham: "I saw this guy Bouton writing everything down and I said he really keeps a good chart on the hitters."

Bob Watson: "I just looked in the index for *Watson*."

Curt Blefary: "I'm not interested."

Well, you can't win 'em all.

The worst part about writing the yearbook story was that the Astros never used it, even though they paid me. Maybe they thought it wouldn't go with the Bibles in the clubhouse. But I'm still proud to be an Astro.

My only regret is that I wasn't free to go back for the Astro's Old Timers' Game. Or, as Norm Miller calls it, "the Alzheimer's Game." But at least I was invited.

That's more than I can say about the Yankees. They still don't invite me back to Old Timers' Day. Now, you might ask, who would carry a grudge for twenty years?

I'm not sure, but I think it may be Mickey Mantle. He once refused to speak to Joe Pepitone for a month because one time Joe jumped ahead of him in batting practice. I know Mantle refuses to discuss *Ball Four* or even mention my name. When someone asks him about me, his response is pretty funny. He just says, "Jim who?" And if Mantle *is* the reason I'm not invited to Old Timers' Day, I'm quite happy to stay home. I wouldn't want to be announced to the fans at Yankee Stadium as the player who caused "The Mick" not to show up.

The funny thing is that what I said about Mantle in *Ball Four* is now part of his legend. Mickey's drinking ability is a running gag around the country. Radio comic Don Imus says that, "when you go to Mickey Mantle's restaurant in New York City at 2 A.M. you can win a free dinner if you guess which table Mickey's under."

Even Bowie Kuhn wrote about Mantle's drinking in his own book, *Hardball: The Education of a Baseball Commissioner.* I mention it here to help his sales, which I figure is only fair. Kuhn said that Mantle and Billy Martin were running around drunk in some hotel trying to round up votes against his reelection. All I've got to say about that is, "Commissioner, how could you? These guys are heroes. You've done the game a grave disservice."

But the guy who has the most fun with Mickey's reputation as a boozer is Mickey himself. On the corporate lecture circuit one of Mickey's standing jokes is, "if I knew I was going to live this long, I would have taken better care of myself."

Lately, people have been asking me if ballplayers today behave worse than the players I wrote about twenty years ago. They are referring to players taking drugs, the Wade Boggs affair with Margo Adams, Steve Garvey fathering several kids out of wedlock and Pete Rose's gambling.

Actually, the players aren't any different today, it's just that the world is a much more dangerous place. And players, as always, are ill-equipped to deal with it.

Years ago, most of the team would go out and drink after a ballgame. A few guys would get drunk and eventually some would become alcoholics. But today, just a few snorts of cocaine at a party can turn any ballplayer into an addict.

It's the same thing with sex. Years ago, we had girlfriends on the road but they were happy just to be girlfriends. It was fair for both sides. The players liked convenient sex and the women liked the status of sleeping with a ballplayer. Our biggest fear was getting the clap.

Now that ballplayers are making big money, some girlfriends want to make a good living, too. That's why this person named Margo Adams sued Boston Red Sox batting champ Wade Boggs for "palimony." Getting the clap is nothing compared to getting clapped with a 12-million-dollar lawsuit.

Why do ballplayers have to take drugs and have girlfriends in the first place? This may come as a shock to some people but it's because they're human beings. Young human beings. Think of a ballplayer as a fifteen-year-old in a twenty-five-year-old body.

Being a professional athlete allows you to postpone your adulthood. You grow up in Heroworld. Parents change the dinner schedule for you, teachers help with grades, coaches fawn over you, cops ask for an autograph and someone else buys the drinks. Or worse. As basketball great Bill Russell put it, "most professional athletes have been on scholarship since the third grade."

And a lifetime spent developing one skill doesn't allow much time to develop others. Lots of athletes can't function in the real world. That's why they only feel comfortable in each other's company. They sense that something is missing in their lives, but they're not sure what. At the same time, they feel invincible because of their success on the field.

This combination of emotional immaturity and physical ability makes athletes uniquely vulnerable to temptation. They can't "just say no." They're too busy trying to fit in and show how great they are at the same time.

Meanwhile, most athletes don't know who their friends are. They think their friend is the guy who picks them up at the airport or gets them a girl in Detroit. Or invites them to a party. The surprise is that there isn't more drug use among professional athletes. These guys *are* the market.

If you think I'm exaggerating, just ask people who deal with professional athletes. Radio station managers, TV producers and booking agents all have stories about athletes showing up drunk or not at all, without even the courtesy of a phone call. People in the business know that to guarantee an appearance by a famous athlete you've got to send a limo, along with someone to make sure the athlete gets into it.

Okay, but do we have to know about all this pandering and philandering? Shouldn't kids have someone to look up to?

Personally, I think kids are better off knowing the truth. I don't believe kids think it's all right to take drugs because some famous athlete did it. Usually, what they see is that the athlete got suspended, ended up in jail or died. I believe the kid figures that if the famous athlete can't handle this stuff, how can he?

The people who get most upset about athletes falling from grace are the ones who built them up in the first place. I'm talking about the league owners and their friends in the media who help sell the sports product. Heroes sell tickets and newspapers and TV advertising.

But why do we need heroes in the first place? A philosopher once said: "Don't pity the nation that has no heroes; pity the nation that needs them." Another problem with heroes is that in order to look up to them, you have to lower yourself.

And what about Pete Rose? People are always asking me, so I'll tell you. I think his lifetime ban for betting on baseball was cruel and unusual punishment. The major league rule against gambling (even on your own team) is an anachronism, adopted as a response to the Black Sox scandal where players actually "threw" the 1919 World Series.

There is no evidence that Pete Rose ever "threw" a ballgame. But it is pretty clear that he's a compulsive gambler, even though he denies it. Today we know that compulsive gambling is an addiction, just like alcohol or drug addiction, and denial is part of the illness. Accordingly,

Rose should have been treated the same as baseball's drug users; a one-year suspension and rehabilitation with Gamblers Anonymous.

The worst thing about the punishment is that it sends the wrong message to kids. Pete Rose gets banned for life for gambling while the drug addicts are allowed back after a year; and then they get extra chances after that. Baseball is saying, in effect, that gambling is worse than drugs. How do kids make sense out of that?

I believe that the real reason Pete Rose was banished for life was that he dared to challenge the authority of the Baseball Commissioner by going to court. When the late Commissioner A. Bartlett Giamatti suspended Rose, he said that no one man is bigger than baseball. This may be true. But it's also true that baseball is big enough to survive without crucifying one man. Especially one sick man.

And how about those sports commentators, criticizing Rose for going on television to sell his memorabilia? The guy's got legal bills and probably gambling debts to pay off. What did those guys expect Rose to do after devoting his life to nothing but baseball—get a job as a television executive?

The feeling against Pete Rose is so strong that NBC balked at his appearance at the first annual Masters Baseball game. Masters Baseball is an idea developed by me and former Dodger pitcher Andy Messersmith. Our idea is to have an eight-team league of recently retired All-Star caliber major league players. The games would be played on weekends during the summer at different stadiums around the country.

We took our idea to NBC and they agreed to televise a one-game pilot of Masters Baseball in May of 1990. If this game is successful we'll probably have another one in September. We hope Masters Baseball will be as popular as the Legends of Golf tournaments that led to the Senior Pro Golf Tour.

In case you're wondering, Masters Baseball is not the same thing as that new Seniors League using retired players in Florida. And it has nothing to do with The Baseball League, which had plans to compete directly with Major League Baseball using current players. But these new leagues are evidence of an expanding market for baseball.

I talk like that now because I'm a businessman. Actually, what I do is invent things and try to sell them. It's a longshot business but it's fun, if you can handle failure. Fewer than two percent of new ideas ever make it. That's why I've got a garage full of ideas that have bombed.

Like the Baseball Brain. This was my idea for a cardboard slide calculator that allowed fans to match up the batter and the pitcher and predict what might happen during a game. I sold 20,000 in a month. Unfortunately, I had manufactured 100,000.

And then there was Rodney's Cube. This was a spoof of the Rubik's Cube that I got Rodney Dangerfield to endorse. It had only three moving parts. "It's so easy I can do it with my eyes open," said Rodney. Rodney's Cube was introduced just after the Rubik's Cube craze died out. It was a lesson in timing.

Fortunately, all you need is one success to keep you trying. Like Big League Chew. This is that shredded bubble gum in a pouch that Rob Nelson and I invented in the bullpen in Portland, Oregon. We licensed it to Amurol Products, a subsidiary of the Wrigley gum company.

The good news is that Big League Chew has had sales of $14 million a year for the past ten years. The bad news is that Rob and I had to file a lawsuit against the Wrigley Company in order the get the royalties we had coming to us.

The good news is that we won about $2 million in damages. The bad news is that it took five years and cost $400,000 in legal bills. And it's still not over yet because Wrigley is appealing the decision. Of course, we'll eventually get our money. "Of course," says Paula. "But not in our lifetime."

Meanwhile, all the people I owe money to—lawyers, banks, friends and family—are rooting very hard for the success of my other ventures, like Big League Cards.

I thought it would be fun to put people on their own baseball cards with their picture on the front and their personal story or stats on the back. So my brother Bob and I set up a company that combines short-run color printing and custom typesetting to make small quantities that people can afford.

We introduced Big League Cards with a full-page ad in a local newspaper showing sample cards with kids pictures on them. Kids wearing baseball and football uniforms. Kids in band uniforms and cheerleading outfits. Kids wearing jeans and bathing suits and school clothes. We covered all the bases.

At a price of $30 for a minimum fifty cards, we needed a hundred orders to break even. We got up a pool in the office to see how many orders we'd get. Highest guess was 650. I said we'd get over 400. Paula guessed only 250 so she wouldn't "jinx us." I had visions of kids on their own Big League Cards chewing Big League Chew.

Would you believe we only got fifty-three orders? And that wasn't the only surprise. Of the fifty-three orders, only twelve were from kids. The rest were from nineteen salespeople, five joggers, four newborn babies, three dentists, two guys and their cars, a motorcycle, a scoutmaster, a wedding picture, an engaged couple, two dogs, a pet monkey and some lady with a snake. I knew we were onto something, but I wasn't sure what.

My latest invention is something I call "Collect-A-Books." It popped into my mind when I was speaking with a publishing company about how to encourage kids to read. I know that kids read baseball cards. So I made a little book the size of a baseball card. "It's interesting," said the publisher, "but we don't make anything like that."

I took it to a dozen other publishers and they said the same thing. "We don't make anything like that." Of course, if they did make anything like that, it wouldn't be a new idea.

Then I showed "Collect-A-Books" to Larry Greenwald of Collectors Marketing Company. "I love it," he said. "Now let's figure out how we can make it." So, Collect-A-Books is coming on the market in 1990. Larry Greenwald should be the president of General Motors.

And if Collect-A-Books doesn't make it, there's Collect-A-Bats. These are ice cream sticks shaped like baseball bats, with major league players' autographs stamped on them. I licensed the idea to Good Humor. All you have to do is eat the right twenty-six Big League Ice Cream bars to collect the complete set.

A friend recently said, "Bouton, the secret of your success is that you have the mind of a nine-year-old." This may be true. A reporter once described my office as "a long table littered with boxes of caramel popcorn, scissors, T-shirts, Silly Putty, paintbrushes, glue, a moldy baseball and other flotsam. It's a third grader's conception of Edison's laboratory."

My best idea may be Table-To-Go, a combination plate, tray and table which allows someone to hold a complete meal and a beverage in one hand, leaving the other hand free to eat with. It's for cookouts and picnics or anywhere people want to be mobile with food. I finally got a patent for it after two years of trying.

I'm convinced that Table-To-Go will be a winner because it's already been turned down by all the major paper and plastic cookware manufacturers. Big companies are the last to know if an idea is any good or not. As an executive at International Paper candidly told me, "Jim, this may be a good idea but we're too big to know if it is or not."

While all the big companies are merging, acquiring and leveraging, I've licensed a small local outfit to market my invention. The Wecolite Company, run by a nice fellow named Ralph Stern, is introducing Table-To-Go in 1990. Still, it's always tempting to bring your idea to a big company first. As my friend Bob Bell at Licensing Corporation of America says, "A big dog takes a big shit."

When I'm not playing Gyro Gearloose (the Donald Duck character with the propeller hat), I give motivational talks to corporations. I tell them that people need to do what they love or find a way to love what they do. That if you focus on the process rather than the goal, you'll achieve the goal more often. Of course, I always mix in a few Joe Schultz stories to keep everybody laughing.

Sometimes Paula joins me if the business meeting is at a nice resort. Or I go along as the spouse when Paula gives one of her Communicational Judo seminars. And I'm learning to live with an independent woman. I always introduce her as Paula Kurman, not Mrs. Bouton. This did not, however, prevent Paula from introducing me once as her husband, "Jim Kurman." It was an accident but I get a lot of mileage out of it.

Yes, the Magic Lady and I are married now. It's lots of fun and we're always learning from each other. Paula has taken up jazz ballet dancing to be more of an athlete and I wheel and deal in the business world with Communicational Judo.

And we try to separate our business from our personal lives, but it's not easy. The other morning at breakfast I said to Paula that the strawberry jam seemed to be "a hot item" because we were "out of stock." She said she couldn't keep the pipeline filled and that the jam "was on back order."

Paula and I are enjoying having the house all to ourselves. The kids are all out on their own now. Lee, twenty-eight, is an attorney with Cravath, Swaine & Moore in New York. We need all the free legal advice we can get. Hollis, twenty-six, is working in the Paris office of McKinsey, the international consulting firm. She covers the European market for us.

Michael, twenty-six, is still very active in politics. He fought to lower car insurance with New Jersey Citizens Action and is now working to save the environment with Greenpeace. Mike is disproving the theory, popular in college, that you can't make a living as a philosophy major.

David, twenty-five, a Phi Beta Kappa from Rutgers, is in a management training program at First Fidelity Bank. And he's learning to speak Korean. We may join David in a trip to Korea to try and find his biological mother.

And Laurie, twenty-four, is back in college, working toward a degree after a couple of years in the business world. When I asked Laurie if she wanted to add any comments, she said, "Just say, 'Laurie Bouton, twenty-four, still as beautiful as ever.' " That's easy. I believe in telling the truth.

It's been quite a decade, with all the ups and downs of steering five kids through their teenage years. Marrying Paula, opening our own businesses and the Wrigley lawsuit.

My mom died of cancer five years ago. She was much too young. Dad remarried sometime later. And then this past summer he had cancer, too. They had to take one and a half kidneys out of him, but tough guy that he is, he was up and on his feet in a week. Now he's back in Florida getting ready to play in the over-seventy softball league. As brother Bob says, "He should be faster, now that he doesn't have to be lugging all those kidneys around."

So, I'm fifty years old but I don't feel any older, although I think I'm a little wiser. I have some wrinkles, but I've been squinting at batters in the sunshine for a lot of years. I've earned them. And when I look at my life I realize how lucky I am. I still have plans and dreams. And everyday is a new adventure.

About five years ago, just to get a little workout, I pitched some batting practice for a local semipro baseball team. One thing led to another and before I knew it I was pitching in a game the next weekend. Today I'm the ace pitcher for the Little Ferry Giants in the North Jersey Metropolitan League. When the knuckleball is working, I'm tough to hit. When it's not, Paula can't stand to watch.

No, I'm not nostalgic about playing in the major leagues. I have no interest in getting on the road again or reliving any part of that. It's just that every year in the spring I get this urge to play some ball in the sunshine. Just for fun. And, while my life is fun, I know it's not that way for most people. There is too much poverty, too much greed, and too much ignorance in the land. As one of the lucky ones, I'd like to help make things better. That's my dream these days.

Thirty Years Later . . . . .

BALL SEVEN

Laurie died on August 15, 1997.

And I'm not the same guy who wrote *Ball Four.* I'm not so cocky, not so sure of myself. I'm anxious about the future. I get nervous when the phone rings. I can't just will things to happen anymore. I worry about losing it. I'm not living a charmed life. I'm not the luckiest guy in the world.

But I was until that night.

It had been a very exciting summer. Paula and I were on top of the world, literally, in our mountain-top home in the Berkshires. Paula had just appeared in a Williamstown Theater production of *Dead End.* I'd just finished a brief stint with a troupe of *Athletes as Dancers* at Jacob's Pillow. Our life was rich with friends and activities. We were feeling good about ourselves, happy as can be.

We had met some friends for dinner and gone to an outdoor performance at Shakespeare & Company. It was a warm summer night with a full moon. It had been a lovely day. When we came home, we had just stepped inside the door, hadn't even taken the messages off the blinking machine, when the phone rang. Paula picked up and it was Lee.

"Oh, no," I heard her say. "Oh, my God! Oh, my God!"

A jolt of terror shot through my body. I had never heard Paula sound like that before. I just hoped it wasn't one of the kids.

"What is it?" I said, my heart hammering. "Who?"

"Laurie's been in a terrible accident," said Paula, who was shaking now and gasping for breath.

"How bad?" I moaned, terrified of the answer.

"Very bad," said Paula, still on the phone, trying to learn more.

"Is she dead?" I heard myself say, not believing I was saying it.

"No. . . but it's very bad . . . ."

I fell on my knees and vomited.

"No, no, no, no . . ." I wailed. "Not my Laurie . . . not my Laurie."

I pounded the floor in my helplessness. Laurie was in danger and there was nothing I could do to fix it. And she was so far away.

"We have to go to the hospital *right now* . . ." said Paula.

I couldn't think straight. How could we get to the hospital in Newark? That's four hours away. Neither one of us could possibly drive in this condition.

Now David was on the car phone with Paula. He and Lee and Lee's fiancee, Elaine Wood, were driving to the hospital from Manhattan and would be there in twenty minutes. Bobbie and her husband, Phil Goldberg, were already at the hospital. Michael and his then fiancee, Melanie Knapper, were being driven from Brooklyn by a friend, Tom Lanier. Hollis was in Europe and couldn't be reached.

"I have to take care of your dad," said Paula, hanging up the phone. "We'll get there somehow."

Somebody has to take charge when things are falling apart, and nobody's better at that than Paula. In minutes she was on the phone to the driver service that takes me to and from airports when I have to fly. It was now after eleven, but a driver showed up in twenty minutes. Just enough time for us to throw some things in a suitcase if we needed to stay over.

It was the longest ride of our lives. We held each other and cried and talked. David had said Laurie was in a coma and would probably never walk again. This was inconceivable for someone like Laurie, "The Unsinkable Molly Brown," girl daredevil. We knew they were doing everything possible to save her. Evidently, a helicopter had flown her to the hospital from the crash scene.

We called the hospital during a pit stop. The news was not any better. Just get there as quickly as possible. The accident had occurred about seven-thirty that night. We wouldn't be there until three in the morning. I didn't want her to go without me being there. If she was still alive, I'd want to hold her hand and try to comfort her. But I didn't want that to be my last memory of her either. We numbed ourselves against the possibilities. The full moon followed us all the way. It's only been recently that I can even look at a full moon.

University Hospital has about a dozen entrances. David had said we should go around to the back, but we didn't know where that was, and we didn't have time to drive all around. So close and yet so far. Then we saw Michael in the distance, waving at our black sedan. Probably waving at any black cars that came along.

The three of us hugged on the run, and Michael led the way through a series of hallways, walking fast, toward the Intensive Care Unit. Laurie was still alive, Michael said, but in a coma, hooked up to monitors. He and David and Bobbie had been taking turns holding her hand. Michael said he'd been singing songs to Laurie—nonsense songs with funny rhymes—that they'd sung together as children. He said the only reaction was a few blips on one of the machines, but he believed she could hear him. Michael had told her I was coming and would be there soon.

I pictured Laurie lying there. I wanted to see her, yet I couldn't stand the thought. I had a flash memory of her as a little girl in a wet bathing suit, returning from lunch to a fenced-in swimming pool, with halves of a peanut butter and jelly sandwich in each hand. Rather than walk around to the gate, which would have taken all of twenty seconds, she chose to climb the chain-link fence using no hands, just elbows, feet and knees, so as not to drop her sandwiches. That was funny enough, but the best part came when she was halfway over, teetering on the balance point, two elbows and a foot straddling the metal pipe, and suddenly discovered a sandwich-half directly in front of her face. Not one to waste an opportunity, Laurie took a bite and proceeded over the fence.

The double doors of the Intensive Care Unit were just ahead. Through the glass windows I could see the distraught faces of Lee and Elaine. Someone from the hospital pushed open the doors and we entered the main room.

"He's here!" I heard someone say.

The room was crowded with mixed-family members, and friends. The last time I'd seen this group together, ironically, was at Laurie's graduation from college. It was eerily silent except for the beeping of machines. Half the faces turned to us, the rest stayed riveted on a smaller room off to our right. But before I could even glance in that direction, I heard the words that ripped my heart out.

"She's gone."

It was Bobbie, face streaked with tears, emerging from the small room. The group of family and friends exploded in a deluge of cries and wails. I rushed over to hug Bobbie and hold her close. This was our little girl and only we could share that particular pain. Then Paula and Phil moved in quickly to hold us both, and the others followed suit, forming a huddle of devastated souls.

"She waited for you, Jim," everyone said. "She waited for you." And I believe she did. Her incredible spirit lived nearly eight hours in a body with no viable organs, according to the surgeons who later declined our offer to donate them. What's more, Laurie chose the precise moment—the very split second—that would make it easiest on me.

I never went in to see her. I relied on what others said later. That she looked beautiful without her make-up. That she looked peaceful.

I'm sure it's been difficult to read this, but I thought you should know. If you've come this far, thirty years' worth, you're practically family.

The only person who would enjoy reading this is Laurie. "You *best* be writing something *good* about me, Dad," I can hear her say, chin jutting from side to side, in that Jersey Girl way of speaking she shared with her friends. And her friends were legion, because she was loyal and caring and extraordinary fun to be around. At the funeral, half a dozen girls claimed "best friend" status with Laurie, who was godmother to several of their children. Laurie herself had no children, and she had never married, but it wasn't for lack of boyfriends, several of whom showed up at the funeral and eyed each other with interest.

Laurie would also want you to know that the accident wasn't her fault. She was the only innocent party, and the only fatality, in a multi-vehicle collision on a New Jersey highway. The police report said she braked to a complete stop, a few feet short of an accident that had just occurred over the crest of a hill, and was hit from behind by another driver who didn't even touch the brakes. "The Unsinkable Molly Brown" never had a chance.

She always liked that nickname. Her other favorite was "Laurie the Great." She liked the recognition that came with *Ball Four*. Even more than her brothers, Laurie loved the baseball life, the travel, adventures, hanging out with the players. And she had fun with the connection to her infamous father. She even enjoyed the fact that she looked like me. "You must be Jim Bouton's daughter," people would say. "That's right," she'd shoot back. "You want my autograph?" She was only half kidding.

Hundreds of people crowded the little funeral parlor. Some of them spoke, those who were able, about special times with Laurie and of her endearing quirks. She seemed to be everywhere in all of their lives. Where did she find the time? Now I understood about the parking tickets, which always got mailed to me because Laurie had never changed the registration on the car I gave her. The reason she couldn't take time to find a parking space, I explained, was that she was always in a hurry to make people happy. So many people, so little time. Everyone nodded in agreement.

But the one who captured Laurie best was her stepsister Hollis, who read a letter she had written on the plane from Amsterdam.

Dear Laurie,

I have decided to write you a letter, not only because it is still an impossibility for me to think of you in the past—but also because letter writing was always one of our favorite forms of communication. Your wonderfully rambling, stream-of-consciousness letters . . . were peppered with the same expressions ("Oh my God," "soooo," "messed up," etc.) as your conversation.

And it is your voice which surrounds me now. I have a sense of your fidgety, high-energy form near me, but it's mostly your voice. As if you too, are sitting with me in pain and disbelief . . . I could use some of your toughness now, your edge. It occurs to me that I may never have seen you cry, although I have seen you hurt. And I have seen you be heartbreakingly tender and kind.

Then there is the spontaneous Laurie. The one who climbs into a sand trench at the beach to be buried up to the neck. Maybe even just for the photo opportunity . . . The one who dons spike heels and a mini-skirt to attend an afternoon brunch down a cobblestone Amsterdam street . . . The one who energetically bumps into a police car . . . in a parking lot. And the one who volunteers to be by her grandfather's side when he most needs her. No questions asked. No juggling priorities. Just go.

Laurie, Laurie, it was not supposed to happen like this. You were supposed to be the one who always got away. You had so much left to do yet. There was so much we all wanted for you. And still do.

It sounds absurd, but I found myself looking for a gift to bring you from Amsterdam . . . A chance to hear you say, at least one more time, "Oh my God . . . it's just what I've always wanted." And to have you throw your arms around my *neck before trotting off to a mirror with your new prize. You bring the pleasures of gift-giving to new heights.*

My clearest, fondest memories are of vacations or visits where we shared a room and stayed up talking late into the night. You were a one-woman slumber party and I was so much looking forward to having you visit [Gert Jan and me] in our new home.

As you can tell from my own rambling letter, I'm afraid to stop writing, to end this exchange, this time with you. It's like not wanting to hang up the phone, to hear the cold click and the dial tone.

I wish I could have been there to hold your hand, or to sweep you away. I hope you didn't have time to be hurt or to be frightened. I'm flying all this way now to tell you that I will always love you . . . my beautiful, wild thing of a little sister, my bridesmaid and my confidante. Your fire burns so bright that it lights and warms us all. And nothing, not even the cruel freak injustice of the road, can ever extinguish it.

With very much love and an aching heart, your sister,
Hollis

Those early days were horrendous. I didn't know I could feel such pain—an aching, empty agony. And I couldn't escape it. Sleep was no help because waking only brought the awful news again, as if for the first time. An early-morning sucker punch to a defenseless heart; my God, that's right, it really *did* happen.

It was too big a blow. I couldn't absorb it. I had to take it in smaller pieces. Spend some time in denial. Force myself to look away, try to occupy my mind, throw myself into some project.

Like my stonework.

It was a hobby I had stumbled into about seven years ago, when Paula and I were still living in New Jersey. An old wooden fence in our yard had fallen down and I decided to replace it with a stone wall that

I'd build myself. I'd never built a stone wall before, but I always liked the way they looked. How hard could it be?

I searched the yellow pages, found a local stone yard, and went down to check it out. They had acres of stones, all different kinds, stacked on pallets held together with chicken wire. I liked what they called "mountain fieldstone" because it looked the most natural—irregular shapes and sizes with a nice mix of colors. I tagged three pallets with my name and walked into the office. "You ever build a stone wall before?" asked the guy behind the counter. I told him no. "Good luck," he said, as he ran my credit card through the machine.

I decided to build a freestanding, dry-laid (no cement) wall about four feet high, two feet wide, and sixty feet, six inches long because the distance felt familiar. A book I got from the library said dry-laid was harder to build because the stones had to fit snugly to keep it from falling down. On the other hand, it wouldn't crack when the ground heaved because it was flexible. I bought some work gloves and a mason's hammer to chip any stones that might not fit.

After a boom truck deposited the pallets in front our house, I unloaded the stones and spread them out on the lawn so I could see what I was working with. This took me half a day. "How long are those stones going to be out there?" asked Paula. "Just a few weeks, Babe," I said. "As soon as I'm finished with the wall."

I learned a lot about stones that first day. The next morning I bought a weight belt, steel-toed boots, goggles, and some aspirin.

It certainly was a challenge. The trick was choosing the right stone the first time so you didn't have to pick up a stone more than once. Or twice. Or six, or a dozen times, when it looked like the damn thing ought to fit somewhere, but never did. Some of the stones weighed more than a hundred pounds. And they didn't have handles. I soon wore large holes in my work gloves and had to buy more. Three pallets became fifteen. A few weeks turned into six months.

But to my surprise, I discovered it was tremendously satisfying. Big rocks sliding into place with the thud of a bank vault door. A giant jigsaw puzzle without a picture on the box. And I was the artist. The work was Zen-like. I'd fall into a trance, looking for a certain stone to fill a particular space, only to spot another stone for a different space I'd

474

been looking to fill earlier. After about a month, I could carry a dozen configurations in my head as I wandered my field of stones.

To give the wall a starting point, I began by building a large pillar, which looked pretty decent until I got going on the wall itself. Then as the wall proceeded, my skills improved and now the pillar didn't look as good as the wall. In fact, the wall looked fantastic and the pillar didn't seem to go with it anymore. Of course, I did the only thing I could do. I tore the pillar down. "What are you doing!?" Paula inquired from an upstairs window. "Don't worry, Babe," I said. "I'll have it rebuilt in a week."

Paula called a lot from the upstairs window that summer. Her favorite was "Do you know what *time* it is?" Not wearing a watch, I'd squint up at the sun if it wasn't raining. But before I could answer, she'd say, "It's three o'clock in the afternoon; you haven't even had lunch yet!" If it was raining, she'd say, "Do you know that it's raining?" If it was nine o'clock at night, she'd say, "It's too dark to work out there!" Paula is a master of the understatement.

I became a nut about it. Not content with just fitting the stones, I had to make designs. I'd stand flat stones on edge to make feathers if the preceding stone looked like a bird. I built Indian totems and other symbols into that wall. There's a fish in there somewhere if you know where to look. Of course, I don't see the wall that often, since we moved. I only drop by once in a while for a visit just to make sure it's still there. It always is.

Leaving my wall behind wasn't easy. I had seriously considered numbering each stone and reassembling the whole thing at the new home we were building in Massachusetts, but cooler heads prevailed. Instead, I elevated my game. Using cement this time, I built a stone veneer foundation, a stone front entrance, and a stone facing on the back of the house. That took four summers. I also built a stone retaining wall and matching pillars at the bottom of the driveway. I have to say it all looks pretty good. The stones fit so tightly you can't see the cement. As the building inspector, Dante Testa, said to me, "You should have been Italian."

It was during the time I was finishing the back of the house that Laurie died.

A few weeks after the funeral, I had placed a large stone in a small grove of trees behind our house, in memory of Laurie. This would be a place I could go to be with her, since her grave in New Jersey was so far away. I remember looking out the window at Laurie's stone, and noticing the debris of my uncompleted work near the house: all the stones spread around, the blue plastic tarp that covered the cement bags, my wheelbarrow, the tree loader I used to cart the bigger stones, the bucket of trowels, my hammers, the metal wall-ties, the sandpile, the scaffolding, and I wondered how I could ever clean up that mess in the state I was in.

It wasn't any better inside the house. The death of a child puts tremendous stress on a marriage. The frequency of divorce is well documented, but it's no help to even be aware of that because fear of the statistic simply adds to the woe. And in a mixed family like ours, it's even worse. I was the father and no suffering could match mine. But in many ways it was harder for Paula. She had to postpone her own grieving to take care of me. And as wonderful a mother as Paula always tried to be for Laurie, she was still just the stepmother. Well-meaning people would stop her on the street and ask, "How's Jim?" as if her pain didn't count.

The house was filled with jagged edges. We grieved at different times, in different ways, and it was hard to be together. When I was crying I wanted Paula to hold me; when I could push it down I wanted to be left alone. When Paula cried, I sometimes saw her as if she was at the end of a long tunnel. "Why can't you hold me when I'm crying?" she once asked. "I have nothing left to give," I said. My heart had ceased to function. We walked a tightrope of emotions, and the slightest breeze would topple us into the abyss, where nothing mattered anymore.

It was during this nowhere time that I decided that rather than clean up the mess outside, I would just finish the job. It was a tricky section that remained, with lots of windows to work around, lots of chipping and fitting. I roamed the yard, measuring the stones through my tears, and talked to Laurie. It was stone therapy, and Paula was glad to have the help. I think it saved us.

Life will never be the same without Laurie, but we do everything we can to keep her close. We have her pictures around and try to find opportunities to talk about her. She always makes an entrance in some hilarious anecdote whenever we have a party. We believe her spirit hovers near. We call on her at important times. "C'mon, Laurie help us out here," we sometimes ask. We give her partial credit for special achievements, and full credit for good weather. And just as the loss of Laurie brings me down, her memory lifts me up. Whenever I get depressed, I hear her voice. "Now, don't you be *sittin'* all day in that chair, Dad."

Back in 1994, when Mickey Mantle's son Billy died, I had sent Mickey a brief note saying how bad I felt for him. I said I had a nice memory of Billy, a polite little boy, running around the Yankee clubhouse during spring training. I also said I hoped Mickey was feeling better about *Ball Four*, that I had never intended to hurt him, and that I looked back on my Yankee years as a great time in my life.

I never expected to hear back from Mickey; I just wanted him to have the note. But about two weeks later I walked into my office and my secretary was standing by the answering machine with an enigmatic smile on her face. She said there was a message I should play for myself. I punched the button.

"Jim, this is Mickey," said that familiar Oklahoma voice. "I just got your letter about . . . you know, saying you're sorry about Billy, and I appreciate it. And I never was really hurt by your book, I think that's been exaggerated a lot . . . and I sure in the hell never did tell the Yankees that if you came to an Old Timers' game, or something, I wasn't going to come; I heard that was out. Anyway, thanks for the letter, and everything's fine with me. Thanks a lot, Bud."

Of course, I saved the tape. I'll leave it for my grandchildren.

It was only after Laurie died that I fully understood why Mickey had called. It was because of the condolence note I had sent about Billy. When Laurie died, I remember how close I felt to anyone who called, or dropped a note, or stopped me on the street to express their sympathy. Especially if they had a particular memory of Laurie, a brief encounter, a story we hadn't heard that would add something to our experience of her, and make her come alive again, if only for a moment. I was deeply grateful for any kind word or gesture.

The death of a child changes you in profound ways. It suddenly moves you to a new level of tolerance and empathy. I take nothing for granted today. I'm no longer so quick to judge a sour face, an angry tone of voice, a slumped demeanor. Who knows what that person's story might be? Maybe it's worse than mine. They say it can make you a better person, but I don't know about that. I only know if I could just have Laurie back, I'd happily return to my former, rotten self.

In 1995, Mickey Mantle himself passed away. Nobody had been surprised to learn it was liver cancer. The surprise was that he lived as long as he did. His famous line, "If I knew I was going to live this long, I would have taken better care of myself," took on added poignancy. His sense of humor was there to the end, but it was his message to kids that lifted The Mick to new heights. "I'm not a role model," he cautioned at a press conference. "Don't do what I did." Then Mickey endorsed the organ donor movement, thereby saving uncounted future lives thanks to the body parts that would be donated by his many fans. Talk about giving something back.

As I watched Mickey shrivel away, twenty-six years after *Ball Four* talked about his drinking, I couldn't help wondering this: If the baseball people who had called the book lies had instead tried to help Mickey, might he still be alive?

Mickey joins Roger Maris, Elston Howard, Steve Hamilton and Dale Long among my Yankee teammates who have passed away. I don't know if it's just me or the fact that I'm getting older, but as time goes by I feel closer to them now than I did back then. My perspective has changed.

I was actually ambivalent in 1998 when Mark McGuire and Sammy Sosa were dueling to break Roger Maris' home run record—his sixty-one homers in '61 had broken Babe Ruth's record. It was not the angry Roger of *Ball Four* that I was pulling for, but the small-town kid from Fargo, North Dakota who had signed out of high school, and never had help dealing with the big city media.

Today I see Elston Howard, not as the less-than-militant fellow portrayed in the book, but as a black man who survived growing up in the '40s and worked his way to the top of what was once a white man's game. I think of Elston behind the plate in his catcher's gear, hunching his big body forward and squatting low to give me a target at the knees. He's a teammate to me now, not a token.

So much has changed. I marvel now at our lack of sophistication back then, how naive we were, how unprepared we were for life in the big leagues. Except for the occasional college guy, invariably nicknamed "The Professor," or in the case of Mike Marshall, "Brains," most players had only high school educations, if that. We were raw, rough, unfinished. Sometimes it could be a problem, but mostly it was fun. When you had a teammate from Alabama or Brooklyn, for example, you got *Alabama*—and *Brooklyn*.

With college baseball replacing the lower minor leagues as a training ground, today's players are more homogenized, more polished. The common experience of having attended college with the mere exposure to education, if not actual learning, has rounded off the corners, blurred regional differences. Players are more savvy about how the world works. They understand that they're more than just athletes—they're entertainers, spokesmen, profit centers. The more successful ones are small industries unto themselves with lawyers, and agents, and accountants.

People are always asking me about baseball today, starting with the money. "Isn't it outrageous," they say, "how much money these players are making?" I tell them the money we made was outrageous; that players are finally getting their share of the revenue, most of which comes from television.

"They're making so much money they don't care anymore," say people who have no clue what it takes to get to the big leagues. The most competitive players in the world—the only ones who make it—are not likely to change their natures because of money. Nobody accuses millionaire businessmen of slacking off.

What people don't understand is that sports is a zero-sum game. A player only does well at another player's expense. No matter how hard they try and no matter how much you pay them, at any given time one-third of the players will be having a good year, one-third will be having an average year, and one-third will be having a bad year. It's like putting

800 Nobel-Prize-winning nuclear physicists in a science class and grading them on a curve.

Then people whine about ticket prices, saying they can't afford to bring their families to the games anymore. I mention that attendance is up, that entire families have replaced what used to be mostly fathers and sons, and that salaries have no effect on ticket prices, which are based solely on what customers are willing to pay.

Next thing out of their mouths is that some team is going to go bankrupt, in spite of the fact that the only team to *ever* go bankrupt in the modern history of the game was the Seattle Pilots, believe it or not, giving them yet one more distinction. And even there, nobody lost money. The franchise was purchased for $5.3 million and sold a year later for $10.8 million. That's a $5.5 million difference, less debt service and expenses which couldn't have been that much, considering what the Pilots saved on salaries, baseballs, and hot water in the clubhouse. The City of Seattle even got another franchise in the bargain.

People say it's hard to have a rooting interest today because players change teams all the time. But players moved around more in the old days. The Seattle Pilots used *fifty-three* players in a single season! Cleveland general manager Frank "Trader" Lane wasn't happy if he hadn't traded three guys before breakfast. The Yankees practically used Kansas City as a farm team. The difference is that back then trades were announced as something good. "We just traded four bums for five phenoms who are gonna help us win the pennant," the GM would say. Today he says, "We can't pay what this guy's asking, so we have to trade him."

The truth is, most players don't want to change teams. They want to settle into a community, put their kids in school, make business contacts. It's the owners who insist on keeping players on a short leash, with two- and three-year deals, and then cry foul when the players shop themselves around.

The latest gripe is that small-market teams don't have a chance. But when did small-market teams *ever* have a chance? In the '40s and '50s, baseball's so-called "golden age," most World Series involved one or two of the three New York teams. While the Yankees were winning twenty-nine pennants in forty-four years, some teams never got out of last place! The truth is, since free agency, more teams have won championships than ever before in the history of baseball.

But people don't want to hear the truth. They prefer their steadfast beliefs, acquired over time and developed into a mantra: "The players are overpaid, teams are losing money, and the game is about to go bankrupt." Where do they get this nonsense? It starts with the owners who are not above trashing their own players every time a union contract comes up for renewal. This is strange marketing. Can you imagine General Motors announcing that its cars are not worth the price?

The owners are encouraged in this effort by the media, which back them up with an unending stream of anti-player rhetoric. It's the theme of every sports talk show in the country, the favorite rant of reporters and so-called journalists, most of whom are employed by companies in partnership with the leagues. Little thought is given to the notion of athletes as entertainers, that owners didn't get rich in their other businesses by overpaying their employees, and that unlike failed businessmen, players don't get stock options when they get released.

Of course, the players don't help themselves very much. Instead of simply saying, "We're entitled to bargain for our services in a free market like any other citizen," a few can always be counted on for gems like, "We're just trying to put food on the table." This is usually uttered by a guy wearing gold chains, climbing out of a limo. Of course, this drives the radio guys nuts, and before long, Larry from Brooklyn is calling to say that, "conducive to what that last caller just said, I would like to remunerate that the owners should just, like, draw a line in the sand, or whatever, and show who's boss by locking up the stadiums and let those prima donnas rot."

The whole exercise is so one-sided that an owner *lockout* is commonly referred to as a player *strike*. Which may explain why a nation of fans is angry at the players. At stadiums today there's an underlying level of hostility that can be quite scary. It's a love-hate relationship with very little patience; booing often starts in the first inning! Fans are not there to enjoy a ball game so much as watch surrogate achievers attempt to provide something that's missing in their own lives.

This is not how it was in the *old*, old days. When I was a kid my brothers and I would go to the Polo Grounds in New York and root for the Giants no matter how badly they played. Willie Mays, Whitey Lockman, Monte Irvin, and my man Sal Maglie; we loved those guys. When they lost we wanted to run down on the field and tell them not to feel bad, that we were still behind them.

So, what's fair between the owners and the players? Ask yourself how things would be if Major League Baseball (or the NFL or NBA) faced competition from another league. There'd be no player draft, no six-year-service requirement, no tax on team spending, and no salary caps. And professional sports would survive—because as long as there are people who like to play and others who like to watch, businessmen will figure out how to make money from that combination. And if not these guys, then the ones waiting in the wings to buy the next available franchise at any price.

Incidentally, if you ever wonder what life would be like without the antitrust laws, these never-ending sports labor wars give you some idea. Meanwhile, the owners and players will blame each other, and the only thing for sure is that no matter what happens, the beauty and the magic of the game will bail them out.

How good are today's players? The truth is, they're better than we were. They're bigger, stronger, and faster. They train with weights and work out year round. We were told not to lift weights because it would make us muscle-bound. We spent our off-seasons trying to earn money to support our baseball habit. On the first day of spring training, today's players look like greyhounds. We went down there to lose weight. Yes, we were better at the little things. We could bunt, hit-and-run, move the runners, hit the cutoff man. But if we played against today's players we'd score three or four runs doing the little things and lose 14-3.

I know I'm going to hear it from the old guys, but I always remember what Johnny Sain used to say on Old Timers' Day when players from the '40s and '50s would tell us how much better *they* were. "The older they get," John would say of his contemporaries, "the better they were when they were younger."

This is not to say that guys forty years ago wouldn't be as good as today's players if we had had the same advantages of diet, training and coaching, etc. It's more a commentary on the general level of play. I'm saying if we walked off a field in the '60s onto a field in 2000, we wouldn't be as successful. Players like Koufax and Mantle would be good, but not great. Our good players would just be average. I'd probably spend two years in the big leagues instead of eight. And some guys, like Whitey Ford, wouldn't even get a chance to play in the first place, on size alone. They're no longer signing 5' 9" pitchers from high schools in the Bronx.

This doesn't diminish Whitey's greatness, or the achievements of any former athletes, for that matter. You can only be great in your time. And greatness in any era is worthy of respect.

While the quality of play has improved, it doesn't mean the game itself is any better. The designated-hitter rule, for example, is awful. It adds offense to a game that doesn't need it, at the expense of that wonderful moment when a manager had to choose whether to leave a good pitcher in a low-scoring game, or take him out for a pinch hitter. And I don't like the shorter fences and all those home runs, not because I'm a pitcher but because it subordinates strategy. What's the value of a bunt or a stolen base in a 14-12 game? Baseball has become a cheaper game, designed for unknowing fans accustomed to gross action over subtle beauty.

It's part of a general dumbing down of society, reflected in shock-jock radio, Jerry-Springer TV, and professional wrestling, which has become the new model for player behavior. Hype and bravado have supplanted truth and humility. Baseball has a cartoonish feel. A batter hits a long drive, pauses at home plate to admire the blast, flips his bat in the air with the flourish of a baton twirler that must be practiced in front of a mirror, and pirouettes around the bases with his arms in the air like he's just discovered a new route to the Far East. And that's on a foul ball!

After a home run today, a player has to point somewhere, to his heart, to the sky, to his agent in the third row. Then there's a curtain call in front of the dugout, insisted upon by delirious fans who don't seem to understand that the game is not over yet. In my day, a player would hit the ball, toss his bat aside, jog around the bases, tip his cap, and sit down. A homer was just a homer—not a religious experience.

World Series celebrations consisted of players slapping each other's backs as they ran off the field. The only perfect game in World Series history rated a mere bear hug between the pitcher and the catcher near home plate. Today's celebrations are staged events in the middle of the field, with the obligatory player pile. Athletes in all sports are now looking to make a statement—ride a police horse around the field, strip off some clothes—with the highlight reel and the magazine cover in mind.

Even umpires are getting into the act with their confrontational demeanor. It's not enough to call a hitter out on strikes today, they have to get in his face and dare him to complain. Or they'll take off their masks and follow a guy back to the dugout, as if hoping for one more word to get him tossed. Years ago the umpires would go out of their way to avoid confrontation. Some of the funniest scenes had umpires constantly turning their backs and walking away, while heated players or managers ran in circles to try and stay in front of them.

The aura of spectacle, along with the booing, lends a Roman Coliseum-like feeling to ballparks today. It's no surprise that the next escalation is the players themselves charging into the stands, as happened recently when some Los Angeles Dodgers waded into the field boxes at Wrigley Field. And why? Well, because a fan had grabbed one of their baseball hats. A *hat*? These guys could buy entire hat companies! At least it's nice to see that they're not any *smarter* than we were.

And what's the deal with all that noise at the stadiums today? As soon as you walk in, you're blasted with music and advertising spots and silly scoreboard games. And this goes on before, during, and after the games; it's relentless. You can't hear yourself think. You can't even talk to the person sitting next to you in a normal tone of voice. The quiet observation, "I think he's going to bunt here," loses something when screamed, "I THINK HE'S GOING TO BUNT HERE!"

When I was a kid, walking into the Polo Grounds during batting practice was like walking into a church. A vast, strangely quiet place where you could hear the crack of a bat on a ball from the far reaches of the upper deck, like mumbled Latin echoing off vaulted ceilings. There was nothing else quite like it, and that was part of the magic. I'm sure today's marketing geniuses have decided they're just giving fans what they want, but I think it's a mistake. Blurring the distinction between a real sport and a phony extravaganza can't be good for the sport in the long run.

At least the players are better cared for today. Pitching, for example, is now a team effort with a bullpen full of specialists with titles like "middle reliever" and "setup man" and "closer." We had a "short man" to pitch the last inning or two, if necessary, and everybody else was a "long man," in case the game got out of reach. Whoever was injured, struggling, or on the shit-list was a "long man." Today they count pitches and rarely let the starter throw more than ninety. We routinely threw a hundred and twenty, or more. We pitched until we dropped. And we did it on three days' rest, not four or five like today.

It wasn't that we were stronger, or the managers more abusive. We simply didn't know any better. There was no throttle on our competitive juices. In '63 I *wanted* to pitch 249 innings; in '64 I *wanted* to start 37 games. I hated to come out, even when I was exhausted. I was the Bulldog; give me the ball. In '65, when my biceps felt like a toothache, I kept pitching. It wasn't an elbow or a shoulder so it couldn't be too serious. Keep pitching, it'll get better. What did we know?

I lost fifteen games that season, but more important, in favoring my arm because of the pain I lost my pitching motion. This was a serious problem. Trying to find a pitching motion, or a batting swing, was like trying to find the lost chord. I didn't know what my motion looked like because *I had never seen myself pitch*. The only film I ever saw—this was before video tape in the '70s—was World Series highlights, which looked like they were shot from a helicopter.

Today a dozen cameras are shooting the games. A hitter strikes out in the first inning, runs up to the clubhouse, watches his swing from three different angles, and corrects the flaw in his next time at bat. We just sat there in the dugout and tried to remember.

And the reason outfielders are making those circus catches halfway up into the stands is that the walls are padded. Players are bouncing off foam rubber. We bounced off cement, bricks, and chain-link fences. Any improvements resulted from sad experience. Mickey Mantle got his spikes caught in the grid of an outfield drain and twisted his knee. That got somebody thinking that it might be a good idea to put rubber covers on the drains.

In *Ball Four* I joked that a team shrink would be more helpful than a team trainer. Whenever we had personal problems we just had to tough it out. Players were told their dying fathers would have wanted them to be at the ballpark. Darrel Brandon lost a starting opportunity with the Pilots when he took a day off because his wife had a miscarriage. Today they often fly players to be with ailing relatives. Teams have psychologists, translators, counselors, and advisors.

Players are treated better today because there's a lot more money invested in them. Other comforts include personal trainers, chartered planes, suites on the road, and no doubleheaders. Players today are like thoroughbred horses.

We were farm animals.

"But we had more fun," said Gary Bell. My fellow beast of burden was on the phone from his home in San Antonio. "We'd go out after the games, five or six guys. Hell, they don't even have roommates anymore."

"You probably could have won twenty games with the Pilots if you didn't have to room with me," I said.

"But then I wouldn't have learned about Mars and Pluto and shit," said Gary.

We laughed. And then we talked about the money in baseball. I asked Gary if he resented what the players are getting today.

"I resent *me* not getting it," he said. "You know, nobody says anything about movie stars getting money. That was then and this is now. I *would* like to see them be a little more humble about things. I'd be pogo-ing around, saying hello to people. Let me get in the stands and sign autographs."

"What do you think of today's players?" I asked.

"Good guys and horses' asses," said Gary. "Just like when we played."

The last time I saw Gary was about five years ago near a sporting goods show he was attending. We threaten to get together more often but we can never coordinate our schedules.

"Hell, I'm doing more shit now than I did when I was playing," said Gary. "With these charity golf tournaments and fantasy camps. I enjoy getting with the guys, dick around, laugh, have a good time. See all the fuckheads again. I was at a fantasy camp with Pepitone a few months ago. Remember that game in New York when we almost had that fight with you guys? Stan Williams had thrown at a couple of our players and Birdie Tebbets told me to drill Pepitone, so I nailed him in the ribs. I hadn't seen him in thirty-five years and the first thing he says to me, in that mafia voice is, 'All my boys in Brooklyn are still looking for you.'"

I asked Gary if he ever decked any doctors or lawyers at the fantasy camps.

"Not with my weak shit," he said. "The last time I pitched was about fifteen years ago in an exhibition game when I threw one of the longest home runs I've ever seen. Some asshole got out of a milk truck, in bib overalls, and hit one over the trees. So Luis Tiant comes walking out to the mound with a bent coat hanger, to give me the hook. I said, 'Get me out of here.'"

I asked Gary about his health and he told me all about his quin-tuple bypass.

"I was sitting on a plane to Las Vegas to appear at a card show with Duke Sims, which is dangerous enough in itself. It was ten minutes before they closed the door and I started to feel nauseous, and I was sweating profusely, so I got off the plane. The stewardess said, 'Where are you going?' I said, 'I'm history,' and I walked down the ramp, got into my car, drove to my office, and called Rhonda. I told her to meet me at the hospital, I was having a heart attack. She said, 'Stay right where you are, I'm sending an ambulance.' I had had an angioplasty about four years ago and she didn't want me to move."

"That probably saved your life," I said.

"The problem was, my cholesterol levels were up, due to a faulty liver. For six months I ate nothing but lettuce and cardboard and my cholesterol was still 246. Tests showed my liver wasn't doing the job. Gee, I don't understand it, because I always took such good care of myself."

We both laughed.

"So this is my second one, Roomie," said Gary. "I'm good for one more, then that's it. I got a zipper from my ankle to my groin where they took an artery, and I got one leg left."

I told Gary that Duke Sims was one of the players in that Masters Baseball game I organized about fifteen years ago with Andy Messersmith.

"Duke was probably happy I couldn't make the card show," said Gary, "so he could collect both fees."

We talked about the phenomenon of fantasy baseball camps, how it gave fans a chance to hang out with players they once idolized, in exchange for giving players a chance to hang out with each other. Seemed like a fair trade.

"These are the last of the golf outings and fantasy camps," said Gary. "You know the current guys aren't going to do shit. They don't have the camaraderie, and they don't need the money."

Maybe it was the notion of camaraderie, or the sense of time passing, but we got to talking about the Seattle Pilots, as we always do.

"Ten times a year," said Gary, "I think about the time you told Joe Schultz you had the feel of your knuckleball and he grabbed his crotch and said, 'Oh yeah? Well, feel this.' I fell back in my locker, I was laughing so hard. I couldn't stand it." We talked about the deaths of Joe Schultz, Gene Brabender and Ray Oyler, but we didn't want to dwell on the subject for very long.

"You know, I still expect to see Oyler walk through the door," said Gary, "and Brabender shootin' a goddamn missile over his head with a blowgun."

We laughed again about all the characters we played with.

"One of these days I'm gonna write a book like that," said Gary, "but I gotta wait till everybody in my family dies."

Then we promised each other that we'd try to get together sometime soon.

"Okay, Rooms," he said. "See you on down the road somewhere."

Down the road is where I found Steve Hovley.

It was about a two-and-a-half hour drive from Long Beach, California, where I had given a motivational talk, to Steve's home in Ojai. I had been looking forward to seeing him for a long time—thirty years to be exact. The last time I'd been with Steve was on that morning in our hotel room in Baltimore when Joe Schultz called with the news that I'd been traded to the Houston Astros.

"Ah, the dreams, the dreams," Steve had said when I woke him up.

When I'd told him that I had to fly to St. Louis that afternoon to meet the Astros, he had said, "You can't go to St. Louis today. You're supposed to go to the Museum of Art this afternoon. You promised."

So I was really looking forward to this visit. Steve and I had kept in touch by phone over the years, and his wife, Lynn, was good about sending cards, but I was anxious to see him in person. Would we have that same connection, as fellow outsiders, that I'd always felt?

Steve said on the phone that he wasn't sure when he'd be getting home from a big plumbing job he'd been working on, but that if he wasn't there I should just go into the house and have a beer and make myself comfortable. He said that Lynn was out of town visiting their grandchildren, but the house wouldn't be locked.

The drive up from Long Beach was magical; all alone in a rented car, tooling north on Ventura Highway, with *America's* tune of the same name playing in my mind, past the citrus and avocado ranches, on into the beautiful Ojai Valley, framed by the Topa Topa Mountains of the Los Padres National Forest. It felt like I was traveling in a novel.

About four o'clock in the afternoon, I pulled into a driveway next to a cozy house on a shady street, on the outskirts of town. I knocked on the door and nobody answered, so I decided to wait in the car and read a newspaper. Twenty minutes later a truck pulled up and a stocky guy with a short beard climbed out. Could that be him? I wondered. The guy was wearing a green T-shirt, work pants, and a nondescript baseball cap. Then I recognized the grin.

"I guess you didn't have any trouble finding the place," said Steve, in that laconic way he has.

We greeted each other with a hug and a handshake combination.

"As soon as I get cleaned up, we can have some Mexican food," he said. "I bought some strip steaks and avocados. I'll grill the steaks and you can make the guacamole."

Steve dumped some charcoal briquettes onto a grill and blasted them with a blowtorch while I chopped garlic and onions for the guacamole.

"So what do you think about baseball these days?" I asked.

"I don't follow it, or anything," said Steve. "I don't enjoy watching it that much. It's a little slow. I like to watch basketball."

"Do the people you work with know that you used to be a major league ballplayer?" I asked.

"It comes up less in conversation than it used to," he said. "It depends on the job. Sometimes I'm able to slide and sometimes I'm not. They ask a few questions and that's the end of that."

"Why do you try to hide from your baseball past?" I asked.

"Because then they want to know why you're not a millionaire. They don't realize how little we got paid."

"What about the money in baseball today?" I asked. "You think it's turned the fans against the players?"

"I haven't been consciously monitoring the thing," said Steve, "but my feeling is it's the same as it always was. I remember people expressing the attitude that the players make too much money, back when we weren't making anything."

Before long, we had polished off the steaks and the guacamole. I don't recall whether we pounded Bud or something else. Then we went for a drive around the area, through some orange groves, and past the Catholic school that Steve went to as a kid. And we talked about religion, among other things.

"Religion is like baseball," said Steve. "Great game, bad owners."

That sounded about right. But what I mostly wanted to talk about was the Seattle Pilots. For example, did he remember the day I was traded and we couldn't go to the museum in Baltimore?

"I remember you were traded," said Steve.

What about the time he stole my pants and I had to walk into the locker room in my bathing suit? Or the "pitcher's fund" money he had planned to steal?

"It's funny how you remember those things," he said.

Didn't he ever think about the Pilots?

"No."

"No?" I said in disbelief. "Don't people ever ask you about them? Or *Ball Four?*"

"I hate to say it," said Steve. "But I think people have forgotten about it."

This was a little hard to accept from one of the main characters in the book, not to mention one of my favorite people. Was Steve living in a bubble—or on some higher plane? Or was I living in a self-involved world of my own making? The possibility was too frightening to consider.

"You know, there's a Seattle Pilots Web site," I said. "Fans get together and talk about the Pilots, exchange memories, leave messages."

"That's kind of like the American Brotherhood of Bobs," said Steve. "They have conventions every year in Cleveland or Waukegan. They figure if your name is Bob, you need someone else to commiserate with."

This will come as harsh news for Pilots junkies.

"Have you ever been on the Internet?" I asked.

"A guy was showing me how amazing it was," said Steve, "so he punches in my name and one of the references said, 'See John Donaldson and Steve Barber.'"

"Why those guys?" I asked.

"I don't know," said Steve. "I guess because they were on the team."

Linked in perpetuity to John Donaldson and Steve Barber. There may be more bizarre things in life, but I can't think of any offhand.

People ask if I keep in touch with old teammates. Very sporadically, I say. Phone calls once in a while. A card or a note. Mostly we bump into each other at sports dinners or golf outings. Occasionally, my old Yankee roommate, Phil Linz, and I will team up for a baseball clinic. Phil gives batting tips to the kids. I tell him he should teach them how to play the harmonica.

I exchange e-mail with my other Yankee roommate, Fritz Peterson. Fritz says he still likes to speed along a freeway playing Spanish music as loud as the radio will go, just as we did on those road trips long ago.

Every once in a while I run into Tommy Davis, another member of the lost tribe. He flies into New York for the Baseball Assistance Team dinner—they raise money for older players in financial need. Tommy is one of Paula's favorite players, even though she knows he doesn't remember her name. She just likes the way he says, "Hey, Baby," when he sees her.

Not long ago I was giving a talk in Chicago and I drove out to nearby Oak Brook to have lunch with Johnny Sain and his wife, Mary Ann. The great pitching coach is still tall and handsome, and very distinguished now, with a mane of white hair and that touch of Arkansas in his voice. And he still works out everyday. "If you don't watch," says John, "as you get older you find yourself saying you can't do this or that, but that's bullshit." I asked John how old he was. "I don't know," he said. "I'll have to think about it."

I finally retired from amateur baseball in the spring of 1997.

Over the years, I had played in a variety of leagues near where I lived. When we moved up to Massachusetts, I switched from the Met League in New Jersey to the Twilight League in Albany, an hour's drive from our new home. These are both very good leagues, made up primarily of college kids and returning minor leaguers. The average age is about twenty-eight, with a few old-timers in their forties. I was the Ancient Mariner—or Pilot—in my fifties.

The kids were nice to me once they saw I was serious. They remembered me from their baseball card collections, or from *Ball Four*. "Are you going to write a book about the Twilight League?" they'd ask. "We got some good stories for you." I told them not to worry, I was only there to pitch.

And I meant it. I didn't want note taking to distract from the experience. Even though these were amateur games, these guys wanted to win. And so did I. It's the reason I could never play in those over-forty leagues where the competition is a little more casual. Those are terrible leagues for a pitcher because the players are too old to do anything but swing a bat. They can't run, throw, or field, which negatively impacts the defense, to put it mildly, and anything hit to the outfield is extra bases. As I said, I never did like 14–12 games.

At first my teammates treated me as a novelty. They'd ask what it was like to play ball with The Mick, and get me to sign stuff for their little brothers. After they got to know me they'd make old-age jokes, or use me to rag on other players. "*Look* at this guy," they'd say to some out-of-shape twenty-year-old. "You should be ashamed of yourself with that body of *yours*."

Of course there were the occasional humiliations. Like the time I was resting on a table in the locker room before a game and heard a visiting-team player who had just arrived ask where I was. "He's taking a nap," said one of my teammates. Not the kind of thing that strikes fear in your opponent. Then there was the occasional home run ball I'd have to autograph after the game. I'd sign it, "To Jason, nice home run*, Jim Bouton." Then underneath that I'd write, "*aluminum bat," to put things in perspective.

The Twilight League games were played at Bleeker Stadium, a concrete-and-wood WPA relic from the 1940s. I pitched for the Heflin Builders, which morphed into Mama's Pizza when the sponsor changed. Occasionally scouts would come to the games with their notebooks and stopwatches. I knew they weren't looking at the old righthander, but I sometimes fantasized about what might happen if I really got my knuckleball going. I wasn't the best pitcher in the league but I wasn't bad either, armed with the knuckler and a few games under my belt.

To keep in shape I'd throw an orange rubber baseball against the wall down in our basement, which is pretty big. I marked off sixty feet, six inches, and drew a box on the cement for a strike zone. Then I set up a series of baffles with leftover plywood so the ball would bounce straight back to me without veering off into the furnace or the stairs. For twenty minutes a day I'd be down there throwing against the wall, imagining a hitter with a bat in his hands. That was the challenge: trying to find a little bit of the magic that had worked so well in my prime.

I'd come upstairs soaking wet, ready for the shower.

"Had a good one today," I'd say to Paula, who had to listen to all those thumps against the wall. "I think my motion's coming back!"

"Really?" she'd ask affectionately. "How terrific *were* you this morning, sweetheart?" Then she'd kiss the tip of my sweaty nose. Just wait until I win a few games, I would think to myself, and I get invited to pitch for a local professional minor league team.

Paula actually came to about half the games. And not just to make sure I didn't fall asleep on the drive home. She liked sitting in the stands and listening to the comments of people who didn't know who she was.

"How old *is* he?" someone would ask.

"Pretty old," some old guy would say. "I saw him pitch when I was a kid."

If I pitched well, people would say, "How does he *do* it?" If I pitched poorly, the same people would say, "He should quit and give the younger players a chance. What's he trying to prove?"

What *was* I trying to prove? I'm not sure exactly. Maybe I was trying to stay young, ward off my own mortality, or just feel connected to my past. All I knew for sure was that it was fun, and that it seemed worth doing for that alone. Every once in a while someone would mention the last line in *Ball Four*.

In any case, I was looking forward to the 1997 season. After having pitched Mama's Pizza into the playoffs the year before, I had ended on a disastrous note by blowing an eight-run lead in a regional tournament. That was something I couldn't ever remember having done before in my life, pro or amateur. I couldn't wait until the next year to prove it was just a fluke.

I was in excellent shape after building a stone facade on the back of the house the previous fall and working out all winter. Just to make things interesting, and get some extra innings, I decided to pitch for *two* teams—Mama's and the Saugerties Dutchmen, a well-known independent team from the Hudson Valley. It mattered little that when the Dutchmen's skipper, twenty-seven-year-old Kiko Romaguera, was told I'd be trying out, he had said, "I never heard of him." The doubts I had lived with that winter would be banished in the spring.

And I would do it in Cooperstown, New York.

It was early May. The Dutchmen were playing the Otsego Macs at legendary Doubleday Field, just behind the Baseball Hall of Fame. The very same field I had played on with the Yankees back in 1965 when we beat the Philadelphia Phillies 7-4 in the annual Hall of Fame exhibition game.

It's about a three-hour drive from our home, across the Hudson River, and through the Catskill Mountains to Cooperstown. Paula and I had left at nine in the morning for a mid-afternoon game, which was scheduled to begin as soon as the twelve o'clock game ended. Doubleday Field was rented out like a catering hall. We arrived in plenty of time for me to relax and take a nap.

This was my kind of game. It was springtime; I had always done well in the spring. It was a beautiful stadium. The sun was shining. The crowd was buzzing. I was as ready as I could possibly be.

And I never got past the second inning.

I don't even remember exactly what happened anymore. The first inning was a fiasco, and it went downhill from there. It began with some walks and a few wild pitches, degenerated into a series of line drives and cannon shots, and culminated in an assortment of mammoth blasts. A late arriver might have thought he'd stumbled into the fireworks display.

This is where the old credentials can really hurt you. Out of respect, Kiko was reluctant to come out to the mound and remove me from the game. I never had a chance to use Fred Talbot's great line, "What kept you?"

It wasn't just a case of not finding my rhythm. The knuckler was moving, it just wasn't moving sharply enough. It was like a balloon up there, floating instead of jumping. There was no pop, no bite. In spite of all those workouts I just didn't have the arm strength anymore. I had reached a new, and lower, plateau in my life. I wasn't simply getting older. I was getting old.

When you're twenty-seven, a bad outing is just a bad outing; chalk it up to a lack of preparation, inexperience, or just give credit to the other team. When you're *fifty*-seven, however, a bad outing becomes an embarrassment. "Get him out of there. Put him out of his misery." It's funny how, with a few swings of the bat by guys named Justin or Tyler, you can be transformed from a guy who just loves to play into a self-deluded old man.

If I could pitch so badly in *my kind of game,* what hope was there for the regular games? In all my years playing amateur ball, this was only the second time that I felt I was spoiling the game for my teammates. The first was that tournament game I had blown to end the previous season. It was a terrible feeling. And I didn't want to feel it again. So at age fifty-seven, I retired for good. I should have quit at my uniform number—fifty-six.

That's fifty years of baseball since I started playing as a kid in Rochelle Park, New Jersey. Half a century!

Nothing ever stopped me from playing ball.

Until I stopped myself.

It was a long ride home, where we had one of those milestone conversations. Paula talked about the significance of my decision; she understood that this was not a small thing for me. I focused on the lighter aspects; no more wicked come-backers in dimly lit ballparks. No more wondering what rain might be doing to a pitcher's mound somewhere.

And I seemed to be okay about it.

Until two weeks later, when I went down to the basement to get something, and I spotted my baseball glove sitting on a stool, with the orange rubber ball in the pocket, like they were waiting for me to play with them again. Suddenly, Puff the Magic Dragon popped into my head and I could feel the tears starting to come. So I went to find Paula because I don't like to cry when she's not holding me.

Instead of pitching, I'm dancing now.

That's ballroom dancing, as in fox-trot, tango and waltz, not to mention swing, rumba, cha-cha, two-step, salsa, and whatever other new dance comes along that Paula finds out about. Granted, it doesn't involve a ball—except in the name—so why would I be interested? Because, as Paula so eloquently communicated to me, dancing is a sport. There are competitions. You can beat other people.

Well, okay then.

We had started back in 1993, shortly before Hollis' marriage to the Dutchman Gert Jan van der Hoeven. (He has two brothers, Robert and Paul; she has to marry the one whose name takes practice.) Anyway, Paula didn't want us (read *me*) to be embarrassed on the dance floor. So we took a few lessons at a local Fred Astaire Dance Studio in New Jersey. And we (read *Paula*) liked it so much we continued to take lessons even *after* we thrilled and amazed everybody at the wedding.

The trick to learning how to dance at those chain studios, we discovered, is to pay for private lessons, which are five times more expensive but twenty times faster. Then what you have to do is pick out a few dances that you want to learn and insist on focusing on only *one* of those dances at each lesson so that you can lock it in. Otherwise, they'll try to teach you a tiny fraction of a dozen different dances at each lesson, that you can never remember, so it takes years of lessons before you get to be any good, which is the whole idea. So if it turns out that you like it, negotiate a package of private lessons and *don't sign any contracts*.

A big problem with beginners is that the woman is often the better dancer, but the man is supposed to lead, ballroom dancing being an old-fashioned enterprise. So what happens is that women try to lead the men into initiating the proper steps.

This was a big problem for Paula and me until we got some marvelous advice from Pierre Dulaine of the American Ballroom Theater: "The man's job is to lead, and the woman's job is to follow his mistakes." Precisely! We are now working on the part about the funny looks whenever I do something weird.

The best thing to happen to our dancing, and one of the best things in our lives, was to meet Marge Champion—of Marge and Gower dance-team fame—also known as America's Dancing Sweetheart. On the classic movie channel, Marge is the one with the huge smile, doing all the tricky steps in those Broadway musicals from the '40s, '50s, and '60s. In person she's a nuclear-powered icon, performer, arts activist, board member, world traveler, mother, grandmother, and dear friend.

As the best ballroom dancer to have pitched for the Yankees—as far as anyone knows—I'm often featured as Marge's dance partner at local fund-raisers. I'm like the talking dog; it's not that the dog speaks well, it's that he speaks at all. Before Marge and I do our number we have to practice in order to look smooth, but more important, so that I don't hurt Marge. Ballroom is not your basic grab-ass dancing, but moving-across-the-floor dancing. Done right, it's like flying. My job is to keep from plunging us into a nosedive.

Sunday, June 21, 1998.
The phone rang at eight in the morning. I picked it up.
"Happy Father's Day."
"Thank you, David," I said.
"Did you see *The New York Times* this morning?"

497

"*The Times*?" I said. "No, we haven't been down to the general store yet."

"Well, there's something you have to read," he said.

"We'll get it later," I said. "We just woke up."

"I think you should read it now," David insisted.

"We'll read it after breakfast," I said. "Whatever it is can wait."

"No, it can't," he said. There was a pause. "Okay, I'll read it to you myself."

Mystified, I motioned for Paula to pick up the other phone.

"It takes up half the page," said David. "There's a big picture of you and Mickey Mantle and another smaller picture of you . . . and Laurie."

I felt a familiar ache in my chest.

"The headline is," said David, "'For Bouton, Let Bygones Be Bygones.'"

This made no sense. I hadn't spoken to any reporters lately.

"Then there's a smaller headline," said David, who was having difficulty speaking. "It says . . . ." David seemed to be choking back tears.

"It says . . . .," continued David, "'Son's Wish on Father's Day . . . Is to See Dad and Yogi Stand with Old Timers.'"

Son's wish?

"By . . . Michael Bouton," said David.

Michael? When did he do this? *The New York Times?* I was too stunned to process it.

Then David began to read his brother's letter over the phone, haltingly at times, as follows:

> *Today is Father's Day, but the date I have circled on my calendar is July 25. That is Old Timers' Day at Yankee Stadium. Traditionally, it is the day when past Yankee stars take their annual curtain call. It is the day my father, Jim Bouton, No. 56, the Bulldog, is snubbed, and not invited back. Although an invitation to attend Old Timers' Day is an honor he can live without, it is what I wish for him this year.*

498

You see, this past August my sister Laurie died in an automobile crash at the age of 31. She was beautiful and sweet. And tough as it is to lose a sibling, I cannot even fathom the loss my parents must feel.

Philosophers say it is because of tragedy that we give such importance to our games. Baseball, seemingly, has always been here for us. The key to baseball's future as America's pastime lies in its continuity between generations.

I realize the big loss for Yankee fans and baseball continues to be the absence of Yogi Berra on Old Timers' Day. Yogi has let it be known that he refuses to be part of the celebration as long as George Steinbrenner is the owner. I have applauded Yogi's decision on this matter of principle, but recently I have had a change of heart and mind.

It is just as petty for Yogi to spite George as it is for George to spite my father. It does not serve the greater good for families, the fans or the sport we supposedly love so much. It does not factor in the human equation.

I know that not having Old Timers' Day on our calendar like a holiday gave us fewer days with Laurie. I wonder if Yogi knows how important it is for his grandchildren to witness him out there under the classic facade of the stadium. There is no substitute for smelling the grass and hearing the cheers. It will be time for dusting off the scrapbook soon enough.

For the fans, their children and grandchildren, the great difference between a regular game and Old Timers' Day cannot be gauged. How many stories from their own lives are triggered by the sight of a player from the past?

The type of story that places them in time, describing what they were doing, say, on that afternoon when Yogi won his first of three most valuable player awards.

Where have you gone, Joe DiMaggio, when you are more remembered as a line in a pop song than for an acrobatic catch or a batting streak? Old Timers' Day is a chance for fans to give back. To forget this aspect will ultimately doom baseball's primacy among sports in America.

It has been nearly thirty years since my father wrote "Ball Four." And for all the hullabaloo about his book, the major detractors have all written their own tell-all books, affirming the validity of what they once called lies. Last year, on the occasion of its 100th anniversary, the New York Public Library listed "Ball Four" as one of the 100 most important books of the century. The question is this: Why do the Yankees feel as if they still have to punish him?

For years, the rumor was that Mickey Mantle had threatened not to attend Old Timers' Day if my father was present. I am thankful that the Mick was big enough to make what amounted to a deathbed call to my father to put that rumor to rest as being untrue. He understood the significance of the snub and wanted no part of it.

So that leaves only George, who was not even the team's owner when "Ball Four" came out in 1970. If George blames "Ball Four" for contributing toward free agency, one would expect a different reaction, because everyone knows it is only through the acquisition of such free agents as Reggie, Catfish, Cone, et al., that Steinbrenner's reign has seen any championships at all.

I'm hoping that a compromise on positions can take place without necessarily a compromise on principles. I mean, if George really hates my father that much, is it good for him to still hold it inside? Wouldn't it be more healthful to have my father there, if only to boo him?

George has said that this year he will be turning over more of the day-to-day operations to his sons Hal, Hank and Harold. Might that be enough for Yogi to return to Yankee Stadium and still save face?

I am hoping to reach George's sons. Despite our different upbringings, I think we have a lot in common. It is never easy growing up the child of a public figure. I know that they have heard mean things said about their father, much the same way I have. I think there have been days when they have been publicly embarrassed by him and there have been times when they have been as proud as any child has ever been about a parent—exactly like me. I'm sure they love their father as much as I love mine. That is what Father's Day is about—celebrating that love.

I see this as an opportunity to get my father some extra hugs at a time in his life when he can use all the hugs he can get. It is something he would never seek for himself—he is going to kill me when he reads this—and maybe the kind of thing only a son or daughter can do for their father.

I am not asking for any favors, just reconsideration. That is all. Life is short. Time is at hand.

I couldn't believe it. What a Father's Day gift! What a beautiful letter.

"Did you know about this, David?" I asked.

"No."

Amazing.

Not just Michael's writing, or that he kept it a secret, but that he had those feelings in the first place. I never knew he cared that much about my not being invited to Old Timers' Day. The kids were little when I wrote *Ball Four,* and they grew up just accepting that their dad was some kind of pariah. The only one who ever said anything was Laurie, who would get personally offended at the Yankees for a few days every summer, and then she'd let it go.

I always tried to joke about it, saying they didn't want me back because fans don't like to see the Old Timers strike out. They're going to wait till I'm the oldest living Yankee; by the time I go back I won't even know I'm there.

I never knew the kids' private thoughts on the matter, never guessed how it might have affected their view of me all these years.

Until now. Evidently it had bothered Michael.

We spoke with David a while longer, I thanked him for his Father's Day wishes, and then we hung up to call Michael. I had this flash thought of him in his Brooklyn apartment with *The New York Times* opened up on the table, examining the layout, checking to see if anything was cut at the last minute, as writers do.

He was waiting by the phone. I could hear the smile in his voice.

"What can I say, Michael?" I stammered. "It was just beautiful. Powerful. A great surprise. Thank you."

"I've wanted to write that letter for a long time," he said, "but I could never finish it. This time I did."

"Well," I said, "that's not something you just knock off in a few hours."

"I had a little help from Laurie, too," said Michael.

"I use her for inspiration myself," I said.

"So, do you think the Yankees are going to invite you back?"

"I don't know, Michael," I said. "But whether they do or not, your letter stands by itself as a wonderful gift. It doesn't have to produce a result to be meaningful."

Then I called *my* dad to tell him what one of his grandsons had done.

For the next few days, Mike and I were on the phone, still buzzing about his letter. I told him about strangers stopping me on the street, mostly men, telling me how they had cried when they read it and how lucky I was to have a son like him. Michael said the Yankees would *have* to invite me back. They had no choice.

I said don't count on it.

A week went by, then two weeks, then three. We went on with our lives. There would be no invitation to Old Timers' Day. The game was only two weeks away; the Yankees would have had to invite me by now.

"It was a great letter, Mike," I said. "But the pen is not always mightier than the sword."

On the morning of July 15, the phone rang.

"Hi, my name is Joe Schillan. I'm the director of Promotions and Special Events for the Yankees. And we'd like to invite you to Old Timers' Day."

There was a short pause. Was this it? Or was this a joke? I'd gotten similar calls over the years from friends.

"Excuse me for hesitating," I said. "This could be any number of guys."

"I understand," said Schillan. "It's not a joke. You can call me back if you want; I'll give you my direct line."

"That's okay," I said. "I'll take your word for it."

"To be honest with you," said Joe, "we read your son's letter in *The New York Times* and we were moved by it. We presented the idea to George and he said, 'Sure, why not? I don't know why we didn't invite him before this.'"

"Well, that's nice," I said. I didn't have the heart for skepticism.

"Old Timers' Day is only ten days away," said Joe. "And the teams are set, with their uniforms and everything, so you'll be introduced in your street clothes."

"That's fine, I don't have to be in uniform," I said. "I think I'm free that day. I'll call back and let you know."

I hung up the phone and tried to absorb what had just happened. I stood up and felt slightly dizzy. Twenty-eight years of exile for writing a book, fewer than ten pages of which mention the Yankees, end with a simple phone call.

I walked into the next room where Paula was sitting.

"Well," I said. "Guess what? That was the Yankees. They invited me back."

"You're going, of course," said Paula. This is a woman who knows how to chaperon a decision.

Over the years, I had toyed with the idea of saying I had a previous engagement if I ever got invited. After Michael's letter, that no longer seemed possible.

"Sure, I'm going," I said. "Let them sweat for an hour."

Then I picked up the phone to make a more important call.

"I knew they would do it," said Michael. "I *knew* it!"

Maybe I was wrong about the pen.

I received my invitation to Old Timers' Day with mixed emotions. I was thrilled for Michael, that he got the result he wanted. Sad for Laurie, because she never got to see it. And for myself, a strange kind of numbness. It wasn't that I was ungrateful, just that I seemed incapable of joy.

Still, everybody else seemed juiced up about it. Within hours of calling the Yankees with my acceptance, the phone started ringing. It must have been a slow news day because every media outlet in New

York, plus a few from around the country, was calling for interviews and comments.

The rocket ship had taken off. That's what it's like when you're involved in an event that's bigger than you are. All you can do is hang on for the ride. And it was some ride. The same people who had welled up over Michael's letter were now shaking my hand and clapping me on the back, as if I had just achieved something.

It was going to be another one of those life-altering events—a happier one this time.

The day after the stories began appearing, I got another call from the Yankees informing me that it had been decided I would now be *in uniform* for the game, and not just introduced in my street clothes. They requested my uniform size. I wanted to say size 34 pants, same as always, but I had to add an inch.

Paula did her part to help the old righthander.

"You'd better start throwing in the basement," she said. "You've only got about a week."

"All I can do in a week, Babe," I said, "is get a sore arm. I'm better off just cranking my arm over my head a few times so it doesn't fly off on my first pitch."

Sunday, July 25, 1998. Old Timers' Day at Yankee Stadium.

It was a beautiful day. The sun was shining. And my heart was beating a little faster than usual as I boarded the players-only bus in front of the hotel. Wives and family would make the trip to Yankee Stadium on a later bus. How would my old teammates treat me, I wondered? I had run into a few the previous night at a cocktail party, and they were very welcoming. Tommy Tresh gave me a hug. Joe Pepitone had a big smile. "Hey, Jim, what's happenin'?" Like nothing happened.

Walking down the aisle of the bus, I realized that most of these Yankees were from other eras. I recognized a few from newspapers and television. Some I had run into at charity golf outings. They all seemed to know each other from previous Old Timers' Days. I was like a guy who had just crawled out of a cave. Then I spotted my old friend and fellow pitcher, Ralph Terry, who had flown in from his home in Kansas.

"Hey, welcome back," he said, sticking out his hand.

It was great to see Ralph again. I took a seat across the aisle.

"You belong here," said Ralph. "Hell, man, you earned it! And the game belongs to the fans, Baby."

I started to think this might turn out to be more fun than I had imagined. Then I noticed Clete Boyer, sitting on the other side of Ralph, working hard to ignore me. You can't win 'em all.

When the bus pulled up to the stadium several hundred fans were already waiting behind wooden barriers flanking the players' entrance. I let most of the others file off first so I could watch the response. With outstretched arms, hands clutching baseballs and autograph books, kids and adults of all ages welcomed the players.

"Goose, Goose," they screamed, when Gossage ambled onto the pavement. "Over here, Goose."

"There's Ron Guidry," someone said. The crowd started hollering "Gator! Just one, pleeease."

"Who's that?" a kid asked.

"Ralph Terry," said an older man.

"Sixty-two World Series!" shouted a guy who remembered Ralph's Game 7 shutout against the Giants.

Most of the players signed a few autographs on their way in. And I was looking forward to it myself. Actually, I was pretty excited, but still a little nervous. I wondered how these genuine Yankee fans, Mickey Mantle fans, would greet me. I took a deep breath and got off.

"Bulldog!" a lot of people hollered. "Welcome back."

Inside, the familiar smell of the stadium washed over me—a distinctive mix of industrial-strength New York air, popcorn, and freshly-hosed cement. I looked for familiar faces—anyone with wrinkles—among the stadium personnel. I recognized a few people, but I couldn't recall any names. Most of them smiled, some shook my hand. The real reception, good or bad, would be down in the clubhouse.

The players' entrance had been moved from the first-base to the third-base side, so the route to the clubhouse was new. I had to follow a blue painted line on the floor through a series of turns, down a narrow concrete hallway. In an open area around a corner, I saw some older men lingering near a door and knew I had found the clubhouse. There are always some older men lingering near clubhouse doors.

And there was Louis Requena, my favorite Yankee photographer! We were practically rookies together back in 1962. Louie, one of the sweetest men you'd ever want to meet, had made a composite picture of me in my Yankee uniform surrounded by the box scores of my first seven wins. I still have it somewhere. I came up behind him and tapped him on the shoulder.

"Jimmy Boy!" he said, as we bear-hugged, "Good to see you back."

Fortified by Louie's reception, I entered the clubhouse.

Whoa!

Instead of players, sitting at their lockers talking and laughing about old times, a mob of sportswriters and photographers and television crews was filling the room. They were all over the place. I was confused. What were they doing here?

Waiting for *me*, I was embarrassed to discover. As I walked to my assigned locker across the room, they followed like minnows darting after a bread crumb. I felt uncomfortable. I wondered what the other players were thinking: "Big-Mouth" gets invited back and screws up Old Timers' Day." I just wanted to slip in quietly, be one of the guys, see what that felt like.

Moose Skowron was sitting on a stool at the locker next to mine. He was wearing his baseball underwear and having coffee, just like he always did. I took a chance and reached out my hand.

"Hey, Jimmy, how are you?" he said, smiling and shaking my hand. Moose was chatting with Hank Bauer, who was before my time, but who I'd seen at a couple of sports dinners.

"Hello there, Mr. Bouton," said Hank in his gravelly Marine voice.

So far, so good, I thought. Then I saw John Blanchard with the same look on his face that Clete Boyer had had on the bus, and I got a twinge of bad feeling. Part of me wanted to talk with them but I knew that wouldn't work. These were not talking guys, at least not with me. Maybe when we're ninety or so, we'll shake hands on a foul line somewhere.

Once at my locker, the clubhouse disappeared from view behind a wall of sportswriters and photographers. The questions tumbled over one another. When did the Yankees contact you? Have you had any response from your teammates yet? Did you ever make peace with Mickey Mantle? What did you think of Michael's letter? And the most frequently asked, "How does it feel to be back?"

"So far, it feels like a press conference," I said nervously. They laughed.

Meanwhile, I kept looking around to see if I could spot any other players. I wanted to be bullshitting with teammates, not answering questions. I appreciated the attention but it's not what I was hoping for. I wanted to *experience* Old Timers' Day, and the questions were getting in the way. I still felt isolated, not really a part of things. This was not what I had in mind.

The barrage of questions continued—a respectful barrage but a barrage nonetheless. When one member of the group had had enough, he was replaced by another who hadn't heard the answers to the previous questions. All the while, I was trying to change into my uniform. The other players were already dressed and on the field. Batting practice would be over before I got out there. I felt panicky. It was like one of those bad dreams where you can't quite get to something. Old Timers' Day was happening without me!

"So how does it feel to be back?" asked the newest arrival.

"Well, if I'm ever going to know that," I said, "I'll have to actually *be* back, so let me get out there and I'll tell you later."

And I headed down the tunnel to the dugout.

Waiting on the steps was another convention of photographers and video crews. I couldn't believe it.

But Joe Pepitone could. Wading into the throng, he put his arm around my shoulder and pointed at me, shouting, "Jim's back! Jim's back! Do I know how to get my picture in the newspapers, or what? Jim's back! Jim's back!"

Everybody laughed. Same old Pepi. Fortunately, pictures are quicker than questions and I was *finally* able to run out onto the field.

This is it, I thought to myself. It's actually happening. I'm running out onto the field on Old Timers' Day at Yankee Stadium. It was not something I had ever missed; at least not consciously. But now, here I was.

I felt quietly pleased.

And a little bit giddy. What should I do? Throw a ball? Run across the outfield? What do you *do* on Old Timers' Day? I was like a kid at an amusement park. I needed something to hang onto. A life preserver.

Tommy Davis was at first base, taking throws from the infielders. I jogged over. Tommy was invited to play for the opposing Los Angeles Dodgers. I love Tommy Davis. Whenever we see each other he says things like "Don't be gettin' too close to me, Bouton. People already think I had something to do with your book." This time he greeted me with a big smile and an exaggerated handshake.

I grabbed a baseball and headed for right field, looking up into the stands as I ran, elated now to be out on the grass "with all the people looking down at you," as Dick Baney once put it. Pretty soon, family members and friends were leaning over the wall, waving and taking pictures. In the upper deck, where I had reserved seats for sixty people, another contingent was hollering and waving. There was so much to see, and do, and feel. It was overwhelming, really. I just sort of floated around, tossing a ball, waving to people, soaking it all up.

That was the fun part. But there was also a sense of vindication; that I had been invited to a place I should have been invited to a long time ago. Twenty-eight years in the principal's office for throwing spitballs was a cruel and unusual punishment. I understand Old Timers' Day is a Yankee event and they can invite whoever they want, but it's also made possible by the fans. As Ralph Terry had said, "The game belongs to the fans, Baby."

Then I'd remember why I was there in the first place and a tremendous sadness would come over me. I was there because my daughter had died. I knew Laurie would have wanted me to have fun, so I didn't feel guilty; but I just couldn't keep the emotions separated for very long.

I'd think of Michael and his Father's Day gift, and feelings of love and pride would well up. I bounced from pleasure to vindication to sadness to pride and back again. How I felt depended on the moment.

When I wasn't waving and smiling, or welling up, I'd try to do some serious throwing with whoever wandered by. I didn't want to embarrass myself if I got into the game. You never know who you might be pitching to. The last thing a '60s guy wants to do is face some guy from the '70s or '80s, not to mention '90s.

As soon as batting practice was over, I jogged in to get ready for the big moment—the introduction of the players. This is actually more important than the game itself, which is an anti-climactic side show. I sat on the top step of the dugout next to Yankee pitching coach and former teammate, Mel Stottlemyre. Mel and his wife Jean had lost their youngest son, Jason, to leukemia in 1981. Mel said it was two years before he could really function again. I had at least another year to go.

"Are you going to lose your hat when you pitch?" Mel asked.

"I don't throw hard enough anymore," I said.

"You have to lose your hat," said Mel. "That's your trademark. Everyone will expect it. Just prop it on your head and make it fall off—otherwise the fans will be disappointed."

Mel is one of the great pitching coaches in baseball.

With the players gathering in the dugout, I scanned the stands behind home plate for Paula's chartreuse jacket; the one she was wearing so I could see her from the field. She was there with Michael and David and my dad and my brother Bob. Lee was out of town on business and Hollis was in Amsterdam. I spotted the jacket, arms flapping as if trying to signal an airplane, and waved back again for about the fifteenth time.

"Good afternoon, ladies and gentlemen," boomed the legendary public-address announcer Bob Sheppard, making it official. "Welcome to the 52nd annual Old Timers' Day." Bob Sheppard's voice has not lost a step.

Sheppard then introduced Yankee announcer Michael Kay, who would introduce the old timers. On Old Timers' Day, players are introduced with their career highlights first, to build suspense and let the fans try to guess who they are. The players wait in the dugout, listening to the highlights, to see whose turn it is to run on the field. I wondered what highlights they'd choose from my career.

"He was a pretty good pitcher in the 1960s . . . but then he wrote a book . . . and became a pariah . . . Let's welcome . . . ."

I moved to the top step of the dugout so I could hear the announcer. They usually introduce the smaller fish early and save the big guys for last, ending with Joe DiMaggio. I just didn't want to be first.

"He spent the mid-1960s with the Dodgers . . .," Michael Kay began, and I knew it wasn't me.

"Only the fourteenth Yankee player to hit three home runs in a game . . ." Nope.

"Played eleven years in the majors . . ." Nope.

Fifteen players later, I was wondering if they had skipped me by mistake. Maybe I was on a list of players to be introduced in street clothes. If they got to the end before realizing the oversight, I'd *never* get introduced; they sure as hell weren't going to bring me out after Joe DiMaggio!

"Remember the Yankee whose hat fell off whenever . . . .?"

A charge went through my body. I waited a second just to be sure.

". . . he rang up twenty-one victories in 1963 . . . ."

I climbed out of the dugout and started for first base. I felt unsteady, like I might topple over. I heard a roar. What if I fell down? I wondered. It seemed as if I was moving in slow motion, or underwater. At some point my hearing went out. I was moving in a white zone, watching myself slap hands with the other players. I took my place at the end of the line, numb, trying to figure out what had happened.

I stood there like that through what must have been two more introductions.

Slowly, I began to focus again. Son of a gun, I thought, I'm really *out* here. On Old Timers' Day. This is great. The other players were being introduced but I paid no attention. I was in my own little world. I looked into the stands again for Paula's green jacket, but I couldn't find it because everyone was standing, blocking the view.

Then I remembered the gang in the upper deck in right field; my brother Pete and his family, my aunt Frances, my cousins, the Goldensohns, the Stanleys, the Elitzers, the Nelsons, Laurie's Girls—

which is what we call her closest friends Noreen, Kay and Grace—some of Mike's friends, and others. Could they see me from that far away? I wondered. Could I see them? I stepped back off the foul line and looked up, waving my arm, oblivious to the ceremonies around me.

And that's when I saw a large blue banner with white block lettering that read, WE LOVE LAURIE, being held aloft by a frantically waving group of people. That must be Laurie's Girls, I figured, who had obviously been waiting for this moment.

It got me right in the heart and I began to cry. Players were being introduced and cheered, and I was crying. Laurie, my poor Laurie, I thought. She would have loved to have been here. And maybe she was, I told myself.

I waved my hat to let the girls know that I'd seen the banner, and I stepped back into the line. After a memorial tribute to Mel Allen, a recitation of Yankee greats enshrined in Monument Park in center field, and the singing of the national anthem by Robert Merrill, the players headed for the dugout to play ball.

That's when I realized something terrible. I had forgotten to acknowledge Michael, whose letter had made it all possible! My plan had been to tip my cap to him as I came out of the dugout. But I was in such a daze, I'd forgotten all about it. Now it was too late. I panicked. What could I do?

Then I remembered that there was going to be a game. I could tip my cap to Michael from the mound. That would actually make more sense. That's when I'd do it *if* I got into the game. But not everybody plays. Old Timers' games are three-inning events, with players shuffling in and out, and some guys never get in. Gene Michael was managing the team. I went over and asked if I was scheduled to play. Fortunately, he wasn't eating a liverwurst sandwich. Gene promised me one hitter. That's all I wanted.

Keith Olbermann, my favorite TV guy, was doing the play-by-play over the PA system. When my name was announced I headed for the mound, and my final curtain. It all went perfectly. The scoreboard flashed the message I had requested earlier that said, THANKS, MIKE. I took off my hat and pointed it to where he was sitting in the stands, holding it there for a moment so everyone understood, and gently placed it back on my head.

Very gently. On my first pitch, the hat popped off as Mel had suggested, and Olbermann called it BALL FOUR! It was fantastic. On a day of ceremony, ritual, and gesture, I was allowed to play my part—not just for the fans, but for me and my friends and family. Then, to top it all off, Jay Johnstone hit a nice little dribbler to second base and I was out of there.

How did it feel the day *after* Old Timers' Day? Like I'd just climbed off one of those paint-mixing machines at the hardware store. A temporary, but welcome, reprieve from the depression I'd been living with since Laurie died. Or, as I say in conversation, "Since Laurie . . . " because I can't stand to hear myself utter those terrible words. But underneath, the depression was still there. In fact, I was so depressed, I didn't realize I was depressed.

I had gone from being a "pathological optimist," as Paula used to call me, to a fearful and panicky person. I'd make an awful decision based on fear, then panic over how to recover from the awful decision. In the old days, when I was on my game, a friend had once said, "You know the expression, 'He's not playing with a full deck?' Well, Jim's playing with extra cards." Now I was playing with half a deck. Or less. I was folding with aces and sticking with a pair of twos.

I didn't care what happened to me anymore. I'd be in an airplane, bouncing around in a storm, and I wouldn't be nervous; just let it go down, I'd think, I've got plenty of insurance. I only wanted to eat comfort foods, like macaroni and cheese and hamburgers and mashed potatoes and peanut butter sandwiches. Which is why Paula never wanted me to drive alone, or pick the restaurants.

Ironically, I only recognized that I was depressed when I was having a really good time. I'd find myself laughing at something, or enjoying a moment on a tennis court, and a noticeable feeling of joy would hit me, a fleeting speck of freedom from care and worry. But I couldn't make it last. At night, instead of nodding off to sleep with hopes and plans for the future as I'd always done, I'd toss and turn with doom and gloom about the past. And feel sorry for myself.

Then on August 20, 1999, a few days past the second anniversary of Laurie's death and just over a year after my return to Old Timers' Day, I was driving to a quarry to pick out some stones and came upon a police roadblock where a bad accident had just occurred. A fire truck and an ambulance were on the scene, about seventy yards up the road, with their lights flashing. As I slowed down I could see it had been a head-on collision between a pickup truck and a gray Jeep.

A bolt of terror struck me. Paula! That was Paula's gray Jeep, the *exact* same color, same model! She had left the house about a half hour before me to do her own errands, in the same direction, *along the same highway!*

In a panic, my heart pounding, I pulled over and jumped out of my car and started running toward the accident. A policeman held up his hand and signaled me to stop. I ran right past him. As I got closer another policeman, seeing me coming, jumped in my path with his arms held out.

"Whoa, stop right there!" he commanded.

"That's my wife in the Jeep!" I shouted, as I dodged around him. "I have to get there."

My eyes were blurring with tears as I ran, my lungs gasping for air. No, no, no, I thought, not Paula, too. My Babe. Just as I got there, the ambulance doors were closing.

"Where is she?" I hollered at the policeman coming toward me.

"Where is who?" he barked, grabbing both my arms.

"My wife!" I said. "I think she was in the Jeep."

"There were no women in this accident," he said. "Two men. That's all."

"Are you sure?" I asked, in disbelief.

"Positive," he said, releasing my arms. "Now go sit over there and calm down." And he directed me to a highway guardrail.

I sat there for about ten minutes, until I stopped wheezing. If I don't get a heart attack now, I thought, I'm never going to get one.

Later, at the house, I couldn't wait for Paula to walk in the door. When she did, I put my arms around her and held her tight. Really held her close and told her what had happened, and how scared I'd been.

"My God, what a terrible experience," said Paula. "But you can relax now. I'm here and everything's okay."

She looked intently at me. "And you're back," she said. "You're back."

I wasn't exactly sure what she meant.

"You haven't been yourself for two years," said Paula. "This is the first time, since Laurie died, that I've felt you're really *with* me. I was afraid I had lost you and that you were never coming back."

In any case, I think I'm getting better. I still carry a handkerchief for sudden tears, and melancholy is still my default setting, but at least I'm not so numb anymore. Sometimes I wake up in the morning and I'm actually glad to be alive. I've got plans to build a stone terrace on the east side of the house. I'll be doing some work with a money-management firm in New York. I'm back on regular foods now and I'm starting to care when the plane jumps around.

And I'm getting invited to more ballparks.

A group I recently spoke to in Seattle arranged to have me throw out the first pitch before a Mariners' game against the Minnesota Twins. On my way to the stadium, I stopped by the Eagle Hardware store, the edifice built on the parking lot that was once Sicks Stadium, home of the immortal Pilots. At least it's recognized as an historic landmark. Just outside the entrance, in a batter's box painted on the cement, stands a bronze statue of a batter hovering over a brass home plate.

"Batter up!" reads the inscription on home plate. "You are standing on the site of Sicks Seattle Stadium, home of the Seattle Raniers and Seattle Pilots. If the year were 1942, you would be in perfect position to knock one out of the park."

It's altogether fitting that the Pilots should have to share credit with a minor league team, and as if that wasn't pitiful enough, the statue is standing *sideways* in the batter's box, as if the pitcher's mound was over by the first-base dugout! A *pop fly* would leave the park—about a hundred feet foul.

Inside the store, near cash register No. 17, sixty feet, six inches away from the batter outside, is a beige circle on the floor representing the pitcher's mound, with a white pitcher's rubber in the middle. There is no inscription on the mound, its location next to a checkout lane being commentary enough.

And not far from the checkout lanes, a Sicks' Stadium display case features photographs and memorabilia of the Seattle Raniers. The only Pilot item is a photo of Don Mincher with the caption: "Don Mincher, Pitcher." It never ends.

While Seattle's Safeco Field lacks the charm of Sicks Stadium, it certainly holds more people. A few of them recognized me standing on the field before the game. They would smile and wave and then nudge the child sitting next to them and point in my direction. What were they telling the kids, I wondered. "You see that man down there? He once had his spikes nailed to the floor."

Before I threw out the first pitch I went over to the Mariners' dugout to say hello to manager Lou Piniella, who was almost a Pilot until he was traded in spring training to the Kansas City Royals. We laughed at the first sight of each other, and the notion that we were together in Seattle under circumstances neither of us could have predicted in 1969.

I asked Lou if he remembered the day Joe Schultz told him he'd been traded.

"Sure," said Lou, "I'll never forget it. Joe called me into his office and said, 'Lou, you're gonna have to pound Bud somewhere else.'"

There should be a statue of Joe Schultz in front of the Anheuser-Busch Inc. headquarters.

I'm sixty-one years old, but in my mind, I'm forty. I turned forty a few years ago when I couldn't get amateur hitters out with my knuckleball. Before that I was twenty-eight. I had turned twenty-eight when I couldn't throw my fastball past major league hitters and had to resort to the knuckler. Before that I was nineteen. I was never in my thirties.

I judge my age in baseball years, but I don't live as a former baseball player. My scrapbooks are stashed in the basement, my trophies are still in boxes. I enjoy my memories, but I don't live in the past. I go there only when someone else brings it up or when I occasionally open *Ball Four* to get a laugh from Joe Schultz or one of the players.

Laughing is important. Laughing, and paying attention to the details, and appreciating things. As I've learned to live with loss, I've also learned to make the most of whatever time I have left, because life is so fragile and we never know when it will end or what awaits us, if anything, when it's over. So I've become a major appreciator of things, large and small.

Right now I'm appreciating a very small person named Georgia Grace, born to Lee and his wife, Elaine, on April 12, 2000. My first grandchild. There is nothing like the joy and wonder of holding a newborn baby. And fear. When they handed Georgia to me in the maternity ward I was afraid I was going to drop her; she was too tiny for my arms and too big for my hands, and with her wobbly head I wasn't sure how to get hold of her. But she sure smelled good. That new-baby smell.

Now Georgia is three months old and grabbing onto my pinkies with her tiny fingers and lifting herself up off my lap. I pretend I'm playing "soooo big," but I'm really strengthening her hands and forearms.

You need a good grip to throw a knuckleball.

THE PILOTS LIVE!
IN CYBERSPACE!

One day I was cruising the web and came upon a treasure trove of Seattle Pilots lore on a site developed by a fan named Mike Fuller. It turns out there are a whole lot of Pilots junkies out there who post letters and photographs and chat with each other on this site. Mike even has an updated Where Are They Now? section on the Pilots. There's another guy named Charles Kapner who may be the world's greatest collector of Pilots' memorabilia. Most of the photos in the back of this book were supplied by Charles. There's also a fellow named Shawn Collins who has a *Ball Four* site in case anyone's interested. I've never met any of these gentlemen, but I'd be happy to link you to their web sites from **jimbouton.com** if I can ever figure out how to set it up.

Maybe one day I'll post the original notes from *Ball Four* which I discovered in a box down in the basement. Except that they're a little hard to read because they were scrawled on spiral notebook paper, hotel stationery, popcorn boxes, ticket stubs, scorecards, bar coasters, air sickness bags, and whatever else was handy at the moment. Ancient scribblings of a lost tribe.

ACKNOWLEDGMENTS

It's not an overstatement to say that this book was a collaboration.

My deepest gratitude goes to the late Leonard Shecter, my friend and editor of the original *Ball Four*. It was Shecter who encouraged me to keep a diary, who helped sell the book to World Publishing and who, with patience and humor, turned a reasonably observant relief pitcher into a writer of sorts.

Next I want to thank my teammates on the Seattle Pilots and Houston Astros who would just as soon not have cooperated but who, nonetheless, contributed their matchless hilarity and enduring humanity. What kind of a book would this be, after all, without Joe Schultz, or Fred Talbot, or Gene Brabender, or Gary Bell? Novelists spend lifetimes trying to invent characters like these.

I also want to thank Michael and David, Lee and Hollis, and my brothers Bob and Pete, for their thoughtful comments and suggestions.

Lastly I thank my wife Paula Kurman, the primary editor of all three updates, and an accomplished writer herself. Always and forever the magic lady, only Paula had the editorial expertise, the intimate knowledge, and the emotional understanding that enabled me to write about the events of the past few years. Thanks, Babe.

ABOUT THE EDITOR

Lenny Shecter died on January 19, 1974. He was only 47 years old. He had leukemia. It says something about Lenny that I was one of his closest friends and I never knew he had the disease. He didn't sit around and cry in his beer that he might die young someday. He probably didn't want anybody to feel sorry for him. He was a courageous man.

I had heard about Lenny Shecter even before I had met him. It was during spring training in 1962 when I was a rookie with the Yankees and he was a sportswriter for the New York *Post*. The veteran players were teaching the rookies about life in the major leagues. "Don't talk to the writers," they would say. "Especially that fuckin' Shecter." That spring I heard "fuckin' Shecter" so many times I thought it was his first name. I expected this guy to be some kind of monster.

Instead, I discovered that he was a jolly fellow with a quizzical smile and a twinkle in his eye. He was also smart and funny and tough and he taught me things about the world that I never learned in a locker room. He had opinions about politics, the war, newspaper reporting, and almost everthing else, and he didn't mind expressing them. He was famous for being irascible but I found that to be part of his charm. We'd have some wonderful, raging debates and I'd always come away tired and happy and a lot wiser. I would rather argue with Lenny Shecter than agree with anyone else.

The establishment hated Shecter because he exposed the hypocrisy, the greed, and the racism in sports. As the sports editor of *Look* magazine, his profile of Vince Lombardi was the first insight into the dehumanizing demands of big time football. Lenny was one of those few reporters who refused to become an extension of the teams' publicity departments. Referring to the stacks of press releases teams would send out, he said the most important tool a reporter could have was a "shit detector."

Lenny insisted upon truth in all matters. When friends would describe him as portly or heavyset, he would laugh. "I'm not heavyset," he would say. "I'm fat. Let's be honest."

As a free lance writer Lenny was one of the first journalists to write about sports as big business. His first book, *The Jocks,* introduced Shecter's First Law of Sport: "Larceny abhors a vacuum." But his books and his other writings also contained funny and loving looks at sports figures like Casey Stengel and an obscure marathon runner named Buddy Edelen. And it was Lenny, writing about the early Mets, who transformed a clumsy first basemen into the legend of Marvelous Marv Throneberry.

What I remember most about Lenny was his guts. He would write a less than complimentary column about Mickey Mantle or Roger Maris, and the Yankee clubhouse would be steaming. Players would b e threatening to tear Shecter apart the next time they saw him, and I'd be sitting over by my locker figuring he wouldn't dare come near the clubhouse for at least a couple of months. Then suddenly the door would pop open and here he'd come, smiling and carrying his notebook like nothing happened. And nobody would say a word.

Lenny Shecter was my friend. I miss him a lot.

Shecter also edited Bouton's second book, I'm Glad You Didn't Take It Personally; *wrote* Roger Maris, *a biography;* Once Upon the Polo Grounds, *a nostalgic history of the first two years of the New York Mets; and* On the Pad, *with by William Phillips, the bribed policeman whose testimony before the Knapp Commission helped uncover corruption in the New York City Police Department.*

OTHER BOOKS BY
JIM BOUTON

I'm Glad You Didn't Take It Personally

Strike Zone
(A novel co-written with Eliot Asinof)

Index

SEATTLE PILOTS

JACK AKER

DICK BANEY

STEVE BARBER

DICK BATES

GARY BELL

GENE BRABENDER

DARRELL BRANDON

GEORGE BRUNET

WAYNE COMER

FRANK CROSETTI

TOMMY DAVIS

JOHN DONALDSON

BILL EDGERTON

JOHN GELNAR

GUS GIL

GREG GOOSSEN

SEATTLE PILOTS

JIM GOSGER

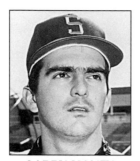

LARRY HANEY

TOMMY HARPER

MIKE HEGAN

BILL HENRY

STEVE HOVLEY

JOHN KENNEDY

BOB LASKO

BOB LEMON

BOB LOCKER

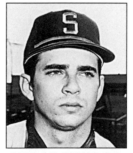

SKIP LOCKWOOD

GORDIE LUND

SAL MAGLIE

MIKE MARSHALL

JOHN McNAMARA

JERRY McNERTNEY

SEATTLE PILOTS

MARVIN MILKES

DON MINCHER

JOHN MORRIS

EDDIE O'BRIEN

JOHN O'DONOGHUE

JIM O'TOOLE

RAY OYLER

JIM PAGLIARONI

MARTY PATTIN

GABE PAUL JR.

LOU PINIELLA

RON PLAZA

CURT RAYER

MERRITT RANEW

RICH ROLLINS

GARRY ROGGENBURK

DIEGO SEGUI

ROLAND SHELDON

JOE SCHULTZ

DICK SIMPSON

SIBBY SISTI

BILL STAFFORD

JERRY STEPHENSON

FRED TALBOT

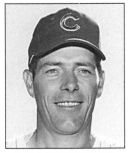

BOB TIEFENAUER

GARY TIMBERLAKE

FREDDIE VELAZQUEZ

JOSE VIDAL

HOUSTON ASTROS

JESUS ALOU

JACK BILLINGHAM

WADE BLASINGAME

CURT BLEFARY

HOUSTON ASTROS

NATE COLBERT

LARRY DIERKER

JOHN EDWARDS

FRED GLADDING

JULIO GOTAY

TOM GRIFFIN

BUDDY HANCKEN

DENNY LEMASTER

LEON McFADDEN

MEL McGAHA

DENIS MENKE

NORM MILLER

JOE MORGAN

JIM OWENS

DOUG RADER

JIMMY RAY

SPEC RICHARDSON

HARRY WALKER

BOB WATSON

DON WILSON

NEW YORK YANKEES

YOGI BERRA

JOHNNY BLANCHARD

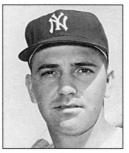

CLETE BOYER

WHITEY FORD

JAKE GIBBS

STEVE HAMILTON

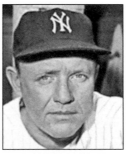

RALPH HOUK

ELSTON HOWARD

JOHNNY KEANE

PHIL LINZ

MICKEY MANTLE

ROGER MARIS

BILLY MARTIN

JOE PEPITONE

FRITZ PETERSON

BOBBY RICHARDSON

JOHNNY SAIN

MEL STOTTLEMYRE

TOM TRESH

JIM TURNER

SUPPORTING CAST

JOE ADCOCK

BRANT ALYEA

EMMETT ASHFORD

ROD CAREW

MIKE EPSTEIN

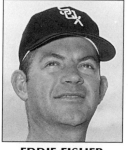

EDDIE FISHER

HAWK HARRELSON

FRANK HOWARD

SUPPORTING CAST

REGGIE JACKSON

AL KALINE

HARMON KILLEBREW

BOWIE KUHN

WILLIE MAYS

MARVIN MILLER

PHIL NIEKRO

FRANK ROBINSON

PETE ROSE

MAYO SMITH

HOYT WILHELM

DOOLEY WOMACK

PHOTOS COURTESY OF:

KANSAS CITY ROYALS   CHARLES KAPNER
NEW YORK YANKEES   GARY TIMBERLAKE
HOUSTON ASTROS   MRS. BOB LASKO
MILWAUKEE BREWERS   BILL SEARS
ANAHEIM ANGELS   PHOTOFILE
BOSTON RED SOX   NEWSDAY

My first ball. Age 2 ½. Notice the right hand gripping the knuckler.

With Mom and Dad, on leave from the navy in 1943.

Pitching for the Yankees in 1964 (when I threw smoke), I set a World Series record by losing my hat 37 times. It looks like my haircut is coming back in style.
(UPI/Bettmann Newsphotos)

This is not what the Yankees did to me after *Ball Four* was published. It was our 1963 pennant-clinching party after I shut out the Minnesota Twins, 2-0.

(Louis Requena)

The Mick and I pose for photographers after I beat St. Louis, 2-1, on Mantle's homer off Barney Shultz in the ninth inning in Game 3 of the 1964 World Series. Calling his shot, Mickey had said, "I'm going to hit one out of here."

Baseball commissioner Bowie "The Ayatollah" Kuhn has just asked me to sign a statement saying that *Ball Four* was not true. I respectfully declined.

BASEBALL
OFFICE OF THE
COMMISSIONER

(AP/ Wide World Photos)

1975, in Robert Altman's movie *The Long Goodbye,* where I was the bad guy.

Mount Everest, 1978. I was just telling the umpire that with the garbage I threw, I couldn't afford to have him make too many bad calls.
(Atlanta Constitution)

Seattle, Washington, 1969. Michael, 5; David, 4; and Laurie, 3. (Seattle Times)

Brooklyn, New York, 1996. Michael, David, Hollis, Lee, and Laurie.

Paula and Jim. Summer 2000.

Laurie's Girls. Old Timers' Day at Yankee Stadium. July 26, 1998. (Newsday)

Grandpa Jim holding Georgia Grace Wood Kurman—6 hours old. April 12, 2000.

Laurie Bouton
1966 - 1997